SECOND CANADIAN EDITION

A Short Guide to
Writing about
Literature

Sylvan Barnet
Tufts University

Reid Gilber
Capilano Colleg

William E. C
Wellesley College

D0555028

PEARSON
Longman

Toronto

National Library of Canada Cataloguing in Publication

Barnet, Sylvan
    A short guide to writing about literature / Sylvan
Barnet, Reid Gilbert, William E. Cain.—2nd Canadian ed.

Includes bibliographical references and indexes.
ISBN 0-321-10569-9

English language—Rhetoric. 2. Criticism—Authorship.
Exposition (Rhetoric) 4. Report writing. I. Gilbert, Reid
II. Cain, William E. III. Title.

PE1479.C7B3 2004   808'.0668   C2003-901452-5

ISBN 0-321-10569-9

Vice-President, Editorial Director: Michael J. Young
Acquisitions Editor: Marianne Minnaker
Marketing Manager: Toivo Pajo
Assistant Editor: Andrew Simpson
Production Editor: Charlotte Morrison-Reed
Senior Production Coordinator: Peggy Brown
Page Layout: Christine Velakis
Art Director: Mary Opper
Interior and Cover Design: Alex Li
Cover Image: Getty Images/Photodisc

1 2 3 4 5   08 07 06 05 04

Printed and bound in Canada.

PEARSON
Longman

Contents

PART 2

Standing Back: Thinking Critically about Literature   63

PART 3
Up Close: Thinking Critically about Literary Forms   127

PART 4

Inside: A Grammar Sketch, Style, Format,
and Special Assignments   253

Preface

Favourable response to the first Canadian edition has allowed me to revise the text originally based on the seventh edition of Sylvan Barnet's *A Short Guide to Writing about Literature*. This new edition is based substantially on the first Canadian edition, and incorporates some changes introduced into the ninth U.S. edition when William E. Cain became a collaborator.

This edition adds a new chapter which has two aims: to present a case study of a contemporary cross-discipline research project employing non-literary sources to explore literary subjects, and to show the process of electronic research. This chapter takes the student step-by-step through a search employing online search engines to locate relevant Web sources. It augments the preceding chapter on traditional research, which is extensively revised from the first edition.

The section on documentation is, of course, heavily revised to include citations of electronic sources and to update the print citations.

As well, I have added a sketch of grammar definitions and common grammar errors. While it was impossible to add a full grammar primer to this already lengthy text, this brief overview will provide students with a quick refresher and reminders of errors to avoid. For many students, this checklist will eliminate the need to purchase a separate grammar textbook.

Throughout, I have revised (and often shortened) the chapters to make them as clear and concise as possible and to update them.

The text retains elements of the first edition that colleagues and students have told us are valuable: examples of preliminary notes, drafts and revisions of drafts, checklists of questions, bibliographies for further reading, and examples of student writing. We believe that all writers gain from the examples of other writers, and that student writers gain confidence both from reading effective essays by their peers and seeing how some of these drafts can be further improved.

Part 1 is based in the premise that good writing requires good reading. The early chapters emphasize annotating a text, brainstorming, and asking questions to generate ideas. Explication and analysis are discussed and illustrated.

Part 2 considers definitions of literature, including contemporary notions of cultural performance and the performative. This section urges students to think critically about literature, considering relationships among interpretation, meaning, and evaluation. It discusses persuasive writing and provides brief introductions to critical approaches employed by contemporary critics, including the post-colonial theories so germane to Canadian criticism. These introductions to critical theories have been revised and updated.

Part 3 considers the three major genres (fiction, drama and poetry) and briefly discusses film. Each chapter provides technical and analytic tools, shows the process of thinking through an analysis, and offers sample essays. We comment upon the sample essays with marginal notations or brief assessments. Chapters conclude with checklists of questions students may ask as they read and think about a work.

Changes to Part 4 have already been mentioned: "Style and Format" now includes matters of grammar; "Writing a Research Paper" is updated and now includes electronic citation styles; a new chapter, "New Approaches to the Research Paper: History and the World Wide Web" explores the relationship between historical and political documents and the writing of Japanese-Canadians interned in camps during World War II. The chapter offers a guide to evaluating sources on the Web and directories of search engines and print guides to electronic sources.

There are three appendices: two stories which are used as the subjects of many of the student essays and a revised glossary of literary terms which provides quick definitions of key terms highlighted throughout the text. The glossary and index were completely reconfigured in the First Canadian edition and this apparatus has been continued and expanded in this second edition.

The book continues to use examples from First Nations' writers, to quote writers from the various ethnic backgrounds that make up Canadian society, and to introduce marginalized voices. It also uses excerpts from early Canadian writers whom we must not forget.

As the preface to the first edition notes, this book assumes "the role of literature in 'making' Canada and Canadians—sometimes in positive and sometimes in negative ways." Literature provides provisional or partial answers to complex questions, and while no one today assumes that literature will offer universal truths, the sharing of stories—told in many voices—allows us to read and reread ourselves. This process of reading and thinking about literature, then, is far more than simply an exercise for school: It is fundamental to our understanding of who we are, where we live, and what we value.

I would like to thank the following reviewers, all of whom offered valuable suggestions: David Hyttenrauch of Mount Royal College, Marlene A. Sawatsky of Simon Fraser University, and Mary Keating of University College of Cape Breton.

The basis of this text is still the work of Sylvan Barnet, to whom generations of students continue to be indebted—as do I. I would also like to thank Marianne Minaker and Andrew Simpson of Pearson Education Canada for their assistance. I thank Michael Young again for the original commission. My thanks also to copy editor Tara Tovell for her keen editorial eye. I thank my colleagues Jean Clifford and Bill Schermbrucker of Capilano College, Alan Filewod of Guelph University and Susan Bennett of the University of Calgary for their advice, and the reference librarians of Capilano College—especially George Modenesi—for their generous assistance. I thank Andrea and Douglas Westcott for a hideaway in which to write. In particular I would like to thank Dorothy Jantzen, of Capilano College, for continuing support and friendship. This second edition is for my parents, and, once again, for James Power.

REID GILBERT

A Key to Types
of Writing Assignments

PART 1

Jumping In

1

The Writer as Reader: Reading and Responding

Learning Objectives

When you've read this chapter, you should be able to

➢ appreciate the link between reading and writing about your reading;

➢ gather ideas and make inferences about your reading that will help you write about it;

➢ mark up a text to help you write about it;

➢ recognize the links between your own interpretation, the writer's purpose, and the responses of your audience; and

➢ see writing as a collaboration.

Learning to write is in large measure learning to read. The text you must read most carefully is the one you write, an **ESSAY** you will ask someone else to read. It may start as a jotting in the margin of a book you are reading or as a brief note in a journal, and it will go through several drafts before it becomes an essay. To produce something that another person will find worth reading, you yourself must read each draft with care, trying to imagine the effect your words are likely to have on your reader. In writing about literature, you will apply some of the same critical skills to your reading, that is, you will examine your responses to what you are reading and will try to account for them.

Let's begin by looking at a very short story by Gilles Vigneault (1928–). Vigneault was born in the village of Natashquan on the north shore of the St. Lawrence River. He has published two volumes of short-short stories, or as they are sometimes called, "postcard" stories. The title of the first collection is translated by Paul Allard as *Tales on Tiptoe* (Press Porcépic, 1972). The second collection, *Contes du coin de l'oeil* (which means "stories from the corner of the eye") has not yet been translated. This story is translated by Jacqueline de Puthod.

THE WALL
Gilles Vigneault

A former mason, sentenced to twenty years' hard labour, was repairing with surprising care the exterior wall of his prison. He was, of course, closely guarded, and although the work was compulsory and under scrupulous surveillance, the taste for perfection he exhibited at it was a source of amazement to passers-by and even to his two guards. Someone expressed his surprise, and the former mason, without lifting his eyes from his work, replied as if he had expected the question all along. "What pleasure would there be in escaping from a prison that was poorly built?"

Then, before the anxious prison guards who had become more watchful than ever, he went on as though talking to himself: "When you've put your own hand to the making of a wall, it tells you more about human freedom than all the philosophers put together."

This saying spread far and wide until it reached the ears of a monk. The monk came to visit the mason. They talked together at length. And the mason, without disturbing a soul, left the prison by the main gate, wearing a habit and a rope belt.

The prison director, a subtle man though he didn't show it, recently asked a professional burglar to repair a window sash. The work was so well done that one feels something is bound to happen, despite the formal order issued that day forbidding anyone to speak to a prisoner at work.

READING AS RE-CREATION

If we were Vigneault's fellow Québecois, we would be very familiar with his POEMS and his songs, lyrics that made him the most popular *chansonnier* of the vital period of the "quiet revolution" in Québec in the 1960s. Indeed, his song *"Mon pays n'est-ce pas un pays; c'est l'hiver"* ("My country isn't a country; it's the winter") became almost an anthem in Québec during this period. But we are not Vigneault's original readers, and we are reading the story in translation, so inevitably we read "The Wall" in a somewhat different way. This difference gets us to an important point about writing and reading. A writer writes, sets forth his or her MEANING, and attempts to guide the reader's responses, as we all do when we write a letter home saying that we are thinking of dropping a course or asking for money or trying to get a commitment. To this extent, the writer creates the written work and puts a meaning in it.

The reader, whether reading as an assignment or for recreation, *re*-creates it according to his or her experience and understanding. For instance, if the letter-writer's appeal for money is indirect, the reader may miss it entirely or may sense it but feel that the need is not urgent. If, on the other hand, the appeal is direct or demanding, the reader may feel irritated or imposed upon, even assaulted. "Oh, but I didn't mean it that way," the writer later protests. Still, that's the way the reader took it. The letter is "out there," between the writer and the reader, but the *meaning* is something the reader, as well as the writer, makes.

Since all readers bring themselves to a written work, they bring something individual. For instance, although many of Vigneault's original readers were familiar with the European folk tradition within which tales of this type fit, and people in Québec were familiar with stories in which monks and priests play a role, they must have varied in their attitudes to the memories and to the iconographic figures that populate this story. For younger Québecois, the story (then as now) seems old-fashioned. The monk who visits the prison is a type, not a real man. But to older readers, the monk might seem like the local parish priest, a man who played an important role in early Québec social history. Before they read a story like this, many of today's readers do not know anything about the subject. For readers from the Prairies and the Pacific coast, in fact, it may seem to be set in a foreign land. Prisons are imagined from television depictions, and they are much more violent and much less personal than this cozy jail. Inmates are more likely to be seen as gang leaders or violent criminals than as homely philosophers. Moreover, even if a present-day reader in Hamilton, Burnaby, or St. John's knows something of Québec folk history, he or she may assume that "The Wall" depicts a way of life still current; a reader from Québec may see in the work a depiction of a lost way of life, a depiction of the good old days (or perhaps of the bad old days, depending on the reader's POINT OF VIEW). Much depends, we can say, on the reader's storehouse of experience.

To repeat: Our reading is a *re*-creation; the author has tried to guide our responses, but inevitably our own experiences, including our ethnic background and our education, contribute to our responses. You may find useful a distinction that E. D. Hirsch makes in *Validity in Interpretation* (1967). For Hirsch, the *meaning* in a TEXT is the author's intended meaning; the *significance* is the particular relevance for each reader. In this view, when you think about meaning you are thinking about what the author was trying to say and to do—for instance, to take an old THEME and treat it in a new way. When you think about significance, you are thinking about what the work does for you—enlarges your mind, offends you by its depiction of women, resonates with IMAGES with which you are familiar as a Canadian, or whatever.

MAKING REASONABLE INFERENCES

If when we read and especially when we talk of significance we are re-creating, is there really no use in talking (or in writing) about literature since all of us perceive it in our relatively private ways, rather like the seven blind men in the FABLE? One man, you will recall, touched the elephant's tail (or was it his trunk?) and said that the elephant is like a snake; another touched the elephant's side and said the elephant is like a wall; a third touched the elephant's leg and said the elephant is like a tree; and so on. Notice that each of the blind men *did* perceive an aspect of the elephant—an elephant is massive, like a wall or a tree, and an elephant is (in its way) remarkably supple, as you know if you have given peanuts to one.

As readers, we can and should make an effort to understand what the author seems to be getting at; that is, we should make an effort to understand the words in their context. We shouldn't look up every word we don't know, at least on the first reading, but if certain unfamiliar words are repeated and thus seem especially important, we will probably want to look them up. (And if we are later writing about the text we will need to look up all words that we don't already know.) It happens that in "The Wall" the word *mason* appears: The word names a skilled worker who builds in stone or a related material, like brick or concrete. This word is crucial, but the context probably makes it clear. Had any reader thought the word referred to a member of the Freemasons' Lodge, for example, he or she would quickly realize that Vigneault is using it in its original meaning. The point is this: The writer is pitching, and he expects the reader to catch. A reader who does not know that a monk's habit (or costume) is traditionally belted with a humble rope, for instance, will miss the subtlety of the escape plan. Although writers tell us a good deal, they do not tell us everything. We know that the prison director is a subtle man, but we don't know exactly what he plans by allowing a burglar to repair a window. Further, Vigneault tells us nothing of the monk's reason for participating in the escape—or whether he does so willingly. It rather *sounds* as though the mason convinces the monk to assist him by his philosophical musings, but readers may disagree. One reader may argue that the monk is impressed by this clever mason and thinks he deserves to be free; another may say that the monk comes to accept a new understanding of freedom and chooses to remain in the prison as a hermit. In short, a text includes INDETERMINACIES (passages that careful readers agree are open to various interpretations) and GAPS (things left unsaid in the story, such as why the mason is in prison in the first place). As we work our way through a text, we keep re-evaluating what we have read, pulling the details together to make sense of them in a process called CONSISTENCY BUILDING.

Whatever the gaps, careful readers are able to draw many reasonable inferences about the mason. We can list some of them:

- He works with "surprising care" even though he has been sentenced to twenty years' punishment.

- He has a taste for "perfection."

- He seems to accept a challenge: "what pleasure would there be in escaping" if it is easy?

- Given this last point, he is patient and thorough.

- He is able to see that his own "hand" is involved in his imprisonment and in his freedom and sees this personal truth as more profound than any philosophy.

You may at this point want to go back and reread "The Wall" to see what else you can say about the mason. And now, what of the monk, or the director, or the burglar? At this point you may want to make a list like the one for the mason for each of these CHARACTERS.

READING WITH A PEN IN HAND

Perhaps the best way to read attentively is to mark the text, underlining or highlighting passages that seem especially interesting, and to jot notes or queries in the margins. Here is the work once more, this time with the marks that a student added after a second reading.

THE WALL
Gilles Vigneault

A former mason, sentenced to twenty years' hard labour, was repairing with surprising care the exterior wall of his prison. He was, of course, closely guarded, and although the work was compulsory and under scrupulous surveillance, the taste for perfection he exhibited at it was a source of amazement to passers-by and even to his two guards. Someone expressed his surprise, and the former mason, without lifting his eyes from his work, replied as if he had expected the question all along. "What pleasure would there be in escaping from a prison that was poorly built?"

why surprise?

check this

odd

repeats l. 1

like "one" mason, in l. 27

contrast between mason and guard

Then, before the anxious prison guards who had become more watchful than ever, he went on as though talking to himself: "When you've put your own hand to the making of a wall, it tells you more about human freedom than all the philosophers put together."

important? works for his own beliefs?

This saying spread far and wide until it reached the ears of a monk. The monk came to visit the mason. They talked together at length. And the mason, without disturbing a soul, left the prison by the main gate, wearing a habit and a rope belt.

repeated subject— echo, like l. 1 + l. 8

Is prisoner religious in some way? Or a philosopher?

The prison director, a subtle man though he didn't show it, recently asked a professional burglar to repair a window sash. The work was so well done that one feels something is bound to happen, despite the formal order issued that day forbidding anyone to speak to a prisoner at work.

nice detail

Compare description of "former mason"

has the lesson been learned?

Who? reader? narrator?

RECORDING YOUR FIRST IMPRESSIONS

After you annotate your text, another useful way of getting at meanings is to write down your initial responses to the story, jotting down your impressions as they come to you in any order—almost as though you are talking to yourself. Since no one else is going to read your notes, you can be entirely free and at ease. You can write in sentences or not; it's up to you. Write whatever comes into your mind, whatever the story triggers in your own imagination, whatever rings true or reminds you of your own experiences.

Here is the response of the student who annotated the text.

```
I like the way the burglar seems to be duplicating the
mason's action.  And I like the way the prison director
seems to know what is going on and tries, on the one
```

hand, to prevent it by "forbidding anyone to talk to a prisoner at work" but, on the other hand, may cause it to happen again when he "asks" a burglar to work on another escape route. I like the mason's attitude to doing his best work and his idea that success is only sweet if earned. I can see these people even though there is so little personal description. I'd like to meet this mason after he leaves prison and ask him what his "freedom" feels like.

Here is another student's first response to "The Wall."

This is a very short story. I didn't know stories were this short, but I like it because you can get it all quickly and it's no trouble to reread it carefully. The shortness, though, leaves a lot of gaps for the reader to fill in. So much is <u>not</u> said. Your imagination is put to work.

But I can see the mason working at his wall-- quietly powerful and precise--no one you would want to argue with. He's formal and distant and asks serious questions. He seems to be building a wall to give himself satisfaction in a job well done, but maybe he's just planning his escape. Maybe he only says these clever things in order to attract the monk to visit, not because he really means them. Maybe he is clever in a different way; he plots to appear philosophical just so he can trap the guards and the monk. Maybe I can develop this idea.

Another thing. I can see that these people are in a prison but it isn't full of serious criminals. It seems more like a small town, or a club. The prisoners are at "hard labour" but they work at their professions. The thief is a "professional burglar," but the mason seems to be more a professional craftsman. This contrast might be important to what the story is saying, or what the prison director is planning. But I don't know enough about this kind of old-fashioned prison to go into this. Their life is different from mine; no one I know is a burglar and no one I know is this patient!

AUDIENCE AND PURPOSE

Suppose you are beginning the process of writing about "The Wall" for someone else, not for yourself. The first question to ask yourself is: For whom am I writing? In other words, Who is my *audience*? (Of course, you probably are writing because an instructor has asked you to do so, but you still must imagine an audience. Your instructor may tell you, for instance, to write for your classmates or for the readers of the college newspaper.) If you are writing with people who are familiar with some of Vigneault's other work, you will not have to say much about the author; certainly if you are writing in Québec you won't. If you are writing for an audience that is interested in the tradition of the folk TALE in Québec (or comparing it to the strong folkloric tradition of the Maritimes), you may want to mention stories by, say, Jacques Ferron or Roch Carrier.

In a sense, as we said at the outset, the audience is your collaborator; your reader helps you decide what you will say. You are helped also by your sense of *purpose*. If your aim is to introduce readers to Vigneault, you will make certain points. If your aim is to tell people what you think "The Wall" means about freedom, or the human sense of accomplishment, you will say different things. If your aim is to have a little fun and to entertain an audience that is familiar with "The Wall," you may write a PARODY (a humorous imitation). If you are working from a particular critical perspective, you will select details that develop that approach.

A WORD ON DISCOURSE

Writers have always known that audience and purpose are important to the pre-writing process. Today, in Canada, writers are interested in the relationships among audience, purpose, and the style of writing they adopt (even the GENRE they employ). Discourse Theory and what is called "The New Rhetoric" argue that the interplay among writer, reader, and style of writing helps to create genres that can then be repeated. Further, these theories suggest that such repetition is part of social process and that genre is part of a complex social construction in which literature (and related forms) play an important role. (See the discussion of CULTURAL MATERIALISM in Chapter 5.) These ideas suggest just how important it is to think carefully about who will read your text and why you want to write it.

A WRITING ASSIGNMENT ON "THE WALL"

The Assignment

Let's assume that you are trying to describe "The Wall" to someone who has not read it. You probably will briefly summarize the ACTION, such as it is, will mention where it takes place and who the characters are (including their relationships), and what, if anything, happens to them. Beyond that, you will probably try to explain as honestly as you can what makes "The Wall" appealing or interesting or boring or whatever.

Here is an essay that a student wrote for this assignment.

A Sample Essay

Finding Freedom

Gilles Vigneault's "The Wall" describes an escape from prison. This escape is not a daring breakout, nor is it the real reason Vigneault is writing. Instead, the story asks the reader to consider what freedom really means and how we can become free in ourselves.

A mason is sent to prison; we don't know why. He is set to work by the Warden to build a wall which he does with surprising care because there would be "no pleasure [. . .] in escaping from a prison that was poorly built." He also comments that building a strong wall makes him think about freedom and what it means. These sayings--which seem to define his pride in his craft and also his challenge to the authorities--become famous. A monk visits. We don't know what the men discuss, but the monk either allows the mason to borrow his habit as a disguise, or the mason takes it from him and escapes. Since Vigneault notes that the mason leaves "without disturbing a soul," it seems that the monk agrees to the switch. Later, in a strange decision, the Warden puts a thief to work repairing a window. Is the Warden setting up another escape? Or is he encouraging the "professional burglar" to ponder the nature of freedom and his role in making himself free?

The story is comic, in an understated way, but it asks important questions. The mason committed some crime, so he must accept a role in his own imprisonment. At the same time, he is free within himself even in jail, because he has pride in his own accomplishment. That sense of self-worth seems to convince the monk that the mason deserves to be physically free because he is already psychologically free. Perhaps the monk decides that committing himself to jail will allow him to free himself mentally or spiritually (as hermits tried to do in medieval times). The burglar, in turn, is challenged

to determine whether his pride lies in being a
"professional" criminal, or in being sure enough of
himself to make good his escape. The Warden is, indeed,
a "subtle man."

These are questions which we are forced to ask
ourselves because the author gives us so little plot and
no real answers. Because so much is left to us to fill
in, the reader is invited to face important questions in
a very intimate way.

Other Possibilities for Writing

Of course, one might write a paper of a very different sort. Consider the
following possibilities:

1. Write a sequel, describing what happens to the burglar. Or describe the
   mason's life outside prison.
2. Write a letter from the monk to the mason, or to the prison director.
3. Imagine that the monk is now an old man, writing his memoirs. What
   does he say about the mason and their secret conversation?
4. Write a narrative based on your own sense of what freedom means and
   how you have obtained it, or how you hope to become free in your life.
5. Write an expository essay about freedom in another country from which
   you came to Canada; how is freedom different here?
6. Write an expository essay considering how reading this story and writing about it may make someone rethink his or her own freedom. Will
   the *act* of writing change this person? (This is an essay related to
   Discourse Theory.)

▭ Suggestions for Further Reading

Aviva Freedman and Peter Medway, *Genre and the New Rhetoric* (1994),
especially Carolyn R. Miller's essays, "Genre as Social Action" (23–42) and
"Rhetorical Community: The Cultural Basis of Genre" (67–78) and Richard
Coe's essay, "'An Arousing and Fulfilment of Desires': The Rhetoric of Genre
in the Process Era—and Beyond" (181–90).

2

The Reader as Writer:
Drafting and Writing

Learning Objectives

When you've read this chapter, you should be able to

➤ use various pre-writing techniques to help you begin to write, in order to find a thesis;

➤ consider keeping a journal to help you generate ideas, in order to find a thesis;

➤ understand the concept of thesis and how to write a thesis;

➤ outline a draft;

➤ help yourself and your colleagues through peer review; and

➤ revise your first draft into a more exact and polished essay.

PRE-WRITING: GETTING IDEAS

How does one "learn to have ideas"? Try reading with a pencil or a set of coloured highlighters in hand so that (as we have already seen) you can annotate the text, or keep a journal in which you jot down reflections about your reading, or talk with others about the reading. Let's take another look at the first method, annotating.

Annotating a Text

In reading, if you own the book do not hesitate to mark it up, indicating (by highlighting or underlining, or by marginal notes) what puzzles you, what pleases or interests you, and what displeases or bores you. Of course, later you'll want to think further about these responses, asking yourself if, on rereading, you still feel this way, and if not, why not, but these first responses will get you started.

Annotations of the sort given on page 15, which chiefly call attention to contrasts, indicate that the student is thinking about writing some sort of **ANALYSIS** of the story. An analysis is an essay in which the parts are examined to see how they relate to each other or in which a part is examined to see how it relates to the whole. Later on, while rereading, you may be able to annotate more fully. One method is to choose a different colour of marker for different aspects you notice. Then, when you go back over the text you quickly see repetitions and patterns, and you can quickly find examples.

More about Getting Ideas: "Marrying the Hangman" by Margaret Atwood

Let's look at a story that is a little longer than "The Wall," and then we'll discuss how, in addition to annotating, one might get ideas for writing about it.

MARRYING THE HANGMAN
Margaret Atwood

She has been condemned to death by hanging. A man may escape this death by becoming the hangman, a woman by marrying the hangman. But at the present time there is no hangman; thus there is no escape. There is only a death, indefinitely postponed. This is not fantasy, it is history.

. . .

To live in prison is to live without mirrors. To live without mirrors is to live without the self. She is living selflessly, she finds a hole in the stone wall and on the other side of the wall, a voice. The voice comes through darkness and has no face. This voice becomes her mirror.

. . .

In order to avoid her death, her particular death, with wrung neck and swollen tongue, she must marry the hangman. But there is no hangman, first she must create him, she must persuade this man at the end of the voice, this voice she has never seen and which has never seen her, this darkness, she must persuade him to renounce his face, exchange it for the impersonal mask of death, of official death which has eyes but no mouth, this mask of a dark leper. She must transform his hands so they will be willing to twist the rope around throats that have been singled out as hers was, throats other than hers. She must marry the hangman or no one, but that is not so bad. Who else is there to marry?

. . .

You wonder about her crime. She was condemned to death for stealing clothes from her employer, from the wife of her employer. She wished to make herself more beautiful. This desire in servants was not legal.

. . .

She uses her voice like a hand, her voice reaches through the wall, stroking and touching. What could she possibly have said that would convince him? He was not condemned to death, freedom awaited him. What was the temptation, the one that worked? Perhaps he wanted to live with a woman whose life he had saved, who had seen down into the earth but had nevertheless followed him back up to life. It was his only chance to be a hero, to one person at least, for the others would now despise him. He was in prison for wounding another man, on one finger of the right hand, with a sword. This too is history.

My friends, who are both women, tell me their stories, which cannot be believed and which are true. They are horror stories and they have not happened to me, they have not yet happened to me, they have happened to me but we are detached, we watch our unbelief with horror. Such things cannot happen to us, it is afternoon and these things do not happen in the afternoon. The trouble was, she said, I didn't have time to put my glasses on and without them I'm blind as a bat, I couldn't even see who it was. These things happen and we sit at a table and tell stories about them so we can finally believe. This is not fantasy, it is history, there is more than one hangman and because of this some of them are unemployed.

. . .

He said: the end of walls, the end of ropes, the opening of doors, a field, the wind, a house, the sun, a table, an apple.

She said: nipple, arms, lips, wine, belly, hair, bread, thighs, eyes, eyes.

They both kept their promises.

. . .

The hangman is not such a bad fellow. Afterwards he goes to the refrigerator and cleans up the leftovers, though he does not wipe up what he accidentally spills. He wants only the simple things: a chair, someone to pull off his shoes, someone to watch him while he talks, with admiration and fear, gratitude if possible, someone in whom to plunge himself for rest and renewal. These things can best be had by marrying a woman who has been condemned to death by other men for wishing to be beautiful. There is a wide choice.

. . .

Everyone said he was a Fool.

Everyone said she was a clever woman.

They used the word *ensnare*.

. . .

What did they say the first time they were alone together in the same room? What did he say when she had removed her veil and he could see that she was not a voice but a body and therefore finite? What did she say when she discovered that she had left one locked room for another? They talked of love, naturally, though that did not keep them busy forever.

The fact is there are no stories I can tell my friends that will make them feel better. History cannot be erased, although we can soothe ourselves by speculating about it. At that time there were no female hangmen. Perhaps there have never been any, and thus no man could save his life by marriage. Though a woman could, according to the law.

. . .

He said: foot, boot, order, city, fist, roads, time, knife.

She said: water, night, willow, rope hair, earth, belly, cave, meat, shroud, open, blood.

They both kept their promises.

"After 29 April 1752, all trace of him and his wife is lost." ("Corolère, Jean," *The Dictionary of Canadian Biography,* Vol. 3).

Brainstorming for Ideas for Writing

Unlike annotating, which consists of making brief notes and small marks on the printed page, *brainstorming*—the free jotting down of ideas—requires that you jot down whatever comes to mind, without inhibition. Don't worry about spelling, about writing complete sentences, or about unifying your thoughts;

just let one thought lead to another. Later, you will review your jottings, deleting some, connecting with arrows others that are related, amplifying still others. For now, you want to get going, and so there is no reason to look back. Thus, you might jot down something about the title:

```
Title--marriage and a hangman.  Weird to put the two
together.
```

And then, perhaps prompted by "marriage," you might happen to add something to this effect:

```
Is this history true?  Could a woman save herself this
way?  What does that say about the institution of
marriage?
```

Your next jotting might have little or nothing to do with this issue; it might simply say:

```
Enjoyed "Marrying" more than "The Wall" partly because
"Marrying" is so shocking.
```

And then you might ask yourself:

```
By shocking, do I mean "improbable," or what?  Come to
think of it, maybe it's not so improbable.  A lot
depends on what the marriage was like.
```

Focused Free Writing

Focused free writing, or directed free writing, is a related method that some writers use to uncover ideas they want to write about. Concentrating on one issue, such as a question that strikes them as worth puzzling over (What kind of person is this woman?), they write at length, non-stop, for perhaps five or ten minutes. They don't pause, or think: they just write.

Writers who find free writing helpful put down everything that has bearing on the one issue or question they are examining. They do not stop at this stage to evaluate the results, and they do not worry about grammar or spelling. They just explore ideas in a steady stream of writing, using whatever associations come to mind. (Fiction is sometimes written in STREAM OF CONSCIOUSNESS, but this is not, as it may appear, free writing. An author has carefully crafted the work to resemble spontaneous association.)

After the free-writing session, these writers usually go back and reread what they have written, highlighting or underlining what seems to be of value. Of course, they find much that is of little or no use, but they also usually find that some strong ideas have surfaced and have received some development. At this point, the writers are often able to make a scratch outline and then begin a draft. Some writers look for a central idea in what they've written, repeat it as the first sentence of a new paragraph, and then free write again. This is called "looping," and it sometimes helps to refine general ideas down into specific ones that lead to an essay.

Here is an example of one student's focused free writing:

What do I know about the woman prisoner? What can I
figure out from what Atwood tells me? When she finds
herself in prison she has no mirror. This woman was
"condemned to death for stealing clothes," for wanting
to be beautiful. So she talks to the voice through the
wall and he becomes her mirror. Is that good? She
perceives that she has to "create" a hangman in order to
marry him in order to escape her "particular death"
which she describes as pretty gruesome. To do so is to
surrender her power to him even though she's created him
in some way. So it's a power issue but it's also a
feminist one. When she makes him she must accept him
sexually and watch him "with admiration and fear." A
woman has to accept these things from a man if she needs
him for his power or if she can only "see" herself in a
mirror that is him. Why can't she see herself for
herself? To do so would mean she was hanged. Is this
the connection with the narrator's friends and their
stories? I wonder what these friends are telling. They
are horror stories. Are they about having no power?
Are these women talking together?

Listing

In your preliminary thinking, you may find it useful to make lists. In the
previous chapter, we saw that listing the traits of characters was helpful in
thinking about Vigneault's "The Wall." For "Marrying," you might list the
woman's traits, or you might list the stages in her story. (Such a list is not the
same as a summary of the PLOT. The list helps the writer see the sequence of
psychological changes.)

She is living "selflessly" ("condemned to death"
  "indefinitely postponed")
lives alone--comes to use voice as mirror
"Who else is there to marry?"
"She uses her voice like a hand [. . .] stroking and
  touching."
He says words that signal freedom and domestic life
She says words that signal sexuality and domestic life
"They both kept their promises"
" [. . .] she had left one locked room for another"
"History cannot be erased"

```
His words change to words of domination and pain--"fist,
   boot, knife"
Her words describe woman's concerns and cycles--"water,
   open, blood"
No trace of them exists--she disappears into a
   historical note.
```

Of course, unlike brainstorming and annotating, which let you go in all directions, listing requires that you first make a decision about what you will be listing—traits of character, images, puns, or whatever. Once you make the decision, you can then construct the list, and, with a list in front of you, you will probably see patterns that you were not fully conscious of earlier.

Asking Questions

If you feel stuck, ask yourself questions. (You'll recall that the assignment on "The Wall" asked you to ask yourself questions about the work—for instance, a question about the relationship between the characters—and about your responses to it: "You will probably try to explain as honestly as you can what makes 'The Wall' appealing or interesting or boring or whatever.")

If you are thinking about a work of FICTION, ask yourself questions about the plot, any SUBPLOT, and the characters: Are they believable? Are they interesting? What does it all add up to? What does the story mean *to you*? (The chapters on the ESSAY, FICTION, **DRAMA**, **POETRY**, and **FILM** include questions on each form.) One student found it helpful to jot down the following questions:

```
Plot
   Ending satisfying?  What is the relationship of the
   stories of the friends to the history?
Character
   Is the woman unfeeling?  Immoral?
   Is she a "clever woman?"  Does she "ensnare?"
   What might her marriage have been like?  No details.
   (Can we tell what her husband was like?)
   And yet they "both kept their promises"
Symbolism
   Cut with stories from present day.  Do the words from
   the historical relationship suggest something to the
   women telling their contemporary "horror" stories?
```

You don't have to be as tidy as this student is. You may begin by jotting down notes and queries about what you like or dislike and about what puzzles or amuses you. What follows are the jottings of another student, Amy Wong. They are, obviously, in no particular order—the student is brainstorming, putting down whatever occurs to her—though it is equally obvious that one note sometimes led to the next:

```
Title sums up the whole story.  Too much?  What might be
   a better title?
Could a woman be so calculating?
Is she heartless?  Did she love him?
Why does he agree to her plan?
Why wasn't she allowed to be beautiful?  Because she was
   a servant?
Are all women servants?
Could this story happen today?  Feminist interpretation?
Tricky ending--but maybe it shouldn't end with realistic
   details.
What happens when couples stop talking about love--"that
   did not keep them busy forever"?
Irony: her imprisonment repeats itself.  She trades one
   "locked room" for another.
```

These jottings will help the reader-writer think about the story, find a special point of interest, and develop a thoughtful argument about it.

Keeping a Journal

A journal is not a diary, a record of what the writer did during the day ("today I read Atwood's 'Marrying.' Weather damp."). Rather, a journal is a place to store some of the thoughts you may have inscribed on a scrap of paper or in the margin of the text, such as your initial response to the title of a work or to the ending. It is also a place to jot down further reflections, such as thoughts about what the work means to you, and what was said in the classroom about writing in general or specific works.

You will get something out of your journal if you write an entry at least once a week, but you will get much more if you write entries after reading each assignment and after each class meeting. You may, for instance, want to reflect on why your opinion is so different from that of another student, or you may want to apply a concept such as CHARACTER or **IRONY** or "plausibility" to a story that you may later write about in an essay. Comparisons are especially helpful: How does this work (or this character, or this **RHYME** scheme) differ from last week's reading?

You might even make an entry in the form of a letter to the author or from one character to another. You might write a dialogue between characters in two works or between two authors, or you might record an experience of your own that is comparable to something in the work.

A student who wrote about "Marrying the Hangman" began with the following entry in his journal. In reading this entry, notice that one idea stimulates another. The student was, quite rightly, concerned with getting and exploring ideas, not with writing a unified paragraph.

```
Seems clever rather than real, not plausible.  The
woman's decision is so businesslike--maybe some women
might respond like this, but probably not most.
```

Does literature deal with unusual people, or with
typical people? Shouldn't it deal with typical? Maybe
not. (Anyway, how can I know?) Is "typical" same as
"plausible"? prob. not.

Anyway, whether this woman is typical or not, could
she talk the guy into becoming a hangman? Think more
about this.

Husband dominated her life but he wanted a decent
life and he "is not such a bad fellow." Is it a crime
to want a partner to admire you? I guess he just
couldn't see how he denied her a private space. Do men
allow women space today? Is this why the friends have
horror stories to tell?

Critical Thinking: Arguing with Yourself

In our discussion of annotating, brainstorming, free writing, listing, asking
questions, and writing entries in a journal, the emphasis has been on responding freely rather than in any highly systematic or disciplined way. Something
strikes you (perhaps an idea, perhaps an uncertainty), and you jot it down.
Maybe even before you finish jotting it down you begin to question it, but
probably not; at this early stage it is enough to put down on paper some
thoughts, rooted in your first responses, and to keep going on.

The almost random play of mind that is evident in brainstorming and in
the other activities already discussed is of course a kind of thinking, but the
term **CRITICAL THINKING** is reserved for something different. When you
think critically, you sceptically scrutinize your own ideas, for example by
searching out your underlying assumptions, or by evaluating what you have
quickly jotted down as evidence. We have already seen some examples of
this sort of analysis of our own thinking in the journal entries, where, for
instance, a student wrote that literature should probably deal with "typical"
people, and then wondered if "typical" and "plausible" were the same, and
then added "prob[ably] not."

Speaking broadly, critical thinking is rational, logical thinking. In thinking critically,

• you scrutinize your assumptions, and

• you test the evidence you have collected, even to the extent of looking
  for counterevidence.

Let's start with assumptions. If, for instance, I say that a story is weak
because it is improbable, I ought at least to think about my assumption that
improbability is a fault. I can begin by asking myself if all good stories—or all
of the stories that I value highly—are probable. I may recall that among my
favourites is *Star Wars* (or *Gulliver's Travels* or *Animal Farm*)—and so I
probably have to withdraw my assumption that improbability in itself makes
a story less than good. I may of course go on to refine the idea, and decide that
improbability is not a fault in science fiction, or in satiric stories, but is a fault

in other kinds, but that is not the same as saying bluntly that improbability is a fault.

The other aspect of critical thinking that we have isolated—searching for counterevidence within the literary work—especially involves rereading the work to see if we have overlooked material or have taken a particular detail out of context. If, for instance, we say that in "Marrying the Hangman" the condemned woman talks the man into marrying her, can we be sure he didn't want a domestic life himself all along? Or a job, even if it was as hangman? Perhaps the original observation will stand up, but perhaps on rereading the story we may come to feel, as we examine their actions and words, that both characters are unconsciously living out roles already prepared for them by "the law."

Of course, different readers may come to different conclusions; the important thing is that all readers should subject their initial responses to critical thinking, testing their responses against all of the evidence. **Remember:** your instructor probably expects you to hand in an essay that is essentially an *argument,* a paper that advances a THESIS of your own. The thesis might be that the story is improbable, or is typical of Atwood, or uses history to illustrate contemporary feminist thinking. Whatever your thesis, it should be able to withstand scrutiny. You may not convince every reader that you are unquestionably right, but you should make every reader feel that your argument is thoughtful. If you read your notes and then your drafts critically, you probably will write a paper that meets this standard.

Just as your first jottings probably won't be the products of critical thinking, your first reading of the literary work probably won't be a critical reading. It is entirely appropriate to begin by reading simply for enjoyment. After all, the reason we read literature (or, for example, listen to music) is to derive pleasure. It happens, however, that in this course you are trying to deepen your understanding of literature, and therefore you are *studying* literature. On subsequent readings, therefore, you will read the work critically, taking careful note of (for instance) the writer's view of human nature, and of the writer's ways of achieving certain effects.

We will discuss critical thinking again, on pages 83–84, in talking about interpretations of literature.

Arriving at a Thesis, and Arguing It

If you think critically about your early jottings and about the literary work itself, you probably will find that some of your jottings lead to dead ends, but some will lead to further ideas that hold up under scrutiny. What the THESIS of the essay will be—the idea that will be asserted and developed or argued (supported with evidence)—is still in doubt, but there is no doubt about one thing: A good essay will have a thesis, a point, an argument. You ought to be able to state your point in a THESIS SENTENCE. Note that a thesis is a *full sentence*, not simply a subject waiting for a verb to complete it. When you have thought out the verb or verbs you need, you will have determined what you want to develop. It is the process of creating a full and accurate thesis sentence that helps you organize the whole essay in your mind.

Consider these candidates as possible thesis sentences:

1. The condemned woman convinces a man to marry her in order to live.

True, but scarcely a point that can be argued or even developed. About the most the essayist can do with this sentence is amplify it by summarizing the plot of the story, a task not worth doing unless the plot is unusually obscure. An essay may include a sentence or two of SUMMARY to give readers their bearings, but a summary is not an essay.

2. The shift from history to the present makes the story universal.

Here is a thesis. The writer will probably suggest that the sketchy details of the historical story illustrate the kinds of emotions and actions that govern men and women and that these can, therefore, serve as examples for the troubles of the modern women telling their "horror" stories.

3. The story is clever but contrived because it is based on an unreal character.

Here, too, is a thesis, a point of view that can be argued. Whether this thesis is true is another matter. The writer's job will be to support it by presenting evidence. Probably the writer will have no difficulty in finding evidence that the story is "clever"; the difficulty probably will be in establishing a case that the CHARACTERIZATION of the condemned woman is "unreal." The writer will have to set forth some ideas about what makes a character real and then will have to show that the woman is an "unreal" (unbelievable) figure. And the writer will have to deal with the historical footnote telling us that a woman like this one actually did live, though we don't know details of her biography. (See glossary entries for ROUND and FLAT CHARACTERS.)

4. The lack of detail of the ending is believable partly because it is a story about all women, not just this historical figure.

It happens that the student who wrote the essay printed on pages 23–24 began by drafting an essay based on the third of these thesis topics, but as she worked on a draft she found that she could not support her assertion that the character was unconvincing. In fact, she came to believe that the woman summed up very believable characteristics of many women. So she shifted to the second thesis topic.

In creating a final thesis, it is a good idea to remember the suggestion by the psychologist and educator, Jean Piaget, that a good thesis should have *resonance* or *dissonance* within it. That is, one part should establish a given against which the other part acts. Often this can be well expressed by using a thesis in the form "Although *a*, then *b*," or "Despite *a*, *b* [. . .]," (dissonance), or "Given *a*, then *b*," or "Because of *a*, *b* [. . .] (resonance).

Numbers 3 and 4 use the form "*a* because *b*," which is another version of the suggested model. Here are some examples. Notice that these put the topics into specific, thesis form:

"Although the condemned woman in Margaret Atwood's 'Marrying the Hangman' convinces a man to marry her in order to live, she trades one prison for another."

"Although the woman in Margaret Atwood's 'Marrying the Hangman' seems unreal, the dilemma in which she finds herself is real for many women."

"Because men and women have been taught how to act out their lives, they trap one another in emotional and legal prisons."

"Despite the changes to women's legal status since 1752, the plight of the historical figure in Margaret Atwood's 'Marrying the Hangman' is real for women today."

Remember: Your thesis needn't slavishly follow this exact formula; these examples show models of an approach to writing a good, dynamic thesis.

Remember: It's not likely that you will quickly find a thesis. Annotating, making entries in a journal, and writing a first draft are *ways of finding* a thesis.

WRITING A DRAFT

After jotting down notes, and further notes stimulated by rereading and further thinking, you probably will be able to formulate a tentative thesis. At this point, most writers find it useful to clear the air by glancing over their preliminary notes and by jotting down the thesis and a few especially promising notes—brief statements of what they think their key points may be, such as key quotations that may help support the thesis.

Here are the selected notes (not the original brainstorming notes, but a later selection from them, with additions) and a draft that makes use of them:

```
title?  Prison for Women (?)  Ironical Freedom (?)
   Ironies for Women (?)
thesis: although the woman escapes hanging, ironically
   she continues a life in prison
chief irony: woman can only get out by marrying and
   being subservient to a man
other ironies:
      1. desire "to make herself more beautiful" is her
         crime and is needed to capture him
      2. woman can only "see" herself in him as a mirror
      3. modern women hearing story are also trapped
```

These notes are in effect a very brief *outline.* Some writers at this point like to develop a fuller outline, but probably most writers begin with only a brief outline, knowing that in the process of developing a draft from these few notes additional ideas will arise. For these writers, the time to jot down a detailed outline is *after* they have written a first or second draft. The outline of the written draft will, as we shall see, help them to make sure that their draft has an adequate organization, and that main points are developed.

A Sample Draft: "Ironies for Women"

Now for the student's draft—not the first version, but a revised draft with some of the irrelevancies of the first draft omitted and some evidence added.

The digits within the parentheses refer to the page numbers from which the quotations are drawn, though when writing about a short work page references are hardly necessary. Check with your instructor to find out if you must always give citations. (Detailed information about how to **DOCUMENT** a paper is given in Chapter 15.)

```
                    Ironies for Women
          After we know how Margaret Atwood's short story,
     "Marrying the Hangman," turns out, we find irony at the
     very start.  The story is about a woman who has been
     condemned to hang because she stole some clothes,
     because she "wanted to make herself more beautiful"
     (50).  She can only escape by marrying a hangman.  So
     she must first convince a man in the next cell to become
     the hangman.  Then he has to marry her.  She does
     convince him and she is released from prison.
          An irony is that she discovers immediately that she
     has "left one locked room for another" (52).  She is now
     his wife and she must obey him and keep his house.  And
     she discovers that love "did not keep them busy forever"
     (52).  Although he "is not such a bad fellow," and wants
     only a simple life, he also wants her to "watch him
     while he talks, with admiration and fear, gratitude if
     possible" (51).
          A deeper irony is the fact that the woman's crime
     was wanting to be beautiful.  Being beautiful was how
     she knew herself.  It is ironic that she is condemned by
     the very things that made her clever enough to convince
     the man and to seduce him.  Also, she has to give up her
     image of herself.  She can no longer see her own beauty.
     She uses him as a mirror.  In the prison she uses his
     voice through a hole in the wall to mirror back to her a
     sense of her identity.  But when she is free, she must
     continue to use him as her mirror.  If she resists, his
     words become harsh: "foot, boot," "fist," "knife" (52).
     This is her real imprisonment.
          The saddest irony in the story is the outer story.
     Some friends tell the narrator stories about abuse.  If
     we are right that one speaker has been raped, it is
     horrible that she didn't have "time to put my glasses
```

```
on" (50) so she couldn't see her attacker.  She is like
the woman speaking through the hole in the wall who was
unable to see the man she had to marry.  Atwood tells
this ironic historical anecdote to point out the
similarity to the contemporary women's lives.  "These
things happen" (51), she says.  The irony is that
history repeats itself.
```

```
                        Work Cited

Atwood, Margaret.  "Marrying the Hangman."  Two-Headed
     Poems.  Toronto: Oxford UP, 1978.
```

Revising a Draft

The draft is not yet a finished essay. The student went on to improve it in many small but important ways. First, the draft needs a good paragraph that will let the *audience*—the readers—know where the writer will be taking them. (Chapter 14 discusses introductory paragraphs.) Doubtless you know, from your own experience as a reader, that readers can follow an argument more easily and with more pleasure if early in the discussion the writer alerts them to the gist of the argument. (The title, too, can strongly suggest the thesis.) Second, some of the paragraphs could be clearer.

In revising paragraphs—or, for that matter, in revising an entire draft—writers unify, organize, clarify, and polish. Writers are assisted in revising if they imagine that they are readers. It helps to read the draft aloud. They try to put themselves into the mind of the imagined audience, asking themselves, "Is this clear?" "Will a reader need another example?" Or, on the other hand, "Will a reader feel that I am talking down, giving more examples than are needed?"

1. UNITY is achieved partly by eliminating irrelevancies. Notice that in the final version, the writer has deleted "an unnecessary transition in the story."
2. ORGANIZATION is a matter of arranging material into a SEQUENCE that will help the reader grasp the point.
3. CLARITY is achieved largely by providing concrete details and quotations to support generalizations and by providing helpful TRANSITIONS ("for instance," "furthermore," "on the other hand," "however").
4. POLISHING is small-scale revision. For instance, you should delete unnecessary repetitions. Similarly, in polishing, combine choppy sentences into longer sentences and break overly long sentences into shorter sentences. (In the third paragraph of the draft, many short sentences repeat the pronoun "she" and the idea of being beautiful. In the final draft, these are combined; secondary thoughts are made subordinate to major thoughts.)

Later, after producing a draft that seems close to a finished essay, writers engage in yet another activity. They edit.

5. EDITING is concerned with such matters as checking the accuracy of quotations by comparing them with the original, checking a dictionary for

accurate spelling, and consulting a grammar handbook for correct punctuation—for instance, whether a comma or a semicolon is needed in a particular sentence.

Outlining a Draft

Whether or not you draw up an outline as a preliminary guide *to writing a draft*, you will be able to improve your draft if you prepare an outline *of what you have written*. For each paragraph in your draft, jot down the gist of the TOPIC SENTENCE or **TOPIC** idea, and under each of these sentences, indented, jot down key words for the idea(s) developed in the paragraph. Thus, to create an outline of the first two paragraphs of the draft we have just looked at you might make these jottings:

```
story ironic from start

• woman wanted to be beautiful
• must convince man in the next cell to marry her to
  escape hanging

central irony

• she is still in prison of marriage
• love can't last forever
• he wants her to be grateful and to serve him
```

An outline of what you have written will help you to see if your draft is adequate in three important ways. The outline will show you

1. the sequence of major topics
2. the degree of development of these topics
3. the argument, the thesis

By studying your outline you may see (for instance) that your first major point (probably after an introductory paragraph) would be more effective as your third point, and that your second point needs to be developed further.

An outline of this sort is essentially a brief version of your draft, perhaps even using some phrases from the draft. But consider making yet another sort of outline, an outline indicating not what each paragraph says but what each paragraph *does*. An attempt at such an outline of the four-paragraph draft of the essay on "Marrying" might look like something like this:

1. she must escape by convincing the man to marry her
2. explains "central irony"
3. relates this irony to "deeper irony" of her wanting to be beautiful
4. shows "saddest irony" that modern women can share same prison

You ought to see a red flag here. The aim of this sort of outline is to indicate what each paragraph *does*, but the jotting for the first paragraph does not tell us what the paragraph does; rather, it more or less summarizes the content of the paragraph. Why? Because the paragraph does not *do* much of anything. Certainly it does not (for example) clearly introduce the thesis, or define a crucial term, or set the story in the context of Atwood's other work. An outline indicating the function of each paragraph will force you to see if your essay has an effective **STRUCTURE**. We will see that the student later wrote a new opening paragraph for the essay.

Peer Review

Your instructor may encourage (or even require) you to discuss your draft with another student or with a small group of students; that is, you may be asked to get a review from your peers. Such a procedure is helpful in several ways. First, it gives the writer a real audience, readers who can point to what pleases or puzzles them, who make suggestions, who may disagree (with the writer or with each other), and who frequently, though not intentionally, *misread.* Though writers don't necessarily like everything they hear (they seldom hear "This is perfect. Don't change a word!"), reading and discussing their work with others almost always gives them a fresh perspective on their work, and a fresh perspective may stimulate thoughtful revision. (Having your intentions *misread* because your writing isn't clear enough can be particularly stimulating.)

The writer whose work is being reviewed is not the sole beneficiary. When students regularly serve as readers for each other, they become better readers of their own work and consequently better revisers. As we stated in Chapter 1, learning to write is in large measure learning to read.

If peer review is a part of the writing process in your course, the instructor may distribute a sheet with some suggestions and questions. An example of such a sheet is shown on page 27.

Final Checks

After you have revised the draft in response to comments by your reviewer, print it out or read it very carefully on the screen. Read with a critical eye: you will probably find that you can improve even this version. Even at this late date you may think of a better title, or you may sense that a quotation doesn't sound quite right, or you might catch a grammar error. You can make small changes by hand, in ink, but if you make a substantial number of changes, print out a clean copy. (Don't worry too much about making the final paper "pretty." It is important that it look professional, but a few hand-written corrections are better than an inaccurate paper. Your instructor is looking for good thought and good writing, not a "neat" paper.)

You may get some help from the computer even at this last stage: use the spelling and grammar checkers. Word processors alert you to **CLICHÉS,** split infinitives, overuse of the passive voice, troublesome pairs of words (like *affect/effect*), certain kinds of grammatical errors, and words and phrases that are potentially sexist. But be careful: Computers are not yet good at understanding language, and you must know the grammar yourself to evaluate suggestions made by the computer. (This can be particularly troublesome for ESL students, who often make more mistakes by misunderstanding the grammar checker than by trusting their own ability.)

QUESTIONS FOR PEER REVIEW

Read each draft once, quickly. Then read it again, with the following questions in mind.

1. What is the essay's topic? Is it one of the assigned topics, or a variation from it? Does the draft show promise of fulfilling the assignment?
2. Looking at the essay as a whole, what thesis is stated or implied? If implied, try to state it in your own words. Should it be clearly stated at the outset?
3. Is the thesis reasonable? How might it be strengthened?
4. Looking at each paragraph separately:
   a. What is the basic point? (If it isn't clear to you, ask for clarification.)
   b. How does the paragraph relate to the essay's main idea or to the previous paragraph?
   c. Should some paragraphs be deleted? Be divided into two or more paragraphs? Be combined? Be put elsewhere? (If you outline the essay by jotting down the gist of each paragraph, you will get help in answering these questions.)
   d. Is each sentence clearly related to the sentence that precedes and to the sentence that follows?
   e. Is each paragraph adequately developed?
   f. Are there sufficient details, perhaps brief supporting quotations from the text?
5. What are the paper's chief strengths?
6. Make at least two specific suggestions that you think will help the author to improve the paper.

Remember: Set your spell checker to "English (Canadian)" or "English (United Kingdom)." Do not leave the default setting of "English (United States)."

Remember: Machines break down, so you need to allow time before your deadline for possible computer and printer glitches.

THE FINAL VERSION

Here is the final version of the student's essay. The essay that was submitted to the instructor was typed, but here, so that you can easily see how the draft has been revised, we print the draft with the final changes written in by hand.

History Repeats Itself
~~Ironies for Women~~

A rereading of Margaret Atwood's short story, "Marrying the Hangman," reveals layers of irony. The story is about a woman who has been condemned to hang because she stole some clothes, because she wanted to make herself more beautiful (13). She can only escape by marrying a hangman and she must first convince a man in the next cell to become the hangman, then to marry her. She does convince him, by promising him sexual favours ("nipple," "belly," "thighs") (14). She is released from prison. Although the woman escapes hanging, ironically she continues to live in prison and so, it seems, do many women today.

~~After we know how Margaret Atwood's story, "Marrying the Hangman," turns out, we find irony at the very start. The story is about a woman who has been condemned to hang because she stole some clothes, because she "wanted to make herself more beautiful" (13). She can only escape by marrying a hangman. So she must first convince a man in the next cell to become the hangman. Then he has to marry her. She does convince him and she is released from prison.~~

"Everyone said she was a clever woman," but by clever everyone meant manipulative or sneaky: "They used the word ensnare" (14). It is ironic that she is condemned by the very things that made her clever enough to convince the man and to seduce him.

The central irony
~~An irony~~ is that she discovers immediately that she has "left one locked room for another" (14). She is now ~~his wife and she must obey him~~ a wife who must obey her husband and keep his house. And she discovers that love "did not keep them busy forever" (14). Although he "is not such a bad fellow," and wants only a simple life, he also wants her to "watch him while he talks, with admiration and fear, gratitude if possible" (14).

A deeper irony, perhaps, is the fact that the woman's crime was wanting to be beautiful. Atwood suggests that her desire for beauty was a way for her to know herself, to give herself worth.

Now, ~~Being beautiful was how she knew herself.~~ ~~Also,~~ she has to give up her image of herself. She can no longer see her own beauty, but must use her husband ~~She uses him~~ as a mirror. In the prison she uses his voice through a hole in the wall to mirror back to her a sense of her identity. But when she is free, she must continue to ~~use him as her mirror~~ see herself through him. If she resists, his words become harsh: "foot, boot," "fist," "knife" (14). This is her real imprisonment.

The ~~saddest~~ irony in the story is, in the outer story. The women who are telling the narrator horror stories are also afraid, and also can't see themselves properly. ~~Some friends tell the narrator stories about abuse.~~ If we are right that one speaker has been raped, it is horrible that she didn't have "time to put my glasses on" so she couldn't see her attacker. In some ways, she ~~She~~ is like the woman speaking through the hole in the wall who was unable to see the man to whom she had to give herself. ~~she had to marry.~~ Atwood tells this ironic historical anecdote to point out the similarity to the lives of contemporary women ~~the contemporary women's lives~~. "These things happen" she says (13). The irony is that history repeats itself.

Work Cited

Atwood, Margaret. "Marrying the Hangman." Two-Headed Poems. Toronto: Oxford UP, 1978.

A Brief Overview of the Final Version

Finally, as a quick review, let us look at several principles illustrated by this essay.

- The *title of the essay* is not merely the title of the work discussed; rather, it gives the reader a clue, a small idea of the essayist's topic. Because your title will create a crucial first impression, make sure that it is interesting.

- The *opening or introductory paragraph* does not begin by saying "In this story [. . .]." Rather, by naming the author and the title it lets the reader know exactly what story is being discussed. It also develops the writer's thesis so that readers know where they will be going.

- The *organization* is effective. The more obvious irony is discussed and then the deeper irony and then the more subtle connection to modern women. The essay does not dwindle but builds up. (Again, if you outline your draft you will see whether it has an effective organization.)

- Some *brief quotations* are used, both to provide evidence and to let the reader hear—even if only fleetingly—Margaret Atwood's writing.

- The essay is chiefly *devoted to analysis, not to summary*. The writer, properly assuming that the reader has read the work, does not tell the plot in great detail. But, aware that the reader has not memorized the story, the writer gives helpful reminders.

- The *present tense* is used in narrating the ACTION: "She does convince him"; "Atwood tells this historical anecdote [. . .]."

- Although a *concluding paragraph* is often useful—if it does more than merely summarize what has already been clearly said—it is not essential in a short analysis. In this essay, the last sentence explains the chief irony and, therefore, makes an acceptable ending.

- *Documentation* is given according to the form set forth in Chapter 15.

- There are no typographical errors. The author has *proofread* the paper carefully.

3

Two Forms of Criticism: Explication and Analysis

Learning Objectives
When you've read this chapter, you should be able to
➢ explicate a text;
➢ analyze a text;
➢ compare or contrast two aspects of a text;
➢ organize evidence as you plan your essay; and
➢ plan, draft, revise, and edit your essay.

EXPLICATION

A line-by-line or episode-by-episode commentary on what is going on in a text is an **EXPLICATION** (literally, unfolding or spreading out). It takes some skill to work one's way along without saying, "In line one [. . .] in the second line [. . .]; in the third line [. . .]." One must sometimes boldly say something like, "The next stanza begins with [. . .] and then introduces [. . .]." And, of course, one can discuss the second line before the first line if that seems to be the best way of handling the passage.

An explication does not deal with the writer's life or times, and it is not a **PARAPHRASE**, a rewording—though it may include paraphrase. Rather, it is a commentary revealing your sense of the meaning of the work. To this end it calls attention, as it proceeds, to the implications of words, the function of rhymes, the shifts in point of view, the development of contrasts, and any other contributions to the meaning.

A Sample Explication: George Bowering's "Forget"

The following short poem is by George Bowering (1935–), who was born in Penticton, BC and was educated at the University of British Columbia. At UBC he was one of the editors of *Tish,* an influential poetry magazine that published a group of writers influenced by the Black Mountain poetry of Charles Olsen and others. Bowering has taught or been writer-in-residence at a number of Canadian universities. He appears regularly on television and radio.

FORGET

We forget those
apartment blocks
were made step-
by-step by
human hands.

The glue on this
envelope too
it tastes like
a pear.

Different readers will respond at least somewhat differently to any particular work. On the other hand, since writers want to communicate, they try to control their readers' responses, and they count on their readers to understand the denotations of words as they understand them. Thus, Bowering assumes that his readers know what large apartment buildings look like, even if they don't know Vancouver's West End, about which he may be writing. Explication is based on the assumption that the poem contains a meaning and that by studying the work thoughtfully we can unfold the meaning or meanings. (This opinion—which has been disputed—will be brought up again at the end of this discussion of explication.)

Let us assume that the reader understands that Bowering is talking about bland or ugly apartment buildings in large cities, and that we forget that real people designed and built them even though they look so impersonal. But Bowering does not say "did not know," he says "forget," and when he shifts to an image of the envelope, he uses the word "glue." You might ask yourself exactly what differences there are between the ideas of ignorance and of forgetting, or what the word *glue* implies. Next, after you have read the poem several times, you might think about which expressions are better in the context, and why.

Working toward an Explication of "Forget"

In preparing to write an explication, type or write by hand the complete text of the work—usually a poem but sometimes a short passage of prose—that you will explicate. Don't photocopy it; the act of typing or writing it will help you to get into the piece, word by word, comma by comma. Type or write it *double-spaced*, so that you will have plenty of room for annotations as you study the piece. It's advisable to print a few copies (or make a few photocopies) before you start annotating, so that if one page gets too cluttered you can continue working on a clean copy. Or you may want to use one copy for a certain kind of annotations—let's say those concerning imagery—and other copies for other kinds of notes—let's say those concerning metre, or wordplay. If you are writing on a word processor, you can highlight words, boldface them, put them in capitals, and so forth.

Let's turn to an explication of the poem, a detailed examination of the whole. Here are the preliminary jottings.

FORGET

who are we? — We forget those — *which? How do we know?*
          apartment blocks *can we see them?*
breaks word   { were made step-
group – sticks   { by-step by ———— *by/by (rhythm)*
        out   human hands.

          The glue on this — *odd. Why shift to glue?*
was also   – envelope too ———— *again, which envelope?*
made by humans. it tastes like
        so?   a pear. —— *does glue taste like pear?*
                why this simile? Glue tastes
                    horrible.

These annotations chiefly get at the structure of the poem, the relationship of the parts. The student notices that the poem speaks from the point of view of "we" and wonders who "we" is, and he also wonders which apartments and which envelope is being discussed. Further, he indicates that the making "step-by-step" is emphasized by breaking up the lines. He questions how glue tastes and asks if the "pear" taste means something important.

Some Journal Entries

The student who made these annotations later wrote an entry in his journal:

Feb. 18. Since the title is "Forget," it's obvious that something that was once known is no longer realized. Also, obvious that Bowering thinks it important that stuff is made by "human hand." I think the glue thing is weird (maybe because I like pears). What's the relationship between an apartment building and glue and a pear. Seem totally different things to me.

Feb. 21. Prof. McCabe said to think of structure or form of a poem as a sort of architecture, a building with a foundation, floors, etc., topped by a roof--but since we read a poem from top to bottom, it's like a building upside down. Title is foundation (even though it's at top); last line is roof, capping the whole. As you read, you add layers. Foundation of poem is the idea of forgetting, or the command "to forget." Then,

set back a bit from foundation, a tall room (5 lines
high); then, on top of this room, built on white space,
another room (4 lines, two statements). Funny; I
thought that in poems all stanzas are the same number of
lines. Then final cap is the unexpected pear taste.

Feb. 21, pm. I get it; one kind of made thing at start,
another in the middle, natural thing at end; so the
contrast with natural things, which taste good, like
pears, and man-made things which seem ugly or impersonal
or taste horrible, like glue. But what we shouldn't
forget is that even functional, impersonal looking
things are also made and someone cares, someone designed
the apartment or dreamed up the glue recipe and took the
trouble to put fake pear taste in it.

Feb 22 am. Thinking about the making of medieval
cathedrals we discussed in History. Those guys made
things step-by-step over generations. We seem to
remember their careful, hard work. Don't we pause to
think of modern workpeople? Don't we notice small
things? What I don't understand is the title. Is it a
comment that we forget or a command to forget? Why
would Bowering tell us to forget when the poem seems to
be asking us to remember, to notice. I'm going to have
to assume it means we forget but we shouldn't.

Drawing chiefly on these notes, the student jotted down some key ideas to guide him through a draft of an analysis of the poem. (The organization of the draft posed no problem; the student simply followed the organization of the poem.)

9 lines; short, but powerful; elusive
Order or comment that we forget
examples of what we forget
pause to realize that buildings are made step-by-step
emphasis on the slow process of building
emphasis on HUMAN hands
white space draws attention to shift to a new
application of the idea
Again, "this" suggests we can see the object
use of pear taste: artificial? natural taste worth
noticing in made object?

The Final Draft

Here is the final essay:

George Bowering's "Forget"

"Forget" is a poem that is only nine lines long, but
it has power because it draws clear pictures of
particular objects. It makes us look at them from a new
perspective. It shows close attention to detail. It
makes directive comments on the man-made objects it
names, but the purpose of the poem seems not only to
describe things. Instead, it challenges the reader's own
ability to see connections and asks the reader if he or
she realizes the human element in what is manufactured
around us. The poem starts out by describing an
apartment building. In urban centres, such buildings are
often ugly. They are almost always impersonal and cold.
We live in cities full of such buildings and we learn to
ignore them, to "forget." Perhaps we are almost ordered
to forget them. Certainly Bowering's title can be read
as an order to forget just as it can be read as a comment
on our tendency to forget. Poems can often be read more
than one way, and this title seems to ask the reader to
consider it in two ways: "You forget" with a "you"
understood--that's a command--or the simple verb,
forget--something we all do.

The possibility of two ways to read the title is
not surprising in a poem that says very little and yet
implies so much. It asks us not to forget, urging us to
look more closely. Often, imagist poems like this one
ask us to pause and look at small details. This poem
does. It makes us slow down, in fact, by its rhythm in
lines three to five. The reader would normally say the
apartments "were made step-by-step." But Bowering
breaks the sentence up, drawing attention to it and
making the reader stop, think, and go

step-
by-step by

Not only must we slow down, but Bowering stresses
the word <u>by</u>. He reminds us that these buildings did not
just appear, but were built by someone. When we see a
huge building we forget that individual men and women
designed the building, financed it, and built it. We
forget that some of them actually cared about how the

building looks or that it might house many people.
Sometimes buildings are just slammed up for profit, but
even then the workers and decorators and tradespeople
tried to do the best job they could in the
circumstances. Like the medieval cathedrals, these new
buildings were build "step- / by-step by / human hands."
The humanity is Bowering's point.

    That is why he moves to a new image of glue on
envelopes. This is a very small image of a dull thing.
We never notice the glue, except that it usually tastes
bad. But this glue tastes good, like "a pear." So we
are asked again to pause and consider that someone made
this glue and tried to make it taste like a real thing,
a natural thing. Bowering makes us stop in our urban
lifestyle and look at things. He reminds us that people
live in these blocks of apartments and make things and
try their best to make them as close to nature as they
can. There might be a negative comment here about how
far our manufactured world is from the real world
(perhaps the boyhood world of Bowering in the orchards
of the Okanagan Valley), but there is also a call for us
to appreciate the humanity that still surrounds us.

    This poem doesn't call for earth-shaking change; it
deals with small attention to details. But it reminds
us of an important fact: that we are human and we must
make the best we can of our world.

Topics for Discussion

The student's explication suggests that even though we have made a world of manufactured things, we can still find humanity in our world. In class, another student suggested that Bowering may be ironic. Fake pear taste isn't the same as real fruit in a natural world. Which explanation do you prefer, and why? What do you think of combining the two?

    Does some method or principle help us decide which interpretation is correct? Can one, in fact, talk about a "correct" interpretation, or only about a plausible or implausible interpretation and an interesting or uninteresting interpretation? *Note:* Another explication (of W. B. Yeats's "The Balloon of the Mind") appears in Chapter 12.

ANALYSIS: THE JUDGMENT OF SOLOMON

EXPLICATION is a method used chiefly in the study of fairly short poems or brief extracts from essays, stories, novels, and plays. Of course, if one has world enough and time one can set out to explicate all of Richler's *The*

Apprenticeship of Duddy Kravitz or Tremblay's *Les Belles Soeurs;* more likely, one will explicate only a paragraph or at most a page of the novel, and a speech or two of the play. In writing about works longer than a page or two, a more common approach than explicating is ANALYZING (literally, separating into parts in order better to understand the whole). An analysis of, say, *The Apprenticeship of Duddy Kravitz* may consider the functions of the SETTING, or the uses that certain minor characters serve; an analysis of *Les Belles Soeurs* may consider the theatrical rhythms, or the Roman Catholic imagery, or the repression of the women shown in their MONOLOGUES.

Analysis is not a process used only in talking about literature. It is commonly applied in thinking about almost any complex matter. Steffi Graf plays a deadly game of tennis. What does her serve do to her opponent? How does her backhand contribute? And so it makes sense, if you are writing about literature, to try to examine one or more of the components of the work, in order to see how they contribute to the whole, either as part of an aesthetic pattern or as part of the meaning. In Chapter 5 we will see, for example, how the line breaks of a poem by Phyllis Webb affect the various ways it may be understood.

A brief analysis of a very short story about King Solomon, from the Bible, may be useful here. Because the story is short, the analysis can consider all or almost all of the story's parts, and therefore the analysis can seem relatively complete. ("*Seem* relatively complete" because the analysis will in fact be far from complete, since the number of reasonable things that can be said about a work is almost as great as the number of readers. And a given reader might, at a later date, offer a rather different reading from what the reader offers today. Recall the discussion in Chapter 1.)

The following story about King Solomon, customarily called "The Judgment of Solomon," appears in what is often termed the Hebrew Bible, in the latter part of the third chapter of the book called 1 Kings or First Kings, probably written in the mid-sixth century BCE. The translation is from the King James Version of the Bible (1611). Two expressions in the story need clarification. (1) The woman who "overlaid" her child in her sleep rolled over on the child and suffocated it; (2) it is said of a woman that her "bowels yearned upon her son," that is, her heart longed for her son. (Among the early Hebrews, the bowels were thought to be the seat of emotion.)

> Then came there two women, that were harlots, unto the king, and stood before him. And the one woman said, "O my lord, I and this woman dwell in one house, and I was delivered of a child with her in the house. And it came to pass the third day after that I was delivered, that this woman was delivered also, and we were together; there was no stranger in the house, save we two in the house. And this woman's child died in the night, because she overlaid it. And she rose at midnight, and took my son from beside me, while thine handmaid slept, and laid it in her bosom, and laid her dead child in my bosom. And when I rose in the morning to give my child suck, behold, it was dead; but when I considered it in the morning, behold, it was not my son, which I did bear."
>
> And the other woman said, "Nay, but the living son is my son, and the dead is thy son." And this said, "No, but the dead is thy son, and the living is my son." Thus they spoke before the king.

Then said the king, "The one said, 'This is my son that liveth, and thy son is dead.' And the other said, 'Nay, but thy son is the dead, and my son is the living.'" And the king said, "Bring me a sword." And they brought a sword before the king. And the king said, "Divide the living child in two and give half to the one, and half to the other."

Then spake the woman whose the living child was unto the king, for her bowels yearned upon her son, and she said, "O my lord, give her the living child, and in no wise slay it." But the other said, "Let it be neither mine nor thine, but divide it."

Then the king answered and said, "Give her the living child, and in no wise slay it. She is the mother thereof."

And all Israel heard of the judgment which the king had judged, and they feared the king, for they saw that the wisdom of God was in him, to do judgment.

Let's begin by analyzing the *form,* or the shape, of the story. One form or shape that we notice is this: The story moves from a problem to a solution. We can also say, still speaking of the overall form, that the story moves from quarreling and talk of death to unity and talk of life. In short, it has a happy ending, a form that (because it provides an optimistic view of life and also a sense of completeness) gives most people pleasure.

In thinking about a work of literature, it is always useful to take notice of the basic form of the whole, the overall structural pattern. Doubtless you are already familiar with many basic patterns, for example TRAGEDY (joy yielding to sorrow) and COMEDY (angry conflict yielding to joyful union). If you think even briefly about verbal works, you'll notice the structures or patterns that govern songs, episodes in soap operas, political speeches (beginning with the candidate's expression of pleasure at being in Lethbridge, and ending with "God bless you all"), detective stories, horror films, and so on. And just as viewers of a science fiction film inevitably experience one sci-fi flick in the context of others, so readers inevitably experience one story in the context of similar stories, and one poem in the context of others.

Second, we can say that "The Judgment of Solomon" is a sort of detective story: There is a death, followed by a conflict in the testimony of the witnesses, and a solution by a shrewd outsider. Consider Solomon's predicament. Ordinarily in literature characters are sharply defined and individualized, yet the essence of a detective story is that the culprit should not be easily recognized as wicked, and here nothing seems to distinguish the two petitioners. Solomon is confronted by "two women, that were harlots." Until late in the story—that is, up to the time Solomon suggests dividing the child—they are described only as "the one woman," "the other woman," "the one," "the other."

Does the story suffer from weak characterization? If we think analytically about this issue, we realize that the point surely is to make the women as alike as possible, so that we cannot tell which of the two is speaking the truth. Like Solomon, we have nothing to go on; neither witness is known to be more honest than the other, and there are no other witnesses to support or refute either woman.

Analysis is concerned with seeing the relationships between the parts of a work, but analysis also may take note of what is *not* in the work. A witness would destroy the story, or at least turn it into an utterly different story. Another thing missing from this story is an explicit editorial comment or interpretation, except for the brief remark at the end, that the people "feared the king." If we had read the story in the so-called Geneva Bible (1557–60), which is the translation of the Bible that Shakespeare was familiar with, we would have found a marginal comment: "Her motherly affection herein appeareth that she had rather endure the rigour of the lawe, than see her child cruelly slaine." Would you agree that it is better, at least in this story, for the reader to draw conclusions than for the storyteller explicitly to point them out?

Solomon wisely contrives a situation in which these two claimants, who seem so similar, will reveal their true natures: The mother will reveal her love, and the liar will reveal her hard heart. The early symmetry (the identity of the two women) pleases a reader, and so does the device by which we can at last distinguish between the two women.

But even near the end there is a further symmetry. In order to save the child's life, the true mother gives up her claim, crying out, "Give her the living child, and in no wise slay it." The author (or, rather, the translator who produced this part of the King James Version) takes these very words, with no change whatsoever, and puts them into Solomon's mouth as the king's final judgment. Solomon too says, "Give her the living child, and in no wise slay it," but now the sentence takes on a new meaning. In the first sentence, "her" refers to the liar (the true mother will give the child to "her"); in Solomon's sentence, "her" refers to the true mother: "Give her the living child [. . .]." Surely we take pleasure in the fact that (1) the very words by which the mother renounces her child are the words that reveal to Solomon the truth, and that (2) Solomon uses these words to restore the child to its mother.

This analysis has chiefly talked about the relations of parts, and especially it has tried to explain why the two women in this story are *not* distinct, until Solomon finds a way to reveal their distinctive natures: If the story is to demonstrate Solomon's wisdom, the women must seem identical until Solomon can show that they differ. But the analysis could have gone into some other topic. Let's consider several possibilities.

A student might begin by asking this question: "Although it is important for the women to be highly similar, why are they harlots?" (It is too simple to say that the women in the story are harlots because the author is faithfully reporting an historical EPISODE in Solomon's career. The story is widely recognized as a folktale (a kind of PARABLE) found also in other ancient cultures.) One possible reason for making the women harlots is that the story demands that there be no witnesses; by using harlots, the author disposed of husbands, parents, and siblings who might otherwise be expected to live with the women. A second possible reason is that the author wanted to show that Solomon's justice extended to all. Third, perhaps the author wished to reject or at least to complicate the STEREOTYPE of the harlot as a thoroughly disreputable person. He did this by introducing another (and truer?) stereotype, the mother as motivated by overwhelming maternal love.

Other Possible Topics for Analysis

Another possible kind of analytic essay might go beyond the structure of the individual work, to the relation of the work to some larger whole. For instance, one might approach "The Judgment of Solomon" from the point of view of GENDER CRITICISM (discussed in Chapter 8): In this story, one might argue, wisdom is an attribute only of a male; women are either deceitful or emotional. From this point one might set out to write a research essay on gender in, say, certain books of the Hebrew Bible. We might also analyze the story in the context of other examples of what scholars call Wisdom Literature (the Book of Proverbs, and Ecclesiastes, for instance). Notice that Solomon's judgment leads the people to *fear* him—because his wisdom is seen as great, formidable, and God-inspired.

We do not know who wrote "The Judgment of Solomon," but the authors of most later works of literature are known, and therefore some critics seek to analyze a given work within the context of the author's life. For some other critics, the larger context would be the reading process, which includes the psychology of the reader. (Biographical criticism and reader-response criticism are discussed in Chapter 8.)

Still another analysis—again, remember that a work can be analyzed from many points of view—might examine two or more translations of the story. You do not need to know Hebrew in order to compare this early seventeenth-century translation with a twentieth-century version such as the New Jerusalem Bible or the Revised English Bible. One might seek to find which version is, on literary grounds, more effective. Such an essay might include an attempt, by means of a comparison, to analyze the effect of the archaic language of the King James Version. Does the somewhat unfamiliar language turn a reader off, or does it add mystery or dignity or authority to the tale, valuable qualities perhaps not found in the modern version?

Topics for Discussion

In the New Revised English Bible, Solomon does *not* exactly repeat the mother's plea. The mother says, "Give her the living child," and Solomon then says, "Give the living child to the first woman." In the New Jerusalem Bible, after the mother says "Let them give her the live child," Solomon says, "Give the live child to the first woman." If you prefer one version to the other two, explain why. What is the literary value of Solomon repeating the exact words (as we discuss above)?

This story comes from the Christian Bible. Do you know a similar story from another religious tradition? If so, you might want to analyze that story to see how it is composed, how the writing affects its meaning. Or you might want to compare or contrast the two tales.

Comparison: An Analytic Tool

Analysis frequently involves comparing and contrasting: Things are examined for their resemblances to and differences from other things. (We tend to use the generic term *comparing* for such analysis, but remember that sometimes this actually implies contrasting.)

Although your instructor may ask you to write a **COMPARISON** or **CONTRAST** of two works of literature, the *subject* of the essay is the works; comparison is simply an effective analytic technique to show some of the qualities in the works. You might compare Atwood's use of a prison in "Marrying the Hangman" (pages 13–14) with the use of a prison setting in Vigneault's "The Wall" (pages 3–4) in order to reveal the subtle differences between the stories, but a comparison of works utterly unalike can hardly tell the reader or the writer anything.

Something should be said about organizing a comparison, say between the settings in two stories, between two characters in a **NOVEL** (or even between a character at the end of a novel and the same character at the beginning), or between the **SYMBOLISM** of two poems. Probably, your first thought after making some jottings would be to discuss one half of the comparison and then go on to the second half. Instructors and textbooks often urge students away from such an organization (sometimes called the A + B MODEL), arguing that the essay breaks into two parts and that the second part involves a good deal of repetition of categories set up in the first part. Usually, they recommend that you organize your thoughts in related pairs or groups. (This is often called the ALTERNATING MODEL.) Here is an example:

1. First similarity
   a. first work (or character, or characteristic)
   b. second work
2. Second similarity
   a. first work
   b. second work
3. First difference
   a. first work
   b. second work
4. Second difference
   a. First work
   b. Second work

and so on, for as many additional differences as seem relevant. If you wish to compare "Marrying the Hangman" with "The Wall," you may organize the material thus:

1. First similarity: the hero is in prison
   a. The mason
   b. The condemned woman
2. Second similarity: both escape
   a. He by convincing a monk to help him
   b. She by convincing a man to become the hangman and marry her
3. First difference: the way in which each convinces the helper
   a. He lays out a philosophical argument that seems to attract help
   b. She must rely on her sexuality to seduce

Another way of organizing a comparison and contrast:

1. First point: the hero is in prison
   a. similarities between the mason and the woman
   b. differences between the mason and the woman
2. Second point: the method of obtaining freedom
   a. similarities between the method of the man and of the woman
   b. differences between the method of the man and of the woman
3. Third point: the degree of success in obtaining real freedom
   a. similarities between the man and the woman
   b. differences between the man and the woman

A comparison need not employ either of these structures. There is even the danger that an essay employing either of them may not come into focus until the essayist stands back from the seven-layer cake and announces in the concluding paragraph that the odd layers taste better.

In your preparatory thinking, you may want to make comparisons in pairs (good-natured humour: the clown in *Othello,* the clownish grave-digger in *Hamlet;* social satire: the clown in *Othello,* the grave-digger in *Hamlet;* relevance to main theme: A and B; comments by other characters: A and B), but you must come to some conclusions about what these add up to before writing the final version. This final version should not duplicate the thought processes; rather, it should be organized so as to make the point—the thesis— clearly and effectively. After reflection, you may believe that although there are superficial similarities between the clown in *Othello* and the clownish grave-digger in *Hamlet,* there are essential differences; then, in the finished essay, you probably will not wish to obscure the main point by jumping back and forth from play to play, working through a series of similarities and differences. It may be better to discuss the clown in *Othello* and then to point out that, although the grave-digger in *Hamlet* resembles him in A, B, and C, the grave-digger also has other functions (D, E, and F) and is of greater consequence to *Hamlet* than the clown is to *Othello.* With some repetition in the second half of the essay ("The grave-digger's puns come even faster than the clown's [. . .].") she will bind the two halves into a meaningful whole, making clear the degree of similarity or difference. The point of the essay presumably is not to list pairs of similarities or differences but to illuminate a work or works by making thoughtful comparisons.

Although in a long essay you cannot postpone until page 30 a discussion of the second half of the comparison, in an essay of, say, fewer than 10 pages nothing is wrong with setting forth one half of the comparison and then, in light of it, the second half. The essay will break into two unrelated parts if the second half makes no use of the first or if it fails to modify the first half, but not if the second half looks back to the first half and calls attention to differences that the new material reveals. It is often preferable to plan a comparison with interwoven comparisons, but remember that a comparison may be written in other ways, too, and no rule says how you must plan your essay.

Remember: The purpose of a comparison is to call attention to the unique features of something by holding it up against something similar but significantly different. You can compare Macbeth with Banquo (two men who hear a prophecy but who respond differently), or Macbeth with Lady Macbeth (a husband and wife, both eager to be monarchs but differing in their sense of the consequences), or Hamlet and Duddy Kravitz (two people who see themselves as surrounded by a corrupt world), but you can hardly compare Duddy with Lady Macbeth—there simply are not enough points of resemblance to make it worth your effort to call attention to subtle differences. If the differences are great and apparent, a comparison is a waste of effort. ("Blueberries are different from elephants. Blueberries do not have trunks. And elephants do not grow on bushes.") Indeed, a comparison between essentially and evidently unlike things can only obscure, for by making the comparison the writer implies that significant similarities do exist, and readers can only wonder why they do not see them. Another danger is that essays that make uninstructive comparisons do break into two halves: The first half tells the reader about five qualities in "Marrying the Hangman," and the second half tells the reader about five different qualities in "The Wall," but no reasonable PRINCIPLE OF COMPARISON connects the two.

FINDING A TOPIC

All literary works afford their own topics for analysis, and all essayists must set forth their own theses, but a few useful generalizations may be made. You can often find a thesis by asking one of two questions:

1. *What is this doing?* That is, why is this SCENE in the novel or play? Why is Beckett's *Waiting for Godot* in two acts, rather than one or three? Why is there Biblical ALLUSION in *Waiting for Godot?* Why does Hamlet delay? Why are these lines unrhymed? Why is this STANZA form employed? What is the significance of the parts of the work? If you don't know where to begin, think about the title, the first part of a work. Titles are often highly significant parts of the work: Ibsen explained that he called his play *Hedda Gabler* rather than *Hedda Tesman* because "She is to be regarded as her father's daughter rather than as her husband's wife." But of course there are other ways of beginning. If the work is a poem without a title, and you don't know where to begin, you may be able to get a start by considering the stanza form, or the chief images. If the work is a story or play, you may get a start by considering the relation between the chief character and the second most important character.

2. *Why do I have this response?* Why do I find this poem clever or moving or puzzling? How did the author make this character funny or dignified or pathetic? How did he or she communicate the idea that this character is a bore without boring me? Why am I troubled by the representation of women in this story? Why do I regard as sexist this lover's expression of his love?

The first of these questions, "What is this doing?" requires that you identify yourself with the author, wondering, for example, whether this opening scene is the best possible for this story. The second question, "Why do I have this response?" requires that you trust your feelings. If you are amused or bored or puzzled or annoyed, assume that these responses are appropriate and follow them up, at least until a rereading of the work provides other responses.

CONSIDERING THE EVIDENCE

Once your responses have led you to a topic ("The Clown in *Othello*") and then to a thesis ("Although he is an Elizabethan dramatic CONVENTION, the clown plays a key role in developing character"), be certain that you have all the evidence. Usually this means that you should study the context of the material you are discussing. For example, if you are writing about "Marrying the Hangman," before you argue that the woman should have escaped her marriage after she has used the man to escape prison, remember that this story is set in the eighteenth century—a historical period during which a woman needed to be married for social and financial status.

ORGANIZING THE MATERIAL

"Begin at the beginning," the King of Hearts in *Alice in Wonderland* said very gravely, "and go on till you come to the end: then stop." This is how your paper should seem to the reader, but it need not have been drafted thus. In fact, unless you are supremely gifted, you will (like the rest of us) have to work very hard to make things easy for the reader.

After locating a topic, converting it into a thesis, and weighing the evidence, a writer has the job of organizing the material into a coherent whole, a sequence of paragraphs that holds the reader's interest (partly because it sets forth material clearly) and that steadily builds up an effective argument. Notice that in the essay on irony in Atwood's "Marrying the Hangman" the student wisely moves from the historical ironies to the contemporary irony. To begin with the chief irony and end with the lesser ironies would almost surely be anticlimactic.

The organization of an essay will, of course, depend on the nature of the essay: An essay on FORESHADOWING in *Macbeth* probably will be organized chronologically (material in the first ACT will be discussed before material in the second act), but an essay on the character of Macbeth may conceivably begin with the end of the play, discussing Macbeth as he is in the fifth act, and then may work backward through the play, arriving at last at the original Macbeth, so to speak, of the beginning of the play. (This is not to suggest that such an organization be regularly employed in writing about a character— only that it might be employed effectively.) Or suppose you are questioning whether Macbeth is a victim of fate. You might state the problem, and then go on to outline one view and then the other. Which view should be set forth first? Probably it will be best to let the reader first hear the view that you will refute, so that you can build to a CLIMAX.

The important point is not that there is only one way to organize an essay, but that you find the way that seems best for the particular topic and argument. Once you think you know more or less what you want to say, you will usually, after trial and error, find what seems the best way of communicating it to a reader. A scratch outline will help you find your way, but don't assume that once you have settled on an outline the organization of your essay finally is established. After you read the draft that you base on your outline, you may realize that a more effective organization will be more helpful to your reader—which means that you must move paragraphs around, revise your transitions, and, in short, produce another draft.

If you look at your draft and you outline it, as suggested on page 25, you will quickly see whether the draft needs to be reorganized.

COMMUNICATING JUDGMENTS

Because a critical essay is a judicious attempt to help a reader see what is going on in a work or in a part of a work, the **VOICE** of the critic usually sounds, on first hearing, impartial; but good criticism includes—at least implicitly—evaluation. The critic may say not only that the setting changes (a neutral expression) but also that "the novelist aptly shifts the setting" or "unconvincingly describes [. . .]" or "effectively juxtaposes [. . .]." These evaluations are supported with evidence. The critic has feelings about the work under discussion and reveals them, not by continually saying "I feel" and "this moves me," but by calling attention to the degree of success or failure perceived. Nothing is wrong with occasionally using "I," and noticeable avoidance of it in jargon such as, "it is seen that," "this writer," "the present writer," "we," and the like, suggests an offensive sham modesty; but too much talk of "I" makes a writer sound like an egomaniac.

Consider this sentence from the opening paragraph in a review of George Orwell's *1984*.

> I do not think I have ever read a novel more frightening and depressing; and yet, such are the originality, the suspense, the speed of writing and withering indignation that it is impossible to put the book down.

Fine—provided that the reviewer goes on to offer evidence that enables readers to share his or her evaluation of *1984*. Simply telling your reader your emotional response is not criticism.

One final remark on communicating judgments: Write sincerely. Any attempt to neglect your own thoughtful responses and replace them with fabrications designed to please an instructor will surely fail. It is hard enough to find the words that clearly communicate your responses; it is almost impossible to find the words that express your hunch about what your instructor expects your responses to be. George Orwell shrewdly commented on the obvious signs of insincere writing: "When there is a gap between one's real and one's declared aims, one turns as it were instinctively to long words and exhausted idioms, like a cuttlefish squirting out ink."

REVIEW: HOW TO WRITE AN EFFECTIVE ESSAY

All writers must work out their own procedures and rituals before writing (Clark Blaise has said "the first sentence of a story is an act of faith," and Desmond, the protagonist of "The Leper's Squint," by Jack Hodgins, waits for the words to run off the end "[. . .] like a fishing line pulled by a salmon."), but the following suggestions may provide some help. The writing process may be divided into four stages—Pre-writing, Drafting, Revising, and Editing—though, as the following discussion admits, the stages are not always neatly separate.

1. Pre-writing

Read the work carefully. You may, on this first reading, want to highlight or annotate certain things, such as passages that please or that puzzle, or you may prefer simply to read it through. In any case, on a second reading you will certainly want to annotate the text and to jot down notes either in the margins or in a journal. You probably are not focusing on a specific topic, but rather are taking account of your early responses to the work.

If you have a feeling or an idea, jot it down; don't assume that you will remember it when you get around to drafting your essay. Write it down so that you will be sure to remember it and so that in the act of writing it down you can improve it. Later, after reviewing your notes (whether in the margins or in a journal) you'll probably find that it's a good idea to transfer your best points to 10 x 15 cm cards (or paper torn in half), writing on one side only. By putting the material on cards, you can easily group related points later.

2. Drafting

After reviewing your notes and sorting them out, you will probably find that you have not only a topic (a subject to write about) but a thesis (a point to be made, an argument). Get it down on paper or into a computer file. Perhaps begin by jotting down your thesis and under it a tentative outline. (If you have transferred your preliminary notes to index cards, you can easily arrange the cards into a tentative organization.)

If you are writing an explication, the order probably is essentially the order of the lines or of the episodes. If you are writing an analysis, you may wish to organize your essay from the lesser material to the greater (to avoid anticlimax) or from the simple to the complex (to ensure intelligibility). If you are discussing the roles of three characters in a story, it may be best to build up to the one of the three that you think the most important. If you are comparing two characters, it may be best to move from the most obvious contrasts to the least obvious.

At this stage, however, don't worry about whether the organization is unquestionably the best possible organization for your topic. A page of paper with some ideas in some sort of sequence, however rough, will encourage you that you do have something to say. If you have doubts, by all means record them. By writing down your uncertainties, you will probably begin to feel your way toward tentative explanations of them.

Almost any organization will help you get going on your draft; that is, it will help you start writing an essay. The process of writing will itself clarify and improve your preliminary ideas. If you are like most people, you can't do much precise thinking until you have committed to paper at least a rough sketch of your initial ideas. Later, you can push and polish your ideas into shape, perhaps even deleting all of them and starting over, but it's a lot easier to improve your ideas once you see them in front of you than it is to do the job in your head. On paper, one word leads to another; in your head, one word often blocks another.

Just keep going; you may realize, as you near the end of a sentence, that you no longer believe it. Okay; be glad that your first idea led you to a better one, and pick up your better one and keep going with it. By trial and error, you are pushing your way not only toward clear expression but also toward sharper ideas and richer responses.

Although we have been talking about drafting, most teachers rightly regard this first effort at organizing your notes and turning them into an essay not as a first draft but as a zero draft, really a part of pre-writing. When you reread it, you will doubtless find passages that need further support, passages that seem out of place, and passages that need clarification. You will also find passages that are better than you thought at the outset you could produce. In any case, on rereading the zero draft you will find things that will require you to go back and check the work of literature and to think further about what you have said about it. After rereading the literary work and your draft, you are in a position to write something that can rightly be called a first draft.

3. Revising

Try to allow at least a day to elapse before you start to revise your zero draft and another day before you revise your first draft. If you come to the material with a relatively fresh eye, you may see, for example, that the thesis needs to be announced earlier or more clearly or that certain points need to be supported by concrete references—perhaps by brief quotations from the literary work. Almost all student writing suffers from too little revision and a rush at the due date. If you can plan your schedule to allow some "down time," your mark will almost assuredly be higher. A review by your peers will give you a good sense of which things need clarification and of whether your discussion is adequately organized.

At this stage, pay special attention to the following matters.

The Title If you haven't already jotted down some tentative title for your essay, now is the time to do so. Make sure that the title is interesting and informative. There is nothing interesting and there is very little that is informative in a title such as "On a Play by Joan MacLeod," or even in "On *Toronto, Mississippi*." Such titles are adequate to get you going, but try, as you think about your draft, to come up with something more focused, such as "Man as Elvis in *Toronto, Mississippi*" (this title announces the topic). Avoid announcing your approach too abruptly. "A Feminist Reading of *Toronto, Mississippi*" is not a good title. Better might be, "Choices for Women in *Toronto, Mississippi*." Because you are still drafting your essay, of course you will not yet settle on a final version of the title, but thinking about the title will help you to write an essay that is focused.

The Opening Try to make sure that your introductory sentences or paragraphs engage the reader's interest. It's usually desirable also to give the reader the necessary information concerning which work you are writing about, to indicate your thesis (this information itself may get the reader's interest), and to indicate what your organization will be. It is usually better to imply the organization than to say "I will point out," or "This essay will examine." Here is a sample that does all of these things:

> Joan McLeod's <u>Toronto, Mississippi</u> is not so much a play about a girl with a mental challenge, as it is a play about the choices open to women. The play shows two women, the challenged girl and her mother, but it shows them in relationship to men. The girl is attracted to a man on her bus with whom she cannot hope to have a relationship. She also loves her father, an Elvis impersonator. Her mother is attracted to a caring man but she is confused by old feelings for the father, her ex-husband. And, of course, she is caught in the myth of Elvis. Joan MacLeod shows that these women, because they live in a world which values the machismo of Elvis, must struggle to find ways to love without losing their own identities. Each of the women and men in the play and each of the relationships shows an aspect of this difficult contemporary struggle.

Again, this opening paragraph identifies the author and the work, and it also indicates the topic (women), the thesis (women must struggle to overcome sexual MYTHS to find love without losing their own identities), and the structure (the final sentence implies that the essay "will examine" each character and explore how the various characters interact). Perhaps because it is so informative, it is at least moderately interesting. Of course an opening need not do all of these things, but in revising your draft, be sure to ask yourself *what* your opening does, and if it does enough. Here is another possible opening, again for an essay on *Toronto, Mississippi*. This passage does less than the previous example, but it seeks to interest the reader by means of brief quotations from the play and by means of a question that hints at the thesis.

> In Joan MacLeod's <u>Toronto, Mississippi</u>, King, the Elvis impersonator, says he is "sick to death of everyone wanting what is bad for them." He says this "ties into the way I feel about women." Bill, the college

instructor, calls himself "a voice for women." Does
Joan MacLeod agree that women want what is bad for them,
or that they need men to speak for them? Or does she
use these portraits to suggest that women can find what
is best for themselves and can find their own voices?

The Thesis and the Organization In addition to announcing your
thesis early—perhaps in the title, or in the opening paragraph—be sure to
keep the thesis in view throughout the essay. For instance, if you are arguing
that MacLeod's depiction of women is multisided, you will say so, and you will
reaffirm the point during the essay, when you present supporting evidence.
Similarly, even if you have announced the organization, you will keep the
reader posted by occasionally saying such things as "One other minor character
must be looked at," and "the last minor character that we will look at," and
"With Janna, the younger woman in the play," and so on. And of course you
will make the organization clear to your readers by using the appropriate
lead-ins and transitions, such as "Furthermore," "On the other hand," and
"The final example [. . .]."

The Closing Say something more interesting than "Thus we see,"
followed by a repetition of the thesis sentence. Among the tested ways of
ending effectively are these:

- glance back to something from the opening paragraph, thus giving
  your essay a sense of CLOSURE;

- offer a new bit of evidence, thus driving the point home;

- indicate that the thesis, now established, can be used in other
  investigations of comparable material, for instance in a discussion
  of MacLeod's later plays.

(For further discussion of concluding paragraphs see pages 277–78.)

4. Editing

Small-scale revision, such as checking the spelling, punctuation, and accuracy
of quotations, is usually called *editing*. Even when you get to this stage, you
may unexpectedly find that you must make larger revisions. In checking a
quotation, for instance, you may find that it doesn't really support the point
you are making, so you may have to do some substantial revising.

Time has run out. Type, write, or print out a clean copy, following the
principles concerning margins, pagination, and documentation set out later
in this book. If you have borrowed any ideas, be sure to give credit to your
sources. Finally, proofread and make corrections as explained on page 281.

The whole process of writing about literature, then, is really a process of
responding and of revising your responses—not only your responses to the
work of literature but also to your own writing about those responses. When
you jot down a note and then jot down a further thought (perhaps even reject-
ing the earlier note) and then turn this material into a paragraph and then
revise the paragraph, you are in the company of Picasso, who said that in

painting a picture he advanced by a series of destructions. You are also following Mrs. Beeton's famous recipe: "First catch your hare, then cook it."

The Dreaded Deadline

When someone asked Duke Ellington why he had not found time to complete a promised piece of music, Ellington replied, "I don't need time. I need a deadline!" When your instructors give you deadlines they are doing you a favour. But they assume that you will take the deadlines seriously *and* that you will begin reading, thinking, drafting, and revising several days—perhaps a week or more—before the deadline. Even a genius like Duke Ellington found that a deadline was a stimulus to creativity. But unless you are a genius, don't count on being able to produce excellent—or even good—work at the last minute. When instructors set deadlines, they assume that students will apportion their work over a period of days. They assume, that is, a process involving the stages outlined, and they will evaluate the final product in terms of that process, not in terms of a last-minute frenzy to meet the deadline.

A WORD ABOUT TECHNICAL LANGUAGE

Literature, like the law, medicine, the dance, and, for that matter, cooking and hockey, has given rise to technical terminology. A cookbook will tell you to boil, or bake, or blend, and it will speak of a "slow" oven (150 degrees), a "moderate" oven (190 degrees), or a "hot" oven (215 degrees). These are technical terms in the world of cookery. In watching a hockey game, we find ourselves saying, "I think that's offside" or "It's a hat trick." We use these terms because they convey a good deal in a few words; they are clear and precise. Further, although we don't use them in order to impress our hearer, they do indicate that we have more than a superficial acquaintance with the game. That is, the better we know our subject, the more likely we are to use the technical language of the subject. Why? *Because such language enables us to talk precisely and in considerable depth about the subject.* Technical language, unlike jargon (pretentious **DICTION** that needlessly complicates or obscures), is illuminating—provided that the reader is familiar with the terms.

In writing about literature you will, for the most part, use the same general language that you use in your other courses, and you will not needlessly introduce the technical vocabulary of literary study. But you *will* use this vocabulary when it enables you to be clear, concise, and accurate. And you will use it when it is necessary to capture a technical point (there's no way to discuss the importance of a pause without words in a poem without using the term **WHITE SPACE**). And you won't use the technical language of another discipline (sociology, for example) except when it also illustrates a literary point (or unless you are using that discipline's methodology as part of your analysis; see Chapter 17).

✓ Editing Checklist: Questions to Ask Yourself

✓ Is the title of my essay at least moderately informative and interesting?

✓ Do I identify the subject of my essay (author and title) early?

✓ What is my thesis? Do I state it soon enough (perhaps even in the title) and keep it in view?

✓ Is the organization reasonable? Does each point lead into the next without irrelevancies and without anticlimaxes?

✓ Is each paragraph unified by a topic sentence or a topic idea? Are there adequate transitions from one paragraph to the next?

✓ Are generalizations supported by appropriate concrete details, especially by brief quotations from the text?

✓ Is the opening paragraph interesting and, by its end, focused on the topic? Is the final paragraph conclusive without being repetitive?

✓ Is the tone appropriate? No sarcasm, no apologies, no condescension?

✓ If there is a summary, is it as brief as possible, given its purpose?

✓ Are the quotations adequately introduced, and are they accurate? Do they provide evidence and let the reader hear the author's voice, or do they merely add words to the essay?

✓ Is the present tense used to describe the author's work and the action of the work ("Shakespeare *shows*," "Hamlet *dies*")?

✓ Have I kept in mind the needs of my audience, for instance by defining unfamiliar terms, or by briefly summarizing works or opinions that the reader may be unfamiliar with?

✓ Is documentation provided where necessary?

✓ Are the spelling and punctuation correct? Are other mechanical matters (such as margins, spacing, and citations) in correct form? Have I proofread carefully?

✓ Is the paper properly identified—author's name, instructor's name, course number, and date?

4

Other Kinds of Writing about Literature

Learning Objectives

When you've read this chapter, you should be able to

➤ write a summary and paraphrase;

➤ write a literary response;

➤ recognize parody and pastiche; and

➤ write a review of a dramatic production or other literary text.

A SUMMARY

The essay on "Marrying the Hangman" in Chapter 2 does not include a summary because the writer knew that all of her readers were thoroughly familiar with Atwood's story. Sometimes, however, it is advisable to summarize the work you are writing about, thus reminding a reader who has not read the work recently, or even informing a reader who may never have read the work. A review of a new work of literature or of a new film, for instance, usually includes a summary, on the assumption that readers are unfamiliar with it.

A SUMMARY is a brief restatement or condensation of the plot. (In non-literary writing, a summary is also often helpful; here, it is a condensation of the author's critical analysis, including a statement of his or her thesis.) Consider the following summary of Atwood's "Marrying the Hangman."

> A woman who has been condemned to death by hanging
> learns that while a man may escape hanging if he agrees
> to become the hangman, a woman can also save herself by
> marrying the hangman. There is no hangman for her to
> marry, so she convinces a man in the next cell--to
> whom she talks through a hole in the wall--to become
> the executioner and then to marry her. Once married,
> she realizes that she has "traded one locked room
> for another." Like the contemporary women who tell
> the narrator "horror stories," this woman has no
> identity outside the man who demands her "gratitude."

```
Like them she is subject to abuse.  Her destiny is
caught up in words and those words show her
imprisonment.
```

Here are a few principles that govern summaries:

1. A summary is *much briefer than the original.* It is not a paraphrase—a word-by-word translation of someone's words into your own. A paraphrase is usually at least as long as the original, whereas a summary is rarely longer than one quarter of the original and is usually much shorter. A novel may be summarized in a few paragraphs, or even in one paragraph.

2. A summary *usually achieves its brevity by omitting almost all of the concrete details of the original* and by omitting minor characters and episodes. Notice that the summary of "Marrying the Hangman" omits the reason the woman was in prison, omits the image of the mirror, and omits the comments on the character of the husband.

3. A summary is *as accurate as possible,* given the limits of space.

4. A summary is *normally written in the present tense.* Thus "A woman is condemned to hanging [. . .]; The friends tell the narrator [. . .]."

5. If the summary is brief (say, fewer than 250 words), it *may be given as a single paragraph.* If you are summarizing a long work, you may feel that a longer summary is needed. In this case, your reader will be grateful to you if you divide the summary into paragraphs. As you draft your summary, you may find *natural divisions.* For instance, the scene of the story may change midway, providing you with the opportunity to use two paragraphs. Or you may want to summarize a five-act play in five paragraphs.

Summaries have their place in essays, but remember that a summary is not an analysis; it is only a summary.

A PARAPHRASE

A PARAPHRASE is a restatement—a sort of translation into the same language—of material that may in its original form be somewhat obscure to a reader. A native speaker of English will not need a paraphrase of "Thirty days hath September," though a non-native speaker might be puzzled by two things, the meaning of *hath* and the inverted word order. For such a reader, "September has thirty days" would be a helpful paraphrase.

Although a paraphrase seeks to make clear the gist of the original, if the original is even a little more complex than "Thirty days hath September" the paraphrase will—in the process of clarifying something—lose something, since the substitution of one word for another will change the meaning. For instance, "Shut up" and "Be quiet" do not say exactly the same thing; the former (in addition to asking for quiet) says that the speaker is rude, or perhaps it says that the speaker feels he can treat his listener contemptuously, but the paraphrase loses all of this.

Still, a paraphrase can be helpful as a first step in aiding a reader to understand a line that includes an obsolete word or phrase, or a word or phrase that is current only in one region, or a word with multiple meanings. For instance, in a poem by Phyllis Webb, titled "Propositions," the following line appears:

the just passion, just encountering

In the *Oxford English Dictionary*, *just* has 22 meanings! Even taking the most common, we realize that the word carries both the meaning of "only" (or "barely"), of "exactly," and of "fair, morally or legally right." So a paraphrase of the line might go thus:

that which is only and exactly love—but is right—simply and precisely coming together in a fair manner.

(And the older definitions include the word as a form of *joust,* so there is also a notion of two lovers parrying with one another, a reading that fits with the theme and with images of the Four Horsemen elsewhere in the poem.) Rendering this beautiful line in such a clumsy paraphrase shows how concentrated poetic language can be, how much can be contained in a few words.

(It's worth mentioning, parenthetically, that you should have at your elbow a good desk dictionary, such as *Gage Canadian Dictionary, The Penguin Canadian Dictionary, The Canadian Oxford Dictionary* or *The Concise Oxford English Dictionary.* Writers—especially poets—expect you to pay close attention to every word. If a word puzzles you, look it up.)

IDIOMS, as well as words, may puzzle a reader. The Anglo-Irish poet William Butler Yeats begins one poem with

The friends that have it I do wrong

Because the idiom "to have it" (meaning "to believe that," "to think that") is unfamiliar to many Canadian readers today, a discussion of the poem might include a paraphrase—a rewording, a translation into more familiar language, such as

The friends who think that I am doing the wrong thing

Perhaps the rest of the poem is immediately clear, but in any case here is the entire poem, followed by a paraphrase:

The friends that have it I do wrong
When ever I remake a song,
Should know what issue is at stake:
It is myself that I remake.

Now for the paraphrase:

The friends who think that I am doing the wrong thing
when I revise one of my poems should be told what the
important issue is; I'm not just revising a poem; rather,
I am revising my own thoughts, my own feelings.

Here, as with any paraphrase, the meaning is not translated exactly; there is some distortion. If English is not your first language, you are very aware of how hard it is to capture true meaning in a paraphrase or translation. For instance, if "song" in the original is clarified by "poem" in the paraphrase, it is also altered; the paraphrase loses the sense of lyricism that is implicit in "song." Further, "Should know what issue is at stake" (in the original), is ambiguous. Does "should" mean "ought," as in (for instance) "You should know better than to speak so rudely," or does it mean "deserve to be informed," as in "You ought to know that I am thinking about quitting"?

Granted that a paraphrase may miss a great deal, a paraphrase often helps you, or your reader, to understand at least the surface meaning, and the act of paraphrasing will usually help you to understand at least some of the implicit meaning. Furthermore, a paraphrase makes you see that the original writer's words (if the work is a good one) are exactly right, better than any words we might substitute. It becomes clear that the thing said in the original—not only the rough "idea" expressed but also the precise TONE with which it is expressed—is a sharply defined experience.

A LITERARY RESPONSE

Of course, anything that you write about a work of literature is a response, even if it seems to be as matter-of-fact as a summary. It's sometimes useful to compare your summary with that of a classmate. You may be surprised to find that the two summaries differ considerably—though when you think about it, this is not really surprising. Two different people are saying what they think is the gist of the work, and their views are inevitably shaped, at least to some degree, by such things as their gender, their ethnicity, and their experience (including, of course, their *literary* experience).

But when we talk about writing a response, we usually mean something more avowedly personal, something (for instance) like an entry in a journal, wherein the writer may set forth an emotional response, perhaps relating the work to one of his or her own experiences. (On journals, see pages 18–19.)

Writing a Literary Response

You may want to rewrite a literary work, for instance by giving it a different ending, or by writing an epilogue in which you show the characters 20 years later. (We have already talked about the possibility of writing a sequel to Vigneault's "The Wall," or of writing a letter from the monk to the mason, or of writing the monk's memoirs.) Or you might want to rewrite a literary work, presenting the characters from a somewhat different point of view. A student who argues in an essay on Davies' *Fifth Business* that Boy Staunton *needs* someone very much like Dunstan Ramsay as a FOIL might well rewrite Davies' novel from Staunton's point of view. The fun for the reader would of course rest largely in hearing the story reinterpreted, in seeing the story turned inside out. It would be a challenge to rewrite "Marrying the Hangman" from the point of view of the husband. What would he say of the voice through the wall and its sexual promises? And what would he say of the woman he subsequently found himself bound to marry? Is he guilty of abuse? Does he really want gratitude from his wife for saving her, or does he just want a "simple life"? Rewriting a story like this could be an entertaining exercise, and it certainly would help you come to understand the author's STYLE and use of detail. It is unlikely, however, that you will be asked to undertake such an exercise (except, perhaps, in a creative writing class).

A PARODY

One special kind of response is the PARODY, a comic form that imitates the original in a humorous way. It is a caricature in words. For instance, a parody may imitate the style of the original—let's say, short, punchy sentences—but apply this style to a subject that the original author would not be concerned with. Thus, because Ernest Hemingway often wrote short, simple sentences about tough guys engaged in activities such as hunting, fishing, and boxing, parodists of Hemingway are likely to use the same style but for their subject they may choose something like opening the mail, or preparing a cup of tea.

Canadians have a great love of parody (as we do of SATIRE). One of the funniest books in early Canadian literature was *Sarah Binks*, a parody by Paul Hiebert of literary styles, literary criticism, and second-rate writing . Hiebert created a fictional poet named Sarah Binks (he called her a poetess and the Laureate of Saskatchewan which, today, adds to the humour) who wrote terrible poems in various derivative styles. She treated absurd subjects and had a funny, repressed relationship with the hired man, Ole. Hiebert made up her poems and then wrote literary criticism of them, lampooning professorial attitudes and vocabulary. Traditional parodies are critical, but they are usually affectionate, too. In the best parodies one feels that the writer admires the author being parodied. Canadians have come to love Sarah Binks, even though they see how foolish she is and how naïve.

Stephen Leacock, an early Canadian humorist, often used parody in his scathing satires. Popular TV shows like the very successful *SCTV*, *The Royal Canadian Air Farce,* and *This Hour Has 22 Minutes* all use parody as one of their vehicles for humour. Not only can literature parody itself, but film and television can also exaggerate and poke fun at the clichés in which they operate. *SCTV*'s parodies of movie classics are hilarious, and characters on *This Hour Has 22 Minutes* are often depicted watching the very programmes they satirize and mimicking the behaviour of characters on these shows. This sort of double parody is very sophisticated.

POSTMODERN PASTICHE AND PARODY

In the last twenty years or so, a new attitude has developed that eclipses or "empties out" parody. Parody may take pieces from various existing literary, dramatic, and filmic sources and "glue" them together into a mixed form

A REVIEW 57

that mimics (or satirizes) the individual styles or beliefs of each "piece." Fredric Jameson, in his influential essay "Postmodernism and Consumer Society," however, describes a contemporary condition in which styles or beliefs—and even language—is no longer seen as individual or living. The writer who takes segments of such empty allusions engages in what Jameson calls a "neutral" mimicry, creating "blank parody." Jameson calls this style of writing PASTICHE and argues that it does not have the same intention to correct, or the same affection for the source, as traditional parody. Many young, urban Canadian writers are creating pastiche.

A REVIEW

A review, for instance of a play or of a novel, is also a response, since it normally includes an evaluation of the work, but at least at first glance it may seem to be an analytic essay. We'll talk about a review of a production of a play, but you can easily adapt what we say to a review of a book.

A Review of a Dramatic Production

Your instructor may ask you to write a review of a local production. A review requires analytic skill, but it is not identical with an analysis. First, a reviewer normally assumes that the reader is unfamiliar with the production being reviewed and also with the play if the play is not a classic. Thus, the first paragraph usually provides a helpful introduction along these lines:

> Morris Panych's award-winning play, 7 Stories, a satire of social, psychological and religious attitudes, shows us a man contemplating suicide. Having been unable to find a parking place, the Man decides he can no longer bear to live in his urban world and plans to leap off a building. On the ledge, he encounters the occupants of the building who slowly lead him to a self-revelation.

Inevitably some retelling of the plot is necessary if the play is new, and a summary of a sentence or two is acceptable even for a familiar play. The review will, however, chiefly be concerned with

describing,
analyzing, and
evaluating.

Some advice:

1. *Save the program*; it will give you the names of the actors, and perhaps a brief biography of the author, a synopsis of the plot, and a photograph of the set, all of which may be helpful.

2. *Draft your review as soon as possible*, while the performance is still fresh in your mind. If you cannot draft it immediately after seeing the play, at least jot down some notes about the setting and the staging, the acting, and the audience's response.

3. *If possible, read the play*—ideally, before the performance and again after it.

4. *In your first draft, don't worry about limitations of space*; write as long a review as you wish, putting down everything that comes to mind. Later, you can cut it to the required length, retaining only the chief points and the necessary supporting details; but in your first draft, try to produce a fairly full record of the performance and your response to it, so that later, when you revise, you won't have to trust a fading memory for details.

A Sample Review: "An Effective *Macbeth*"

If you read reviews of plays in *Maclean's* or a newspaper, you will soon develop a sense of what reviews normally do. Newspaper reviews, however, are usually not as concerned with analysis as you might be in a critical review for class. The following example, an undergraduate's review of a production of *Macbeth,* is typical except in one respect. As has been mentioned, reviews of new plays customarily include a few sentences summarizing the plot and classifying the play (a tragedy, a FARCE, a rock musical, or whatever), perhaps briefly putting it into the context of the author's other works. Because *Macbeth* is so widely known, however, the reviewer need not tell her readers that the play is a tragedy by Shakespeare.

Preliminary Jottings
During the two intermissions and immediately after the end of the performance, the reviewer made a few jottings, which she rewrote later:

```
Compare with last year's Midsummer Night's Dream
Set: barren;
      pipe framework at rear. Duncan exits on it.
        Useful?
witches: powerful, not funny
stage: battlefield? barren land?
costume: earth-colored rags
      they seduce--even caress--Mac.
Macbeth
      witches caress him
      strong; also gentle (with Lady M)
Lady Macb.
      sexy in speech about unsexing her
      too attractive? Prob. ok
Banquo's ghost: naturalistic; covered with blood
Duncan: terrible; worst actor except for Lady Macduff's
  boy
costumes: leather, metal; only Duncan in robes
pipe framework used for D, and murder of Lady
  Macduff
forest: branches unrealistic; stylized? or cheesy?
```

The Finished Version

The published review follows, accompanied by some marginal notes commenting on its strengths.

Sandra Santiago

An Effective <u>Macbeth</u>

Title conveys information about thesis.

Opening paragraph is informative, letting the reader know the reviewer's overall attitude. Note that this review is of a production in the US and the spelling is American, not Canadian.

<u>Macbeth</u> at the University Theater is a thoughtful and occasionally exciting production, partly because the director, Mark Urice, has trusted Shakespeare and has not imposed a gimmick on the play. The characters do not wear cowboy costumes as they did in last year's production of <u>A Midsummer Night's Dream</u>.

Reviewer promptly turns to a major issue.

Probably the chief problem confronting a director of <u>Macbeth</u> is how to present the witches so that they are powerful supernatural forces and not silly things that look as though they came from a Halloween party. Urice gives us ugly but not absurdly grotesque witches, and he introduces them most effectively. The stage seems to be a bombed-out battlefield littered with rocks and great chunks of earth, but some of these begin to stir--the earth seems to come alive--and the clods move, unfold, and become the witches, dressed in brown and dark gray rags. The suggestion is that the witches are a part of nature, elemental forces that can hardly be escaped. This effect is increased by the moans and creaking noises that they make, all of which could be comic but which in this production are impressive.

First sentence of this paragraph provides an effective transition.

The witches' power over Macbeth is further emphasized by their actions. When the witches first meet Macbeth, they encircle him, touch him, caress him, even embrace him, and he seems helpless, almost their plaything. Moreover, in the scene in which he imagines

that he sees a dagger, the director has
arranged for one of the witches to appear,
stand near Macbeth, and guide his hand toward
the invisible dagger. This is, of course, not
in the text, but the interpretation is
reasonable rather than intrusive. Finally,
near the end of the play, just before Macduff
kills Macbeth, a witch appears and laughs at
Macbeth as Macduff explains that he was not
"born of woman." There is no doubt that
throughout the tragedy Macbeth has been a
puppet of the witches.

Paragraph begins with a broad assertion and then offers supporting details.

Macbeth (Stephen Beers) and Lady Macbeth
(Tina Peters) are excellent. Beers is
sufficiently brawny to be convincing as a
battlefield hero, but he also speaks the lines
sensitively, and so the audience feels that in
addition to being a hero he is a man of
insight and imagination, and even a man of
gentleness. One can believe Lady Macbeth when
she says that she fears he is "too full of the
milk of human kindness" to murder Duncan.

Reference to a particular scene.

Lady Macbeth is especially effective in the
scene in which she asks the spirits to "unsex
her." During this speech she is reclining on
a bed and as she delivers the lines she
becomes increasingly sexual in her bodily
motions, deriving excitement from her own
stimulating words. Her attachment to Macbeth
is strongly sexual, and so too is his
attraction to her. The scene when she
persuades him to kill Duncan ends with them
passionately embracing. The strong attraction
of each for the other, so evident in the early
part of the play, disappears after the murder,
when Macbeth keeps his distance from Lady
Macbeth and does not allow her to touch him.

The acting of the other performers is effective, except for Duncan (John Berens), who recites the lines mechanically and seems not to take much account of their meaning.

Description, but also analysis.

The set consists of a barren plot at the rear on which stands a spidery framework of piping, of the sort used by construction companies, supporting a catwalk. This framework fits with the costumes (lots of armor, leather, heavy boots), suggesting a sort of elemental, primitive, and somewhat sadistic world. The catwalk, though effectively used when Macbeth goes off to murder Duncan (whose room is presumably upstairs and offstage) is not much used in later scenes. For the most part it is an interesting piece of scenery but it is not otherwise helpful. For instance, there is no reason why the scene with Macduff's wife and children is staged on it. The costumes are not in any way Scottish--no plaids--but in several scenes the sound of a bagpipe is heard, adding another weird or primitive tone to the production.

Concrete details.

Summary

This <u>Macbeth</u> appeals to the eye, the ear, and the mind. The director has given us a unified production that makes sense and that is faithful to the spirit of Shakespeare's play.

Documentation

Work Cited

<u>Macbeth</u>. By William Shakespeare. Dir. Mark Urice. Perf. Stephen Beers, Tina Peters, and John Berens. University Theater, Medford, MA. 3 Mar. 1990.

The marginal notes call attention to certain qualities in the review, but three additional points should be made:

1. The reviewer's feelings and evaluations are clearly expressed, not in such expressions as "furthermore I feel," and "it is also my opinion," but in such expressions as "a thoughtful and occasionally exciting production," "excellent," and "appeals to the eye, the ear, and the mind."
2. The evaluations are supported by details. For instance, the evaluation that the witches are effectively presented is supported by a brief description of their appearance.
3. The reviewer is courteous, even when (as in the discussion of the cat-walk, in the next-to-last paragraph) she is talking about aspects of the production she doesn't care for.

📖 Suggestions for Further Reading

Fredric Jameson, "Postmodernism and Consumer Society," *The Anti-Aesthetic* (1983). Jameson's idea of pastiche is further discussed in "Postmodernism: The Cultural Logic of Late Capitalism," *New Left Review* 146 (1984).

PART 2

Standing Back:
Thinking Critically
about Literature

5

What Is Literature?

Learning Objectives

When you've read this chapter, you should be able to

➤ come to your own conclusions about what defines *literature*;

➤ expand your definitions of *literature* to include other cultural discourses;

➤ understand the relationships among content, form, and meaning in literary texts; and

➤ understand the current debate about the literary canon—and decide for yourself what you might include in a Canadian canon.

Perhaps the first thing to say is that it is impossible to define *literature* in a way that will satisfy everyone. And perhaps the second thing to say is that in the last twenty years or so, some serious thinkers have argued that it is impossible to set off certain verbal or written works from all others, and to designate them as *literature* on some basis or other. For one thing, it is argued, a work is just marks on paper or sounds in the air. The audience (reader or listener) turns these marks or sounds into something with meaning, and different audiences will construct different meanings out of what they read or hear. There are *texts* (birthday cards, sermons, political speeches, magazines, novels that sell by the millions and novels that don't sell at all, poems, popular songs, editorials, and so forth), but nothing that should be given the special title of *literature*. John M. Ellis argues, in *The Theory of Literary Criticism* (1974), that the word *literature* is something like the word *weed*. A weed is just a plant that gardeners for one reason or another don't want in the garden, but no plant has characteristics that clearly make it a weed and not merely a plant.

An important school of criticism known as CULTURAL MATERIALISM argues that what is commonly called literature and is regarded with some awe as embodying eternal truths is in fact only a "cultural construct," part of a huge project to make society and each person in it fit patterns that evolve through history. (The French thinker Michel Foucault has urged a whole new way of reading history that places events and even ways of understanding ourselves within constructions that evolve from the application of power.) According to cultural materialism, the writers of literature are the products of their age, and they are producing a product for a market, and the critic therefore ought to be concerned chiefly not with whether the text is beautiful or true—these ideas themselves are only social constructions—but, rather, with how writers are shaped by their times. Critics might consider, for instance, how the physical conditions of the Elizabethan playhouse and how the attitudes of the Elizabethan playgoer influenced Shakespeare, and how writings work upon the readers and thus help to shape the times. We will discuss this notion of context in Chapter 8 and in Chapter 16.

Although there is something to be said for the idea that *literature* is just an honorific word and not a body of work embodying eternal truths and eternal beauty, let's make the opposite assumption, at least for a start. Let's assume that certain verbal works are of a distinct sort—whether because the author shapes them, or because a reader perceives them a certain way—and that we can call these works *literature*. But what are these works like?

LITERATURE AND FORM

We know why we value a newspaper or a textbook or an atlas, but why do we value a work that doesn't give us the latest news or information about business cycles or the names of the capitals of nations? About a thousand years ago, a Japanese woman, Lady Murasaki, offered an answer in *The Tale of Genji*, a book often called the world's first novel. During a discussion about reading fiction, a character offers an opinion as to why a writer tells a story. (This is an early example of **METAFICTION**.)

> Again and again something in one's own life, or in the life around one, will
> seem so important that one cannot bear to let it pass into oblivion. There must
> never come a time, the writer feels, when people do not know about this.

Literature is about human experiences, but the experiences embodied in literature are not simply the shapeless experiences—the chaotic passing scene—captured by a mindless, unselective camcorder. Poets, dramatists, and storytellers find or impose a shape on scenes (for instance, the history of two lovers), giving readers things to value—written or spoken accounts that are memorable not only for their content but also for their *form*—the shape of the speeches, of the scenes, of the plots. (In a little while, we will see that form and content are inseparable, but for the moment, for textbook purposes, we can talk about them separately.)

Ezra Pound said that literature is "news that *stays* news." Now, "John loves Mary," written on a wall, or on the front page of a newspaper, is news, but it is not news that stays news. It may be of momentary interest to the friends of John and Mary, but it's not much more than simple information and there is no particular reason to value it. Literature is something else. The Johns and Marys in poems, plays, and stories—even though they usually are fairly ordinary individuals, and in many ways they often are rather like us—somehow become significant as we perceive them through the writer's eye and ear. The writer selects what is important (or what the writer has learned to value as important), and makes us care about the characters. Their doings stay in our mind.

To say that their doings stay in our minds is *not* to deny that works of literature show signs of being the products of particular ages and environments. It is only to say that these works are not exclusively about those ages and environments; they speak to later readers. The love affairs that we read about in the newspaper are of no interest a day later, but the love of Romeo and Juliet, with its joys and sorrows, has interested people for over four hundred years. Those who know the play may feel, with Lady Murasaki's spokesman, that there must never come a time when these things are not known. It should be mentioned, too, that readers find, on rereading a work, that the works are still of great interest but often for new reasons. That is, when as adolescents we read *Romeo and Juliet* we may value it for certain reasons, and when in maturity we reread it we may see it differently and we may value it for new reasons. It is *news* that remains news.

As the example of *Romeo and Juliet* indicates, literature need not be rooted in historical fact. Although guides in Verona find it profitable to point out Juliet's house, the play is not based on historical characters. Literature is about life, but it may be fictional, dealing with invented characters. In fact, almost all of the characters in literature are imaginary—though they *seem* real. In the words of Picasso,

> Art is not truth. Art is a lie that makes us realize truth. [. . .] The artist must know the manner whereby to convince others of the truthfulness of his lies.

We can put it this way: Literature shows *what happens,* rather than what happened. It may indeed be accurate history, but the fact that it is factual is unimportant.

One reason that literary works endure (whether they show us what we are or what we long for or dread) is that their form makes their content memorable. In Picasso's terms, the artist knows how to shape lies (fictions, imagined happenings) into enduring forms. Because this discussion of literature is brief, we will illustrate the point by looking at one of the briefest literary forms, the **PROVERB**. (Our definition of literature is not limited to the grand forms of the novel, tragedy, and so on. It is wide enough, and democratic enough, to include brief, popular, spoken texts.) Consider this statement:

> A rolling stone gathers no moss.

Now let's compare it with a paraphrase (a restatement, a translation into other words), for instance "If a stone is always moving around, vegetation won't have a chance to grow on it." What makes the original version more powerful, more memorable? Surely much of the answer is that the original is more concrete and its form is shapelier. At the risk of being heavy-handed, we can analyze the shapeliness thus: *Stone* and *moss* (the two nouns in the sentence) each contain one syllable; *rolling* and *gathers* (the two words of motion) each contain two syllables, each with the **ACCENT** on the first of the two syllables. Notice, too, the nice contrast between stone (hard) and moss (soft).

The reader probably *feels* this shapeliness unconsciously, rather than perceives it consciously. That is, these connections become apparent when one starts to analyze, but the literary work can make its effect on a reader even before the reader analyzes. As T. S. Eliot said in his essay on Dante (1929), "Genuine poetry can communicate before it is understood." Indeed, our *first* reading of a work, when we are all eyes and ears (and the mind is highly receptive rather than sifting for evidence), is sometimes the most important reading. Experience proves that we can feel the effects of a work without yet understanding *how* the effects are achieved.

Probably most readers will agree that the words in the proverb are paired interestingly and meaningfully. And perhaps they will agree, too, that the sentence is not simply some information but is also a composition, a careful arrangement of words. What the sentence *is,* we might say, is no less significant than what the sentence *says.* The sentence as a whole forms a memorable picture, a small but complete world, hard and soft, inorganic and organic, inert and moving. The idea set forth is simple—partly because it is highly focused and therefore it leaves out a lot—but it is also complex. By virtue of the contrasts, and, again, even by the pairing of monosyllabic nouns and of disyllabic words of motion, it is unified into a pleasing whole. For all of its specificity and its compactness—the proverb contains only six words—it expands our minds.

At this point, it must be said that many contemporary critics deny that unity is a meaningful concept. They argue that because each reader reads a text in his or her own way—in effect, each reader constructs or creates the text—it is absurd to talk about unity. Unity may be illusory. Or, on the other hand, if unity is real it is unwanted, a repressive cultural convention. We will discuss the point later, in Chapter 8, especially in conjunction with Deconstruction and Reader-Response theory, but here we will cite one example. In *Literary Theory* (1983), Terry Eagleton says, "There is absolutely no need to suppose that works of literature either do or should constitute harmonious wholes, and many suggestive frictions and collisions of meaning must be blandly 'processed' by literary criticism to induce them to do so" (81). Like many contemporary critics, Eagleton assumes that our society is riven with contradictions and that the art it produces is therefore also contradictory, fissured, fractured. Since the works are produced by a particular society and are consumed by that society, they are, in effect, propaganda for the present Late Capitalist economy, whether the authors know it or not. According to this view, critics who look for artistic unity falsify the works.

Contradictions are not always evident; it is sometimes fair for a critic to point out "absences" or "silences" or "omissions." That is, the critic may argue that certain material is not actually in the text, but its absence shows that the author has sought to repress the contradiction. Thus, a poem, story, or play about heterosexual romantic love may be seen as embodying a contradiction because it does *not* include any reference, say, to gay or lesbian love, or to marriage as a patriarchal construction that oppresses women. This view denies that any work is unified.

On the other hand, it is entirely legitimate to think about the choices a writer makes, and to wonder why *this* is included in the work whereas *that* is not. Shakespeare chose, in his *King Lear,* to alter his source (*King Leir*) essentially; he dropped the happy ending (in the source, *Leir* is restored to the throne, and his beloved daughter Cordelia does not die). An examination of this sort of choice—which ending is more suitable—is another equally valuable way to read literature.

   A Brief Exercise: Take a minute to think about some other proverb, for instance "Look before you leap," "Finders keepers," "Haste makes waste," "Absence makes the heart grow fonder," or whatever. Paraphrase it, and then ask yourself why the original is more interesting, more memorable, than your paraphrase. *what was oft thought / but n'er so well expressed*
                                                                  – A. Pope

LITERATURE AND MEANING

We have seen that the form of the proverb pleases the mind and the tongue, but what about content or MEANING? We may enjoy the images and the sounds, but surely the words add up to something. (It should be noted that some sound poets are more interested in the sound of words than their meaning. They try to show that meaning breaks down when the auditor concentrates on sound.) Probably most people would agree that the content or the meaning of "A rolling stone gathers no moss" is something like this: "If you are always on the move—if, for instance, you don't stick to one thing but you keep switching schools, or jobs—you won't accomplish much." Now, if this statement approximates the meaning of the proverb, we can say two things: (1) the proverb contains a good deal of truth, and (2) it certainly is not always true. Indeed this proverb is more or less contradicted by another proverb, "Nothing ventured, nothing gained." Many proverbs, in fact, contradict other proverbs. "Too many cooks spoil the broth," yes, but "Many hands make light the work"; "Absence makes the heart grow fonder," yes, but "Out of sight, out of mind"; "He who hesitates is lost," yes, but "Look before you leap." The claim that literature offers insights, or illuminates experience, is not a claim that it offers irrefutable and unvarying truths, covering the whole of our experience. Of course literature does not give us *the truth* (a concept some critics deny); rather it wakes us up, makes us see, helps us feel intensely some aspect of our experience and perhaps evaluate it. The novelist Franz Kafka said something to this effect, very strongly, in a letter of 1904:

> If the book we are reading does not wake us, as with a fist hammering on our skull, why then do we read it? [. . .] What we must have are those books which come upon us like ill-fortune, and distress us deeply, like the death of one we love better than ourselves. [. . .] A book must be an ice-axe to break the sea frozen inside us.

Arguing about Meaning

In Chapter 6, we will discuss at length the question of whether one interpretation—one statement of the meaning of a work—is better than another, but a word should be said about it now. Suppose that while discussing "A rolling stone gathers no moss" someone said to you,

I don't think it means that if you are always on the move you won't accomplish anything. I think the meaning is something like the saying, "There are no flies on him." First of all, what's so great about moss developing? Why do you say that the moss more or less represents worthwhile accomplishments? And why do you say that the implication is that someone should settle down? The way I see it is just the opposite: The proverb says that active people don't let stuff accumulate on them, don't get covered over. That is, active people, people who accomplish things (people who get somewhere) are always unencumbered, are people who don't stagnate.

What reply can be offered? Probably no reply will sway the person who interprets the proverb this way. Perhaps, then, we must conclude (as the critic Northrop Frye said) that reading is a picnic to which the writer brings the words and the reader brings the meanings. The remark is witty and is probably true. Certainly readers over the years have brought very different meanings to such works as the Bible and *Hamlet*. Even if readers can never absolutely prove the truth of their interpretations, all readers have the obligation to make as convincing a case as possible. When you write about literature, you probably will begin (in your marginal jottings and in other notes) by setting down random expressions of feeling and even unsupported opinions, but later, when you are preparing to share your material with a reader, you will have to go further. You will have to try to show your reader *why* you hold the opinion you do. In short,

- you have to offer plausible supporting evidence, and
- you have to do so in a coherent and rhetorically effective essay.

That is, you'll have to make the reader in effect say, "Yes, I see exactly what you mean, and what you say makes a good deal of sense." You may not thoroughly convince your readers, but they will at least understand *why* you hold the views you do.

FORM AND MEANING

Let's turn now to a work not much longer than a proverb—a very short poem by Phyllis Webb. It is the twelfth in a group of poems titled "Non Linear":

I have given up
complaining

but nobody
notices

Read the poem aloud once or twice, physically experiencing Webb's wonderful use of language. Notice that it is possible to read the poem as a kind of prose sentence, but that the line breaks ask you to pause at key places. Notice that the poem could be read as a humorous comment that friends don't notice that the speaker has finally stopped complaining. But it seems—because, perhaps, of the line breaks—that a more sober reading is intended. The speaker has given up complaining, but those who do not notice her (or him) don't notice even that fact. These comments assume you read the first two lines together: "I have given up complaining." But if you read them as totally separate comments—"I have given up." "[I am] complaining"—then the speaker is giving up because "nobody notices." No two readers will read the lines in exactly the same way, and that gives the poem its elusive strength. Let's consider how the lines may break:

1. I have given up complaining. No one notices that I've done so.
2. I have given up because nobody notices my complaints.
3. I have given up. I am complaining. But I have nobody. But nobody notices.
4. I have given up totally because when I gave up complaining nobody noticed.
5. I am complaining that nobody notices that I've given up.
6. I have given up complaining and, in fact, I've just plain given up, but as there is nobody out there, no one notices.

Each of these readings is possible, though some are more likely than others. The point is that this poem allows a READER-RESPONSE that is partly controlled by how the reader puts meaning to the line lengths.

The reader can also read the poem aloud, or with the mind's ear, in a number of ways. How would you STRESS this poem that doesn't use a conventional METRE? Again, there are various possibilities:

I have given up
COMPLAINING

but nobody
NOTICES

and

I have GIVEN UP
complaining

but NObody
notices

and so on. These two examples might prompt the humorous or sombre interpretations mentioned at the outset. Other emphases allow for more nuanced interpretations:

I have GIven UP
complaining

BUT NObody
NOTICES.

Consider how you first read the poem. Have you changed your reading? How does your way of stressing words alter your sense of what the poet is saying? Do you see that the more subtly you stress syllables or leave weak notes, the more possible ways you have to understand multiple meanings in the poem? Older poems with conventional rhythms sometimes forced a reader to a certain way of responding. (Think of Tennyson, for example, who urges patriotism in "The Charge of the Light Brigade" even though the subject matter calls for a renunciation of nationalism: "Half a league, Half a league, Half a league onward / All in the valley of death / Rode the six hundred.") Most contemporary poems do not prescribe a reading, but invite individual responses. **DECONSTRUCTION**, which we discuss in Chapter 8, urges readers to observe the "free play" between meanings.

Notice also that there is WHITE SPACE between the first two lines and the last two. This blank space is also part of the poem. How will you "speak" it? Is it a pause? Or does it cause you to emphasize the second **COUPLET**? It seems to ask for a pause, and it also highlights the two couplets—both linking them and pushing them apart. That might ask for the readings, "I have given up complaining" and "But nobody notices." Or it might act to link "complaining" and "But nobody," the lines that border the white space. Or it might highlight "complaining" and "But nobody" by putting no other words near these statements. It certainly allows you to read each couplet as complete in itself and then as part of the larger poem. So we have three tiny poems here that are really all part of one. The space is an active part of the form of this poem, even though it seems just to be "nothing."

The single words and short comments of these lines make the reader slow down, pronounce each piece, and think about it. That may bring about a sense of despair that no one notices what we do or say. Or, again, it may cause us to link the fragments together: "But there is nobody. Nobody notices. = There is nobody to notice." This way, the same word operates in two different groupings. Does the isolation of each word or word group invite these double linkages?

Part of what makes the poem effective is that the theme is *not* stated explicitly, not belaboured. Readers have the pleasure of making the connection for themselves—under Webb's careful guidance. Or let's put it this way: Other people may have noticed that they are alone, or that friends have stopped listening to their problems, but perhaps only Webb thought (to use Lady Murasaki's words), "There must never come a time [. . .] when people do not know about this." And, fortunately for all of us, Webb had the ability to put this perception into memorable words. Skill in handling language, obviously, is indispensable if the writer is to produce literature. A person may be feeling emotions like these, but emotion is not enough equipment with which to write even a four line poem. Poems, like other kinds of literature, are produced by people who know how to delight us with what the American poet Robert Frost called, "a performance in words." Once you have read or heard the poem, you can never again hear a complaint, or notice a friend is remaining silent, in quite the way you used to—and probably the poem will keep coming to mind as you notice your own solitude. Fairness requires us to mention, however, that many thoughtful people disagree, and argue that literature and art entertain us but do not really influence us in any significant way. In trying to resolve this debate, perhaps you can rely only on your own experience.

We can easily see that Phyllis Webb's poem is a work of literature—a work that uses language in a special way—if we contrast it with another short work in rhyme:

Thirty days hath September,
April, June, and November;
All the rest have thirty-one
Excepting February alone,
Which has twenty-eight in fine,
Till leap year gives it twenty-nine.

This information is important, but it is only information. The lines rhyme, giving the work some form, but there is nothing very interesting about it. (This is a matter of opinion; perhaps you will want to take issue.) It is not news that stays news, probably because it only *tells* us facts rather than *shows* or *presents* human experience. We all remember the lines, but they do not hold our interest. "Thirty Days" does not offer either the pleasure of an insight or the pleasure of an interesting tune. It has nothing of what the poet Thomas Gray said characterizes literature: "Thoughts that breathe, and words that burn."

As we will see, there are many ways of writing about literature, but one of the most interesting is to write not simply about the author's "thoughts" (or ideas) as abstractions but about the particular *ways* in which an author makes thoughts memorable, chiefly through the manipulation of words that at least glow if they don't "burn."

The poet W. H. Auden once defined literature as "a game of knowledge." Games have rules, forms; and conformity to the rules is part of the fun of playing a game. We don't want the hockey player to pick up the puck and skate away with it, or the tennis player to tear down the net. The fun in writing literature comes largely from performing effectively within the rules, or from introducing new rules and then working within them. For Auden, a work of art is "a verbal contraption," and in every work of art (as in a game), "Freedom and Law, System and Order are united in harmony" (*The Dyer's Hand* [1968], 50, 71).

We don't play (or watch) games because they teach us to be good citizens, or even because they will make us healthier; we play and watch them because they give us pleasure. But Auden's definition of literature is not simply "a game"; it is "a game of knowledge." When Auden speaks of knowledge, he is speaking of the writer's understanding of human experience. We are back to Lady Murasaki's comment that "there must never come a time, the writer feels, when people do not know" about certain experiences. This knowledge that Lady Murasaki and Auden speak of is conveyed through words, arranged as in a performance or a game. The performance may be very brief, as in the highly structured proverb about a rolling stone, or it may be extended into a novel of a thousand pages. Many of the later pages in this book will be devoted to talking about structure in fiction, drama, and poetry.

THE LITERARY CANON

You may have heard people talk about the CANON of literature; that is, talk about the recognized body of literature. *Canon* comes from a Greek word for a *reed* (it's the same as our word *cane*); a reed or cane was used as a yardstick, and certain works were said to measure up to the idea of literature. Many plays by Shakespeare fit the measure and were accepted into the canon early (and they have stayed there), but many plays by his contemporaries never entered the canon—in their own day they were performed, maybe applauded, and some were published, but later generations have not valued them. In fact, some plays by Shakespeare, too, are almost never taught or performed, for instance *Cymbeline* and *Timon of Athens*. And, conversely, some writers are known chiefly for a single work, although they wrote a great deal. The canon, in actuality, has always been highly varied. Because, until fairly recently, in the Euro–North American world white males were the people doing most of the publishing, white males controlled the publishing industry and white males were deemed to have value that other people were deemed not to have, the canon chiefly contained the work of white males. Much was written by women and people of colour, but very little of it was published, and the few examples that entered the canon did so because they fit the established assumptions of the canonical world. Even in the traditional male-dominated canon, however, the range was great, including, for instance, ancient epic poems by Homer (who is now thought not to have been a single person), tragedies and comedies by Shakespeare, brief lyrics by Wordsworth, and short stories and novels by James Joyce and Virginia Woolf. In Canada, a canon has been forming through the twentieth century. As it happens, the process of its creation is coinciding with the move to disband canons, making the development of a Canadian canon a conflicted one. There are writers who are clearly part of a Canadian canon: Robertson Davies, Alice Munro, Margaret Atwood, Margaret Laurence, Jack Hodgins, Michael Ondaatje, Dorothy Livesay, Phyllis Webb, Michel Tremblay, George Walker, Judith Thompson, Tomson Highway—the list is much, much longer. And some of these writers have joined larger, international canons. But the process of becoming known has been different for these writers than for earlier European and American writers who entered already established canons.

Further, the canon—the group of works esteemed by a community of readers—keeps changing, partly because in different periods somewhat different measuring rods are used. For instance, Shakespeare's *Troilus and Cressida*—a play about war, in which heroism and worthy ideals are in short supply—for several hundred years was performed only rarely, but during the Vietnam War it became popular in the United States, doubtless because the play was seen as an image of that widely unpopular war. More important, however, than the shifting fortunes of individual works is the recent inclusion of material representing newly valued kinds of experiences. In our day, we have become increasingly aware of the voices of women and of members of minority cultures, for instance First Nations Peoples, Canadians of colour, lesbians, and gay men. As a consequence, works by these people—giving voice to identities previously ignored by the larger society—are now taught in litera-ture classes.

What is or is not literature, then, changes over the years; in the language of today's criticism, "literature" as a category of "verbal production and reception" is itself a "historical construction" rather than an unchanging reality. Insofar as a new generation finds certain verbal works pleasing, moving, powerful, memorable, compelling, they become literature. Today, a course in Canadian literature may include works by Hiromi Goto, Roo Borson, or Wayde Compton, but it probably will also include works by long-established favourites such as Munro, Purdy, and Findley.

Some works have measured up for so long that they probably will always be valued; that is, they will always be part of a literary canon, though it is unlikely that there will be only one recognized canon. (Indeed, many young critics are suspicious even of the notion of canon.) But of course one cannot predict the staying power of new works. Doubtless some stories, novels, poems, and plays, as well as some television scripts and popular songs, will endure. Most of the literature of *any* generation, however, measures up only briefly; later generations find it dated, uninteresting, unexciting.

LITERATURE, TEXTS, DISCOURSES, AND CULTURAL STUDIES

These pages have routinely spoken of *literature* and of literary *works*, terms recently often supplanted by *text*. Some say that *literature* is a word with elitist connotations. They may say, too, that a *work* is a crafted, finished thing, whereas a TEXT, in modern usage, is something that in large measure is cre-ated (i.e., given meaning) by a reader. Further, the word *text* helps to erase the line between what traditionally has been called literature—for instance, canonized material—and popular verbal forms such as science fiction, Westerns, political addresses, interviews, advertisements, comic strips, and bumper stickers—and, for that matter, nonverbal products such as sports events, architecture, fashion design, automobiles, and the signs in a shopping mall. Texts or DISCOURSES of this sort (said to be parts of what is called a DISCURSIVE PRACTICE or a **SIGNIFYING PRACTICE**) in recent years have increas-ingly interested many people. They are the texts of cultural studies. In this approach, the emphasis is not on artefacts inherently valuable and taught apart from the conditions of their production. Rather, the documents—whether plays by Shakespeare or comic books—are studied in their social and political contexts, especially in view of the conditions of their produc-tion, distribution, and consumption. Thus, *Hamlet* would be related to the economic and political system of England around 1600, and *also* to the context today—the educational system, the theatre industry, and so on—that produces the work. (We discuss New Historicism in Chapter 8.) Some claim that studying a work otherwise—studying a literary work as an aesthetic object, something to be enjoyed and admired apart from its context, "sacralizes" it: treats it as a sacred thing, and in effect mummifies it.

IN BRIEF: A CONTEMPORARY AUTHOR SPEAKS ABOUT LITERATURE

Finally, in an effort to establish an idea of what literature is, let's listen to the words of Margaret Laurence, an author of stories and novels. Laurence, as a highly successful writer, could of course be examined in the context of cultural studies: How are her novels promoted? What sorts of people (race, class, gender) read Laurence? To what extent did her success jibe with the currency of the subjects she treated? But Laurence's own abundant comments about writing are almost entirely concerned with aesthetic matters, as in the following passage. She is talking about her story "The Loons," but we can apply her words to all sorts of literature:

> History for me, as with social issues, is personalized—these events happen to real people; people with names, families and places of belonging. [. . .] And so, by some mysterious process which I don't claim to understand, the story gradually grew in my mind until it found its own shape and form.

▢ Suggestions for Further Reading

Subsequent chapters will cite a fair number of recent titles relevant to this chapter, but for a start a reader might first turn to an old but readable, humane, and still useful introduction, David Daiches, *A Study of Literature* (1948). Another book of the same generation, and still a useful introduction, is a businesslike survey of theories of literature, by René Wellek and Austin Warren, *Theory of Literature*, 2nd ed. (1956). For a fairly recent, readable study, see Gerald Graff, *Professing Literature: An Institutional History* (1987).

Some basic reference works should be mentioned. An introductory dictionary of movements, critical terms, literary periods, and genres is C. Hugh Holman, *A Handbook to Literature*, 6th ed. (1992). For fuller discussions of critical terms, see John Peck and Martin Coyle, *Literary Terms and Criticism* (1993), and Wendell V. Harris, *Dictionary of Concepts in Literary Criticism and Theory* (1992), each of which devotes several pages to each concept and gives useful reading lists for each entry. See also: Irene Makaryk, ed., *Encyclopedia of Contemporary Literary Theory: Approaches, Scholars, Terms* (1993), and Michael Groden and Martin Kreiswirth, eds., *The Johns Hopkins Guide to Literary Theory and Criticism* (1994), and Jeremy Hawthorn, *A Concise Glossary of Contemporary Literary Theory* (1994). More topics are discussed in *The New Princeton Encyclopedia of Poetry and Poetics*, eds. Alex Preminger and T. V. F. Brogan (1993), which offers lucid entries (with suggestions for further reading) on such terms as "allegory," "criticism," "canon," and "irony." For a collection of essays on the canon, see *Canons*, ed. Robert von Hallberg (1984); see also an essay by Robert Scholes, "Canonicity and Textuality," in *Introduction to Scholarship in Modern Languages and Literatures*, ed. Joseph Gibaldi, 2nd ed. (1992), 138–58. Gibaldi's collection includes essays on related topics, for instance literary theory (by Jonathan Culler) and on cultural studies (by David Bathrick). For essays specific to the Canadian canon, see Robert Lecker, ed., *Canadian Canons: Essays in Literary Value* (1991), a very valuable collection that urges reconsideration of the way Canadian literature has been read and valued in the past.

6

What Is Interpretation?

Learning Objectives

When you've read this chapter, you should be able to

➤ interpret a literary text persuasively;

➤ ensure that your interpretation is reasonable given the contexts of the work, the author, the period in which the text was written, and our own period;

➤ avoid the fallacy of thinking you know the author's intention;

➤ find evidence and counterevidence in the text for your thesis; and

➤ read other interpretations critically, evaluating what is reasonable and well evidenced and what is not.

INTERPRETATION AND MEANING

We can define **INTERPRETATION** as a setting forth of the meaning, or, better, a setting forth of one or more of the meanings of a work of literature. This question of *meaning* versus *meanings* deserves a brief explanation. Although some critics believe that a work of literature has a single meaning—the meaning it had for the author—most critics hold that a work has several meanings: for instance the meaning it had for the author, the meaning(s) it had for its first readers (or viewers, if the work is a drama or film), the meaning(s) it had for later readers, and the meaning(s) it has for us today. Take *Hamlet* (1600–01), for example. Perhaps this play about a man who has lost his father had a very special meaning for Shakespeare, who had recently lost his own father when he wrote the play. Further, Shakespeare had earlier lost a son named Hamnet, a variant spelling of Hamlet. The play, then, may have had important psychological meanings for Shakespeare—but the audience could not have shared (or even known) these meanings.

What did the play mean to Shakespeare's audience? Perhaps the original audience of *Hamlet*—people living in a monarchy, presided over by Queen Elizabeth I—were especially concerned with the issue (specifically raised in *Hamlet*) of whether a monarch's subjects ever have the right to overthrow the sovereign. But obviously for twentieth-century Canadians the interest in the play lies elsewhere and the play must mean something else. If we are familiar with Freud, we may see in the play a young man who has a confused sexual response to his mother and seeks to kill his father (in the form of Claudius, Hamlet's uncle). Or we may see the play as largely about an alienated young man in a bourgeois society. Or—but the interpretations are countless.

IS THE AUTHOR'S INTENTION A GUIDE TO MEANING? *the Intentional Fallacy*

Shouldn't we be concerned, one might ask, with the intentions of the author? The question is reasonable, but there are difficulties, as justices of the Supreme Court find when they must interpret the intent of the Charter of Rights. First, for older works, we almost never know what the intention was. Authors did not leave comments about their intentions. We have *Hamlet,* but we do not have any statement of Shakespeare's intention concerning this or any other play. One might argue that we can deduce Shakespeare's intention from the play itself, but to argue that we should study the play in the light of Shakespeare's intention, and that we can know his intention by studying the play, is to argue in a circle. We can say that Shakespeare must have intended to write a tragedy (if he intended to write a comedy, he failed) but we can't go much further in talking about his intention.

Even if an author has gone on record, expressing an intention, we may think twice before accepting the statement as decisive. The author may be speaking facetiously, deceptively, mistakenly, or (to be brief) unconvincingly. For instance, Thomas Mann said, probably sincerely and accurately, that he wrote one of his novels merely in order to entertain his family—but we may nevertheless take the book seriously and find it profound.

IS THE WORK THE AUTHOR'S OR THE READER'S?

A good deal of recent critical theory argues that writers—usually quite unconsciously and despite how independent they may think they are—largely reflect the ideas of their age. In current terminology, to accept the artist's statements about a work is "to privilege intentionalism." The idea that the person who seems to have created the work cannot comment definitively on it is especially associated with Roland Barthes (1915–80), author of a much-reprinted essay entitled "The Death of the Author," and Michel Foucault (1926–84), author of an equally famous essay entitled "What Is an Author?" (Barthes's essay may be found in his *Image-Music-Text,* and Foucault's in *Foucault Reader.*) Foucault, for example, assumes that the concept of the author is a repressive invention designed to impede the free circulation of ideas. In Foucault's view, the work belongs—or ought to belong—to the *perceiver,* not to the alleged maker.

Much can be said on behalf of this idea—and much can be said against it. On its behalf, one can again say that we can never entirely recapture the writer's intentions and sensations. Suppose, for instance, we are reading an early work by Earle Birney, the poet and educator who wrote as a Marxist as a young man. None of us can exactly recover Birney's attitudes; we cannot exactly recreate in our minds what it was like to be Birney in the 1930s and 1940s—the period during which his early novel, *Down the Long Table,* was suppressed by the government. We can read his texts, but we necessarily read them through our own eyes and in our own times, whether during the popularity of Marxist criticism in the 1960s, or now, after the collapse of the Soviet bloc countries.

Similarly, we can read or see a performance of an ancient Greek tragedy (let's choose Sophocles' *Oedipus the King*), but surely we cannot experience the play as did the Greeks, for whom it was part of an annual ritual. Further, a Greek spectator probably had seen earlier dramatic versions of the story. The Oedipus legend was, so to speak, part of the air that the Greeks breathed. Moreover, we know (or think we know) things that the Greeks did not know. In the twenty-first century, familiar as we are with Freud's view of the Oedipus complex—the idea that males wish to displace their fathers by sleeping with their mothers—we probably cannot experience Sophocles' *Oedipus the King* without seeing it through Freud's eyes, as we earlier said was true of modern viewings of *Hamlet*.

However, *against* the idea that works have no inherent core of meaning that all careful readers can perceive, one can argue that a competent writer shapes the work so that his or her meaning is largely evident to a competent reader—that is, to a reader familiar with the language and with the conventions of literature. (Writers of course do not mindlessly follow conventions; they can abide by, challenge, or even violate conventions, putting them to fresh purposes. But to deeply enjoy and understand a given work—say, an **ELEGY**—one needs some familiarity with other works of a similar kind.) Many people who write about literature assume a community of informed readers, and indeed it seems to be supported by common sense.

WHAT CHARACTERIZES A GOOD INTERPRETATION?

Even the most vigorous advocates of the idea that meaning is indeterminate do not believe that all interpretations are equally significant. Rather, they believe that an interpretative essay is offered against a background of ideas, shared by essayist and reader, as to what constitutes a *persuasive argument*. Thus, an essay (even if it is characterized as "interpretative free play" or "creative engagement") will have to be coherent, plausible, and rhetorically effective. The presentation as well as the interpretation is significant. This means (to repeat a point made in Chapter 2) that the essayist cannot merely set down random expressions of feeling or unsupported opinions. The essayist must, on the contrary, convincingly *argue* a thesis—must point to evidence so that the reader will not only know what the essayist believes but will also understand why he or she believes it.

There are lots of ways of making sense (and even more ways of making nonsense), but one important way of helping readers to see things from your point of view is to do your best to face all of the complexities of the work.

Put it this way: Some interpretations strike a reader as better than others because they are *more inclusive,* that is, because they *account for more of the details of the work.* The less-satisfactory interpretations leave a reader pointing to some aspects of the work—to some parts of the whole—and saying, "Yes, but your explanation doesn't take account of [. . .]." This does not mean, of course, that a reader must feel that a persuasive interpretation says the last word about the work. We always realize that the work—if we value it highly—is richer than the discussion, but, again, for us to value an interpretation we must find the interpretation plausible and inclusive.

Interpretation often depends on making connections not only among various elements of the work (for instance among the characters in a story, or among the images in a poem), and among the work and other works by the author, but also on making connections between the particular work and a cultural context. The cultural context usually includes other writers and specific works of literature, since a given literary work participates in a tradition. That is, if a work looks toward life, it also looks toward other works. A SONNET, for example, may be about a human experience, but it is also part of a tradition of sonnet-writing. The more works of literature you are familiar with, the better equipped you are to interpret any particular work. Here is the way the American poet Robert Frost put it, in the preface to *Aforesaid*:

> A poem is best read in the light of all the other poems ever written. We read A the better to read B (we have to start somewhere; we may get very little out of A). We read B the better to read C, C the better to read D, D the better to go back and get something more out of A. Progress is not the aim, but circulation. The thing is to get among the poems where they hold each other apart in their places as the stars do.

Given the views (1) that a work of literature may have several or even many meanings, that (2) some meanings may be unknowable to a modern spectator, and that (3) meaning is largely or even entirely determined by the viewer's particular circumstances, some students of literature prefer to say that they offer a "commentary" on the "significance" of a work rather than an "interpretation" of the "meaning."

AN EXAMPLE: INTERPRETING PATRICK LANE'S "THE CHILDREN OF BOGOTA"

Let's think about interpreting a short poem by Patrick Lane, written in 1975.

THE CHILDREN OF BOGOTA

The first thing to understand, Manuel says,
is that they're not children. Don't start feeling
sorry for them. There are five thousand
roaming the streets of this city.

4

and just because they look innocent
doesn't make them human. Any one
would kill you for the price of a meal.
Children? See those two in the gutter   8

behind that stall? I saw them put out
the eyes of a dog with thorns because
it barked at them. Tomorrow it could be you.
No one knows where they come from   12
but you can be sure they're not going.
In five years they'll be men and tired of killing
dogs. And when that happens you'll be the first
to cheer when the carabineros shoot them down.   16

Perhaps most readers will agree that the poem dramatizes a conversation between, say, a taxi driver and visitors to Bogotá, Colombia. It is likely that most Canadian readers will interpret the visitors as tourists. The cabby or tour guide presents shocking information to the rather naïve tourists. It seems likely that the visitors expressed concern for street children and this reply disabuses the visitors of any romantic notions. (Lane is not saying that *all* taxi drivers have this opinion; he has simply invented one speaker who says such-and-such. Of course *we* may say that Lane says all residents of Bogotá have this opinion, but that is our interpretation.) The poem states that the visitors must "understand" the life of these children and their violent response to it against the lives we expect (or hope) for children. The poem highlights the word *children* and puts a question mark after it. The speaker almost laughs at the unheard use of the word by the visitors in relation to these violent youths. Lane breaks down any romantic notions by the image of a dog whose eyes have been put out. This is an ugly image, and an image that offends most Canadians, who are fond of animals. We are reminded that these youths have no pets, no families, no love: They live by their wits and bodies on the streets and they will lash out at anything that gets in their way. On the other hand, Lane also makes a strong link between the horrible blinding of a hapless dog and the equally unfair plight of these children who are not considered "human."

One can see other comments in the poem: It is also a warning. These children are a powder keg, ready to go off. There are "five thousand" of them, representing a serious threat to any society. And, of course, also to the developed countries that allow these injustices to continue. The speaker—who now seems frightened himself—warns that in "five years" these children will be men and might turn to killing what? Visitors? The speaker cynically adds that these tourists will, themselves, then cheer when the police shoot the dangerous thugs. It is a chilling comment on the difference between a fantasy of innocence and our instinctive response to protect ourselves.

A reader might seek Lane out, and ask him why he put the word "dogs" at the beginning of the penultimate line, rather than at the end of the line above, but Lane might not be willing to answer, or he might say that he doesn't really know why, it just seemed right when he wrote the poem. Most authors do in fact take this last approach. When they are working as writers, they work by a kind of instinct, a kind of feel for the material. Later they can look critically at their writing, but that's a different experience.

To return to our basic question: What characterizes a good interpretation? The short answer is, evidence, and especially evidence that seems to cover all relevant issues. In an essay, it is not enough merely to assert an interpretation. Your readers don't expect you to make an airtight case, but because you are trying to help your reader to understand a work—to see a work the way you do—you are obliged

- to offer reasonable supporting evidence, and
- to take into account what might be set forth as counterevidence to your thesis.

Of course, your essay may originate in an intuition or an emotional response, a sense that the work is about such-and-such, but this intuition or emotion must then be examined, and it must stand a test of reasonableness. (It's usually a good idea to jot down in a journal your first responses to a work, and in later entries to reflect on them.) It is not enough in an essay merely to set forth your response. Your readers will expect you to *demonstrate* that the response is something that they can to a large degree share. They will want you to *develop* your ideas, not merely list them. They may not be convinced that the interpretation is right or true, but they must at least feel that the interpretation is plausible and in accord with the details of the work, rather than, say, highly eccentric and irreconcilable with some details.

THINKING CRITICALLY ABOUT LITERATURE

Usually you will begin with a strong response to your reading—interest, boredom, bafflement, annoyance, shock, pleasure, or whatever. Fine. Then, if you are going to think critically about the work, you will go on to examine your response in order to understand it, or to deepen it, or to change it.

How can you change a response? CRITICAL THINKING involves seeing an issue from all sides, to as great a degree as possible. As you know, in ordinary language *to criticize* usually means to find fault, but in literary studies it does not have a negative connotation. Rather, it means *to examine carefully*. (The word *criticism* comes from a Greek verb meaning *to distinguish, to decide, to judge*.) Nevertheless, in one sense the term *critical thinking* does approach the usual meaning, since critical thinking requires that you take a sceptical view of your response. You will, so to speak, argue with yourself, seeing if your response can stand up to doubts.

Let's say that you have found a story implausible. Question yourself:

- Exactly what is implausible in it?
- Is implausibility always a fault?
- If so, exactly why?

Your answers may deepen your response. Usually, in fact, you will find supporting evidence for your response, but in your effort to distinguish and to decide and to judge, try also (if only as an exercise) to find COUNTER-EVIDENCE. See what can be said against your position. (The best lawyers, it is said, prepare two cases—their own, and the other side's.) As you consider the counterevidence, you will sometimes find it necessary to adjust your thesis. Writing is a process, so changing your mind is perfectly acceptable. You may even find yourself developing an entirely different response. That's also fine, though of course the paper that you ultimately hand in should clearly argue one thesis.

Critical thinking, in short, means examining or exploring one's own responses, by questioning and testing them. Critical thinking is not so much a skill (though it does involve the ability to understand a text) as it is a habit of mind, or, rather, several habits, including

- open-mindedness
- intellectual curiosity, and
- willingness to work.

It may involve, for instance, the willingness to discuss the issues with others, and to do research, a topic that will be treated separately in Chapter 15, on writing a research paper.

THREE STUDENT INTERPRETATIONS OF EARLE BIRNEY'S "THE BEAR ON THE DELHI ROAD"

Read Birney's poem, "The Bear on the Delhi Road," and then read the first interpretation, written by a first-year student. This interpretation is followed by a discussion that is devoted chiefly to two questions:

- What is the essayist's thesis?
- Does the essayist offer convincing evidence to support the thesis?

Two additional essays by first-year students, offering different interpretations of the poem, provide further material for you to analyze critically.

THE BEAR ON THE DELHI ROAD
Earle Birney

Unreal   tall as a myth
by the road the Himalayan bear
is beating the brilliant air
with his crooked arms
About him two men   bare   5
spindly as locusts   leap

One pulls on a ring
in the great soft nose   His mate
flicks   flicks with a stick
up at the rolling eyes   10

They have not led him here
down from the fabulous hills
to this bald alien plain
and the clamorous world   to kill
but simply to teach him to dance   15

They are peaceful both   these spare
men of Kashmir   and the bear
alive is their living   too
If far on the Delhi way
around him galvanic they dance   20
it is merely to wear   wear
from his shaggy body the tranced
wish forever to stay
only an ambling bear
four-footed in berries   25

It is no more joyous for them
in this hot dust to prance
out of reach of the praying claws
sharpened to paw for ants
in the shadows of deodars   30
It is not easy to free
myth from reality
or rear this fellow up
to lurch   lurch with them
in the tranced dancing of men   35

A Student Essay and Commentary

Surinder Sihota

On the Road to the World of Men

Earle Birney's "The Bear on the Delhi Road" is about
what the title says, and it is also about something more
than the title says. When I say it is about what the
title says, I mean that the poem really does give us a
picture of two peasant men from Kashmir and a bear that
they are leading down the road. We are told it is the
road to Delhi, the capital of India, a huge city teeming
with people. In line 13 the narrator says the men have
come from "fabulous hills" down to "this alien plain."
The plain is full of "hot dust." So it is clear that
these men have left a beautiful mountainous region where
it is probably cool to come down onto the great central
plain of India where it is very hot. The heat makes

their rough condition worse. In line 19, we are told
that they have already come "far on the Delhi way" so we
know that the journey has been going on for some time
and that they are, in fact, well into this part of the
country that is "alien" to them.

But in what sense is the poem about <u>more</u> than the
title? The title does not tell us anything about the
men who are on "the Delhi Road," but the narrator's
meditation on the scene tells us a lot about them. In
the first stanza he reveals that the men are "bare" and
"spindly as locusts." This means that they are very
thin and semi-naked. They are poor and they don't seem
to be part of the main society to which they are
travelling. The second stanza gives the information
that they are "mates" and the fourth that they are
"peaceful men." Perhaps each is the only friend the
other man has. They seem very alone, except for the
bear. These men dance and "prance" around the bear.
The image of the men is not typical of North American
images of men who aren't usually seen dancing and
wouldn't want to be described as "pranc[ing]." Men are
always afraid of any suggestion that they aren't
masculine. The rules by which men live say how they can
move and what occupations are "manly." These two are
quiet, want no trouble and just want to keep out of the
way of anything that will hurt them: they keep "out of
the reach of the praying claws."

The bear doesn't fit in, either. The bear is also
lonely. He wants to remain in a trance, pretending that
he is just hunting for berries in his old home. These
men have forced the bear to come to the main society and
to perform. It is important that this is a male bear.
The narrator shows him as a big, "shaggy" creature,
strong, but trapped and held in check by a ring through
his nose. The nose is described as a "great, soft
nose." Again, the strength of the bear is contrasted
with his soft nose and his desire just to be "ambling /
four-footed in berries." The bear is being made to
conform to standards that aren't natural for him and is
being made to earn a living for the men. He wants to be
free to forage for berries but our society doesn't allow
him to live his own life. He must work and he must
submit to the power of the men who control him.

>   Birney may be saying that the two men who have
> power over the bear--another male creature--don't have
> any power themselves. They are forced to make a living,
> too, and they can't just be peaceful "mates." What they
> are having to do is not "joyous" for them. When the
> bear dances, he just "lurches," but so do they. And the
> bear is being made to give up one trance for another.
>   What does Birney mean by the "tranced dancing of
> men"? Does he mean that all people live in a myth and
> are drugged by common beliefs? Or does he really mean
> "men" are? I think the poem is speaking about men.
> These two men might want to be "peaceful" and live in
> the hills as mates. Perhaps they are even lovers. But
> our modern world says everyone must work, everyone must
> come to cities and all men must obey rules of conduct.
> The reality of their lives might be one thing, but they
> are forced to live in the myth of what men are. The
> poem may be talking about peasants on a road in India,
> but the lack of freedom for men to be themselves, to be
> with a friend, and to be different is true in our world,
> as well. Society has every man by a ring in his nose.

Let's examine this essay briefly.

The title is interesting. It gives the reader a good idea of which literary work will be discussed ("On the Road") and it arouses interest, in this case by suggesting a destination that isn't literal and extends the comment outside India. A title of this sort is preferable to a title that merely announces the topic, such as "An Analysis of Birney's 'The Bear on the Delhi Road'" or "On a Poem by Earle Birney." (Notice that the title is centred, has no period at the end, and is not enclosed in quotation marks or underlined.)

The opening paragraph helpfully names the exact topic (Earle Birney's poem) and arouses interest by asserting that the poem is about something more than its title. The writer's thesis presumably will be a fairly specific assertion concerning what else the poem is "about."

The body of the essay, beginning with the second paragraph, begins to develop the thesis. (The THESIS perhaps can be summarized thus: "The men, like the bear, are trapped males in a world that demands they live by certain rules.") The writer's evidence in the second and third paragraphs is that these men are poor, maybe because they don't live in the "mainstream society," that they are friends who are close enough to be called "mates," and that they are "peaceful men." Readers of Sihota's essay may at this point be unconvinced by this evidence, but probably they suspend judgment. In any case, he has offered what he considers to be evidence in support of his thesis.

The next paragraph turns to the bear and links him with the men. The bear, Sihota says, wants to remain in his own "trance" but is being made to conform. He is strong, but is kept in place by a ring in a nose, which—in its own right—is soft. Do we agree with Sihota's assertion, in the last sentence of this paragraph, that Birney is suggesting that "men must work and submit to the power of other men"? Clearly this is the way Sihota takes the poem, but do you agree with his response to these lines? After all, Birney is talking about a bear. Is it fair to link his position to that of the men? And if so, does it matter that these are males, or just that animals and people have differing power? Is Sihota finding political comment that is not in the poem, or is his reading justified? The next paragraph amplifies the point that the men are living a life that is not "joyous," and "lurch" through life like the bear. No doubt most readers would agree that Birney makes this point, that the text lends support to Sihota's view.

The concluding paragraph effectively reasserts and clarifies Sihota's thesis, saying that all people live in a myth and are controlled by their masters and their societies. But Sihota restates his opinion that this problem is somehow special for men. Then he reiterates that the men are friends and suggests they may be lovers. In doing so, Sihota alters his thesis, suggesting that gay men are especially forced to live a "myth" that is not their own. The rest of the paragraph speaks about men in general again, but Sihota specifies that the freedom to "be with a friend, and to be different" is also denied to men—or, perhaps, to gay men. This may very well be true, and it is certainly possible to write an essay from a gay point of view. But the question is, has Sihota offered a response that is private? It is *his* response—and perhaps you share it. But perhaps you do not. Is this shading of his thesis argued convincingly? It certainly is argued, not merely asserted, but how convincing is the evidence? Has he helped you to enjoy the poem by seeing things that you may not have noticed—or has he said things that seem to you not to be in close contact with the poem as you see it? If so, is it because there is concrete evidence for his argument about men (or people) but less evidence (some might say no evidence) that these mates are gay? Sihota's observation about hegemonic controls on gay people is valuable, but is this the essay in which to develop it? It is important that you always question whether your interpretation is drawn from evidence in the work under study, or whether you are working out a concern of your own and forcing the writing to accommodate it. If you adopt various filters to view your texts (the filters we will discuss in Chapter 8), it is crucial that you first undertake a CLOSE READING of the text and ensure that your theoretical reading is entirely reasonable in terms of the evidence contained in the fictional text itself.

The documentation for this short essay on a short poem need not be overly elaborate. The opening paragraph informs us of the author and title, so we know that all references will be to this poem. You may wish to give a line number in the text, as Sihota does when he writes, "In line 13 the narrator says [. . .]." You may wish to indicate line numbers after quotations from the poem, but it is probably not necessary.

Remember: in a larger essay with more than one source, it is always necessary to indicate page and line numbers. If you are using line numbers, indicate that fact in the first reference with the full word—(line 18)—and subsequently simply use the number. If you are using both line and page references for different texts, you must always indicate what each number signifies.

Two More Student Essays

Here are two other interpretations of the same poem. You will see that these two essays also develop specific theses and reflect opinions of their writers, but each works with the evidence of the poem carefully. These are good, brief analyses of the poem.

Notice that Ms. Gifford's title is actually a quotation from the poem; that is why it is contained in quotation marks. Her *own* title would not appear in quotation marks because this is not a published essay. Mr. Hawford's title contains his own words and a quotation; notice how it is punctuated.

Barbara Gifford
                    "These Spare Men of Kashmir"
Earle Birney's poem "The Bear on the Delhi Road"
presents strong images of the captured bear and his
captors. None seem very happy and all are, as Birney
puts it, "tranced." These poor men of Kashmir are
forced by poverty to bring a bear down from the
"fabulous hills" with a "ring / in the great soft nose,"
but they are also on an "alien plain" and they must
"prance" in "hot dust." Although the poem presents
exotic images, it is really a poem about poverty and
social injustice.

        India is a society that has a strong caste system.
Although modern India is developing and there is no
doubt more opportunity for many people, there is still
an enormous population of peasants and uneducated people
trapped in centuries old beliefs and social systems.
For these people, the modern world does not exist.
Birney paints a vivid picture of the deprivation in
which these men live: they are "bare," meaning partly
dressed; they are "spindly," meaning thin; they are like
"locusts," meaning they are insect-like. Birney says
"it is no more joyous for them" than for the captive
bear. They have been forced by economic necessity to
give up their home, "in the shadows of deodars," which
are aromatic and shady trees, and come down to the
"clamorous world" of a more advanced India nearer to the

capital, Delhi. They are not participating in the urban
life of Delhi, however, but out in the dusty plain. The
actions of the men also show their low status. Although
they are by nature "peaceful," they are tormenting the
bear by flicking a stick at his eyes because their own
poverty necessitates teaching him to dance. They have
to keep out of the "praying claws / sharpened to paw for
ants." They also have to keep out of the way of the
modern world which is steamrollering its way forward
without providing any economic security for people like
these Kashmir peasants. Because they have no money,
they have no power. They can only "lurch, lurch"
forward to an uncertain future.

It is words like "lurch" and "tranced" and
"spindly" that create the tone of despair and poverty.
It is images like "beating the air / with his crooked
arms," "the rolling eyes," to "wear, wear / from his
shaggy body the tranced wish" that show how worn out and
beaten down the bear and the men have become by their
plight.

Earle Birney's poem presents foreign images, but
the story he tells is true around the world and even in
Canada. Poor people have no power and do whatever they
can to survive. If they want to survive, they must
attempt to exploit the even more disadvantaged, if any
exist. For these men, the only thing lower is a bear.
"The Bear on the Delhi Road" is a call for change.
The tone of defeat suggests that these conditions
cannot continue. The poor have reached the bottom
rung and Birney helps us to see the injustice of that
fact.

Exercises
1. What is the thesis of the essay?
2. Does the essayist offer convincing evidence to support the thesis?
3. Do you consider the essay to be well written, poorly written, or something in between? On what evidence do you base your opinion?

Ed Hawford
    "The Tranced Dancing of Men": Living in Myth
Although on the surface there is nothing about religion
in Earle Birney's "The Bear on the Delhi Road," the poem
is, in fact, talking about the myths in which humans

live.　There are social comments in this poem and economic ones, too, but the aim of the poem is to investi-
gate the "tranced dancing of men," the power of religion
and myth in human lives.

Right from the beginning, Birney introduces the
idea of myth and tells us that the images he presents
are "Unreal."　It is powerful to begin a poem with the
word unreal because it tells the reader that what is to
follow is a story, but also that there is a parallel,
unreal world to the world in which we live.　In the real
world, these men must capture and train a bear in order
to make a poor living.　But, in fact, they are as
trapped as he is by their own belief systems.

We think that the human mind is very different from
the mind of a bear.　This bear doesn't know why he is
captured; he just follows the "ring" in his "great soft
nose."　He can't help it.　And he doesn't really dance,
he just rears back and "lurches" to avoid a stick which
the men "flick" at his eyes.　He is being trained and he
doesn't understand why.　It is easy to see the comment
on animal cruelty here, but the more important comment
is that the bear is being forced to give up one
"trance," his

> wish forever to stay
> only an ambling bear
> four-footed in berries

for another trance.　In this new myth, the men will feed
him and will not kill him if he performs for them.
After a while, he will imagine this has always been his
life and will have learned that jumping about brings
food and water and no pain.

The men live a similar life, despite the human
belief that we are "higher animals."　They have also
left one life in the "fabulous hills" and find
themselves on an "alien plain."　But while they know
they must break down the will of the bear, "wear" him
down, they don't realize that they live in a similar
myth.　Birney doesn't tell us what religion they

practice, but that isn't important. What is more important than the particular religion is the fact that they, like the bear, live in a set of myths, the myths that govern us as humans. Birney calls them the "tranced dancing of men." These men also don't understand; they are also pawns of larger forces. They aren't "joyous" and they, too, dance around in the dust and "prance," just like the bear. They are dancing to a set of beliefs that pulls them along by a metaphorical ring in the nose. They are in a sort of trance, but it is the trance in which we all live, a trance that says life is a certain way, that humans and animals occupy certain positions, that some people have money and live in the capital city while some must live in the dust and train dancing bears to survive. These men don't question the way they live; they just enter the trance and dance through it.

Birney says it is "not easy to free / myth from reality." These men are trapped in a hard reality, but they survive it by remaining "peaceful" in their trance. By training the bear to dance, they make him look human. But they only <u>look</u> human, themselves. Far from governing their own lives, they just dance. By repeating the word <u>lurch</u> Birney really drives home the point that human life is a stumbling, drugged existence. We "lurch" forward, half asleep and trained into a dance by our own myths and beliefs. Centuries of beliefs have worn down our "shaggy bodies" and taken away whatever "wish" we might have once had. Like "The Bear on the Delhi Road," human life is "unreal" and we are only trained "in the tranced dancing of men."

Exercises

1. What is the thesis of the essay?
2. Does the essayist offer convincing evidence to support the thesis?
3. Do you consider the essay to be well written, poorly written, or something in between? On what evidence do you base your opinion? What do you think of the variety of sentence lengths in this essay? Would you rewrite any sentences?

◻ Suggestions for Further Reading

The entries on "interpretation" in the reference works listed at the end of Chapter 5 provide a good starting point, as does Steven Mailloux's entry on "interpretation" in *Critical Terms for Literary Study*, eds. Frank Lentricchia and Thomas McLaughlin (1990). You may next want to turn to a short, readable, and highly thoughtful book by Monroe Beardsley, *The Possibility of Criticism* (1970). Also of interest are E. D. Hirsch, *Validity in Interpretation* (1967), Paul B. Armstrong, *Conflicting Readings: Variety and Validity in Interpretation* (1990), and Umberto Eco, with Richard Rorty, Jonathan Culler, and Christine Brooke-Rose, *Interpretation and Overinterpretation* (1992). This last title includes three essays by Eco, with responses by Rorty, Culler, and Brooke-Rose, and a final "Reply" by Eco. See also Joseph Margolis, *Interpretation Radical but Not Unruly: The New Puzzle of the Arts and History* (1995); and *Texts and Textuality: Textual Instability, Theory, and Interpretation*, ed. Philip Cohen (1997).

7

What Is Evaluation?

Learning Objectives

When you've read this chapter, you should be able to

➤ differentiate between the evaluation and the criticism of texts;

➤ determine what standards you apply to your criticism;

➤ decide your opinion of the roles played by morality, truth, realism, and emotion in writing; and

➤ separate emotional from sentimental writing, evaluating the effectiveness of emotive writing.

CRITICISM AND EVALUATION

Most literary criticism is not concerned with evaluation even though, as noted previously, in ordinary usage *criticism* implies finding fault, and therefore implies evaluation—"this story is weak." Rather, it is chiefly concerned with *interpretation* (the setting forth of meaning) and with *analysis* (examination of relationships among the parts, or of causes and effects). For instance, an interpretation may argue that, in David Fennario's *Balconville*, the characters are victims of an unequal capitalistic economy, while an analysis may show how the symbolic setting of the play (the balconies of the tenement houses, which are the only vacation destination available to these workers in the heat of summer) contributes to the meaning. In our discussion of "What Is Literature?" we saw that an analysis of Phyllis Webb's "Non Linear" poem (pp. 70–72) called attention to the line breaks, which guide the reader to certain interpretations of the number of possible readings. We noticed that you can read these lines in (at least) two different ways:

> I have given up
> complaining

and noted that it makes a great deal of difference if you read the two lines as one grammatical unit or as two separate lines.

In our discussion, we did not worry about whether this poem deserves an A, B, or C, nor about whether it was better or worse than some other poem by Webb, or by some other writer. And, to repeat, if one reads books and journals devoted to literary study, one finds chiefly discussions of meaning. For the most part, critics assume that the works they are writing about have value and are good enough to merit attention, and so critics largely concern themselves with other matters.

Evaluative Language and the Canon

Still, some critical writing is indeed concerned with evaluation—with saying that works are good or bad, dated or classic, major or minor. (The language need not be as explicit as these words are: evaluation can also be conveyed through words such as *moving, successful, effective, important,* or, on the other hand, *tedious, unsuccessful, weak,* and *trivial.*) In reviews of plays, books, movies, musical and dance performances, and films, professional critics usually devote much of their space to evaluating the work or the performance, or both. The reviewer seeks, finally, to tell readers whether to buy a book or a ticket—or to save their money and their time. In short, although in our independent reading we read what we like, and we need not argue that one work is better than another, the issue of evaluation is evident all around us.

ARE THERE CRITICAL STANDARDS?

One approach to evaluating a work of literature, or, indeed, to evaluating anything at all, is to rely on personal taste. This approach is evident in a statement such as "I don't know anything about sound poetry, but I know what I like." The idea is old, at least as old as the Roman saying, *De gustibus non est disputandum* ("There is no disputing tastes"). If we say, "This is a good work," or "This book is greater than that book," are we saying anything beyond "I like this" and "I like this better than that"? Are all expressions of evaluation really nothing more than expressions of taste? Most people believe that if there are such things as works of art, or works of literature, there must be standards by which they can be evaluated, just as most other things are evaluated by standards. The standards for evaluating a pair of scissors, for instance, are perfectly clear: They ought to cut cleanly, ought not to need frequent sharpening, and ought to feel comfortable in the hand. We may also want them to look nice (perhaps to be painted—or on the contrary to reveal stainless steel), and to be inexpensive, rustproof, and so on, but in any case we can easily state our standards. There are agreed-on standards for many categories, but the influence of personal taste and changing fashion is almost always lurking under the surface. There should be a standard for athletic performance, for example, but judging in figure skating suggests this standard is highly subjective. There is an agreed upon standard for fluency in language, for example, but in Canada today not everyone agrees upon what the standard language actually is in a multicultural society.

But what are the standards for evaluating literature? In earlier pages we have implied one standard: In a good work of literature, all of the parts contribute to the whole, making a unified work. Some people would add that mere unity is not enough; a work of high quality must not only be unified but must also be complex. The writer is presenting a work of art, and when we read, we can see if the writer has successfully kept all of the juggler's clubs in the air. If, for instance, the stated content of the poem is mournful, yet the metre jingles, we can probably say that the performance is unsuccessful; at least one of the inept juggler's clubs is clattering on the floor. Here are some of the standards commonly set forth:

Personal taste
Truth, realism
Moral content
Aesthetic qualities

Let's look at some of these in detail.

Morality and Truth as Standards

"It is always a writer's duty to make the world better." Thus writes Dr. Samuel Johnson, in 1765, in his "Preface to Shakespeare." In this view, *morality* plays a large role; a story that sympathetically treated lesbian or gay love might be regarded as a bad story by a reader committed to a traditional Judeo-Christian perspective, or at least be thought less worthy than a story that celebrated heterosexual married love. On the other hand, readers adhering to other points of view might regard the story highly because, in such readers' views, it helps to educate people and thereby does something "to make the world better."

But there are obvious problems in determining value based on moral principles. A gay or lesbian story might strike even a reader with traditional values as a work that is effectively told, with believable and memorable characters, whereas a story of heterosexual married love might be unbelievable, awkwardly told, trite, sentimental, or whatever. (More about sentimentality in a moment.) How much value does one give to the ostensible content of the story, the obvious moral or morality, and how much value does one give to the artistry exhibited in telling the story?

People differ greatly about moral (and religious) issues. Edward FitzGerald's translation of *The Rubáiyát of Omar Khayyám* suggests that God doesn't exist, or—perhaps worse—if He does exist, He doesn't care about us. That God does not exist is a view held by many moral people; it is also a view opposed by many moral people. The issue then may become a matter of *truth*. Does the value of the poem depend on which view is right? In fact, does a reader have to subscribe to FitzGerald's view to enjoy (and to evaluate highly) the following stanza from the poem, in which FitzGerald suggests that the pleasures of this world are the only paradise that we can experience?

A book of verses underneath the bough,
A jug of wine, a loaf of bread—and thou
Beside me singing in the wilderness—
Oh, wilderness were paradise enow!

Some critics can give high value to a literary work only if they share its beliefs, if they think that the work corresponds to reality. They measure the work against their vision of the truth.

Other readers can highly value a work of literature that expresses ideas they do not believe, arguing that literature does not require us to believe in its views. Rather, this theory claims, literature gives a reader a strong sense of *what it feels like* to hold certain views—even though the reader does not share those views. Take, for instance, a LYRIC POEM in which Christina Rossetti (1830–94), a devout Anglican, expresses both spiritual numbness and spiritual hope. Here is one stanza from "A Better Resurrection":

My life is like a broken bowl,
   A broken bowl that cannot hold
One drop of water for my soul
   Or cordial in the searching cold;
Cast in the fire the perished thing;
   Melt and remould it, till it be
A royal cup for Him, my King:
   O Jesus, drink of me.

One need not be an Anglican suffering a crisis to find this poem of considerable interest. It offers insight into a state of mind, and the truth or falsity of religious belief is not at issue. Similarly, one can argue that although *The Divine Comedy* by Dante Alighieri (1265–1321) is deeply a Roman Catholic work, the non-Catholic reader can read it with interest and pleasure because of (for example) its rich portrayal of a wide range of characters, the most famous of whom perhaps are the pathetic lovers Paolo and Francesca. In Dante's view, they are eternally damned because they were unrepentant adulterers, but a reader need not share this belief to appreciate his writing.

Other Ways to Think about Truth and Realism

Other solutions to the problem of whether a reader must share a writer's beliefs have been offered. One extreme view says that beliefs are irrelevant, since literature has nothing to do with truth. In this view, a work of art does not correspond to anything "outside" itself, that is, to anything in the real world. If a work of art has any "truth," it is only in the sense of being internally consistent. Thus Shakespeare's *Macbeth*, like, say, "Rock-a-bye Baby," isn't making assertions about reality. *Macbeth* has nothing to do with the history of Scotland, just as (in this view) Shakespeare's *Julius Caesar* has nothing to do with the history of Rome, although Shakespeare borrowed some of his material from history books. These tragedies, like lullabies, are worlds in themselves—not to be judged against historical accounts of Scotland or Rome—and we are interested in the characters in the plays only as they exist *in the plays*. We may require, for instance, that the characters be consistent, believable, and engaging, but we cannot require that they correspond to historical figures. Literary works are neither true nor false; they are only (when successful) coherent and interesting. The poet William Butler Yeats perhaps had in mind something along these lines when he said that you can refute a philosopher, but you cannot refute the song of sixpence. And indeed, "Sing a song of sixpence, / Pocket full of rye," has endured for a couple of centuries, perhaps partly because it has nothing to do with truth or falsity; it has created its own engaging world.

Many literary critics hold the view that we should not judge literature by how much it corresponds to our view of the world around us. For instance, some argue that there is no fixed, unchanging, "real" world around us; there is only what we perceive, what we ourselves "construct," and each generation, indeed each individual, constructs things differently. In this view, the reality to which literature has traditionally pointed is, itself, a kind of "text," a writing supported by a **METANARRATIVE** of history, social and religious custom, and human sexuality.

And yet one can object, offering a commonsense response or qualification: Surely when we see a play, or read an engaging work of literature, whether it is old or new, we feel that somehow the work says something about the life around us, the real world. True, some of what we read—let's say, detective fiction—is chiefly fanciful; we read it to test our wits, or to escape, or to kill time. But most literature seems to be connected somehow to life. This commonsense view, that literature is related to life, has an ancient history, and in fact almost everyone in the Western world believed it from the time of the ancient Greeks until the nineteenth century, and of course many people—including authors and highly skilled readers—still believe it today. The question to pose, perhaps, is the extent to which a material reality overlaps with a fictional reality (in a literary text) and the roles both play in the "text" of history and human relations.

The desire for accuracy characterizes much writing. Many novelists do a great deal of research, especially into the settings in which they will place their characters. And they are equally concerned with style—with the exactness of each word that they use. Flaubert is said to have spent a day writing a sentence and another day correcting it. The German author Rainer Maria Rilke has a delightful passage in *The Notebooks of Malte Laurids Brigge* (1910), in which he mentions someone who was dying in a hospital. The dying man heard a nurse mispronounce a word, and so (in Rilke's words) "he postponed dying." First he corrected the nurse's pronunciation, Rilke tells us, and "then he died. He was a poet and hated the approximate."

[margin note: Pound's "morality"]

Certainly a good deal of literature, most notably the realistic short story and the novel, is devoted to giving a detailed picture that at least *looks like* the real world. One reason we read the fiction of Susanna Moodie is to find out what "the real world" of Upper Canada in the mid-nineteenth century was like—as seen through Moodie's eyes and class, of course. (One need not be a Marxist to believe, with Karl Marx, that one learns more about Industrial England from the novels of Dickens and Mrs. Gaskell than from economic treatises.) Writers of stories, novels, and plays are concerned about giving plausible, indeed precise and insightful, images of the relationships among people. Writers of lyric poems presumably are specialists in presenting human feelings—the experience of love, for instance, or of the loss of faith. And presumably we are invited to compare the writer's created world to the world in which we live.

Even when a writer describes an earlier time, the implication is that the description is accurate, and especially that people *did* behave the way the writer says they did—and the way our own daily experience shows us that people do behave. Here is George Eliot at the beginning of her novel *Adam Bede* (1859):

> With a single drop of ink for a mirror, the Egyptian sorcerer undertook to reveal to any chance comer far-reaching visions of the past. This is what I undertake to do for you, reader. With this drop of ink at the end of my pen, I will show you the roomy workshop of Jonathan Burge, carpenter and builder in the village of Hayslope, as it appeared on the 18th of June, in the year of Our Lord, 1799.

Why do novelists such as George Eliot give us detailed pictures, and cause us to become deeply involved in the lives of their characters? Another novelist, D. H. Lawrence, offers a relevant comment in the ninth chapter of *Lady Chatterley's Lover* (1928):

> It is the way our sympathy flows and recoils that really determines our lives. And here lies the vast importance of the novel, properly handled. It can inform and lead into new places the flow of our sympathetic consciousness, and it can lead our sympathy away in recoil from things gone dead. Therefore, the novel, properly handled, can reveal the most secret places of life [. . .].

In Lawrence's view, we can evaluate a novel in terms of its moral effect on the reader. The good novel, Lawrence claims, leads us into worlds—human relationships—that deserve our attention, and leads us away from "things gone dead," presumably relationships and values (whether political, moral, or religious) that no longer deserve to survive. To be blunt, Lawrence claims that good books improve us. His comment is similar to a more violent comment, quoted earlier, by Franz Kafka: "A book must be an ice-axe to break the frozen sea inside us." Again, not all critics hold this view today; thinkers reasonably ask what a verb like "improve" means in this context. "Improve" how, and in whose terms? Nonetheless, even quibbles are moral questions, so it seems that literature does, generally, incite moral response.

REALISM, of course, is not the writer's only tool. In *Gulliver's Travels*, Swift gives us a world of Lilliputians, people about six inches tall. Is his book pure fancy, unrelated to life? Not at all. We perceive that the Lilliputians are (except for their size) pretty much like ourselves, and we realize that their tiny stature is an image of human pettiness, an *un*realistic device that helps us to see the real world more clearly.

Some argue that, if a work distorts reality, the work is inferior. For example, some critics have charged that the "Rez plays" of Tomson Highway take up important issues of First Nations politics, but create poorly realized female characters who perpetuate stereotypes of Native women. One might reply, however, that in these plays distorted or exaggerated portraits of women (and men) aim to bring this very debate to the viewers' attention by creating a world that appears simultaneously real and fantastic. In this view, the portraits are not poorly drawn because they do not exactly duplicate material reality; indeed, they are more complex and layered artistic creations. By playing with the spectators' views of reality, Highway asks his audience to consider the very issues to which these critics point.

The view that we have been talking about—that writers do connect us to the world—does not require realism, but it does assume that writers see, understand, and give us knowledge, thus deepening our understanding and perhaps even improving our characters.

As we said earlier, some critics believe that convincing portraits of a supposed reality actually point only to previous texts of a constructed reality. The issue is complex. To say that a work of literature is convincing (and to evaluate its success in these terms) is not to determine whether the reality against which it is being measured does or does not actually exist. It is to determine whether the writer can bring any given world to life. A writer of science fiction is not describing a real colony on a real planet, but we can remark on whether he or she manages to make the colonists appear true. In a similar manner, a writer like Lawrence can bring the northern English countryside to vivid life (and point to truisms in the human spirit in the process), but that does not mean that the real working-class men and women whom he copied were free of the "signifying practices"—the values and social systems—of their day. (For more on this complicated subject, you might want to read works by Michel Foucault or Michel de Certeau.)

Although we *need* not be concerned with an evaluation, we may *wish* to be concerned with it, and, if so, we will probably find, perhaps to our surprise, that in the very process of arguing our evaluation (perhaps only to ourselves) we are also interpreting and reinterpreting. That is, we find ourselves observing passages closely, from a new point of view, and we may therefore find ourselves seeing them differently, finding new meanings in them.

IS SENTIMENTALITY A WEAKNESS— AND IF SO, WHY?

The presence of **SENTIMENTALITY** is often regarded as a sign that a writer has failed to perceive accurately. Sentimentality is usually defined as excessive emotion, especially an excess of pity or sorrow. Today, feminist and other critics are resuscitating the term *sentimental*, especially as it has been used to denigrate domestic issues traditionally of concern to women or emotional responses previously thought appropriate only for women. But when one thinks about it, who is to say when an emotion is "excessive"?

Adam Gopnik relates an emotionally charged experience during his sojourn in Paris:

> [. . .] in Le Soufflé, on a Saturday afternoon in December, in the back room, with [his son] Luke sleeping in his *poussette*, and the old couple across the neighboring banquette, who had been coming for forty years, there with their small blind dog. The waiters in their white coats [. . .] and the smell (aroma is too fancy a word) of mingled cigarettes and orange liqueurs. I am aware that this is what is called sentimental, but then we went to Paris for a sentimental

re-education [. . .] even though the sentiments we were instructed in were not the ones we were expecting to learn, which I believe is why they call it an education.

—*Paris to the Moon* (New York, 2000) 18.

Gopnik, who is often quite acerbic elsewhere in the book, acknowledges that here he is enjoying piling image upon image to create a sensuous description that gains its effect precisely because it is sentimental. He *uses* the sentiment, you'll notice, to make his point about education—and that point actually turns back upon the sentiment to draw a realistic conclusion. And his love of the restaurant, *la vie Parisienne*, and his son seems genuine.

Perhaps it is more useful to ask whether the writer has captured a truly powerful emotion or is trotting out a stock emotion or a fake one. Or is making the level of sadness extreme but is not giving the reader the clues needed to empathize with the emotion, so it seems overdone. In other words, what each reader can say is that the *expression* of grief in a particular literary work is or is not successful, convincing, engaging, moving. Surely (to take an example) parents can be grief-stricken by the death of a child; just as surely they may continue to be grief-stricken for the rest of their lives. Consider the following poem by Eugene Field (1850–95):

LITTLE BOY BLUE

The little toy dog is covered with dust,
    But sturdy and staunch he stands;
And the little toy soldier is red with rust,
    And his musket moulds in his hands.
Time was when the little toy dog was new,
    And the soldier was passing fair;
And that was the time when our Little Boy Blue
    Kissed them and put them there.
"Now, don't you go till I come," he said,
    "And don't you make any noise!"
So, toddling off to his trundle-bed,
    He dreamt of the pretty toys;
And, as he was dreaming, an angel song
    Awakened our Little Boy Blue—
Oh! the years are many, the years are long,
    But the little toy friends are true!
Ay, faithful to Little Boy Blue they stand,
    Each in the same old place—
Awaiting the touch of a little hand,
    The smile of a little face;
And they wonder, as waiting the long years through
    In the dust of that little chair,
What has become of our Little Boy Blue,
    Since he kissed them and put them there.

Why do many readers find this poem sentimental, and of low quality? Surely not because it deals with the death of a child. Many other poems deal with this subject sympathetically, movingly, interestingly. Perhaps one sign of weak writing in "Little Boy Blue" is the insistence on the word *little*. The boy is little (five times, counting the title), the dog is little (twice), the toy soldier is little (once), the toys collectively are little (once), and Little Boy Blue has a "little face," a "little hand", and a "little chair." Repetition is not an inherently bad thing, but perhaps here we feel that the poet is too insistently tugging at our sympathy, endlessly asserting the boy's charm yet not telling us anything interesting about the child other than that he was little and that he loved his "pretty toys." (Gopnik uses a similar diminutive in describing the "small blind dog," but he only uses it once, and he avoids telling us anything sweet about his infant son except that he is asleep.) Real writers don't simply accept and repeat the greeting card view of reality. Children are more interesting than "Little Boy Blue" reveals, and adults react to a child's death in a more complex way.

Further, the boy's death is in no way described or explained. A poet of course is not required to tell us that the child died of pneumonia, or in an automobile accident, but since Field did choose to give us information about the death we probably want something better than the assertion that when a child dies it is "awakened" by an "angel song." We might ask ourselves if this is an interesting, plausible, healthy way of thinking of the death of a child. In talking about literature we want to be cautious about using the word "true," for reasons already discussed, but can't we say that Field's picture of childhood and his explanation of death simply don't ring true? Don't we feel that he is talking nonsense? And finally, can't we be excused for simply not believing that the speaker of the poem, having left the arrangement of toys undisturbed for "many" years, thinks that therefore "the little toy friends are true," and that they "wonder" while "waiting the long years through"? More nonsense. If we recall D. H. Lawrence's comment, we may feel that in this poem the poet has *not* properly directed "the flow of our sympathetic consciousness."

In other poems, the pain of death seems very honest. In such poems, mourners truly notice and feel the death, unlike the strangely absent parents of Little Boy Blue. Their reactions, however, are more balanced: The deceased person is not rendered perfect, and memories of loss are mixed with memories of both good and bad times. Death in a family, for example, often prompts recollections of the pain of living together as well as grief at the passing. In Field's poem, the death of the child is almost a beautiful thing, but real death more honestly involves pain and guilt and sometimes the lost opportunity to make amends between estranged people. A poem such as Miriam Waddington's "Ten Years and More" captures such mixed emotions brilliantly. Robertson Davies' *World of Wonders* (as an example from another genre) takes on the complex implications of the death of Boy Staunton, to which various characters react quite differently. The same complex of reactions is possible in a short poem, skillfully written.

Let us reconsider one more poem about death. In the last chapter, we read Patrick Lane's "The Children of Bogota." Here is an excerpt from that poem (the whole text is on page 80–81):

[. . .] Children? See those two in the gutter

behind that stall? I saw them put out
the eyes of a dog with thorns because
it barked at them. Tomorrow it could be you.
No one knows where they come from
but you can be sure they're not going.
In five years they'll be men and tired of killing
dogs. And when that happens you'll be the first
to cheer when the carabineros shoot them down.

The image of death here is of a dog, but it is very horrifying. (Consider the plight of this blinded dog and the privileged blind dog eating treats in Le Soufflé in Paris!) Not only is it graphic in its violence, but it depicts a totally unnecessary and cruel death. For this reason, the horrible possibility that "tomorrow it could be you" seems very real in its menace. It would be just as senseless and haphazard were the tourist to be killed. The possibility of violent death is everywhere in this poem; it is not a contained, literary contrivance as it is in "Little Boy Blue." The inevitable death of some of these street children is communicated not only by what the poem explicitly says but also by what it does not say, or, rather, by what it shows. While the tourists are saddened by the death of a dog, the speaker suggests they will not be sorry at the death of these children once they have grown up into dangerous men. Is the death of children a sadder spectacle than the death of adults? Is it even sadder to see these youths move almost inescapably toward an early death, barely to escape death in childhood only to die as young adults? Is the plainly stated juxtaposition of the deaths of an animal, of victims of crime and of the criminals themselves what makes death seem so real in this work? Yet can't we say that the poem communicates the sadness of the waste of human lives, without tearfully tugging at our sleeve? Don't we feel that although the poet sympathizes with these young men (and all others who resemble them), he nevertheless does not try to sweeten the facts and take us into an unreal Little-Boy-Blue world where we can feel good about our response to death? Lane does not sentimentalize; he looks without flinching, and he tells it straight. Perhaps we can even say that although these youths may be inventions in "The Children of Bogota," the poem is a fiction that speaks the truth.

No one can tell you how you should feel about these two poems, but ask yourself if you agree with some or all of what has been said about them. Also ask yourself on what standards you base your own evaluation of them. Perhaps one way to begin is to ask yourself which of the poems you would prefer to read if you were so unfortunate as to have lost a child, or a spouse, or to hear of the death of any young person. Then explain *why* you answered as you did.

📖 Suggestions for Further Reading

Most of the reference works cited at the end of the discussion of "What Is Literature?" (page 76) include entries on "evaluation." But for additional short discussions see Chapter 18 ("Evaluation") in René Wellek and Austin Warren, *Theory of Literature,* 2nd ed. (1948); Chapter 5 ("On Value-Judgments") in Northrop Frye, *The Stubborn Structure* (1970); and Chapter 4 ("Evaluation") in John M. Ellis, *The Theory of Literary Criticism* (1974). For a longer discussion, see Chapters 10 and 11 ("Critical Evaluation" and "Aesthetic Value") in Monroe C. Beardsley, *Aesthetics* (1958). Also of interest is Joseph Strelka, ed., *Problems of Literary Evaluation* (1969). In Strelka's collection, you may find it best to begin with the essays by George Boas, Northrop Frye, and David Daiches, and then to browse in the other essays. For a discussion of new theories of sentimentality, see Eve Kosofsky Sedgwick, *Epistemology of the Closet* (1990).

8

Writing about Literature: An Overview

Learning Objectives

When you've read this chapter, you should be able to

➤ appreciate that contemporary critics employ various perspectives or filters when they read;

➤ define the following types of criticism: formalist, deconstructive, reader-response, archetypal, Marxist, New Historicist, biographical, psychological, feminist, gay and lesbian, and post-colonial; and

➤ employ some aspects of these critical approaches in your own reading of texts.

THE NATURE OF CRITICAL WRITING

In everyday talk, the commonest meaning of CRITICISM is something like "finding fault." And to be critical is to be censorious. But a critic can see excellences as well as faults. Because we turn to criticism with the hope that the critic has seen something we have missed, the most valuable criticism is not that which shakes its finger at faults but that which calls our attention to interesting things going on in the work of art.

SOME CRITICAL APPROACHES

Whenever we talk about a work of literature, or even about a movie or television show, what we say depends in large measure on certain conscious or unconscious assumptions that we make: "I liked it; the characters were very believable" (here the assumption is that characters ought to be believable); "I didn't like it; there was too much violence" (here the assumption is that violence ought not to be shown, or if it is shown it should be made abhorrent); "I didn't like it; it was boring" (here the assumption is that there ought to be a fair amount of fast-paced physical action and changes of scene, rather than characters just talking). Whether we realize it or not, we judge the work from a particular viewpoint.

Professional critics, too, work from assumptions, but their assumptions are usually highly conscious, and the critics may define their assumptions at length. They read texts through the lens of a particular theory, and their focus enables them to see things that otherwise might go unnoticed. It should be added, however, that if a lens or critical perspective or interpretative strategy helps us to see certain things, it also limits our vision. Many critics therefore regard their method not as an exclusive way of thinking but only as a useful tool.

What follows is a brief survey of the chief current approaches to literature. You may find, as you read these pages, that one or another approach sounds especially congenial, and you may therefore want to make use of it in your reading and writing. On the other hand, it's important to remember that works of literature are highly varied, and we read them for various purposes—to kill time, to enjoy fanciful visions, to be amused, to explore alien ways of feeling, and to learn about ourselves. It may be best to respond to each text in the way that the text seems to require rather than to read all texts according to a single formula. You'll find, of course, that some works will lead you to think about them from several angles. A play by Shakespeare may stimulate you to read a book about the Elizabethan playhouse, and another that offers a Marxist interpretation of the English Renaissance, and still another that offers a feminist analysis of Shakespeare's plays. All of these approaches, and others, may help you to deepen your understanding of the literary works that you read. There is no "correct" way to read.

Formalist Criticism (New Criticism)

FORMALIST CRITICISM emphasizes the work as an independent creation, a self-contained unity, something to be studied in itself—not as part of some larger context, such as the author's life or an historical period. This kind of study is called *formalist criticism* because the emphasis is on the *form* of the work, the relationships between the parts—the construction of the plot, the contrasts between characters, the functions of rhymes, the point of view, and so on. Formalist critics are concerned to show how particular words in a particular order create unique, complex structures that set forth particular meanings.

Cleanth Brooks, a distinguished American formalist critic, in an essay in the *Kenyon Review* (1951), set forth what he called his "articles of faith":

> That literary criticism is a description and an evaluation of its object.
> That the primary concern of criticism is with the problem of unity—the kind of whole which the literary work forms or fails to form, and the relation of the various parts to each other in building up this whole.
> That the formal relations in a work of literature may include, but certainly exceed, those of logic.
> That in a successful work, form and content cannot be separated.
> That form is meaning.

Formalist criticism is, in essence, intrinsic criticism, rather than extrinsic, for it concentrates on the work itself, independent of its writer and the writer's background—that is, independent of biography, psychology, sociology, and history. The discussions of a proverb ("A rolling stone") and of a short, "non-linear" poem by Phyllis Webb in Chapter 5 are brief examples. The gist is that a work of literature is complex, unified, and freestanding. In fact, of course, we usually bring outside knowledge to the work. For instance, a reader who is familiar with, say, *Hamlet,* can hardly study some other tragedy by Shakespeare without bringing to the second play some conception of what Shakespearean tragedy is or can be. A reader of Rohinton Mistry's *Tales from Firozsha Baag* inevitably brings unforgettable outside material (perhaps the experience of being an Indo-Canadian, or at least some knowledge of immigration) to the literary work. It is very hard to talk only about *Hamlet* or *Tales from Firozsha Baag* and not at the same time talk about, or at least have in mind, aspects of human experience.

FORMALIST CRITICISM, of course, begins with a personal response to the literary work, but it goes on to try to account for the response by a CLOSE READING of the work. It assumes that the author shaped the poem, play, or story so fully that the work guides the reader's responses. The assumption is that the "meaning" lies in the work itself. But, in fact, formalist critics approached their texts with a set of expectations and assumptions, so it may well be that the criticism of F. R. Leavis and the NEW CRITICS in America did not arise as objectively from the text as they may have believed it to do. Many literary critics today, in fact, argue that the active or subjective reader (or even what Judith Fetterley, a feminist critic, has called "the resisting reader"), and not the author of the text, makes the meaning. Still, even if one grants that the reader is active, one can hold with the formalists that the author is active, too, constructing a text that in some measure controls the reader's responses. Of course, during the process of writing about our responses we may find that our responses change. A formalist critic would say that we see with increasing clarity what the work is really like, and what it really means. Those who have moved away from formalism would argue that we have entered a process in which we "write" the text by rereading it and finding more and more connections between it and other of our experiences. Formalist criticism assumes that a work of art is stable; many contemporary critical approaches do not. An artist constructs a coherent, comprehensible work, the formalists say, thus conveying to a reader an emotion or an idea. T. S. Eliot said that the writer can't just pour out emotions onto the page. Rather, Eliot said in an essay entitled "Hamlet and His Problems" (1919), "The only way of expressing emotion in the form of art is by finding an 'objective correlative'; in other words, a set of objects, a situation, a chain of events which shall be the formula of the *particular* emotion." Contemporary critics, on the other hand, notice contradictions and multiple meanings, so their criticism may, itself, be provisional and undecided and still be useful.

In practice, formalist criticism usually takes one of two forms, either EXPLICATION (the unfolding of MEANING, line by line or even word by word) or ANALYSIS (the examination of the relations of parts). The essay on Yeats's "The Balloon of the Mind" (Chapter 12) is an explication, a setting forth of the implicit meanings of the words. The essay on Judith Thompson's *Lion in the Streets* (Chapter 11) is an analysis. The three essays on Birney's "The Bear on the Delhi Road" (Chapter 6) are chiefly analyses but with some passages of explication.

Formalist criticism, also called the **NEW CRITICISM** (to distinguish it from the historical and biographical writing that in earlier decades had dominated literary study), began to achieve prominence in the late 1920s, and was the dominant form from the late 1930s until about 1970. American NEW CRITICS looked for a moral order in the work they studied and, some people argue, chose short lyrics and other works that would provide evidence for what they had preconceived. British formalist critics did not study the text as closely, nor with the same objectives. Canadian criticism until about 1970 tended to be a mix of these two related approaches. Today, most students still employ the approach when beginning to study a work of literature. Formalist criticism can empower a student by allowing an immediate confrontation with the work, and removing the need to first spend days reading related background material. On the other hand, you should neither assume that the text in front of you is complete within itself, nor that there is a "correct" way to decode it. Outside reading and your own experience are valuable critical tools that you should learn to use and to trust. We provide a case study of a research project based in historical and political research in Chapter 16.

Deconstruction

DECONSTRUCTION begins with the assumptions that language is unstable, elusive, unfaithful. (Language is all of these things because meaning is largely generated by opposition: "Hot" means something in opposition to "cold," but a hot day may be 30 degrees whereas a hot oven is at least 200 degrees; and a "hot item" may be of any temperature—indeed, a "hot" item can be "cool.") Deconstructionists seek to show that a literary work (usually called "a text" or "a discourse") inevitably is self-contradictory. Unlike formalist critics, deconstructionists hold that a work has no coherent meaning at the centre. Jonathan Culler, in *On Deconstruction* (1982), says that "to deconstruct a discourse is to show how it undermines the philosophy it asserts" (86). (Johnson and Culler provide accessible introductions, but the major document is Jacques Derrida's seminal, and difficult work, *Of Grammatology* 1967, trans. 1976). Derrida believed that language is a system of signs without fixed meaning, to which we have arbitrarily assigned unified meaning in an effort to locate a "centre." He uses the term LOGOCENTRIC for this attitude. A **SIGN**, or SIGNIFIER, is the marker that points to a signified that stands for an original referent (a "real" thing.) Derrida and others point out, however, that the signified is itself a signifier of an earlier signified in an infinite chain. Derrida wittily created the term *différance* (which, in French carries both the meanings "to defer" and "difference") to suggest that words in this chain are distinct from others but defer meaning to the earlier sign. As a result, texts are "indeterminate," "open," and "unstable."

Deconstructionist interpretations share with various POSTSTRUCTURALIST theories the idea that authors are "socially constructed" from the "discourses of power" or "signifying practices" that surround them. Deconstructionists "interrogate" a text, using a double reading. They try to show what the author selected to order the text—sometimes in a straightforward explication—and then show the contradictions and gaps that prevent the text from becoming a neat, closed universe. (A good example of such a reading is Jennifer Harvie's article on Thompson's play: "Constructing Fictions of an Essential Reality, or 'This Pickshur is Niiiice': Judith Thompson's *Lion in the Streets*," *Theatre Research in Canada* 13 (1992): 81–93.) In this way, deconstruction—like the New Criticism—encourages close, rigorous attention to the text. Furthermore, in its rejection of the claim that a work has a single stable meaning, deconstruction has had a positive influence on the study of literature. A problem with deconstruction, however, is that too often it can be reductive, telling the same story about every text—that here, yet again, and again, we see how a text is incoherent and heterogeneous. Deconstructionists are aware that their emphasis on the instability of language implies that their own texts are unstable or even incoherent. Taken to the limit, deconstruction implies that no language can contain meaning and, therefore, that criticism itself cannot hold meaning. But in practice, the sense of INDETERMINANCY in their criticism allows most such critics freedom to push the limits of their readings, to explore what Derrida calls "the free play of signification." They exuberantly multiply meanings, and to this end they may use PUNS, IRONY, **ALLUSIONS**, and **INTERTEXTUAL** elements somewhat as a poet might. Such criticism can become a form of art itself. Indeed, for many deconstructionists, the traditional conception of "literature" is merely an elitist "construct." All "texts" or "discourses" (novels, scientific papers, a Barbie doll, watching TV, suing in court) are similar in that all are unstable systems of signifying, all are fictions, all are "literature."

Reader-Response Criticism

Probably all reading includes some sort of response—"This is terrific"; "This is a bore"; "I don't know what's going on here"—and probably almost all writing about literature begins with some such response, but specialists in literature disagree greatly about the role that response plays, or should play, in experiencing literature and in writing about it.

At one extreme are those who say that our response to a work of literature should be a purely aesthetic response—a response to a work of art—and not the response we would have to something comparable in real life. To take an obvious point: If in real life we heard someone plotting a murder, we would intervene, perhaps by calling the police or by attempting to warn the victim. But when we hear Macbeth and Lady Macbeth plot to kill King Duncan, we watch with deep interest; we hear their words with pleasure, and maybe we even look forward to seeing the murder and to seeing what the characters then will say and what will happen to the murderers.

When you think about it, the vast majority of the works of literature do not have a close, obvious resemblance to the reader's life. Most readers of *Macbeth* are not Scots, and no readers are Scottish kings or queens. (It's not just a matter of older literature: no readers of Timothy Findley's *Not Wanted on the Voyage* were present with Noah during the Flood.) The connections readers make between themselves and the lives in most of the books they read are not, on the whole, connections based on ethnic or professional identities, but, rather, connections with states of consciousness. For instance, a reader may share a sense of isolation from the family, or a sense of joy or guilt for sexual experiences. Before we reject a work either because it seems too close to us ("I'm a woman and I don't like the depiction of this woman"), or on the other hand too far from our experience ("I'm not a woman, so how can I enjoy reading about these women?"), we probably should try to follow the advice of Virginia Woolf (1882–1941), who said, "Do not dictate to your author; try to become him." Nevertheless, some literary works of the past may today seem intolerable, at least in part. There are passages in nineteenth-century Canadian literature that deeply upset us today. We should, however, try to reconstruct the cultural assumptions of the age in which the work was written. If we do so, we may find that if in some ways it reflected its age, in other ways it challenged that culture.

READER-RESPONSE CRITICISM, then, says that the "meaning" of a work is not merely something put into the work by the writer; rather, the "meaning" is an interpretation created or constructed or produced by the reader as well as the writer. In *Is There a Text in This Class?* (1980), Stanley Fish, an early exponent of reader-response theory, puts it this way: "Interpretation is not the art of construing but of constructing. Interpreters do not decode poems; they make them" (327).

Critics who use this approach differ. At one extreme, the reader is said to construct or reconstruct the text under the firm guidance of the author. That is, the author so powerfully shapes or constructs the text—encodes an idea—that the reader is virtually compelled to perceive or reconstruct or decode it the way the author wants it to be perceived. (We can call this view the **OBJECTIVE VIEW**, since it essentially holds that readers look objectively at the work and see what the author put into it.) At the other extreme, the reader constructs the meaning according to his or her own personality—that is, according to the reader's psychological identity. (We can call this view the SUBJECTIVE VIEW, since it essentially holds that readers inevitably project their feelings into what they perceive.) An extreme version of the subjective view holds that there is no such thing as literature; there are only texts, some of which some readers regard in a particular way. How to reconcile these extremes?

It seems clear that all writers carefully select what they hope is the exactly correct word for the exactly correct spot for some particular reason, but there are always GAPS or INDETERMINACIES, to use the words of Wolfgang Iser. Readers always go beyond the text, drawing inferences and evaluating the text in terms of their own experience. To return to Phyllis Webb's poem "Propositions," which we discussed in Chapter 4, we saw that the word *just* has a number of meanings. Each reader can assign one (or more) of these meanings and each will alter the reading of the poem. If the sense of "justified, with justice" is taken, the "passion" that is being proposed is quite different than if the sense of "only, or simply" is taken. Doubtless much depends on the reader, and there is no doubt that readers "naturalize"—make natural, according to their own ideas—what they read. But does every reader see his or her individual image in each literary work? A contemporary Canadian of Asian heritage may well be able to "see herself" in the company of the British immigrant Susanna Moodie, and her experience will colour her reading of this

nineteenth-century story of immigration, but can the same woman "see herself" among the male hockey players of Rick Salutin's *Les Canadiens* (1977)?

Many people who subscribe to one version or another of reader-response
theory would agree that they are concerned not with all readers but with
what they call INFORMED READERS or COMPETENT READERS. Such readers are
familiar with the conventions of literature. They understand, for instance,
that in a play such as *Hamlet* the characters usually speak in VERSE. Such
readers, then, do not express amazement that Hamlet often speaks metrically, and that he sometimes uses rhyme. These readers understand that
verse is the normal language for most of the characters in the play, and therefore such readers do not characterize Hamlet as a poet. Informed, competent
readers, in short, know the rules of the game; a writer works within a "landscape" that is shared by readers. As readers, we are familiar with various
kinds of literature, and we read or see *Hamlet* as a particular kind of literary
work, a tragedy, a play that evokes (in Shakespeare's words) "woe or wonder."
Knowing (to a large degree) how we *ought* to respond, our responses are not
merely private. Some critics, however, like Carolyn R. Miller (in "Genre as
Social Action," *Quarterly Journal of Speech* 10 [1984]: 151–67) argue that
genre, therefore, becomes one of the ways institutions wield power; READER-
RESPONSE criticism can, to some extent, free the reader of such control.

Archetypal (or Myth) Criticism

Carl G. Jung, the Swiss psychiatrist, in *Contributions to Analytical Psychology*
(1928), postulates the existence of a "collective unconscious," an inheritance
in our brains consisting of "countless typical experiences [such as birth, escape
from danger, selection of a mate] of our ancestors." Few people today believe
in an inherited "collective unconscious," but many people agree that certain
repeated experiences, such as going to sleep and hours later awakening, or the
perception of the setting and of the rising sun, or of the annual death and
rebirth of vegetation, manifest themselves in dreams, myths, and literature—
in these instances, as stories of apparent death and rebirth. These universal
experiences and symbols are called **ARCHETYPES**. For example, the archetypal plot of death and rebirth may be seen in Coleridge's *The Rime of the
Ancient Mariner.* The ship suffers a deathlike calm and then is miraculously
restored to motion, and, in a sort of parallel rebirth, the mariner moves from
spiritual death to renewed perception of the holiness of life. Another archetypal plot is the quest, which usually involves the testing and initiation of a
HERO, and thus essentially represents the movement from innocence to experience. In addition to archetypal plots, there are archetypal characters, since
an archetype is any recurring unit of significant importance to human stories. Among archetypal characters are the Hero (saviour, deliverer—about
whom Joseph Campbell writes extensively), the Scapegoat, the Terrible
Mother (witch, stepmother—even the wolf "grandmother" in the tale of
Little Red Riding Hood), the binary Madonna/Whore and a series of other versions of the Woman, the Wise Old Man (father figure, magician), the Sleeping
Prince, and others.

Because, the theory holds, both writer and reader share unconscious memories, the tale an author tells (derived from the collective unconscious) may strangely move the reader, speaking to his or her collective unconscious. As Maud Bodkin puts it, in *Archetypal Patterns in Poetry* (1934), something within us "leaps in response to the effective presentation in poetry of an ancient theme" (4). But this emphasis on ancient (or repeated) themes has made archetypal criticism vulnerable to the charge that it is reductive. The critic looks for certain characters or PATTERNS OF ACTION, and values the work if the motifs are there, meanwhile overlooking what is unique, subtle, distinctive, and truly interesting about the work. A second weakness in some archetypal criticism is that in the search for the deepest meaning of a work the critic may crudely impose a pattern, seeing (for instance) The Quest in every walk down the street.

Although archetypal criticism is less often used today, it is nevertheless true that one of its strengths is that it invites us to use comparisons, and comparing is often an excellent way to see not only what a work shares with other works but what is distinctive in the work. The most successful practitioner of archetypal criticism was the late Northrop Frye (1912–91), whose numerous books help readers see fascinating connections among works. Frye, who was a professor at the University of Toronto, has had an enormous impact on Canadian criticism. Some current critics accuse Frye of attempting to fit Canadian literature to the patterns he found in European and Classical literature, charging that his way of seeing patterns prevented early critics from seeing something unique or indigenous in our writing. For Frye's explicit comments about archetypal criticism, as well as for examples of such criticism in action, see especially his *Anatomy of Criticism* (1957) and *The Educated Imagination* (1964).

Marxist Criticism

A school of criticism based largely in the writings of Karl Marx (1818–83) and developed particularly in the 1930s took Marx's name. **MARXIST CRITICISM** today is varied, but essentially it sees history primarily as a struggle between socio-economic classes, and it sees literature as the product of its period, specifically as the product of economic forces. For Marxists, economics is the "base" or "infrastructure"; on this base rests a "superstructure" of ideology (law, politics, philosophy, religion, and the arts, including literature), reflecting the interests of the dominant class. Thus, literature can be seen within this perspective as a material product, produced in order to be consumed in a given society. Marxist critics reject notions of "masterpiece" or "genius," asserting that these notions are part of a bourgeois myth of the individual that detaches the text from its economic context. (Joining these ideas, some critics employ terms that link aesthetic perceptions to economic concepts, terms like the SPECTATORIAL ECONOMY and others.) In this view, like every other product, literature is the product of work, and it does work. A bourgeois society, for example, will produce literature that in one way or another celebrates bourgeois values. In the 1930s, critics such as the American

Granville Hicks asserted that the novel must show the class struggle. (Canadian writers such as dramatist David Fennario present such struggles in explicitly Marxist terms and critics of Fennario's plays must either agree with his position or challenge it—producing a kind of Marxist critique in either case.) Such a doctrinaire view, however, has not been much seen in Marxist criticism since World War II. More recent Marxist critics treat the text as a special kind of document that allows a reader to stand apart and view a society. The criticisms, of course, must follow the overall ideology of Marx, though this too has been variously treated. Today, many Marxist critics have responded to POSTSTRUCTURALIST criticism and now regard the text itself as a form of ideology. Louis Althusser, Pierre Macherey, and Terry Eagleton are critics who have been very influential in theorizing literature itself from a Marxist perspective. Few critics of any sort would disagree that works of art in some measure reflect the age that produced them, but most contemporary Marxist critics go further. They assert—in a repudiation of what has been called "'vulgar' Marxist theory"—that the deepest historical meaning of a literary work is to be found in what it does *not* say, what its ideology does not permit it to express. Macherey, for example, looks to the GAPS in texts to reveal to the reader what the text hides; Althusser looks for contradictions in the text, which occur when the ideology that supports the writing fails. While dedicated Marxists use such readings to call for change, many non-Marxists also use this form of criticism—Marxist criticism informs many later critical schools. For these critics, the approach allows the critic to stand outside the received values of a society and interrogate its foundations. For an introduction to Marxist criticism, see Terry Eagleton, *Marxism and Literary Criticism* (1976).

Historical Criticism

HISTORICAL CRITICISM studies a work within its historical context. Thus, a student of *Julius Caesar, Hamlet,* or *Macbeth*—plays in which ghosts appear— may try to find out about Elizabethan attitudes toward ghosts. We may find, for instance, that the Elizabethans took ghosts more seriously than we do, or, on the other hand, we may find that ghosts were explained in various ways, sometimes as figments of the imagination and sometimes as shapes taken by the devil in order to mislead the virtuous. Similarly, an historical essay concerned with *Othello* may be devoted to Elizabethan attitudes toward Moors, or to Elizabethan ideas of love, or to Elizabethan ideas of a daughter's obligations toward her father's wishes concerning her suitor. The historical critic assumes that writers, however individualistic, are shaped by the particular social contexts in which they live. One can put it this way: The goal of historical criticism is to understand how people in the past thought and felt. It assumes that such understanding can enrich our understanding of a particular work. The assumption is, however, disputable, since one may argue that the artist— let's say Shakespeare—may *not* have shared the age's view on this or that. All of the half-dozen or so Moors in Elizabethan plays other than *Othello* are villainous or foolish, but this evidence, one can argue, does not prove that Othello is, therefore, villainous or foolish. Fewer literary critics today

SOME CRITICAL APPROACHES   113

use quite this type of historical approach. Most critics—like most historians—now use a form of "New Historicism."

The New Historicism

Since about 1980, a school of scholarship called the **NEW HISTORICISM** has become a widespread approach to study. New Historicism holds that there is no "history" in the sense of a narrative of indisputable past events. Rather, there is only our version—our narrative, our representation—of the past. Here is an example: In the nineteenth century and in the twentieth, almost up to 1992, Columbus was represented as the heroic benefactor of humankind who discovered the New World. But even while plans were being made to celebrate the five-hundredth anniversary of his first voyage across the Atlantic, voices were raised in protest: Columbus did not "discover" a new world; after all, the indigenous people knew where they were, and it was Columbus who was lost, since he thought he was in India. Similarly, ancient Greece, once celebrated by historians as the source of democracy and rational thinking, is now more often regarded as a society that was built on slavery and on the oppression of women. The history of the Christian church is being reconsidered in the light of modern attitudes toward women, human sexuality, and many other issues.

In some ways, NEW HISTORICISM was a reaction against DECONSTRUCTION, but like most POSTSTRUCTURALIST criticisms it shares many of DECONSTRUCTION's ideas about language. The British critic Raymond Williams has been highly influential, developing a school of criticism called CULTURAL MATERIALISM, which is much like New Historicism and shares with it a sense that the study of the past is not isolated. New historicists try to read history in light of their commitments to various projects in the present. In Stephen Greenblatt's words:

> Writing that was not engaged, that withheld judgments, that failed to connect the present with the past seemed worthless. Such connection could be made either by analogy or causality; that is, a particular set of historical circumstances could be represented in such a way as to bring out homologies with aspects of the present or, alternatively, those circumstances could be analyzed as the generative forces that led to the modern condition. (*Learning to Curse* 167)

Perhaps most influential in the development of NEW HISTORICISM is the work of Michel Foucault, who re-examined the idea of the self by a rereading of history. It would be impossible to overestimate the importance of Foucault's work in contemporary criticism. After him, almost all critics have regarded history differently, looking not simply at political events, but at agencies of power (Foucault speaks of "strategies of power") and attempts to impose or subvert that power.

On the NEW HISTORICISM, see H. Aram Veeser, ed., *The New Historicism* (1989) and *The New Historicism Reader* (1994). For an excellent application of the method, see Ric [Richard Paul] Knowles, "Voices (off): Deconstructing the Modern English-Canadian Dramatic Canon," or Denis Salter, "The Idea of a National Theatre" both in Robert Lecker, ed., *Canadian Canons: Essays in Literary Value* (1991).

Biographical Criticism

One kind of historical research is the study of *biography*, which for our purposes includes not only biographies but also autobiographies, diaries, journals, letters, and so on. What experiences did (for example) Susanna Moodie undergo? Are all of the hardships of women pioneers in Prairie fiction true to the real lives of such women? The really good biographies not only tell us about the life of the author but they enable us to return to the literary texts with a deeper understanding of how they came to be what they are. The diaries of Virginia Woolf, for example, throw wonderful light on this complex woman and her equally complex writing. A fascinating example of biography mixing with fiction is the work of Frederick Philip Grove who, in 1927, published *A Search for America*, claiming it to be a revision of a draft from 1894. The book came to be regarded as an autobiography of this early Canadian settler. Douglas Spettigue, however, has shown that the book was written as late as 1920 and is not, in fact, autobiographical. Such literary detective work warns us about taking biographies too literally and reminds that all writing (as the New Historicists suggest) is a mix of fact and fantasy.

Psychological (or Psychoanalytic) Criticism

PSYCHOLOGICAL or **PSYCHOANALYTIC CRITICISM** developed from the framework of Freudian psychology. Recently, psychological criticism has become widespread, partly as a result of twentieth century interest in psychology, partly because such study connects with other poststructural criticisms, partly because it offers a theoretical explanation of human responses to art.

A central doctrine of Sigmund Freud (1856–1939) is the Oedipus complex, the view that all males unconsciously wish to displace their fathers and to sleep with their mothers. According to Freud, hatred of the father and love of the mother, normally repressed, may appear disguised in dreams.

A classic example of psychological biography read into literature is Ernest Jones's *Hamlet and Oedipus* (1949). Amplifying some comments by Freud, Jones argues that Hamlet delays killing Claudius because Claudius (who has killed Hamlet's father and married Hamlet's mother) has done exactly what an Oedipal Hamlet himself wanted to do. For Hamlet to kill Claudius, then, would be to kill himself. Jones influenced the famous film version of the play with Lawrence Olivier and almost all productions of *Hamlet* since have explored an Oedipal relationship (consider, for example, the overt sexuality of the Mel Gibson version with Glenn Close as the mother).

Jungian criticism, which we discussed earlier, is an evolution from some of Freud's ideas. Even more important recently has been the work of the French neo-Freudian, Jacques Lacan, whose theories have attracted many literary and film critics. In Lacan, Freud is reinterpreted in terms of language, the preoccupation with sexual repression and the "id," and the idea of the self. Lacan believes there is no unified self, that the inner being (the *je*) seeks to see itself, seeing instead images of an ideal self (the *moi*) which forever disappear. As a result, we "suture," or sew together, an image of self that mixes the ideal with the symbolic. For film critics, such a view of the GAZE and the self has been highly suggestive. Lacan bases his ideas in a "phallo-centric" view of language and the nature of thought: Some feminists argue against Lacan as a result; some employ his theories; some use them to work against themselves. The question is how we define what Lacan calls the *phallus*, by which he does not mean the penis. Is such an agency of (male) power at the base of our ideas of self, or is this a notion left over from Freud's preoccupation with the genitals and, particularly, with male sexuality? Lacanian criticism is asking some very important questions about the nature of human perception, self, and society. It also asks whether males and females read the same way.

Feminist Criticism

FEMINIST CRITICISM can be traced back through the work of Simone de Beauvoir (*The Second Sex*, 1949), Virginia Woolf (chiefly *A Room of One's Own*, 1928), the efforts of the suffragettes at the turn of this century, the earlier writing of Mary Wollenstonecraft (*A Vindication of the Rights of Woman*, 1792) and much earlier to the writings of such women as Margery Kempe and Hildegard von Bingen. But a major impetus was the Women's Movement of the 1960s. The call for a reappraisal of the position of women resulted—in literary studies—in work such as *Sexual Politics* (1970), by Kate Millet, which called attention to the misogynist attitudes in canonical litera-ture. There was also a new appreciation for women's literature and female writers, many of whom were shown to have been undervalued by a society that values men. Feminists have argued that certain forms of writing have been especially the province of women—for instance journals, diaries, and letters; and predictably, these forms have not been given adequate space in the traditional, male-oriented canon. As well, many female writers who were known in their day were forgotten as the canon formed. (Consider, as Anne K. Mellor points out, our view of Romanticism based on five male writers [see *Romanticism and Feminism*, 1988.]) In 1972, in an essay entitled "When We Dead Awaken: Writing as Re-Vision," the poet and essayist Adrienne Rich effectively summed up the matter:

> A radical critique of literature, feminist in its impulse, would take the work first of all as a clue to how we live, how we have been living, how we have been led to imagine ourselves, how our language has trapped as well as liberated us; and how we can begin to see—and therefore live—afresh. [. . .] We need to know the writing of the past and know it differently than we have ever known it; not to pass on a tradition but to break its hold over us.

The Women's Movement initially argued that women and men are very similar and therefore should be treated equally. Later feminist criticism emphasized and explored the differences between men and women. Because the experiences of the sexes are different, the argument goes, their values and sensibilities are different, and their responses to literature are different. By the 1980s, however, feminist discussions had become widely varied.

Works written by women are seen by some feminist critics as embodying the experiences of a minority culture—a group marginalized by the dominant male culture; some critics, therefore, place political issues at the forefront. Some critics, like Judith Fetterley in 1978, argued that women should resist the meanings (that is, the visions of how women ought to think or behave) that male authors—or female authors who have inherited patriarchal values—bury in their books. Fetterley pointed out that the canon "insists on its universality in specifically male terms." Fetterley argued that a woman must read as a woman, "exorcising the male mind that has been implanted in women." In resisting the obvious meanings—for instance, the false claim that male values are universal values—women may discover more significant meanings. Fetterley (who was also a reader-response critic) began a debate that has since opened the canon. (It is important to note that it is not only women who have been underrepresented in the canon: so have racial and other minorities.)

Other feminist critics explore more theoretical questions of the very nature of women and men. French theorists such as Julia Kristeva, Luce Irigaray, and Hèléne Cixous used (and reacted against) Lacan and Derrida, attempting to find a new way to write outside a patriarchal structure. They argued for an ÉCRITURE FÉMININE, a "feminine writing."

The work of Michel Foucault has influenced another school of feminist critics who seek to redefine gender and to examine the role of social agencies in the construction of the category "the woman." North American feminism tends more toward this position than toward the reconsidered language of French feminism. Recent criticism by feminist and gay critics has suggested that all gender is a PERFORMATIVE, an act of construction. The ideas of Judith Butler (Gender Trouble: Feminism and the Subversion of Identity, 1990, and the 1993 Bodies That Matter, discussed later) have been highly influential in this debate. The point is that critics disagree as to whether gender is "materialist" or constructed, though most thinkers today agree that historical and cultural context affects how women and men see themselves and, therefore, how they read and write. At this point it should also be said that some theorists, who hold that identity is socially constructed, strongly dispute the value of establishing "essentialist" categories such as woman or man, gay or lesbian—a point we will consider in the next section.

In Canada, Barbara Godard has called for "ex-centric" readings—readings that move from (ex) the centre and are "eccentric" or idiosyncratic. (See Godard, "Ex-centriques, Eccentric, Avant-Garde," Room of One's Own 8 [1984] and also Barbara Harlow, Resistance Literature, 1987.) Susan Bennett urges female writers to "endeavour to destabilize the complacency of spectators who are terrifyingly well trained to conduct their own silent surveillance" (Canadian Theatre Review 76 [1993]: 39). Today, FEMINIST CRITICISM influences every other kind of criticism and has fundamentally altered the way we look at ourselves and, therefore, at our art.

Lesbian and Gay Criticism

LESBIAN AND GAY CRITICISM have their roots in FEMINIST CRITICISM; that is, FEMINIST CRITICISM introduced many of the questions that these other, newer developments are now exploring.

In 1979, in a book called *On Lies, Secrets, and Silence*, Adrienne Rich reprinted a 1975 essay on Emily Dickinson, "Vesuvius at Home." In her new preface to the reprinted essay she said that a lesbian-feminist reading of Dickinson would not have to prove that Dickinson slept with another woman. Rather, lesbian-feminist criticism "will ask questions hitherto passed over; it will not search obsessively for heterosexual romance as the key to a woman artist's life and work" (157–58). Obviously such a statement is also relevant to a male artist's life and work.

Lesbian criticism and gay criticism are not symmetrical. Lesbian literary theory has often found an affinity more with feminist theory than with gay theory; that is, the emphasis has often been on questions of gender (male/female) rather than on questions of sexual orientation (homosexuality/bisexuality/heterosexuality/transgenderation)—but this generalization is, itself, open to debate.

Critics ask various questions:

- Do lesbians and gays read in ways that differ from the ways straight people read?
- Do they write in ways that differ from those of straight people? (For instance, Gregory Woods argues in *Lesbian and Gay Writing: An Anthology of Critical Essays* (ed. Mark Lilly, 1990), that "modern gay poets [. . .] use [. . .] paradox, as weapon and shield, against a world in which heterosexuality is taken for granted as being exclusively natural and healthy" [176].
- How have straight writers portrayed lesbians and gays, and how have lesbian and gay writers portrayed straight women and men?
- What strategies did lesbian and gay writers use to make their work acceptable to a general public in an age when lesbian and gay behaviour was unmentionable? And how are they writing today in the face of continuing homophobia?

Questions such as these have stimulated critical writing, especially about bisexual and lesbian and gay authors (for instance Shakespeare—and not only the sonnets which praise a beautiful male friend—Virginia Woolf, Gertrude Stein, Elizabeth Bishop, Walt Whitman, Oscar Wilde, E. M. Forster, Timothy Findley, Tennessee Williams, Jovette Marchessault, Stan Persky), but they have also led to important writing on other subjects. Robert Wallace, for example, asks why certain plays are produced in Canada and others are not (*Producing Marginality: Theatre and Criticism in Canada*, 1990) and considers gay plays as part of his answer.

Examination of matters of gender can obviously help to illuminate literary works, but some critics write also as activists, reporting their findings not only to help us to understand and to enjoy the works of such writers as Bryden MacDonald, Shawna Dempsey and Lori Millan, Brad Fraser, and Walt Whitman, but also to change society's view of sexuality. Thus, in *Disseminating Whitman* (1991), Michael Moon is impatient with earlier critical rhapsodies about Whitman's universalism. It used to be said that Whitman's celebration of the male body was a sexless celebration of brotherly love in a democracy, but the gist of Moon's view is that we must neither whitewash Whitman's poems with such high-minded talk, nor reject them as indecent; rather, we must see exactly what Whitman is saying about a kind of experience that society had shut its eyes to, and we must take Whitman's view seriously.

Many of the critics who raise these questions are, of course, themselves gay or lesbian, but it should also be pointed out that today there are straight critics who study lesbian or gay authors and write about them insightfully. One assumption in much lesbian and gay critical writing is that although gender greatly influences the ways in which we read, reading is a skill that can be learned, and therefore straight people—aided by lesbian and gay critics—can learn to read lesbian and gay writers with pleasure and profit. This assumption of course also underlies much feminist criticism, which often assumes that men must stop ignoring books by women and must learn (with the help of feminist critics) how to read them, and, in fact, how to read—with newly opened eyes—the sexist writings of men of the past and present.

Many critics discuss the concept of sexual identity itself.[1] Drawing upon the work of Foucault and others, critics such as David Halperin (*One Hundred Years of Homosexuality and Other Essays on Greek Love*, 1990) and Judith Butler (*Bodies That Matter: On the Discursive Limits of Sex*, 1993) explore how various categories of identity, such as "heterosexual" and "homosexual," represent ways of defining human beings that are distinct to particular cultures and historical periods. These critics, who are "social constructionists," argue that however a given society interprets sexuality will determine the particular categories within which individuals come to understand and to name their own desires. For such critics, the goal of a lesbian or gay criticism is not to define the specificity of a lesbian or gay literature or modes of interpretation, but to show how the ideology, the normative understanding, of a given culture makes it seem natural to think about sexuality in terms of such identities as lesbian, gay, bisexual, or straight.

Because such critics have challenged the authority of the opposition between heterosexuality and homosexuality, and have read it as a historical construct rather than as a biological or psychological absolute, they have sometimes resisted the very terms "lesbian" and "gay." Many now name their perspective QUEER THEORY in an attempt to mark their resistance to the categories of identity they see our culture imposing upon us. A special issue of the journal *English Studies in Canada* 20 (1993) discusses the concept of QUEER THEORY and uses it to explore a range of texts; a special issue of *Modern Drama* 39 (1996) provides a number of useful articles using such theory to discuss Canadian drama. Deconstructionist or psychoanalytic thought often influences this mode of criticism.

---

[1] This paragraph and the next are adapted from three paragraphs originally written by Lee Edelman of Tufts University, which appear on pp. 137–38 of the first edition of this text. The Canadian citations have been added and the original text reduced.

Post-colonialism

Because of Canada's colonial history and the immigration of many new Canadians from other former colonies, many critics in Canada are interested in issues broadly grouped as POST-COLONIAL THEORY. The term embraces a complex of questions arising from the colonial process and extending from the effects of early contact to political, social, and literary reactions to independence. In *The Post-colonial Studies Reader* (Routledge, 1995), Bill Ashcroft, Gareth Griffiths, and Helen Tiffin warn against restricting the term only to "after-colonialism," or "after-independence," pointing out that all post-colonial societies are still subject to "overt or subtle forms of neo-colonial domination." [2]

Critics using this approach consider many questions:

- migration and the diaspora of Native peoples;
- slavery;
- resistance to imperial control;
- the metanarratives or "master discourses" of Europe (or other imperial powers);
- relationships among power, race, gender, and place;
- social and national constructions and questions of representation; and
- uses of language (and literature) as tools of imperialism and of resistance.

Ashcroft, Griffiths and Tiffin point out that it is in the "fundamental experiences of speaking and writing" [2] that these interconnected issues come into being and express their power.

The most influential theorists include Edward Said, whose study *Orientalism* (1977) was one of the beginning points for post-colonial discourse, Gayatri Spivak, who extended post-colonial analysis to issues of feminism and race, and the Australian team of Ashcroft, Griffiths, and Tiffin, (mentioned above) whose *The Empire Writes Back* (1989) is a standard introduction to the field.[2] Homi K. Bhabha extended the discourse in the 1990s. His important books, *Nation and Narration* (1990) and *The Location of Culture* (1994) explore how "literature both enforces and subverts the relations of dominant and colonized cultures" (Filewod).

Bhabha raises the dynamic tension between the mimicry of imperial presence and opposition to this presence. For Bhabha, this inevitable duality creates a "transparency," a hybrid state in which the dominant power paradoxically confirms what it seeks to master. Edward Said theorizes the "contrapuntal" relationship between margin and centre, the interplay between dominance and opposition (*Culture and Imperialism*, 1993: 259). Abdul R. JanMohamed (in "The Economy of Manichean Allegory: The Function of Racial Difference in Colonialist Literature, *Critical Inquiry*, 1985) and others

[2] Alan Filewod of Guelph University contributed an overview to the first edition of this text, on pp. 138–39. Where his comments reappear (often in summary form) in this expanded discussion, they are identified.

also point out the self-contradictions implicit in all colonial binaries (self–other; civilized–Native, and the like), urging readers to recognize both polarities. simultaneously as they actively read and, as a result, calling for a resistance reading. (You will recall similar calls by feminist critics, by Marxist critics, and by gay and lesbian critics.) By recognizing the crucial role of writing in the formation of identity, all these critics understand that writing can also be a tool of social reformation. These complex notions open the debate to larger issues of power relations of many kinds, of nation states, and of performance.

Some critics, however, feel that such theories reduce the political passion of earlier "national liberation" movements. (A similar argument is heard in feminist, gay and lesbian criticisms where some believe that intellectual theory sidelines the fight for political rights.) Others counter, saying that even these notions of liberation and entry to the "mainstream" depend upon definitions grounded in colonial language and values. This is a difficult, but important, debate in many poststructural criticisms: On the one hand, most thinkers today agree that identity and our sense of what is "real" is constructed within historical, social, and gender contexts, but—on the other hand—to detach "reality" from the material facts of its production would be to efface cultural difference. (You may wish to read more about this debate, or it may be sufficient to learn that it is a major discussion among thinkers today. At any rate, post-colonialism, like other critical lenses, alerts you to the need to read very carefully and to seek out the very serious implications in what is presented as mere fiction.)

In Canada, post-colonial speculation invites us to consider the concepts of "nation" and "national identity," terms that have been discussed by Canadians since Confederation and are part of the narrative of federation. As Alan Filewod explains, within this discourse, the concept of "identity" itself is exposed as a theoretical proposition shaped by historical experience, rather than an essential, "natural" condition of nationhood. In the preoccupation with national distinctiveness, and in the literary strategies developed to articulate the complexities of settlement and the displacement of aboriginal cultures, Canadian writing bears many similarities to that of the other "settler colonies" of the former British Empire. Post-colonialism enables critics to understand Canadian history and culture as part of a larger historical process, and to challenge the dominant focus on British and American literatures as the product of imperial experience.

The appearance of writing in English by Canadians from a variety of ethnic and cultural backgrounds further urges a rethinking of the definition of "national identity." The links among many English-speaking peoples arise within language not only because people share common, or similar, lexicons, but because a shared experience as colonials has formed that language into an imitation of, and a variance from, British English ("the Queen's English").

The idea of the "universal" has marginalized many people (whose own stories now insist to be heard); post-colonial theory, by exposing the "universal" as an imperial construct, opens the way for many to express themselves in hybrid or oppositional texts. It is not, however, a simple evolution. As Ashcroft, Griffiths, and Tiffin conclude, "All are agreed, in some sense, that the main problem is how to effect agency for the post-colonial subject. But the contentious issue of how this is to be attained remains unresolved" (9).

A Final Word

This chapter began by making the obvious point that all readers, whether or not they consciously adopt a particular approach to literature, necessarily read through particular lenses. More precisely, a reader begins with a frame of interpretation—historical, psychological, sexual, or whatever—and from within the frame a reader selects one of the several competing methodologies. Sometimes the point is made that readers decode a text by applying a grid to it; the grid enables them to see certain things clearly. Of course, such a grid or lens—an angle of vision or interpretative frame and a methodology—may also prevent a reader from seeing certain other things. We must not deceive ourselves by thinking that our keen tools enable us to see the whole. Each approach may illuminate aspects neglected by others. Used carefully, these filters may help you achieve the kind of satisfying reading which Richard Rorty says can occur from an "encounter" with a work of art "which has made a difference to the critic's conception of who she is, what she is good for, what she wants to do with herself [. . .]" (in Umberto Eco, *Interpretation and Overinterpretation*, 1992: 107).

📖 Suggestions For Further Reading

Because a massive list of titles may prove discouraging rather than helpful, it seems advisable here to give a short list of basic titles. (Titles already mentioned in this chapter—which are good places to begin—are not repeated in the following list.)

A collection of essays that re-evaluate the notion of a canon in Canadian literature may be found in *Canadian Canons: Essays in Literary Value*, ed. David Lecker (1991). A good sampling of contemporary criticism can be found in *The Critical Tradition: Classic Texts and Contemporary Trends*, ed. David H. Richter (1989), and *The Norton Anthology of Literary Theory and Criticism*, ed. Vincent B. Leitch, et al. (2001). A good handbook with short entries for these terms (and many other literary terms) is Jeremy Hawthorn, *A Concise Glossary of Contemporary Literary Theory*, 2nd. ed. (1994).

For a readable introduction to various approaches, written for students who are beginning the study of literary theory, see Steven Lynn, *Texts and Contexts*, 3rd ed. (2000); also, Chapter 6 of John Peck and Martin Coyle, *Literary Terms and Criticism* (1993), which offers a useful British perspective. For a more advanced survey, that is, a work that assumes some familiarity with the material, see a short book by K. M. Newton, *Interpreting the Text: A Critical Introduction to the Theory and Practice of Literary Interpretation* (1990). For a collection of essays on Shakespeare written from a number of critical points of view see Patricia Parker and Geoffrey Hartman, eds., *Shakespeare and the Question of Theory* (1985); John Drakakis, ed., *Shakespearean Tragedy* (1992); or *Hamlet*, ed., Susanne L. Wofford, (1994)—which collects a group of essays on the play, each from a different perspective; such a collection is an excellent way to compare approaches. Brian Vickers, *Appropriating Shakespeare: Contemporary Critical Quarrels* (1993) offers stringent appraisal of such theoretical readings of Shakespeare.

Discussions (usually two or three pages long) of each approach, with fairly extensive bibliographic suggestions, are given in the appropriate articles in the four encyclopedic works by Harris, Makaryk, Groden, and Kreiswirth, and by Preminger and Brogan, listed at the end of Chapter 5, though only Groden and Kreiswirth (*Johns Hopkins Guide*) discuss lesbian and gay criticism. For essays discussing feminist, gender, Marxist, psychoanalytic, deconstructive, and New Historicist criticisms—as well as other topics not covered in this chapter, such as cultural criticism—see Stephen Greenblatt and Giles Gunn, eds., *Redrawing the Boundaries: The Transformation of English and American Literary Studies* (1992).

Formalist Criticism (New Criticism)

Cleanth Brooks, *The Well Wrought Urn: Studies in the Structure of Poetry* (1947), especially Chapters 1 and 11 ("The Language of Paradox" and "The Heresy of Paraphrase"); W. K. Wimsatt, *The Verbal Icon* (1954), especially "The Intentional Fallacy" and "The Affective Fallacy"; Murray Krieger, *The New Apologists for Poetry* (1956); and, for an accurate overview of this kind of criticism, Chapters 9–12 in volume 6 of René Wellek, *A History of Modern Criticism: 1750–1950.*

Deconstruction

Christopher Norris, *Deconstruction: Theory and Practice*, rev. ed. (1991); Vincent B. Leitch, *Deconstructive Criticism: An Advanced Introduction and Survey* (1983); Christopher Norris, ed., *What Is Deconstruction?* (1988); Christopher Norris, *Deconstruction and the Interests of Theory* (1989); and *Deconstruction: A Reader*, ed. Martin McQuillan (2001). A good introduction to Derrida in comic book format is Jim Powell, et al. *Derrida for Beginners* in the Writers and Readers Documentary Comic Book series. (This series provides good, approachable introductions to many critics and thinkers, including some we mention: Freud, Lacan, Foucault, and Marx.)

Reader-Response Criticism

Consider Wolfgang Iser, *The Act of Reading: A Theory of Aesthetic Response* (1978); Wolfgang Iser, *Prospecting: From Reader Response to Literary Anthropology* (1993); Susan Sulleiman and Inge Crossman, eds., *The Reader in the Text* (1980); Jane P. Tompkins, ed., *Reader-Response Criticism* (1980); Norman N. Holland, *The Dynamics of Literary Response* (1973, 1989); Steven Mailloux, *Interpretive Conventions: The Reader in the Study of American Fiction* (1982); and Susan Bennett, *Theatre Audiences: A Theory of Production and Reception* (1990). For genre implications: Aviva Freedman and Peter Medway, eds. *Genre and the New Rhetoric* (1994).

Archetypal Criticism

See G. Wilson Knight, *The Starlit Dome* (1941); Richard Chase, *Quest for Myth* (1949); Murray Krieger, ed., *Northrop Frye in Modern Criticism* (1966); Robert D. Denham, *Northrop Frye and Critical Method* (1978); Frank Lentricchia, *After the New Criticism* (1980); "Archetypal Patterns," in Norman Friedman, *Form and Meaning in Fiction* (1975).

Marxist Criticism

Raymond Williams, *Marxism and Literature* (1977); Tony Bennett, *Formalism and Marxism* (1979); Lydia Sargent, ed., *Women and Revolution: A Discussion of the Unhappy Marriage of Marxism and Feminism* (1981); Daniel Aaron, *Writers on the Left: Episodes in American Literary Communism*, new ed. (1992); Barbara Foley, *Radical Representations: Politics and Form in U.S. Proletarian Fiction, 1929–1941* (1993). Ric Knowles, *The Theatre of Form and the Production of Meaning: Contemporary Canadian Dramaturgies* (1999) is an excellent application of a generally Marxist perspective to Canadian drama and performance.

Historical Criticism

For a brief survey of some historical criticism of the first half of this century, see René Wellek, *A History of Modern Criticism: 1750–1950*, Vol. 6, Chap. 4 ("Academic Criticism"). E. M. W. Tillyard, *The Elizabethan World Picture* (1943) and Tillyard's *Shakespeare's History Plays* (1944), both of which related Elizabethan literature to the beliefs of the age, are good examples of the historical approach. (Note that Tillyard is today criticized for taking too neat a view of his period.)

New Historicism

N. H. New, *Among Worlds* (1975); Stephen Greenblatt, *Renaissance Self-Fashioning from More to Shakespeare*, (1980)—especially the first chapter; Deiter Riemenschneider, ed., *The History and Historiography of Commonwealth Literature* (1983); Brook Thomas, *The New Historicism and Other Old-Fashioned Topics* (1991), and Catherine Gallagher, *Practicing New Historicism* (2000).

Biographical Criticism

Estelle C. Jellinek, ed., *Women's Autobiography: Essays in Criticism* (1980); James Olney, *Metaphors of Self: The Meaning of Autobiography* (1981); and *Women, Autobiography, Theory: A Reader*, ed. Sidonie Smith and Julia Watson. There are many excellent biographies of writers: remember that you can enter an author's name as subject (not author) in a search engine or card catalogue and titles of books on the author, including biographies, will emerge.

Psychological (or Psychoanalytic) Criticism

Edith Kurzeil, and William Philips, eds., *Literature and Psychoanalysis* (1983); Maurice Charney and Joseph Reppen, eds., *Psychoanalytic Approaches to Literature and Film* (1987); Madelon Sprengnether, *The Spectral Mother: Freud, Feminism, and Psychoanalysis* (1990); Frederick Crews, *Out of My System* (1975); Kaja Silverman, *Male Subjectivity at the Margins* (1992).

Feminist Criticism

A good first source: *Encyclopedia of Feminist Literary Theory*, ed. Beth Kowaleski-Wallace (1997). For specific studies, see Gayle Greene and Coppèlia Kahn, eds., *Making a Difference: Feminist Literary Criticism* (1985), including an essay by Bonnie Zimmerman on lesbian criticism; Catherine Belsey and Jane Moore, eds., *The Feminist Reader: Essays in Gender and the Politics of Literary Criticism* (1989); Toril Moi, ed., *French Feminist Thought* (1987); Elizabeth A. Flynn and Patrocinio P. Schweikart, eds., *Gender and Reading: Essays on Readers, Texts, and Contexts* (1986); Barbara Christian, *Black Feminist Criticism: Perspectives on Black Women Writers* (1985); Shoshana Felman, *What Does a Woman Want? Reading and Sexual Difference* (1993); Sandra Gilbert and Susan Gubar, *The Madwoman in the Attic: The Woman Writer and the Nineteenth Century Literary Imagination* (1979); Julia Kristeva, *Desire in Language: A Semiotic Approach to Literature and Art* (1980); Elaine Showalter, ed., *Speaking of Gender* (1989); Jill Dolan, *Presence and Desire* (1993).

Lesbian and Gay Criticism

General introductions: *The Gay & Lesbian Literary Companion*, ed. Sharon Malinowski and Christa Vrelin (1995); *The Gay and Lesbian Literary Heritage: A Reader's Companion to the Writers and Their Works, from Antiquity to the Present*, ed. Claude J. Summers (1995); and Henry Abelove et al., eds., *The Lesbian and Gay Studies Reader* (1993). See also Summers, *Gay Fictions: Wilde to Stonewall: Studies in Male Homosexual Literary Tradition* (1990); *Novel Gazing: Queer Readings in Fiction*, ed. Eve Kosofsky Sedgwick (1997); Gregory Woods, *A History of Gay Literature: The Male Tradition* (1998); Annamarie Jogose, *Queer Theory: An Introduction* (1996); Alan Sinfield, *Cultural Politics—Queer Readings* (1994); and *Feminism Meets Queer Theory*, ed. Elizabeth Weed and Naomi Schor (1997); Diana Fuss, ed., *inside/out: Lesbian Theories, Gay Theories* (1991); Vito Russo, *The Celluloid Closet: Homosexuality in the Movies*, rev. ed. (1981); Eve Kosofsky Sedgwick, *Epistemology of the Closet* (1990); Jonathan Dollimore, *Sexual Dissidence: Augustine to Wilde, Freud to Foucault* (1991); Peggy Phelan, *Unmarked: The Politics of Performance* (1993); Lee Edelman, *Homographesis: Essays in Gay Literary and Cultural Theory* (1993); Robert Vorlicky, *Act Like a Man* (1995); R. Jeffrey Ringer, ed., *Queer Words, Queer Images: Communication and the Construction of Homosexuality* (1994); Sue-Ellen

Case, Philip Brett, and Susan Leigh Foster, eds., *Cruising the Performative: Interventions into the Representation of Ethnicity, Nationality, and Sexuality* (1995).

Post-colonial Criticism

For an encyclopedic collection of essays, including Canadian scholars, see Diana Brydon, ed., *Postcolonialism: Critical Concepts in Literary and Cultural Studies (5 vols. 2000). See also* Linda Hutcheon, *The Canadian Postmodern: A Study of Contemporary English-Canadian Fiction* (1988); Bill Ashcroft, Gareth Griffiths, and Helen Tiffin *The Empire Writes Back: Theory and Practice in Post-colonial Literatures* (1989); Homi K. Bhabha, *The Location of Culture* (1994); Francis Barker, Peter Hulme, and Margaret Iversen, eds., *Colonial Discovery: Post-colonial Theory* (1994); Edward W. Said, *Culture and Imperialism* (1993); Elleke Boehmer, *Colonial and Post colonial Literature: Migrant Metaphors* (1995); Benedict Anderson, *Imagined Communities: Reflections on the Origin and Spread of Nationalism* (1983); Ngugi wa Thiong'o, *Writers in Politics* (1981); Gayatri Chakravorty Spivak, *In Other Worlds: Essays in Cultural Politics* (1988). See also the entry for Deiter Riemenschneider under New Historicism, above.

PART 3

Up Close:
Thinking Critically
about Literary Forms

9

Writing about Essays

Learning Objectives

When you've read this chapter, you should be able to

➤ identify the chief kinds of essays and understand their uses;

➤ recognize an essayist's persona and notice the effect of this "voice" on the essay; and

➤ analyze an essayist's style.

The word *essay* entered the English language in 1597, when Francis Bacon called a small book of ten short prose pieces *Essays*. Bacon borrowed the word from Michel de Montaigne, a French writer who, in 1580, had published some short prose pieces under the title *Essais*—that is, "testings" or "attempts," from the French verb *essayer*, "to try." Montaigne's title indicated that his graceful and personal jottings—the fruit of pleasant study and meditation—were not fully thought-out treatises but rather sketches that could be amplified and amended.

If you keep a journal, you are working in Montaigne's tradition. You jot down your tentative thoughts, perhaps your responses to a work of literature, partly to find out what you think and how you feel. Montaigne said, in the preface to his book, "I am myself the subject of my book," and in all probability you are the real subject of your journal. Your entries, recorded responses to other writers and your reflections on those responses, require you to examine yourself.

SOME KINDS OF ESSAYS

If you have already taken a course in composition (or even if you haven't), you are probably familiar with the chief kinds of essays. Essays are usually classified—roughly, of course—into the following modes: *expressive essays* (*meditation* or *speculation* or *reflection*); *exposition* (or *information*); *argument* (or *persuasion*); *narration* and *description*.

Of these, the EXPRESSIVE (or MEDITATIVE or SPECULATIVE or REFLECTIVE) essay is the closest to Montaigne. In an expressive essay, the writer seems chiefly concerned with exploring an idea or a feeling. The organization usually seems casual, not a careful and evident structure but a free flow of thought—what the Japanese (who wrote with brush and ink) called "following the brush." The essayist is thinking, but he or she is not especially concerned with arguing a case, or even with being logical. We think along with the essayist, chiefly because we find the writer's tentative thoughts engaging. Of course the writer may in the long run be pressing a point, advancing an argument, but the emphasis is on the free play of mind, not on an orderly and logical analysis.

In the EXPOSITORY essay (of which there are a number of kinds) you are chiefly concerned with giving information. For example: in a PROCESS essay, you might show how to read a poem, or how to use a word processor; in a COMPARISON/CONTRAST essay, you may outline the contrasting NATO responses in the Gulf War and in the former Yugoslavia; in a CLASSIFICATION essay, you may differentiate the populations of people who support or do not support private health care in Canada; in a CAUSAL essay, you may lay out the health benefits of a vegetarian diet. Clear organization is important in these essays in order to help your reader gain information little by little, in a helpful order.

In the ARGUMENTATIVE (or PERSUASIVE) essay, the organization is apparent, and is reasonable—that is, it follows the rules of formal logic or critical thinking. For instance, you may announce a problem, define some terms, present and refute solutions you consider to be inadequate, and then, in a powerful ending, offer what you consider to be the correct solution. (This order produces what is sometimes called an INDUCTIVE ESSAY, ostensibly because it loosely follows what philosophers call inductive logic, in which the premises point to a valid conclusion but do not guarantee it.) Or, you may present a carefully thought-out thesis, move through a set of premises, data, and authoritative opinion that establishes the thesis, and then restate your conclusion. This form is usually called the DEDUCTIVE ESSAY, because it aims to follow deductive logic, in which a set of sound premises must arrive at a true conclusion.

NARRATIVE and DESCRIPTIVE essays are really types of expressive essays. For instance, a narrative essay may recount some happening—often a bit of autobiography—partly to allow the writer and the reader to meditate on it. Similarly, a description—let's say of an exhilarating ski down a mountain, or a family Christmas dinner—usually turns out to be offered not so much as information, but as something for the writer and reader to enjoy in itself, and perhaps to think about further.

Of course, most essays are not pure specimens. For instance, a process (informative) essay—let's say on how to use a cell phone—may begin with a paragraph that seeks to persuade you to use this particular model. Or it might begin with a very brief narrative, an anecdote of someone who switched from a standard phone to a web-ready digital phone, again in order to persuade the reader to buy the product. Similarly, an argument—and probably most of the essays that you write in English courses will be arguments advancing a thesis concerning the MEANING or STRUCTURE of a literary work—may well include some EXPOSITION. For instance, you might include a very brief summary in order to remind the reader of the gist of the work about which you will be arguing.

THE ESSAYIST'S PERSONA

Many of the essays that give readers the most pleasure are, like entries in a journal, chiefly reflective. An essay of this kind sets forth the writer's attitudes or states of mind, and the reader's interest in the essay is almost entirely in the way the writer sees things. It's not so much *what* the writer sees and says as *how* she says what she sees. Even in narrative essays—essays that recount biographical events—our interest is more in the essayist's *response* to the events than in the events themselves. When we read an essay, we almost say, "So that's how it feels to be you," and "Tell me more about the way you see things." The bit of history is less important than the memorable presence of the writer. Of course, a formal argumentative essay will reveal less of the writer—stressing, instead, rigorous logic and careful conclusions. But even in an informative essay with much data or a powerful argument it is pleasant to have a sense of the writer behind the words. Try to develop a VOICE that expresses who you are.

When you read an essay, try to imagine the kind of person who wrote it, the kind of person who seems to be speaking it. Then slowly reread the essay, noticing *how* the writer conveyed this personality or PERSONA (even while he or she was writing about a topic "out there"). The writer's persona may be revealed, for example, by common or uncommon words, by short or long sentences, by literal or FIGURATIVE LANGUAGE, or by offering familiar or erudite examples.

Let's take a simple example of words that establish a persona. John Diefenbaker, the Prime Minister of Canada from 1957–63, always made speeches with a highly oratorical ring, full of allusions to the Bible and to early Canadian history. For example, in 1942, Diefenbaker began a speech to a party convention: "We meet in Winnipeg, the beginning of the plains. One hundred and thirty years ago my mother's forebears came to this very spot. [. . .]" He might have simply said, "We meet in Winnipeg"—but the language would have lacked the pioneering echo, and the persona would have been that of an ordinary person rather than that of a man who has about him something of the tone of a founder of the nation. The reference to his mother intensifies this link with the pioneers and also suggests that he is a dutiful son. He might simply have said, "My family arrived here in 1812," but in stating the number of years he makes his ancestry seem longer and gives himself something of the persona of an Old Testament prophet. As well, if he been precise in saying his family arrived in 1812, he might have triggered a reference to the War of 1812 in the minds of some listeners, changing the connotations of his announcement. What do you think of his use of the word *plains* rather than *prairies?* Why did he make this choice? Was it a wise choice for a Canadian politician speaking in Winnipeg to use the more American term for our flatlands?

Tone

By such devices as the *choice of words*, the *length of sentences*, and the *sorts of evidence* offered, an author sounds to the reader solemn or agitated or witty or genial or severe. Only by reading closely can we hear in the mind's ear the writer's TONE—whether it is ironic or earnestly straightforward. While speakers can guide the responses of their audience by body language and gestures, by facial expressions, and by changes in tone of voice, writers have only words in ink on paper. As a writer, you are learning control of tone; that is, you take pains in your choice of words, in the way you arrange sentences, and even in the punctuation marks that you may find yourself changing in your final draft. These skills will pay off doubly if you apply them to your reading by putting yourself in the place of the writer whose work you are reading.

As a reader, you must make some effort to "hear" the writer's tone as part of the meaning the words communicate. Skimming is not adequate to that task. Thinking carefully about a piece of writing means, first of all, reading it carefully, listening for the sound of the speaking voice so that you can respond to the persona—the personality or character the author presents in the essay.

WRITING ABOUT AN ESSAYIST'S STYLE

Since much of the pleasure we receive from an essay is derived from the essayist's STYLE—the *how* with which an essayist conveys an attitude toward some aspect of reality that is revealed—your instructor may ask you to analyze the writer's style.

Read the following essay by David Suzuki. While reading it, annotate it wherever you are inclined (you may want to express responses in the margin and to underline puzzling words or passages that strike you as especially effective or as especially clumsy). Then reread the essay; since you will now be familiar with the essay as a whole, you may want to make further annotations, such as brief comments on Suzuki's diction, his use of repetition, or his tone.

David Suzuki, one of the best-known Canadian broadcasters, is also a geneticist, and journalist. He was born in 1936, taught at the University of British Columbia, and has hosted television programs such as *Science Magazine* and *The Nature of Things*. His writings appear in a number of magazines and other publications. He is always concerned with the link between science, human values, and the ecology.

A PLANET FOR THE TAKING
David Suzuki

Canadians live under the remarkable illusion that we are technologically   1
advanced people. Everything around us denies that assumption. We are, in many ways, a Third World country, selling our natural resources in exchange for the high technology of the industrialized world. Try going through your home and looking at the country of origin of your clothes, electrical appliances, books, car. The rare technological product that does have Canada stamped on it is usually from a branch plant of a multinational company centred in another country. But we differ from traditional Third World countries. We have a majority population of Caucasians and a very high level of literacy and affluence. And we have been

able to maintain our seemingly advanced social state by virtue of an incredible bounty of natural resources.

Within the Canadian mystique there is also a sense of the vastness of this land. The prairies, the Arctic, the oceans, the mountains are ever present in our art and literature. This nation is built on our sense of the seeming endlessness of the expanse of wilderness and the output of nature and we have behaved as if this endlessness were real. Today we speak of renewable resources but our "harvest" procedures are more like a mining operation. We extract raw resources in the crudest of ways, gouging the land to get at its inner core, spewing our raw wastes into the air, water and soil in massive amounts while taking fish, birds, animals and trees in vast quantities without regard to the future. So we operate under a strange duality of mind: we have both a sense of the importance of the wilderness and space in our culture and an attitude that it is limitless and therefore we needn't worry.

Native cultures of the past may have been no more conservation-minded than we are but they lacked the technology to make the kind of impact that we do today. Canadians and Americans share one of the great natural wonders, the Great Lakes, which contain 20 percent of the world's fresh water, yet today even this massive body of water is terribly polluted and the populations of fish completely mixed-up by human activity. We speak of "managing" our resources but do it in a way that resembles the sledgehammer-on-the-head cure for a headache. On the west coast of Canada, Natives lived for millennia on the incredible abundance of five species of salmon. Today, the massive runs are gone and many biologists fear that the fish may be in mortal jeopardy because of both our fishing and management policies. Having improved fishing techniques this century to the point of endangering runs yet still knowing very little of the biology of the fish, we have assumed that we could build up the yield by simply dumping more back. But it wasn't known that sockeye salmon fry, for example, spend a year in a freshwater lake before going to sea. Millions of sockeye fry were dumped directly into the Fraser River where they died soon after. In Oregon, over-fishing and hydroelectric dams had decimated coho populations in the Columbia River. In one year, over 8 million fry were released of which only seven were ever caught. No one knows what's happening to the rest.

We act as if a fish were a fish, a duck a duck or a tree a tree. If we "harvest" once, we renew it by simply adding one or two back. But what we have learned is that all animals and plants are not equivalent. Each organism reflects the evolutionary history of its progenitors; in the case of salmon, each race and subrace of fish has been exquisitely honed by nature to return to a very specific part of the Pacific watershed. Similarly, in the enormous area of prairie pothole country in the centre of the continent, migratory birds do not just space themselves out according to the potholes that are empty. Scientists have discovered that the birds have been selected to return to a very restricted part of that area. And of course, our entire forestry policy is predicated on the ridiculous idea that a virgin stand of fir or cedar which has taken millennia to form and clings to a thin layer of topsoil can be replaced after clear-cut logging simply by sticking seedlings into the ground. How can anyone with even the most rudimentary understanding of biology and evolution ignore the realities of the complex interaction between organisms and the environment and attempt to manipulate wild populations as if they were tomato plants or chickens?

I believe that in large part our problems rest on our faith in the power of science and technology. At the beginning of this century, science, when applied by industry and medicine, promised a life immeasurably better and there is no doubt that society, indeed the planet, has been transformed by the impact of new ideas and inventions of science. Within my lifetime I've seen the beginning of television, oral contraception, organ transplants, space travel, computers, jets, nuclear weapons, satellite communication, and polio vaccine. Each has changed society forever and made the world of my youth recede into the pages of history. But we have not achieved a technological utopia. The problems facing us today are immense and many are a direct consequence of science and technology. What has gone wrong?

I believe that the core of our 20th century dilemma lies in a fundamental   6 limitation of science that most scientists, especially those in the life sciences, fail to recognize. Most of my colleagues take it for granted that our studies will ultimately be applicable to the "big picture," that our research will have beneficial payoffs to society eventually. This is because the thrust of modern science has been predicated on the Newtonian idea that the universe is like an enormous machine whose entire system will be reconstructed on the basis of our understanding of the parts. This is the fundamental reductionist faith in science: the whole is equal to the sum of its parts. It does make a lot of sense—what distinguishes science from other activities that purport to provide a comprehensive "world view" is its requirement that we focus on a part of nature isolated to as great an extent as possible from the rest of the system of which it is a part. This has provided enormous insights into that fragment of nature, often accompanied by power to manipulate it. But when we attempt to tinker with what lies in the field of our view, the effects ripple far beyond the barrel of the microscope. And so we are constantly surprised at the unexpected consequences of our interference. Scientists only know nature in "bits and pieces" and assume that higher levels of organization are simply the expression of the component parts. This is what impels neurobiologists to study the chemical and electrical behaviour of single neurons in the faith that it will ultimately lead to an understanding of what creativity and imagination are, a faith that I don't for a moment think will ever be fulfilled (although a lot of useful information will accrue).

Physicists, who originally set this view in motion, have this century, with   7 the arrival of relativity and quantum theory, put to rest the notion that we will ever be able to reconstruct the entire universe from fundamental principles. Chemists know that a complete physical description of atoms of oxygen and hydrogen is of little value in predicting the behaviour of a water molecule. But biologists scream that any sense that there are properties of organization that don't exist at lower levels is "vitalism," a belief that there is some mystical life force in living organisms. And so biochemists and molecular biologists are intent on understanding the working of organisms by learning all they can about sub-cellular organization.

Ironically, ecology, long scorned by molecular biologists as an inexact science,   8 is now corroborating physics. In studying ecosystems, we are learning that a simple breakdown into components and their behaviour does not provide insight into how an entire collection of organisms in a natural setting will work. While many ecologists do continue to "model" ecosystems in computers in the hope that they will eventually derive a predictive tool, their science warns of the hazards of treating it too simply in management programs.

At present, our very terminology suggests that we think we can manage   9 wild plants and animals as though they were domesticated organisms. We speak of "herds" of seals, of "culling," "harvesting," "stocks." The ultimate expression of our narrow view (and self-interested rationalizations) is seen in how we

overlook the enormous environmental impact of our pollution, habitat destruction and extraction and blame seals and whales for the decline in fish populations
or wolves for the decrease in moose—and then propose bounties as a solution!

But Canadians do value the spiritual importance of nature and want to   **10**
see it survive for future generations. We also believe in the power of science to
sustain a high quality of life. And while the current understanding of science's
power is, I believe, misplaced, in fact the leading edges of physics and ecology
may provide the insights that can get us off the current track. We need a very
profound perceptual shift and soon.

Annotations and Journal Entries

While reading the essay a second time, one student planning to write on
Suzuki's style noticed the word choices in the second paragraph and marked
them:

myth of endless supply

Within the Canadian mystique there is also a sense
of the vastness of this land. The prairies, the
Arctic, the oceans, the mountains are ever present
in our art and literature. This nation is built on
our sense of the seeming (endlessness) of the expanse
of wilderness and the output of nature and we have

repeats fake words

behaved as if this (endlessness) were real. Today we
speak of (renewable resources) but our ("harvest")
procedures are more like a mining operation. We
extract raw resources in the crudest of ways,

strong words

gouging the land to get at its inner core, spewing
our raw wastes into the air, water and soil in
massive amounts while taking fish, birds, animals

long sentence

and trees in vast quantities without regard to the
future. So we operate under a strange (duality) of
mind: we have both a sense of the importance of
the wilderness and space in our culture and an

thesis

attitude that it is (limitless) and therefore we
needn't worry.

He marked other paragraphs in more or less the same way, and then,
while brainstorming, made some jottings:

```
Myth--endless supply "endlessness" of Canada/space/
    resources
        Everything in Canada denies this myth
        3rd world country but with huge resources:  but not
            endless
```

          land here for "millennia"--repeats word
          also repeats "harvest"
      --language covers up the destruction: "harvest,"
        "managing"
              strong words against destruction: "crudest";
                "gouging"; "spewing"; "raw wastes"
      Style: Suzuki's diction shows his concern; makes the
        reader pay attention
              long sentence--46 words--to show the harm we do
              --Really pulls reader along. Words make the long
                sentence OK and quick
              role of technology--can do more harm now
              ecology--everything has a role
              but buzz words cover up this ancient balance
              technology and science as solution? Misses big
                picture
              surprised at connections of human "interference"
      Part One: language tough, loaded
      Part Two; language changes--less loaded, more scientific
        words
              --"rudimentary"; "utopia"; "reductionist faith";
                "impels"; "accrue"
              --real long sentences here: 52 words, 53 words.
                Harder words make these sentences move slower,
                doesn't pull reader along; makes you think but
                less emotion
      Part Three: return to strong diction to make point.
        Here the repeated word "harvest"
              --long sentence again--53 words--a mix of tone.
                Less scientific but less loaded
              Comes back to idea of myth
      Last two sentences: good rhythm.
              --One longish, then final sentence short and
                strong.
              We need a shift--need to see importance of ecology
              words work to hide and reveal problem--need clear
                words to make change, I guess
              Is this the "perceptual shift"?

A Sample Essay on David Suzuki's Style

Ultimately, the student wrote the following short essay. You'll notice that it
draws heavily on the notes on style and hardly at all on the notes on the

technology and science. Notes written during pre-writing are a source to draw on. Resist the temptation to work in, at all costs, everything you've produced.

David Suzuki's Style: Shifting to the Truth

David Suzuki feels passionately about the ecology of the planet. He tries, in his essay, "A Planet for the Taking," to warn his readers that living in a myth will lead to our destruction. Canadians believe in "the seeming endlessness of the expanse of wilderness and the output of nature" (133), but Suzuki warns that this is not true. Although he presents reasoned arguments for his opinion, the strength of the essay is in Suzuki's diction; by choosing very strong words in the right places he tries to make his reader feel the truth of what he says.

Suzuki begins by speaking of the "illusion" in which we live. He uses words like "remarkable" and repeats the word millennia in two different ways. In his first use, he points out that "Natives lived for millennia on the incredible abundance" of nature. But in his second use, he warns that it will take "millennia to form" new forests to replace those carelessly cut down. By repeating this word, Suzuki reminds the reader of the eons it has taken nature to evolve the richness we take for granted and how foolish we are to assume we can easily or quickly duplicate her work. He underlines this point by repeating the word harvest as well.

As Suzuki points out, this word implies the management (133; 134) of a renewable resource. If we can convince ourselves that we control our land and can manage it, then poor forest or mining methods seem more acceptable. After all, we can always replace or regrow a product. He uses words like "herds," "culling," and "stocks" (134) to illustrate this attitude which comes partly from our "reductionist faith in science" (134). But, Suzuki argues, we do control the ecosystem and we must see ourselves as part of a huge chain in which each part is important.

He uses words and phrases like "crudest of ways," "gouging," "spewing," "raw wastes" and "vast" (133) to make his reader pay attention to the severity of our destructive practices. He says we have only a "rudimentary understanding of biology" (133) and are not creating the "utopia" (133) we hope to achieve.

He uses long sentences where he wants special effects. In the first case, the long sentence provides a rhythm to carry the reader along. The sentence, full of words like gouging, is 46 words long but it is quickly read because of its powerful, loaded diction. Later in the essay he has two very long sentences, of 52 and 53 words, but these sentences have harder words in them and slow the reader down. Here, he chooses scholarly words: our belief "impels" us to study bits of the puzzle, assuming the parts will add up to the whole; only small chunks of knowledge "will accrue" (134). This diction encourages the reader to think about Suzuki's comments on science.

The urgency of his message is again suggested in the final section where he returns to modifiers like "ultimate," "narrow," and "self-interested" (134) He warns us that we live in "rationalizations" (134) rather than observable facts. And the pace quickens.

It is by his careful word choice that David Suzuki urges his reader to join him in concern for the ecology of the planet. We don't just understand his warning; we feel the danger around us. We agree that a "perceptual shift" is needed "soon" (135).

📖 Suggestions for Further Reading

For collections of essays, with useful introductions, see Philip Lopate, ed., *The Art of the Personal Essay: An Anthology from the Classical Era to the Present* (1994); Neil Waldman and Sarah Norton, eds., *Canadian Content*, 4th ed. (2000); Eva C. Karpinski and Ian Lea, *Pens of Many Colours: A Canadian Reader* (1993). This last collection offers essays by Canadians of a wide range of racial and ethic backgrounds.

On the essay, see also Graham Good, *The Observing Self: Rediscovering the Essay* (1988); Alexander J. Butrym, ed., *Essays on the Essay: Redefining the Genre* (1989).

10

Writing about Fiction:
The World of the Story

Learning Objectives

When you've read this chapter, you should be able to

➤ analyze plot in a work of fiction and understand techniques of organization;

➤ analyze character in a work of fiction;

➤ understand the use of foreshadowing, setting, atmosphere, symbolism, point of view, and theme;

➤ gather ideas for writing about fiction; and

➤ write an essay on any of these aspects of analysis

PLOT AND CHARACTER

PLOT has two chief meanings: (1) what happens, the gist of the narrative (called in formalist criticism, the *fabula*), and (2) the writer's arrangement or structuring of the material into a story (*sjuzet*). Thus, in the first sense all tellings of the life of Prime Minister Mackenzie King have the same plot, but in the second sense a writer who begins with the sensational publication of King's diaries and then gives the earlier material is setting forth a plot that differs from one given by a writer who begins at the beginning. It is usual to say that a plot has an INTRODUCTION, a COMPLICATION, and a RESOLUTION; that is, it gets under way, then some difficulty or problem or complexity arises (usually a CONFLICT of opposed wills or forces), and finally there is some sort of settling down. A somewhat metaphoric way of putting it is to say that the plot can often be seen as the tying and then the untying of a knot; the end is the DÉNOUEMENT (French for "untying").

Still another way of looking at the organization of the happenings in many works of fiction is to see the plot as a pyramid or triangle. The German critic Gustav Freytag, in *Techniques of the Drama* (1863), introduced this concept in examining the five-act structure of plays, but it can be applied to some fiction, too. In this view, we begin either with an unstable situation or with an apparently stable situation that is soon disrupted. The early happenings, with their increasing tension, constitute a RISING ACTION, which culminates in a CLIMAX or CRISIS or TURNING POINT. (The word *climax* comes from a Greek word meaning "ladder." Originally, the climax was the entire rising action, but the word has come to mean the high point or end of the rising action.) What follows the decisive moment is the FALLING ACTION, which ends in a stable situation—a situation that the reader takes to be final. Of course, the characters need not die; the reader feels, however, that nothing more is to be said about them. Here is a diagram showing Freytag's Pyramid. Remember, however, that a story *need* not have this structure and, indeed, many contemporary writings do not.

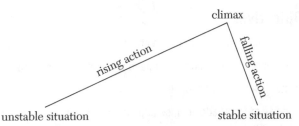

Early fiction tends to have a good deal of physical action—wanderings, strange encounters, births, and deaths. But in some fiction, particularly since the short stories of Chekhov, little seems to happen. These apparently plotless stories, however, usually involve a *mental action*—a significant perception, a decision, a failure of the will—and the process of this mental action is the plot.

The sense of causality is in part rooted in character. Things happen, in most good fiction, at least partly because the people have certain personalities or characters (moral, intellectual, and emotional qualities) and, given their natures, because they respond plausibly to other personalities. What their names are and what they look like may help you understand them, but probably the best guide to characters is what they do. As we get to know more about their drives and goals—especially the choices they make—we enjoy seeing the writer complete the portraits, finally presenting us with a coherent and credible picture of people in action. In this view, plot and character are inseparable. Plot is not simply a series of happenings, but happenings that come out of character, that reveal character, and that influence character. Henry James said: "What is character but the determination of incident? What is incident but the illustration of character?" But, of course, characters are not defined only by what they do. The narrator often describes them, and the characters' words and dress reveal aspects of them.

You may want to set forth a character sketch, describing some person in the story or novel. You will probably plan to convey three things:

> appearance,
> personality, and
> moral or ethical values.

In preparing a character sketch, take these points into consideration:

1. What the person says (but remember that what he or she says need not be taken at face value; the person may be hypocritical or self-deceived or biased)
2. What the person does
3. What others (including the narrator of the story) say about the person
4. What others *do* (their actions may help indicate what the person could do but does not do)
5. What the person looks like—face, body, clothes. These may help convey the personality, or they may in some measure help disguise it. Details of this type are called CODES in poststructuralist criticism. A detail may be an **INDEX** to an established type of character or to a set of cultural assumptions which readers use to name characters. These SIGNS are often based in types and much contemporary criticism questions the validity of such signs while recognizing their power. They can create characters that *appear* essential in some way because cultural codes substitute for a person's real self. It seems less and less likely that character is, in fact, an essential quality.

Writing about a Character

A character sketch such as "Caravaggio, the 'Fifth Business'" may be complex and demanding, especially if the character is complex. In the example, the writer sees that Caravaggio can be viewed as a character himself, but that his true role is to reveal other characters.

An essay on a character, you will recall, is necessarily in some degree an interpretation, and, thus, even such an essay has a thesis or argument holding it together. Usually, however, you will want to do more than set forth your view of a character. Probably, you will discuss the character's function or contrast him or her with other characters or trace the development of personality. (One of the most difficult topics, the character of the narrator, will be discussed later in this chapter, under the heading "Point of View.") You probably will still want to keep in mind the five suggestions above for getting at a character, but you will also want to go further, relating your findings to additional matters of the sort we will examine now.

Organizing an Analysis of a Character

As you read and reread, you will highlight and annotate the text and will jot down notes, recording (in whatever order they come to you) your thoughts about the character you are studying. Reading with a view toward writing, you'll want to

1. jot down traits as they come to mind ("kind," "forgetful," "enthusiastic"); and
2. look back at the text, searching for supporting evidence (characteristic actions, brief supporting quotations), and of course you will also look for counterevidence so that you may modify your earlier impressions.

Brainstorming leads to an evaluation and a shaping of your ideas. Evaluating and shaping lead to a tentative outline. A tentative outline leads to the search for supporting evidence—the material that will constitute the body of your essay. When you set out to write a first draft, review your annotations and notes, and see if you can summarize your view of the character in one or two sentences:

> Because X is [. . .], [something occurs].

or

> Although X is [. . .], she is also [. . .].

That is, try to formulate a thesis sentence or a thesis paragraph—a proposition that you will go on to support. (Review the thesis sentence, discussed in Chapter 2.)

You want to let your reader know early, probably in your first sentence—and almost certainly by the end of your first paragraph—which character you are writing about and what your overall thesis is.

The body of your essay will be devoted to supporting your thesis. If you have asserted that although so-and-so is cruel and domineering, he nevertheless is endowed with a conscience, you will go on in your essay to support those assertions with references to passages that demonstrate them. This support does *not* mean that you tell the plot of the whole work; an essay on a character is by no means the same as a summary of the plot. Since you must support your generalizations, you will have to make brief references to specific episodes that reveal his personality, and almost surely you will quote an occasional word or passage.

An essay on a character may be organized in many possible ways. Much will depend on your purpose and thesis. For instance, you may want to show how the character develops—gains knowledge or matures or disintegrates. Or you may want to show what the character contributes to the story or play as a whole. Or, to give yet another example, you may want to show that the character is unbelievable. Still, although no single organization is always right, two methods are common and effective.

One effective way of organizing an essay on a character is to let the organization of your essay follow closely the sequence of the literary work; that is, you might devote a paragraph to the character as we first perceive him or her and then in subsequent paragraphs go on to show that this figure is later seen to be more complex than he or she at first appears. Such an essay may trace your changing responses. **Warning:** This organization can tempt you into giving plot summary, which you must avoid. If you move from point of development to point of development in your character, be sure that you are not reproducing the plot in the process.

A second effective way of organizing an essay on a character is to set forth, early in the essay, the character's chief traits—let's say the chief strengths and two or three weaknesses—and then go on to study each trait you have listed. The organization would (in order to maintain the reader's interest) probably begin with the most obvious points and then move on to the less obvious, subtler points. The body of your essay, in any case, is devoted to offering evidence that supports your generalizations about the character.

What about a concluding paragraph? The concluding paragraph ought not to begin with a lead-in as obvious as, "Thus, we see," or "In conclusion," or "I recommend this story because [. . .]." In fact, after you have given what you consider to be a sound sketch of the character, it may be appropriate simply to quit. Especially if your essay has moved from the obvious traits to the more subtle and more important traits, and if your essay is fairly short (say, fewer than 500 words), a reader may not need a conclusion. Further, why blunt what you have just said by adding an unnecessary and merely repetitive summary? If you do feel that a conclusion is necessary, you may find it effective to write a summary of the character, somewhat as you did in your opening. For the conclusion, relate the character's character to the entire literary work; that is, try to give the reader a sense of the role that the character plays. Do not repeat the points you have already made.

A Sample Essay on a Character: "Caravaggio, the 'Fifth Business'"

Jane L. McDonald decided to write about Caravaggio, the "extra character" of Michael Ondaatje's *The English Patient*, for an English 104 class. Before writing, she reread the novel, highlighting certain passages about the character. She then reviewed the text and jotted down some key ideas, reproduced here.

```
Other characters fulfill roles of hero, lover,
protector
          Caravaggio is "fifth business"
              --(an opera term, cf. Robertson
          Davies's novel, Fifth Business)
he is necessary--we see other characters through him
he doesn't seem to care about his own identity
he does not speak--he listens intently
he helps people identify "ghosts" from their pasts and
     bury them in "sacred" places
he reveals the secret of the patient's identity
```

This material provided much of the first draft, which was submitted to peer review. The student then revised the draft, partly in accordance with the suggestions offered and partly in the light of her own further thinking. Here is the final version.

```
          Caravaggio, the "Fifth Business"

The English Patient by Michael Ondaatje often feels

like a classic play.  As it unfolds, Kip is seen as the

hero, the lover, the protector; Hana is the heroine,
```

also lover, also protector. Almasy is the villain, both as cuckold and as enemy. Katharine is confidante to Almasy, his counterpart. Caravaggio takes the fifth role. We are allowed to know about the other characters because Caravaggio seeks to discover their identities. He is essential.

We know little of Caravaggio except that the World War is over for him; he has lost his work along with his thumbs. He withdraws and spends his days sitting in darkness, watching others but revealing nothing of himself (27).

It seems Caravaggio's own identity is of little interest to him. When asked his name he remains silent, only writing down his serial number (27). In hospital, however, he hears Hana's name and learns that she is in trouble. Now Caravaggio has a purpose: he must travel to Villa San Girolamo to find this daughter of his old friend and help her. He must discover who she is.

This actor is named only when he comes into Hana's company; then we learn he is "the man named Caravaggio" (31). He arrives at the Villa in silence, with "no clatter of footsteps [. . .] not a sound on the floor" (30). Nothing emanates from this character, not even noise. He begins to take identity only as Hana's father's friend, her "uncle from childhood" (55).

Ondaatje portrays Caravaggio as keen observer and listener. Even the use of the painter's name alerts the reader to his intensity of focus. Like the painter, his man sees people in different lights. Through him we see past Hana of the cold heart and past the accent of the burned man. In fact, because of his attention, Hana is eventually made whole again.

Caravaggio is indeed intrigued by all who surround him. His first night is spent on the roof, looking over the Italian countryside (31). When he becomes familiar with the exterior landscape, he turns his attention (and ours) to the interior landscape.

As the story progresses, we realize that not only Hana, but the other players as well are without identity. Caravaggio reveals their past lives; because of him Katharine's body, for example, is identified and her soul laid to rest.

In a room filled with false images of trompe l'oeil, the "English" patient awaits his death. This Englishman, whose existence is as false as the garden which surrounds him, will be made real by his death. He will remain forever unnamed and mourned only by Hana. Ondaatje moves Caravaggio into the presence of the burned man and it becomes the listener's job to piece together the stories which finally reveal the truth: "Let me tell you a story," Caravaggio says to Hana, "There was a Hungarian named Almasy [. . .]. I think the English patient is not English" (163).

Through Caravaggio, then, a number of tragedies are averted. The unidentified Englishman, who speaks of flower beds in Gloucestershire (163), vanishes. We see that he was never really there. And Almasy, the man who knows the mystery of Katharine's death, is found.

Although Caravaggio has lost his thumbs and probably his profession as thief, he is the one character who has not lost his own identity. He has only secreted it: "Caravaggio watches Hana, who sits across from him looking into his eyes, trying to read him [. . .] sniffing him out, searching for the trace"

```
(39).  But while others seek to discover him, his

presence allows them to be revealed.  The intensity with

which he listens gives them a reason to speak.  When we

last see him, he is walking away from the Villa San

Girolamo on a tightrope, momentarily caught in a flash

of lightning (297).  Then, having played out his role,

he is gone.


                     Work Cited

Ondaatje, Michael. The English Patient. Toronto:

     Vintage, 1993.
```

A few comments on this essay:

1. The title is informative and intriguing—more interesting, for example, than "The Character of Caravaggio."
2. The writer cites passages to illustrate her points, using the form prescribed by the instructor.
3. The final paragraph concludes with the departure of the character. Thus the essay more or less echoes the chronology of the book, but these last sentences are not mere plot-telling. Rather, they solidify the writer's view of Caravaggio's character and his importance to the novel.

FORESHADOWING

The writer of fiction provides a coherent world in which the details work together. FORESHADOWING, which eliminates surprise or at least greatly reduces it and thus destroys a story that has nothing except a surprise ending to offer, is a powerful tool in the hands of the writer of serious fiction. In a story such as Faulkner's classic, "A Rose for Emily," in which we are surprised to learn near the end that Miss Emily has slept beside the decaying corpse of her dead lover, we somehow expect something strange from the outset. We are not surprised by the surprise, only by its precise nature. The first sentence of the story tells us that after Miss Emily's funeral (the narrator begins at the end) the townspeople cross her threshold "out of curiosity to see the inside of her house, which no one save an old manservant [. . .] had seen in at least ten years." As the story progresses, we see Miss Emily prohibiting people from entering the house, and we hear that after a certain point no one ever sees Homer Barron again, that "the front door remained closed," and (a few paragraphs before the end of the story) that the townspeople "knew that there was one room in that region above the stairs which no one had seen in forty years." The paragraph preceding the revelation that "the man himself lay in bed" is devoted to a description of Homer's dust-covered clothing and toilet articles. In short, however much we are unprepared for the precise revelation, we are prepared to discover something macabre in the house; and, given Miss Emily's purchase of poison and Homer's disappearance, we have some idea of what will be revealed.

Joyce's "Araby" (Appendix A) is another example of a story in which the beginning is a preparation for all that follows. Consider the first two paragraphs:

> North Richmond Street, being blind, was a quiet street except at the hour when the Christian Brothers' school set the boys free. An uninhabited house of two stories stood at the blind end, detached from its neighbours in a square ground. The other houses of the street, conscious of decent lives within them, gazed at one another with brown imperturbable faces.
>
> The former tenant of our house, a priest, had died in the back drawing-room. Air, musty from having been long enclosed, hung in all the rooms, and the waste room behind the kitchen was littered with old useless papers. Among these I found a few paper-covered books, the pages of which were curled and damp: *The Abbot*, by Walter Scott, *The Devout Communicant* and *The Memoirs of Vidocq*. I liked the last best because its leaves were yellow. The wild garden behind the house contained a central apple-tree and a few straggling bushes under one of which I found the late tenant's rusty bicycle pump. He had been a very charitable priest; in his will he had left all his money to institutions and the furniture of his house to his sister.

Of course, the full meaning of the passage will not become apparent until you have read the entire story. In a sense, a story has at least three lives:

- when we read the story, sentence by sentence, trying to turn the sequence of sentences into a consistent whole;

- when we have finished reading the story and we think back on it as a whole, even if we think no more than "That was a waste of time"; and

- when we read a story, knowing already—even as we read the first line—how it will turn out at the end.

Let's assume that you have not read the whole of "Araby." On the basis only of a reading of the first two paragraphs, what might you highlight or underline? Here are the words that one student marked:

blind	musty
quiet	kitchen was littered
set the boys free	leaves were yellow
brown imperturbable faces	wild garden [. . .] apple-tree
priest	charitable priest

No two readers will come up with exactly the same list (if you live on North Richmond Street, you will probably underline it and put an exclamation mark in the margin; if you attended a parochial school, you'll probably underline "Christian Brothers' school"), but perhaps most readers, despite their varied experience, would agree that Joyce is giving us a picture of what he elsewhere called the "paralysis" of Ireland. How the story will turn out is, of course, unknown to a first-time reader. Perhaps the paralysis will increase, or perhaps it will be broken. Joyce goes on adding sentence to sentence, trying to shape the reader's response and the reader goes on reading, making meaning out of the sentences.

As we read further in the story, we are not surprised to learn that the boy for a while manufactured quasi-religious experiences, religion being dead—remember the dead priest and his rusty bicycle pump. In his ears, shop-boys sing "litanies," his girlfriend's name springs to his lips "in strange prayers," and his vision of her is a "chalice" that he carries "safely through a throng of foes." He plans to visit a bazaar, and he promises to bring her a gift. After he has with some difficulty arrived at the bazaar, however, he is vastly disappointed by the trivial conversation of the attendants, by the counting of the day's receipts (money-changers in the temple), and by the darkness ("the upper part of the hall was now completely dark"). In the last line of the story he realizes: "Gazing up into the darkness I saw myself as a creature driven and derided by vanity; and my eyes burned with anguish and anger." Everything in the story coheres; the dead-end street, the dead priest, the rusty pump—all are perfect preludes to this story about a boy's recognition of the nothingness that surrounds him. The "vanity" that drives and derides him is not only the egotism that moved him to think he could bring the girl a fitting gift, but also the nothingness that is spoken of in the biblical "Vanity of vanities, all is vanity."

In preparing to write about foreshadowing:

- Reread the story; now that you know how it ends, you will be able to see how certain early details are relevant to the ending.

- Underline or highlight these details, and perhaps jot down brief notes in the margins, such as "images of emptiness" or "later turns out ironically."

- Jot down on a sheet of paper key phrases from the text and annotate them with such comments as "The first of many religious images" and "same image appears later."

Organizing an Essay on Foreshadowing

What is the best way to organize an essay on foreshadowing? Probably you will work through the evidence chronologically, though your initial paragraph may discuss the end and indicate that the remainder of the essay will be concerned with tracing the way in which the author prepares the reader for this end and simultaneously maintains the right amount of suspense. Again, be wary of plot summary in any chronological order. You may want to move around within the sequence of the plot, pulling out examples of foreshadowing that illustrate particular aspects of your thesis. If the suspense is too slight, we stop reading, not caring what comes next. If it is too great, we are perhaps reading a story in which the interest depends entirely on some strange happening rather than a story with sufficiently universal application to make it worthy of a second reading.

Your essay may study the ways in which details gain in meaning as the reader gets farther into the story. Or it may study the author's failure to keep details relevant and coherent, the tendency to introduce material for its momentary value at the expense of the larger design. An essay on an uneven story may do both: It may show that although there are unfortunate irrelevancies, considerable skill is used in arousing and interestingly fulfilling the reader's expectations. If you feel that the story is fundamentally successful, the organization of your thoughts may reflect your feelings. After an initial paragraph stating the overall position, you may discuss the failures and then go on at greater length to discuss the strengths, ending strongly on your main point. If you feel that the story is essentially a failure, perhaps first discuss its merits briefly and then go on to your main point—the unsatisfactory nature of the story. To reverse this procedure would be to leave the reader with an impression contrary to your thesis.

SETTING AND ATMOSPHERE

Foreshadowing normally makes use of SETTING. The setting or environment in the first two paragraphs of Joyce's "Araby" is not mere geography, not mere locale: It provides an ATMOSPHERE, an air that the characters breathe, a world in which they move. Narrowly speaking, the setting is the physical surroundings—the furniture, the architecture, the landscape, and the climate— and these often are highly appropriate to the characters that are associated with them. Thus, in Emily Brontë's *Wuthering Heights* the passionate Earnshaw family is associated with Wuthering Heights, the storm-exposed moorland, whereas the mild Linton family is associated with Thrushcross Grange in the sheltered valley below. King's "Borders" also has two settings: the Canadian border town, Coutts, and the American town, Sweetgrass. A reader of the story probably agrees with King that the descriptive name, "Sweetgrass," sounds more Canadian and the abrupt name more American; the fact that the reverse is true assists the story's theme that borders are arbitrary.

Broadly speaking, setting includes not only the physical surroundings but also a point or several points in time. The background against which we see the characters and the happenings may be specified as morning or evening, spring or fall, and this temporal setting in a good story will probably be highly relevant; it will probably be part of the story's meaning, perhaps providing an ironic contrast or exerting an influence on the characters. (Think of the normally convivial dinner party setting in Timothy Findley's "Dinner Along the Amazon," a story of miscommunication and loneliness within partnerships.)

Note: Although your instructor may ask you to write a paragraph describing the setting, more often he or she will want something more complicated, such as an essay on the *function* of the setting. For such an essay, you may find it useful to begin with a paragraph or two describing the setting or settings, but be sure to go on to analyze the significance of this material.

Symbolism

Writers of fiction do not write only about things that have happened to them. They write about things they have seen or heard, and also about thoughts and emotions. Inevitably, writers use SYMBOLS. Symbols are neither puzzles nor colourful details but are among the concrete embodiments that give the story whatever accuracy it has. For instance, in "The Wall," in Chapter 1, Vigneault may only be creating verisimilitude by having his mason work on "the exterior wall of his prison," but as we read the story we probably feel—because of the emphasis on the *strength* of the wall—that it in some way emphasizes the imprisonment, the interior space, and the mental space occupied by the mason. The occupation of the visitor, who is a monk, is also loaded with special significance and strikes the reader as a clue to a deeper meaning. Noticing these signs, readers may see more than the narrator sees or says.

Let's assume that if writers use symbols, they want readers to perceive—at least faintly—that certain characters or places or seasons or happenings have rich implications, stand for something more than what they are on the surface. Indeed, Baudelaire once described literature as a *forêt de symboles* (forest of symbols). How do writers help us to perceive these things? By emphasizing them—for instance, by describing them at some length, or by introducing them at times when they might not seem strictly necessary, or by calling attention to them repeatedly.

Consider, for example, the name tag with a small Canadian flag at one end and a small American flag at the other worn by the duty-free shop manager, Mel, in King's "Borders" (Appendix B). Because both flags appear on the same tag, but at either end, the national symbols become literary ones. Working in the space between two border stations, Mel inhabits the same "non-country" inhabited by the mother but he can return to whichever country he lives in without subjugation. She must compromise her "Blackfoot" heritage to claim citizenship in Canada. Once this symbol is read, other national symbols like the flagpoles, the water towers, and the guards' guns become more powerful. They are not just details added for realism. King seems to put considerable emphasis on these items and, indeed, on many apparently minor details. But here is a caution. To say that the detail of the relative size of the water towers on each side of the border stands for a larger debate about the North American obsession with size, the Canadian sense of inferiority in the face of the "big" United States, and the congruent Canadian belief that our abundant water resource gives us power is not to say that whenever water appears in a story it stands for resources or national pride. Indeed, water is a primitive symbol that often stands for renewal and can also stand for the "river of death."

Does the water in some way stand for renewal here? For the rebirth of Aboriginal pride? Probably not—though readers might disagree. The legends of Coyote that the mother tells the narrator do suggest pride in racial heritage and the fact that the mother "expected me to remember each one" underlines their importance. The arrival of television vans in the morning contrasts a symbol of modern North American life with these ancient mythical symbols. King reinforces this point by telling us that the television lights "hurt my eyes." It seems King does wish to talk about the enormous cultural power of television, but this theme is secondary to his interest in the Native sense of time and place between "borders." He does not, therefore, invest the television crews or their paraphernalia with much symbolic significance—though it is certainly ironic that the media seems to end the standoff. He gives much more attention to the guns worn by the guards, showing us thumbs "jammed into gun belts" and "notches" in pistol grips. King might have developed these symbols further or even considered guns as Freudian symbols of male potency and power over the Native woman and her boy child, but that would have created a different story. (It would have invited a psychoanalytic interpretation.) **ALLEGORY** is an older, more direct comparison where a concrete object stands for a quality. Do not confuse allegory with symbol.

A Sample Essay on Setting as Symbol

The following essay is about Thomas King's "Borders" (Appendix B). If you have not yet read the story, take a moment now to do so.

Here is a scratch outline. Not all of the notes ended up in the final version, of course, but they obviously were a great help in shaping the essay.

```
thesis: setting here not geographical place, but
        political, cultural place
title?
        King and Borders
        First Canadian Sense of Place
        Flagpoles and Place
        A Mother's Pride
        Setting as Symbol
        Setting as Symbol: Borders in [ ... ]
        Moving Between Countries
        Moving Between: Setting in King's [ ... ]
Setting in "Borders":
        Define setting??? place and time
King gives age of narrator, not date
King gives careful details of the physical setting and
        of Alberta and Salt Lake City; also names Coutts
        and Sweetgrass
"You'll be able to see the tops of the flagpoles, too.
        That's where the border is"
"It's the water.  From here on down, they got lousy
        water"
"I found her sitting on her blanket leaning against the
        bumper of the car"
```

why the guns on the crossing guards? authority? violence
    of American life? Child's viewpoint? Influence of
    TV Cop shows on the narrator????

~~Salt Lake City is where Mormons live in the USA.   Is~~
    ~~there a contrast with Christianity and the Native~~
    ~~beliefs the Mother tells in the Coyote legend?~~

old way of life
"If you tried to look [. . .] in certain directions, you
    couldn't see a thing"
Slides in and out of present time and memory time
Mother's stories come from old time; TV crew comes from
    contemporary time
End with a quotation? Or with something about being
    trapped or having no borders?

*Title implies
thesis.*

                    Moving Between:

        Setting in Thomas King's "Borders"

        In reading Thomas King's "Borders," a
reader is aware exactly where the story is set
but is not always clear on when the action is
taking place. The narrator, a twelve-year-old

*Opening
paragraph
identifies author
and story. Topic
(setting) is
introduced.*

First Nations boy, remembers the events which
led to his sister, Laetitia, leaving the
family home on a reservation in Alberta and
moving to Salt Lake City in the USA. He also
recounts the events over a three-day period in
the present during which he and his mother are
trapped between the USA and Canada, living in
the neutral zone between two border crossings.

        The narrator tells us many details about
the geographical setting. When Laetitia wants
to move, her mother points out the natural
beauty of their home: "You can still see the
mountains from here" (360). The reader sees
"the prairies move in the sunlight" (366) in
Canada, while later, looking into the United
States, "all you could see was an overpass

*Quotations
support points.*

that arched across the highway [. . .] "

(360-361). The mother points out that Canada
already has all the glamorous-sounding things
which the sister is hoping to find in Utah.
Her boyfriend, who has been in Salt Lake,
shows the Mormon Tabernacle and the skiing
mountains on a map. The mother replies that
people "come from all over the world to ski at
Banff. Cardston's got a temple, if you like
those kinds of things" (363). The mother's
pride in Canada is important, because later

Transition ("but")
leads to
significance of
setting.
Introduces thesis.

she will deny being a Canadian. The symbols
of the Canadian setting are important to her,
but more important is her native heritage as a
Blackfoot. The story is full of symbols of
place which are also symbols of heritage and
belonging.

     In Coutts, the Canadian border town, King
not only points out the typical convenience
store and gas station, but a museum which
(significantly) is boarded up. Museums hold
people's histories and memories; in Canada we
are not good at remembering our history and
that is one of the themes which King wants to
convey by his symbolic setting. By putting
the action in between the two countries, King
asks the reader to consider whether

Thesis

nationality has to do with political
boundaries or with a sense of belonging, a
familiarity. The tribal memories conveyed in
the Coyote legends are what the mother expects
the boy "to remember" so she "tell[s] them
slow, repeating parts" (366). King wants his
narrator (and the reader) to understand that
it is this sense of "place" within myth that
really defines our identity, not the physical
space we inhabit. And yet he is also subtle
enough to point out that even the Mother has
another kind of identity in her pride of being

Canadian and her dislike for the American way of life. The story does not pretend that we each identify in only one way.

Transition to second aspect of setting.

The time of the story is also laid out carefully, but it shifts. Within the past and present time, King blurs details. Right at the beginning the boy tells us "When I was twelve, maybe thirteen, my mother announced we were going to Salt Lake City to visit my sister" (359). He says that "over time" (364) Laetitia gained her mother's approval for the move. This vague time is also part of King's theme. In Native folklore, time is less precise than in Western history and since the Mother insists she is "Blackfoot" rather than Canadian (or American), we expect her to live in the fluid time of her people. In an interview, King said of his fiction that "I don't make any distinction between the past and the present" (qtd. Geddes). By moving in time, the story emphasizes that time is less important than belonging. The mother is "slow" when she tells her ancient stories. The boy has a more contemporary sense of time, just as he likes hamburgers. He comments that the second night sleeping in the car was "not as much fun" (365) as the first night, but it is all still an adventure for him. The basic necessities are available (water, some food, cover at night) so the two are able to live outside either country and, somehow, outside time, as well. The time is symbolic in the same way the space is. The two travellers are frozen in time by the refusal of the authorities to let them enter either country, but their Blackfoot identity doesn't operate in the same linear time the guards experience, anyway. Time and place together form setting,

Quotation from author supports thesis.

Thesis is hammered home.

but the particular sense of time and place in this story also symbolize the different perception of the Blackfoot family.

It is her insistence on recognition, summed up in her view of time and place, which marks the Mother's pride. It is also the lesson the narrator learns. As he says, "Pride is a good thing to have, you know. Laetitia had a lot of pride, and so did my mother. I figured that someday, I'd have it, too" (364).

Concluding paragraph wraps up essay; reiterates key idea of pride.

Works Cited

Documentation

Geddes, Gary, ed. The Art of Short Fiction: An International Anthology. Toronto: HarperCollins, 1993. 379.

King, Thomas. "Borders" Rpt. in Sylvan Barnet, Reid Gilbert, and William E. Cain. A Short Guide to Writing about Literature. Second Canadian ed. Don Mills, ON: Pearson Education Canada, 2004. 359-367

POINT OF VIEW

The Dublin in "Araby" is the Dublin that James Joyce thought existed, but it must be remembered that although an author *writes* a story, someone else *tells* it. The story is seen from a particular POINT OF VIEW, and this point of view in large measure determines our response to the story. A wide variety of terms has been established to name differing points of view, but the following labels are among the commonest. We may begin with two categories: third-person points of view (in which the narrator is, in the crudest sense, not a participant in the story) and first-person points of view (in which the "I" who narrates the story plays a part in it).

Third-Person Narrators

The THIRD-PERSON POINT OF VIEW itself has several subdivisions. At one extreme is the **OMNISCIENT NARRATOR**, who knows everything that is going on and can tell us the inner thoughts of all the characters. The omniscient narrator may editorialize, pass judgments, reassure the reader, and so forth, in which case he or she may sound like the author. Here is Thomas Hardy's editorially omniscient narrator in *Tess of the D'Urbervilles,* telling the reader that Tess was mistaken in imagining that the countryside proclaimed her guilt:

> But this encompassment of her own characterization, based upon shreds of convention, peopled by phantoms and voices antipathetic to her, was a sorry and mistaken creation of Tess's fancy—a cloud of moral hobgoblins by which she was terrified without reason.

Still, even this narrator is not quite Hardy; he does not allude to his other books, his private life, or his hope that the book will sell. If he is Hardy, he is only one aspect of Hardy, quite possibly a fictional Hardy, a disembodied voice with particular characteristics.

Another sort of third-person narrator, the **SELECTIVE OMNISCIENT**, takes up what Henry James called a "center of consciousness," revealing the thoughts of one of the characters but (for the most part) seeing the rest of the characters from the outside only. Wayne Booth, in a thoughtful study of Jane Austen's *Emma,* explains the effectiveness of selective omniscience in this novel. He points out that Emma is intelligent, witty, beautiful, and rich. But she is flawed by pride, and, until she discovers and corrects her fault, she almost destroys herself and her friends. How may such a character be made sympathetic, so that we will hope for the happy conclusion to the comedy? "The solution to the problem of maintaining sympathy despite almost crippling faults," Booth says,

> was primarily to use the heroine herself as a kind of narrator, though in third person, reporting on her own experience [. . .]. By showing most of the story through Emma's eyes, the author insures that we shall travel with Emma rather than stand against her. It is not simply that Emma provides, in the unimpeachable evidence of her own conscience, proof that she has many redeeming qualities that do not appear on the surface; such evidence could be given with authorial commentary, though perhaps not with such force and conviction. Much more important, the sustained inside view leads the reader to hope for good fortune for the character with whom he travels, quite independently of the qualities revealed.

—*The Rhetoric of Fiction,* 2nd ed. (Chicago: U of Chicago P, 1983) 245–46.

Booth goes on to point out in a long and careful analysis that "sympathy for Emma can be heightened by withholding inside views of others as well as by granting them of her."

In writing about point of view, one tries to suggest what the author's choice of a particular point of view contributes to the story. Wayne Booth shows how Jane Austen's third-person point of view helps keep sympathetic a character who otherwise might be less than sympathetic. Notice that Booth states the problem—how to draw an intelligent but proud woman so that the reader will wish for a happy ending—and he presents his answer convincingly, moving from "It is not simply [. . .]." to "Much more important [. . .]." (To reverse the order would cause a drop in interest.) He then moves from a discussion of the inside treatment of Emma to the outside treatment of the other characters, thus substantiating and enlarging his argument.

POINT OF VIEW 157

Possibly, one could reverse this procedure, beginning with a discussion of the treatment of the characters other than Emma and then closing in on Emma, but such an essay may seem slow in getting under way. The early part may appear unfocused. The reader will for a while be left wondering why in an essay on point of view in *Emma* the essayist does not turn to the chief matter, the presentation of the central character.

The **THIRD-PERSON NARRATOR**, then, although not in the ordinary sense a character in the story, is an important voice in the story, which helps give shape to it. Another type of third-person narrator is the so-called **EFFACED NARRATOR**. (Some critics use the term DRAMATIC POINT OF VIEW or OBJECTIVE POINT OF VIEW.) This narrator does not seem to exist, for (unlike the editorially omniscient narrator) he or she does not comment in his or her own voice and (unlike the omniscient and selective omniscient narrators) does not enter any minds. It is almost improper to speak of an effaced narrator as "he" or "he or she," for no evident figure is speaking. The reader hears **DIALOGUE** and sees only what a camera or a fly on the wall would see. The following example is from Morley Callaghan's *A Fine and Private Place:*

> At the door he fumbled for his key.
> "My God," Al said. "That's Shore."
> "Are you sure?"
> "It's the same hat he had on in the picture" (25).

But even an effaced narrator has, if we think a moment, a kind of personality. The story the narrator records may seem "cold" or "reportorial" or "objective," and such a TONE or VOICE (the attitude of the narrator, as it is detected) may be an important part of the story. Rémy de Gourmont's remark, quoted in Ezra Pound's *Literary Essays,* is relevant: "To be impersonal is to be personal in a special kind of way [. . .]. The objective is one of the forms of the subjective."

In writing about a third-person narrator, speak of "the narrator" or "the speaker," not of "the author." ✳

First-Person Narrators

To turn to **FIRST-PERSON**, or PARTICIPANT, POINTS OF VIEW, consider the "I" who narrates "Araby." You may recall that the narrator says, at the end, "I saw myself as a creature driven and derided by vanity," when he experiences an **EPIPHANY**. In "Araby," this "I" is a major character; so he is in Bill Schermbrucker's *Mimosa.* He may, however, also be a minor character, a mere witness. (Dr. Watson narrates tales about Sherlock Holmes, Maureen narrates the other characters' lives in Alice Munro's "Open Secrets.") Of course, the narrator, even when a relatively minor character, is still a character, and, therefore, in some degree the story is about him or her. Although "Open Secrets" is primarily about the mystery of a missing girl, it is also about Maureen's changing perception of the townsfolk.

First-person narrators may not fully understand their own report. Take the narrator of Munro's story, "The Albanian Virgin." In telling us about the old woman she visits in the hospital, she uses an **INNOCENT EYE**, a device in which a good part of the effect consists in the discrepancy between the narrator's imperfect awareness and the reader's superior awareness. We see the connection between the mysterious heroine of the inner story, "Lottar," and the old woman's name, "Charlotte"—or we think we do. But we are uncertain if Charlotte is truly proposing a movie plot (as she says she is doing) or narrating her own exotic life. In short, Charlotte is an **UNRELIABLE NARRATOR**. One of the intriguing aspects of this story is the conflict between these two styles of narration; the **MAGIC REALISM** of the story arises from the juxtaposition of the apparently honest details of the persona's narration of her life with Charlotte's exotic narration. These levels of realism are further complicated for some readers who know that Munro herself moved from Southern Ontario to Victoria just as her **PERSONA** says she did. At what point is Alice Munro using first-person narration to tell her own story, at what point is her persona telling a fiction from her own **INNOCENT EYE**, and at what point is Charlotte actually telling the story but keeping certain facts from the reader? Of course the effect of the story comes from the fact that all these points of view operate together, linking the various levels of perception of each narrator.

On the other hand, we sometimes feel that a first-person narrator (Conrad's Marlow in several novels is an example) is a very thinly veiled substitute for the author. Nevertheless, the words of a first-person narrator require the same kind of scrutiny that we give to the words of the other characters in a story or play. The reader must deduce the personality from what is said. For instance, the narrator of "Araby" never tells us that he was a good student, but, from such a passage as the following, we can deduce that he was a bookish boy until he fell in love: "I watched my master's face pass from amiability to sternness; he hoped I was not beginning to idle."

A first-person narrator is not likely to give us the help that an editorially omniscient narrator gives. We must deduce from this passage from "Araby" that the narrator's uncle drinks too much: "At nine o'clock I heard my uncle's latchkey in the hall-door. I heard him talking to himself and heard the hall-stand rocking when it had received the weight of his overcoat. I could interpret these signs." In a first-person narrative it is sometimes difficult for the reader to interpret the signs. In a sense, the author has given the reader two stories: the story the narrator tells and the story of a narrator telling a story.

An essay on point of view in a first-person story will probably characterize the narrator at some length. For instance, it will point out that the narrator is a not-too-bright adult who is eagerly telling a new acquaintance something about life in this town. The essay will then go on to show how this narrator's character colours the story that he or she tells. The essay will, for instance, explain that because the narrator is rather simple, he does not understand that he is in fact recounting a story about murder and not—as he thinks—a curious accident; that is, the essay will discuss how the reader's response resembles or differs from the narrator's.

In writing about point of view in a first-person narrative such as Robertson Davies' *Fifth Business*, after an introductory remark to the effect that Dunstan Ramsay narrates the story, use the character's name or a pronoun ("Ramsay realizes the importance of Mrs. Dempster in his life.") in speaking of the narrator.

Caution: Essays on narrative point of view have a way of slipping into essays on what the story is about. Of course, point of view *is* relevant to the theme of the story, but if you are writing about point of view, keep this focus in sight, explaining, for instance, how it shapes the theme.

NOTES AND A SAMPLE ESSAY ON NARRATIVE POINT OF VIEW IN JAMES JOYCE'S "ARABY"

Here are some of the notes—a journal entry and a rough outline—and the final version of an essay on the narrator in Joyce's "Araby" (Appendix A). Doubtless some of the notes were based on passages that the student had underlined or highlighted in the text.

```
1st person point of view, but what sort of person?

    Several sorts
            Opening paragraph seems objective point of view
    Boy is sensitive to beauty: likes a book because

        pages are yellow (191); plays in stable where he

        hears "music from the buckled harness" (192);

    Boy is shy: hardly talks to girl: "I had never

        spoken to her" (192); "At last she spoke to me"

        (193) Here, narrator is personal, not objective omniscient

        But he plays with other boys; they don't seem

            to regard him as different.  Typical boy?

            Prob. not.  "My eyes were often full of

            tears" (193).  But not from "the rough tribes from
                                        the cottages."
        But narrator is no longer a kid; grownup, looking

        back on childhood, sometimes he seems almost

        amused by his childhood ("Her name sprang to my

        lips at moments in strange prayers and praise

        which I myself did not understand, 192-93);

        sometimes seems a bit hard on his earlier self:

        ("all my foolish blood"; "What innumerable follies

        laid waste my waking and sleeping thoughts,"

            193); My soul luxuriated" (193) So, a third aspect to
                                                       narrator
        Ending: very hard on self: "I saw myself as a
The third aspect,
 or maybe even creature driven and derided by vanity" (196).
 a fourth But opening is very different, unemotional.  In
```

fact, come to think of it, opening isn't even
clearly a first-person narrator. But there _is_ a
special personality in semi-comic comment that houses
themselves were conscious of decent lives within them.

The Three First-Person Narrators of Joyce's "Araby"

James Joyce's "Araby" is told by a first-person
narrator, but this point of view is not immediately
evident to a reader. The story at first seems to be
told by an objective third-person narrator:

> North Richmond Street, being blind, was a
> quiet street except at the hour when the
> Christian Brothers' School set the boys free.
> An uninhabited house of two stories stood at
> the blind end, detached from its neighbours in
> a square ground. The other houses of the
> street, conscious of decent lives within them,
> gazed at one another with brown imperturbable
> faces (271).

These words seem objective and omniscient, but the very
next paragraph begins by saying, "The former tenant of
our house [...]." The word "Our" indicates that the
narrative point of view is first-person. On rereading
the first paragraph of the story, a reader probably
still feels that the paragraph is chiefly objective, but
perhaps the reader now gets a little sense of an
individualized speaker in the passage about the houses
being "conscious of decent lives within them," and the
houses have "imperturbable faces." That is, the
narrator personifies the houses, making them "conscious"
and rather smug. Apparently he is detached, and
somewhat amused, as he thinks back to the middle-class
neighbourhood of his childhood.

In many passages, however, the narrator describes
his romantic childhood without any irony. For instance,
he says that when he was in love with the girl, his
"body was like a harp and her words and gestures were
like fingers running upon the wires" (355). We can say,
then, that so far the narrator has two aspects: (1) an

adult, who looks back objectively, or maybe with a little sense of irony, and (2) an adult who looks back almost nostalgically at himself when he was a child in love.

But there is a third aspect to the narrator, revealed in several passages. For instance, he says that the girl's name was "like a summons to all [his] foolish blood" (354) and that he engaged in "innumerable follies" (355). What may seem to be the strongest passage of this sort is at the very end of the story, and it is the strongest partly because it is in such an emphatic place: "Gazing up into the darkness I saw myself as a creature driven and derided by vanity [...]" (358). But this passage is <u>not</u> exactly what it first seems to be. The narrator is not condemning himself, saying that as a child he was "driven and derided by vanity." He is saying, now, as an adult, that <u>at the time of the experience</u> he saw himself as driven and derided by vanity.

The fact that he says "I saw myself" is almost a way of saying "I saw myself, <u>falsely</u>, as [...]." That is, the narrator makes it clear that he is giving the child's view, and the reader understands that the child was unusually sensitive. In several passages the narrator has distanced himself from the child (as in the "foolish blood" passage) but the reader does not see the child as foolish, just as highly romantic. The very fact that the narrator calls the child "foolish" is enough for a reader mentally to come to the child's defense, and in effect say, "Oh, no, don't be so hard on yourself."

The earlier passages in which the narrator condemns his childhood experience thus serve to help the reader to take the child's part. And now, at the end of the story, when the narrator reports the child's severe judgment on himself, the reader leaps to the child's defense. If the narrator had <u>not</u> occasionally commented negatively on his childhood, readers might themselves have thought that the child was acting absurdly, and also thought that the narrator was too pleased with himself, but since the narrator occasionally passes a negative judgment on the child, and ends by telling us that the child judged himself severely too, the reader almost certainly wants to reassure the child that his behaviour was not nearly so bad as he thought it was-- and in fact it was really quite touching.

In some ways, then, this narrator is an unreliable narrator. Such a narrator is usually a naive person, who doesn't understand what is really going on in the story. The narrator of "Araby" is not naive--he is obviously a very sophisticated person--but sometimes is an unreliable guide so far as his own childhood goes. But because the narrator sometimes takes a very critical view of his childhood, a reader mentally defends the child. The third (critical) aspect of the narrator, then, actually serves to make the reader value the child's behavior rather than judge it negatively.

Work Cited

Joyce, James. "Araby." Rpt. in <u>An Introduction to Literature</u>. Eds. Sylvan Barnet, et al. 11th ed. New York: Longman, 1993. 271-75.

A few comments on this essay may be useful:

1. *The title* is engaging—the idea of *three* first-person narrators at first sounds paradoxical. And it probably is enough if a title is engaging and proves to be relevant. But keep in mind that the best title often is one that gives the reader a hint of your thesis. Here, for instance, the title might have been "How Reliable Is the Narrator in 'Araby?'" or perhaps "Reliable and Unreliable Narrators in Joyce's 'Araby.'" This last version catches a reader's attention for two reasons: It speaks of narrators in the plural (most readers will wonder who narrates the story other than the narrator they have in mind), and it raises the issue of reliability (most readers probably assume that the narrator is reliable). Again, none of this is to say that the student's title is weak. The point here is to indicate that the choice of a title is important.

2. *The organization* is reasonable. It begins with the beginning and it ends with the end. Such an organization is not a requirement, but it is not to be shunned. Do not, however, allow such an organization to turn what

should be an analytic essay into a long summary of the story. You are arguing a thesis, not writing a summary.

3. *The proportions are appropriate.* The thesis is that the third, or critical, voice in the essay is important in (paradoxically) getting sympathy for the boy, and so the third voice is given the most space.

4. *Quotations* are used in order to let the reader know exactly what the writer is talking about. They are used as part of the argument, not as padding.

THEME: VISION OR ARGUMENT?

Because modern fiction makes subtle use of it, point of view can scarcely be neglected in a discussion of THEME—what a story is about. Modern criticism usually prefers not to hear the author's voice directly, as the reader often did in older fiction. We would rather see than be lectured. We are less impressed by

> It was the stillness of an implacable force brooding over an inscrutable intention

(from Conrad's *Heart of Darkness*) than by this passage from the same book:

> Black shapes crouched, lay, sat between the trees, leaning against the trunks, clinging to the earth, half coming out, half effaced within the dim light, in all the attitudes of pain, abandonment, and despair. Another mine on the cliff went off, followed by a slight shudder of the soil under my feet. The work was going on. The work! And this was the place where some of the helpers had withdrawn to die.

The second quotation, but not the first, gives us the sense of reality that we have come to expect from fiction. Thomas Hardy's novels in particular have been censured on this account; the modern sensibility is uneasy when it hears Hardy's own voice commenting on the cosmic significance of the happenings, as when in *Tess of the D'Urbervilles* the narrator says: "In the ill-judged execution of the well-judged plan of things, the call seldom produces the comer, the man to love rarely coincides with the hour for loving." The passage goes on in this vein at some length. Even in passages of dialogue, we sometimes feel that we are getting not a vision of life but a discourse on it, as in this famous exchange between Tess and her brother:

> "Did you say the stars were worlds, Tess?"
> "Yes."
> "All like ours?"
> "I don't know; but I think so. They sometimes seem to be like the apples on our stubbard-tree. Most of them splendid and sound—a few blighted."
> "Which do we live on—a splendid one or a blighted one?"
> "A blighted one."

Partly, we feel that overt commentary (even when put into the mouths of the characters) leaves the world of fiction and invites us to judge it separately as philosophy. Partly the difficulty is that twentieth-century novelists and readers have come to expect the novel to do something different from what Hardy and his contemporaries expected it to do. As the novelist Flannery O'Connor puts it in *Mystery and Manners* (1957), we expect a storyteller to speak "*with* character and action, not *about* character and action" (76).

Determining and Discussing the Theme

First, we can distinguish between STORY and THEME in fiction. Story is concerned with "How does it turn out? What happens?" Theme is concerned with "What does it add up to? What MOTIF holds the happenings together? What does it make out of life, and, perhaps, what wisdom does it offer?" A theme in a literary work is sometimes distinguished from a THESIS, an arguable message such as "People ought not to struggle against Fate." The theme, it might be said, is something like "The struggle against Fate" or "The Process of Maturing" or "The Quest for Love." In any case, the formulation of a theme normally includes an abstract noun or a phrase, but it must be remembered that such formulations as those in the previous sentence are finally only shorthand expressions for highly complex statements. (We discuss theme further in the chapter on drama.)

In a good work of fiction, the details all contribute to the writer's general purpose. In Robertson Davies' *Fifth Business,* for example, there are many references to religion, the circus, and magic. These references contribute to our sense of the reality in Davies' depiction of Canada in the first half of the twentieth century, but they do more: They help comment on the ignorance of the people who consider Ramsay to be a boring and inconsequential Canadian schoolteacher, the shallowness of the religion Ramsay was taught as a boy as opposed to the deep spirituality he finds in his travels, and the role in his life of his "fool Saint." They prepare the reader for a Jungian reading of Ramsay's life, a reading that Davies seems to invite. One might study the author's references to the relation of magic, religion, and character in hopes of a deeper understanding of the novel.

Preliminary Notes and Two Sample Essays on the Theme of Thomas King's "Borders"

Here are the notes and the final essays of two students who chose to write about the theme of King's "Borders" (Appendix B).

The first student, after reading and rereading the story, jotted down the following notes as a sort of preliminary outline. Some of the notes were based on passages he had underlined. Notice that the jottings include some material specifically on the story and other material—references to the outside world—that is relevant to what the student takes to be the theme of the story. When he reviewed his notes before starting on a first draft, the student deleted some of them, having decided that they were not especially useful for his essay. Still, they were worth jotting down; only in retrospect can a writer clearly see which notes are useful.

Canadians and Americans need labels

> --citizenship

Need symbols of these labels so they can locate
themselves in a universe they understand. These form
much of pop culture.

> --nationalities
>
> --guns
>
>> --"guy in a dark blue suit"
>>
>> --"Thank you," he said, his fingers patting the
>> butt of his revolver.
>>
>> --"swaying back and forth" are like "two
>> cowboys headed for a bar or a gunfight"
>
> --border stations
>
> --pins with flags on them and names
>
> --names of towns

"a name tag with a tiny American flag on one side and a
tiny Canadian flag on the other" Americans and
Canadians share many of these pop culture symbols

> --hamburgers, pop
>
> --TV

and he wants the symbols of North American pop culture:
("But we can stop at one of those restaurants, too,
right?"; "Hamburgers would be even better because they
got more stuff for energy.") Mother doesn't want these
things. Sister wants a less "boring" life than on the
reserve. ~~Canadian life is boring vs. American
lifestyle is exciting.~~
~~"Sister's boyfriend has visited Salt Lake; So has her
friend, Charlotte, although it's not clear when she
was there~~
~~Salt Lake City is symbol of American way of life~~
Possible title:

> First Nations People See Different Signs
> Lost in Symbol
> Icons at the Border
> We All Need Signs of Who We Are

After writing a draft and then revising it, the author submitted the revision
to a group for peer review. Ultimately, he turned in the following essay.

Icons at the Border

The young narrator and his mother in Thomas King's "Borders" find themselves trapped between the Canadian and American border crossings. But they also find themselves trapped between competing symbols of two related ways of life. Neither are the heritage or lifestyle that the mother wants for her family. In fact, the symbols they encounter are so strong that they can be seen as icons for the two North American ways of life. King tells us that these images are not appropriate for his First Nations narrator, even though the boy and his sister are drawn to them.

The story concerns a Blackfoot family who has to decide whether to live in Canada or the United States. The sister moves to Salt Lake City, claiming that "life around here is too boring" (365). She is interested in the American city because it is larger--"Oh, this one is real big" (363)--and has features like the Temple, but the reader notices that her descriptions also point out undesirable features of American life: "They got armed guards and everything." Laetitia moves into an apartment with a swimming pool even though, as the mother tells her friend, "[...] she can't even swim" (360). She is seeking an urban life.

The images of American life, however, are not that different from the images of Canadian life off the reserve. The mother points out that the lifestyles are similar: Canadians ski and go to Church just like people in Utah. The two border towns are so close together they seem to be one city. The names of these two towns suggest Canadian and American values but, in fact, the names are reversed from what the boy expects, the "nice name" of Sweetgrass being on the American side even though it reminds the boy of Canadian names like Medicine Hat and Moose Jaw. The father is American; the mother is Canadian.

It seems that the boy and his sister are drawn to these images of urban, North American life. He wants to go to "one of those restaurants" (360) and he wants a hamburger. The American border guards have guns and King makes a point of drawing our attention to them, but for the young boy, they seem fascinating rather than dangerous. For him the border guards "swaying back and forth" are like "two cowboys headed for a bar or a gunfight" (362). He sees things in terms of American movies and TV. Both border stops have flagpoles that announce the symbols of each country, but they seem somewhat interchangeable. The mother warns Laetitia that she won't get "good coffee" because "from here on down, they got lousy water" (360), but the reader realizes the sister can buy her "water in bottles" (360). In modern North American life consumers believe they can compensate for whatever is missing in their lives.

The TV crews stand for the intrusion of media in people's lives in North America. The boy says their lights "hurt my eyes" but he doesn't seem to realize the life he has in "a nice house on the reserve," and "a couple of horses we rode when we went fishing" (366) is more satisfying than the manufactured world represented by TV.

It is the mother who refuses to accept either country as her natural place. Her refusal leads to the humorous entrapment between borders, but the theme is not funny. It is very important to her that the son learn his native legends; she tries to speak to her daughter in Blackfoot even though the girl replies in English. She is secretly fond of Canada, but at heart she is Blackfoot. The icons of urban, North American life that tempt the sister and fascinate the little boy do not seduce the mother. She knows that the TV lights prevent her from seeing "a thing" (366) and that she can only see herself by looking inward. King wants the reader to see more than the innocent eye of his narrator shows us. He wants us to reject the easy symbols of urban life and look for real values.

Work Cited

King, Thomas. "Borders." Rpt. in Sylvan Barnet, Reid
    Gilbert, and William E. Cain. A Short Guide to
    Writing about Literature. Second Canadian Edition.
    Don Mills, ON: Pearson Education Canada, 2004.
    359–367.

Now for the notes and the essay by a second student. This writer came to a very different conclusion about the theme of "Borders." After reading this student's notes and her essay, you may want to compare the two essays. Do you find one essay more interesting than the other? More persuasive? If so, why? You may feel that even though the essays come to different conclusions, the two essays are equally interesting and equally valid.

Assumptions about each side of the border
~~names~~
~~rude people~~
~~"I had to dress up, too, because my mother didn't~~
~~want us crossing the border looking like~~
~~Americans."~~

"But must belong to one group or the other "But you have
to be American or Canadian."
"Boy thinks of himself as Canadian" ("I told Stella we
were Blackfoot and Canadian.")
"a name tag with a tiny American flag on one side and a
tiny Canadian flag on the other"

> Mother is Canadian; father is American (so sister
> can go where she pleases)
> Which side? "Canadian side or American side?" asked
> the guard. "Blackfoot side," she said
> Guard can't understand her reply: Citizenship =
> Blackfoot
>> --"Ma'am?"
>> "Blackfoot," my mother repeated.
>> "Canadian?"
>> "Blackfoot."

Would have been easier to say Canadian, (boy will) but
Mother refuses.
Coyote is also symbol of Native religion

> Coyote = trickster, same as Raven and Nanabush
> Coyote isn't always wise or good, but is
> responsible for the world the way we find it.
> Cf. Sheila Watson, Double Hook--also about Coyote
> legends

time and space are more fluid--connections are to
family.
TV as anchor of North American life/religion/
communication
TV lights "hurt" the boys eyes; sometime if he looks "in
certain directions," you couldn't see a thing. He
doesn't "see" his mother's stories but hears them--
"slow" and as if they mean something.
~~TV is quick and glib~~
Mother anchors herself in old stories and in her sense
of her race. But boy is less certain of his position.
Other people in the story see them as displaced:

THEME: VISION OR ARGUMENT?

```
"reporters would come over and ask me questions about
how it felt to be an Indian without a country." (Boy
misses point of the question)
Possible title:
      Thomas King's Mythology
      Do We Share the Land?
      Coyote Went Fishing
      Under the Stars
```

When you read the essay, you'll notice that for a title the author settled on the last of her four tentative titles. The first title, "Thomas King's Mythology," is too broad since the essay is not on all of King's work but on only one story. The second tentative title, "Do We Share the Land?" is acceptable, but it sounds a bit clumsy, so the choice came down to the last two titles or to some entirely new title that the writer might discover during the process of revising her drafts. The two final choices are less descriptive than the title of the last example essay, but they capture a sense of the theme within the language of the story itself. They imply rather than state the thesis. They aim to intrigue the reader. Sometimes titles of this type are a powerful choice.

Notice also that some points mentioned in the preliminary notes—for instance, the reference to Americans being rude or dressing badly—are omitted from the essay. The reference to a well-known Canadian novel which also deals with Coyote was not developed (nor did the student research other stories by King which also deal with Coyote) because the student recognized that it would make the essay too long if she were to move away from her primary source. (If the assignment were to write a longer essay, these references could be pursued to expand the evidence for the thesis.) And some points scarcely mentioned in the outline are emphasized in the essay. In drafting and revising the essay, the writer found that certain things weren't relevant to her point, and so she dropped them and found that others required considerable amplification.

```
Gabrielle Kirstley
English 212-03
Prof. Robert Hartborn
January 14, 2003


                     Under the Stars
The choice of Salt Lake City as the destination for
the narrator's sister's escape from her reservation
life is a key to the theme of Thomas King's
"Borders." This city is the centre of Mormon life in
the United States. As the Mother points out, there
is also a temple in Cardston, Alberta, "if you like
those kinds of thing" (363). Christian churches can
be found in either country; she doesn't value them.
First Nations' myth and the legends of Coyote form
the basis of the mother's belief system.
```

Coyote was a great chief of the ancient days
before people came to the earth and animals lived
alone. He had many powers, but he was unlike the
Christian God. King has said in the introduction to
his anthology of Native fiction, <u>All My Relations</u>,
that the First Nations' philosophy depends on strong
family ties, ties that extend beyond the nuclear family to include the "extended relationship we share
with all human beings." These relationships go
further:

> the web of kinship extending to the animals,
> to the birds, to the fish, to the plants, to
> all the animate and inanimate forms that can
> be seen or imagined. More than that, "all my
> relations" is an encouragement for us to
> accept the responsibilities we have within
> this universal family [. . .]. (ix)

The mother wants her son to learn about these legends
so she tells them to him "slow, repeating parts as
she went, as if she expected me to remember each one"
(366). The setting is most important here. The
mother tells these stories at night, under the stars,
in the space between Canada and the United States, in
a space without a European nationality. She remembers when her grandmother used to take her "and my
sisters out on the prairies and tell us stories about
all the stars" (366).

The boy is only partly interested in her stories.
He hopes the duty free store manager, Mel, will bring
him a hamburger. He is always interested in details
of modern life--hamburgers, pop, guns, TV, a "fancy
car" (366). This is realistic for a boy of "twelve
maybe thirteen" (359), but it also shows King's
concern that young native people will forget their
heritage. But King's point is subtler. The boy's
lack of real interest does not mean he rejects the
mother's values. He has simply not yet learned
enough about his own myths and values. He does not
yet have the "pride" his mother has (364).

The setting forces the issue of citizenship. From
the point of view of the guards, they must claim
nationality. The first guard can't even understand
the mother's reply because he is so used to hearing a
response that fits with his sense of nation and myth:

"Citizenship?"

"Blackfoot," my mother told him.

"Ma'am?"

"Blackfoot," my mother repeated.

"Canadian?"

"Blackfoot." (361)

The guards can't understand the mother's refusal to name a country and "it didn't take them long to lose their sense of humour" (362). Even though they remain outwardly polite, it is clear that the mother's refusal to obey the rules of the dominant North American culture has annoyed the guards: "The one guard stopped smiling altogether" (362). They make the family wait a long time. They send a woman to speak to the mother (perhaps trying to be non-threatening), but this American woman has a gun, too.

The problem is all about legalities and technical-ities. "Everyone who crosses our border has to declare their citizenship. Even Americans. It helps us keep track [. . .]" (362). "It's a legal techni-cality, that's all" (362). "But you have to be American or Canadian" (364). But the mother isn't being difficult. She feels more connection to Canada than the USA, but she truly believes herself to be Blackfoot first and foremost. This sense of identity stems from her sense of aboriginal mythology, her connection to the land. In the non-native system, connections are political and geographical and rules must be obeyed. In the mother's system time and space are more fluid and connections are to family.

King repeatedly points out that they are in no-man's land. The shopkeeper has "a name tag with a tiny American flag on one side and a tiny Canadian flag on the other" (365) and he inhabits the world between. But Mel can return to whichever side of the border he lives in at the end of his day. That is because he plays by the rules. The guards, Mel, and the TV reporters assume that the family has no place, that they are without a country. But the important comment King makes is that these two First Nations people actually "own" both countries and can inhabit either because they are stewards of the land, itself. The boy doesn't quite realize this fact, but his mother does. And King wants the readers to understand, too. Far from having no country, the mother rejects systems that name countries. Since the father is an American citizen, the children can move to either country and every person does actually have a legal citizenship. But the refusal of the mother to name herself as Canadian suggests to those ignorant of her belief system that she has no home. The reporters ask the boy "how it felt to be an Indian without a country" (366). He misunderstands their question because he knows he has a home "on the reserve" (366). The mother, however, knows that a home on a reserve in Canada or the USA is still a kind of prison between the borders of the native and non-native world, and she also knows that reserves are a product of the value system of the European cultures. Even the word Indian is a European misunderstanding of who these people are. That is why she is so anxious that her son understand his own legends and find his own place. It is in knowing his own religion that the boy will understand his place.

Time seems to move slowly for the family. The story also moves back and forth in time. A strict sense of time is part of the North American way of life. The mother moves in a slower time, connected to the rhythms of the stars. She knows that the same sky is over Canada and the USA and that the legendary sisters and grandmother moon shine down on all people. She has a kind of peace despite the inconvenience of sleeping in the car and being kept a prisoner. This is the peace which King wants the boy and the reader to understand. It is a peace that comes from pride in her beliefs even if those beliefs are not respected by the dominant culture.

The sister may move to Salt Lake City, which is home to Mormon Christians, and there may also be a temple in Cardston, but for the mother in Thomas King's "Borders" a deeper truth exists outside, "sitting on her blanket" (366). It is the truth in the land and it exists even when the land rolls "over a hill" (367) and the flagpoles disappear.

List of Works Cited

King, Thomas. "Borders." Rpt. in Sylvan Barnet, Reid
    Gilbert, and William E. Cain. A Short Guide to
    Writing about Literature. 2nd Canadian ed. Don Mills,
    ON: Pearson, 2004. 359–367.

---. All My Relations: An Anthology of Contemporary
    Canadian Native Fiction. Toronto: McClelland, 1990.

Suggestions for Further Reading

E. M. Forster's *Aspects of the Novel* (1927) remains an engaging introduction to the art of prose fiction, by an accomplished practitioner. Other highly readable books by story writers and novelists include: Flannery O'Connor, *Mystery and Manners* (1969); William Gass, *Fiction and the Figures of Life* (1971); Eudora Welty, *The Eye of the Story* (1977).

For academic studies, see also Robert Scholes and Robert Kellogg, *The Nature of Narrative* (1966), on oral as well as written fiction; Robert Liddell, *Robert Liddell on the Novel* (1969), a volume combining two earlier books by Liddell, *A Treatise on the Novel* and *Some Principles of Fiction*; Norman Friedman, *Form and Meaning in Fiction* (1975); Seymour Chatman, *Story and Discourse* (1978); Wayne C. Booth, *The Rhetoric of Fiction*, 2nd ed. (1983); Gerald Prince, *Narratology* (1982).

For essays defining the short story and sketching its history see Susan Lohafer, and Jo Ellyn Clarey, eds., *Short Story Theory at a Crossroads* (1989). Also helpful is Valerie Shaw, *The Short Story: A Critical Introduction* (1983).

Among journals devoted to narrative are: *Journal of Narrative Technique, Modern Fiction Studies; Novel: A Forum; Studies in Short Fiction;* and *Journal of Canadian Fiction.* Although they publish articles on all genres, the journals, *Canadian Literature* and *SCL (Studies in Canadian Literature/Études en littérature canadienne)* offer frequent essays on fiction.

A study of how writers explore voice, character, and such aspects, from a Canadian writer's point of view, is Jack Hodgins' *A Passion for Narrative* (1993).

Useful studies of Canadian fiction from a feminist perspective include Elizabeth Abel, *The Voyage In: Fiction of Female Development* (1983); Rachel Blau DuPlessis, *Writing Beyond the Ending: Narrative Strategies of Twentieth Century Women Writers* (1985); and *A Mazing Space: Writing Canadian/Women Writing* (1986).

For contemporary theoretical approaches, see Linda Hutcheon, *The Canadian Postmodern* (1988); James Phelan, and Peter J. Rabinowitz, eds., *Understanding Narrative* (1994); Frank Davey, *Reading Canadian Reading* (1988); or Lorna Irvine, *Subversion* (1986).

For post-colonial readings, see Smaro Kamboureli, ed., *Making a Difference: Canadian Multicultural Literature* (1996); or Victor J. Ramraj, ed., *Concert of Voices: An Anthology of World Writing in English* (1995).

✓ A Checklist: Getting Ideas for Writing about Fiction

Here are some questions that may help to stimulate ideas about stories. Not every question is, of course, relevant to every story, but if after reading a story and thinking about it, you then run your eye over these pages, you will probably find some questions that will help you to think further about the story—in short, that will help you to get ideas.

It's best to do your thinking with a pen or pencil in hand. If some of the following questions seem to you to be especially relevant to the story you will be writing about, jot down—freely, without worrying about spelling—your initial responses, interrupting your writing only to glance again at the story when you feel the need to check the evidence.

Title

✓ Is the title informative? What does it mean or suggest? Did the meaning seem to change after you read the story? Does the title help you to formulate a theme?

✓ If you had written the story, what title would you use?

Plot

✓ Does the plot grow out of the characters, or does it depend on chance or coincidence? Did something at first strike you as irrelevant that later you perceived as relevant? Do some parts continue to strike you as irrelevant?

✓ Does surprise play an important role, or does foreshadowing? If surprise is very important, can the story be read a second time with any interest? If so, what gives it this further interest?

✓ What conflicts does the story include? Conflicts of one character against another? Of one character against the setting, or against society? Conflicts within a single character?

✓ Are the conflicts resolved? If so, how?

✓ Are certain episodes narrated out of chronological order? If so, were you puzzled? Annoyed? On reflection, does the arrangement of episodes seem effective? Why or why not? Are certain situations repeated? If so, what do you make out of the repetitions?

✓ List the major structural units of the story. In a sentence or two summarize each unit that you have listed.

✓ In a sentence summarize the conclusion or resolution. Do you find it satisfactory? Why or why not?

Character

✓ List the traits of the main characters.

✓ Which character chiefly engages your interest? Why?

✓ What purposes do minor characters serve? Do you find some who by their similarities and differences help to define each other or help to define the major character? How else is a particular character defined— by his or her words, actions (including thoughts and emotions), dress, setting, narrative point of view? Do certain characters act differently in the same, or in a similar, situation?

✓ How does the author reveal character? By explicit authorial (editorial) comment, for instance, or by revelation through dialogue? Through depicted action? Through the actions of other characters? How are the author's methods especially suited to the whole of the story?

✓ Is the behaviour plausible—that is, are the characters well motivated?

✓ If a character changes, why and how does he or she change? (You may want to jot down each event that influences a change.) Or did you change your attitude toward a character not because the character changes but because you came to know the character better?

✓ Are the characters round or flat? Are they complex, or, on the other hand, highly typical (for instance, one-dimensional representatives of a social class or age)? Are you chiefly interested in a character's psychology, or does the character strike you as standing for something, such as honesty or the arrogance of power?

✓ How has the author caused you to sympathize with certain characters?

✓ How does your response—your sympathy or lack of sympathy—contribute to your judgment of the conflict?

Point of View

✓ Who tells the story? How much does the narrator know? Does the narrator strike you as reliable? What effect is gained by using this narrator?

✓ How does the point of view help shape the theme?

✓ Does the narrator's language help you to construct a picture of the narrator's character, class, attitude, strengths, and limitations? (Jot down some evidence, such as colloquial or—on the other hand—formal expressions, ironic comments, figures of speech.) How far can you trust the narrator? Why?

Setting

✓ Do you have a strong sense of the time and place? How and at what points in the story has the author conveyed this sense? If you do not strongly feel the setting, do you think the author should have made it more evident?

✓ What is the relation of the setting to the plot and the characters? (For instance, do houses or rooms or their furnishings say something about their residents? Is the landscape important?) Would anything be lost if the descriptions of the setting were deleted from the story or if the setting were changed?

Symbolism

✓ Do certain characters seem to you to stand for something in addition to themselves? Does the setting have an extra dimension?

✓ Do certain actions in the story—for instance entering a forest at night, or shutting a door, or turning off a light—seem symbolic? If so, symbolic of what?

✓ If you do believe that the story has symbolic elements, do you think they are adequately integrated within the story, or do they strike you as being too obviously stuck in?

Style

✓ How would you characterize the style? Simple? Understated? Figurative? Or what?

✓ How has the point of view shaped or determined the style?

✓ Do you think that the style is consistent? If it isn't—for instance, if there are shifts from simple sentences to highly complex ones—what do you make of the shifts?

Theme

✓ Do certain passages—the title, some of the dialogue, or some of the description, the names of certain characters—seem to you to point especially toward the theme? Do you find certain repetitions of words or pairs of incidents highly suggestive and helpful in directing your thoughts toward stating a theme? Flannery O'Connor, in *Mystery and Manners,* says, "In good fiction, certain of the details will tend to accumulate meaning from the action of the story itself, and when that happens, they become symbolic in the way they work." Does this story work that way?

✓ Is the meaning of the story embodied in the whole story, or does it seem stuck in, for example in certain passages of editorializing?

✓ Suppose someone asked you to state the point—the theme—of the story. Could you? Is there only one theme, or a number of (related) themes? Would you say that the theme of a particular story reinforces values you hold, or does it to some degree challenge them? (It is sometimes said that the best writers are subversive, forcing readers to see something that they do not want to see.)

11

Writing about Drama

Learning Objectives

When you've read this chapter, you should be able to

➢ respond to a play as drama, or theatre, or as both;

➢ differentiate tragedy and comedy;

➢ understand conventional terms used to analyze tragedy, comedy, and tragicomedy;

➢ write about theme, plot, characterization, motivation, costume, gesture, and setting in drama; and

➢ recognize some theatrical conventions.

The essays you write about plays will be similar in many respects to analytic essays about fiction. You may, however, be asked to treat performance aspects of the play as well as textual ones, if your class is reading drama as text-in-performance, as well as reading it as literature. (Contemporary critics differentiate *drama*, the literary text, from *theatre*, the play in performance.) Unless you are writing a review, however, you won't try to write about all aspects of the play; you'll choose some significant topic. For instance, if you are writing about Judith Thompson's *Lion in the Streets*, you might contrast the aspirations of Sue with those of Karen, or you might compare the sexual illusions of the mistress, Lily, with those of the challenged woman, Scarlett, or the victim, Sherry. Or you might examine the symbolism, perhaps limiting your essay to the "Lion" itself, but perhaps extending it to include other symbols, such as the telephone, the wheelchair, or the stick Isobel carries throughout the play. Or you might consider the religious symbolism. Similarly, if you are writing an analysis, you might decide to study the construction of one scene of a play, or even the construction of the entire play. In Thompson's play, for example, you might explore the way the numerous short scenes form recurring patterns that lead to the final resolution.

The list of questions at the end of the chapter may help you find a topic for the particular play you choose.

A SAMPLE ESSAY

The following student essay discusses *Lion in the Streets*. While in a second-year course, Christopher Walker examined how Thompson explores evil by the use of language and a kind of MAGIC REALISM, using illustrations from the central play and also from Thompson's earlier play, *White Biting Dog*. He mentions various characters, but, since his concern is with the use of language and states of consciousness, he does not (for instance) examine any of the characters in detail. An essay might well be devoted to examining (for example) Thompson's assertion that "I don't want to write industrial plays that play to psychology classes," but Walker is careful not to allow his essay to become a character study or simply a discussion of states of mind: Instead, he turns the evidence to illustrate how Thompson captures an audience and makes it consider the evil in society.

Preliminary Notes

After deciding to write on evil in the play, with an eye toward seeing how the author makes her spectators look at the issue, Walker reread *Lion in the Streets,* jotted down some notes, and then typed them. On rereading the typed notes, he added a few observations in handwriting.

```
1. begins by making the audience confront its own
   knowledge of evil in society
   a. does this in both plays
2. Thompson captures the audience
   a. uses very poetic language
   b. uses high speed action--nothing seems quite real
   c. moves audience into a dream-world--Magic Realism
3. language is the key--attacks the mind of the auditor
   a. language shows characters' need to escape evil and
      get "grace"
4. language is very musical
   a. central Canadian dialect; very naturalistic speech
   b. has effect of drawing in audience--hypnotizes
      listeners
   c. What is it about this musical       - good question to ask
      language that hooks the audience?
5. Collective unconscious
   a. dream-like state of both plays seems to be action
      from the coll. uncon.
6. What is revealed when we dream with Thompson?
   a. her/our inner child
   b. plays show contrast--innocence of inner child and
      evil of adult society
```

7. Real problem in society is that we *— deny capacity for evil*
   deny this contrast
   a. examples from the plays of people who can be mean
      to others
8. Solution is for everyone to admit their potential
   evil, find their child's good side
   a. Cape and his mother face death;
      may learn to love *even her own death* ⟍
   b. Isobel overcomes hatred of her killer and forgives
      --achieves grace
   Forgives audience.
9. Thompson shows that language, dreams can lead
   to grace

Here's the essay written from these notes:

Title is focused; it
announces topic
and thesis.

A Reality in Dreams:

Thompson's Moral Quest

In an interview with Eleanor Wachtel in
Brick, Judith Thompson reveals the purpose of
her plays' focus on evil:

Opening
paragraph closes
in on thesis.

Well, because it's theatrical, it's
what's true, and it's like the
purpose the church used to serve:
for an hour a week we would confront
our spirits [. . .]. In the theatre
I think what we must do is confront
the truth, confront the emotional
truth of our lives, which is mixed
in the swamp of minutiae, everyday
minutiae. (37)

Organization:
starts with first
element of thesis.

Such a mix occurs in Thompson's White
Biting Dog and Lion in the Streets. Thompson
captures the audience with poetic dialogue and
erratic action that invades the unconscious.
Once inside the world she creates, the
theatregoer cannot escape her moral attack on
the nature of society, and her belief that

grace, the freedom of the spirit, is what must be achieved to rid ourselves of evil.

Highly poetic language is what captures the unconscious of the spectators. Kathy Chung, in a review of <u>Lion in the Streets</u>, describes Thompson's dialogue as a place where "her characters seem to lose the division between a private and public self" (132). Chung pinpoints Thompson's ability to show a character's private need to achieve grace and the emotions and thoughts that go along with that need. This need for grace is at the centre of the conflict in a scene in <u>Lion in the Streets</u> when Christine, a reporter, interviews Scarlett, a cerebral palsy patient, and exploits her. Scarlett condemns Christine; Christine physically attacks her and says, "The way you, you, you talked to me like that. Like, like, like you belong. In the world. As if you belong. Where did you get that feeling? I want it. I need it" (<u>Lion</u> 49).

Brief but effective quotations.

Thompson's language is also very musical. The central Canadian dialect, combined with an acute sense of the rhythms of language creates hypnotic speech in her plays. A disclaimer at the beginning of <u>White Biting Dog</u> illustrates Thompson's commitment to this kind of dialogue: "Because of the extreme and deliberate musicality of this play, any attempts to go against the textual rhythms [. . .] are disastrous" (ii). Interviews reveal the music in Thompson's own speech: "It's acknowledging that, yes, it's a jungle out there, there's a war, but we have our wonderful spirits and great strength, and yes, we have the Force [. . .]" (qtd. in Wachtel 41). So, what is it about the exposure of the

Reduces focus to musical language.

Rhetorical question.

private self in a musical language that seizes the person experiencing Judith Thompson?

"We do share a collective unconscious and we have as much in common with [. . .] the so-called deranged fellow [. . .] as you and I have with each other," Thompson tells Wachtel (40). She captures this collective unconscious and burdens it with moral questions in the dream states of her plays. The world of <u>White Biting Dog</u> for example, consists of such nightmarish things as Glidden covering his stomach in peat moss, the dead dogs being kept in the deep-freeze for years, a talking dog, and action that is in constant, incongruous flux. <u>Lion in the Streets</u> is even more dream-based. Rodney, a gay businessman, acts out an imagined confrontation with his boyhood lover; he kills this man--and the audience witnesses it--but it is just a daydream. Where <u>White Biting Dog</u> is dream-like in dialogue and

Evidence from both plays supports thesis.

atmosphere, <u>Lion in the Streets</u> makes the characters' dreams part of the play's reality, reality and dream often get blurred in our own dreams, and this is how Thompson taps into the collective unconscious. Just as a powerful dream can weigh on our minds for days, so do these plays. The difference is that Thompson's plays also have direct access to the conscious mind and thus they are more immediate and permanent than are dreams. She writes in a kind of magic realism.

Moves to next thesis element.

Central to the conflicts in these two plays is the inner-child. "Children," says Thompson, "are a huge part of ourselves They're the beautiful, pure god in us [. . .] we try to beat it down and make it cower [. . .] [but] it takes over in a terrible way, too--the terrible tyrant it can be" (qtd. in Wachtel 40).

While Thompson recognizes how tyrannical the
inner-child can be, she also says of her
characters in <u>Lion in the Streets</u>: "All of
them have something they find precious and
beautiful" (qtd. in Wachtel 40). This ability
to see the beauty in things contrasts with the
tyrannical and selfish actions that dominate
Thompson's work. The characters who are able
to see the beauty, and are thus made better,
purer, provide a target for the tyranny and
thus show its horrible nature. Pony, in <u>White
Biting Dog</u>, embodies this wondrous purity: "I
was lying on my fold-out in my furnished
bachelor on Albany and I got this UNRESISTIBLE
urge to get up and go for a walk. And when
urges like that come along, I listen to them
so I did. I just walked where my feet took
me" (<u>White</u> 11). This kind of freedom of self
is part of being a child. Pony provides Cape,
a character who embodies tyranny, with a means
to expose his evil; he, in effect, uses up her
goodness to save his own soul.

    This evil, found in Cape, is found also
in a great many of Thompson's characters.
There is something that makes this evil
possible, something that Thompson calls "a
pathological state of denial" in which we, "as
a society, as a culture," are living: "Just
having to walk past homeless people, having
to--just deny, deny, deny" (qtd. in Wachtel
38). Thompson's characters exhibit the
ability to deny compassion to others who are
in pain, as do most people in the real world.
It is this denial that allows Christine to
exploit Scarlett's fantasy on the grounds that
"I have a job, Scarlett, I have a child to
support [. . .]" (<u>Lion</u> 48). The characters

The essayist is thinking and commenting, not merely summarizing the plot.

Extends point to include other plays.

are so trapped in states of denial that they become pathological. Cape is so trapped that he cannot love; he cannot have any kind of a genuine mutual relationship with anyone. Thompson describes the kind of person Cape represents: "So these are people I find Horrifying because they can distance themselves from a person and you think they're laughing with you but actually they're watching you" (qtd. in Tomc 20).

Thompson condemns this tyranny and denial and offers a solution in what she calls "grace." In White Biting Dog grace is a starting point on a path towards resolution. Cape and his mother face the deaths of people who love them and, in their pain and sorrow, may themselves begin to find the ability to love.

Last part of thesis is introduced.

In Lion in the Streets, grace is the final resolution. When Isobel tells her murderer that she loves him, she receives grace, and, in turn, sends a message to the audience to seek such peace: "I take my life. I want you all to take your life. I want you all to have your life" (63). She is, in fact, telling people to escape and control their fears, their "lions." Thompson describes to Wachtel what this scene with Isobel means: "It's very hopeful [. . .]. It's the triumph of the spirit" (40). It is the freedom of the spirit.

Useful, thoughtful summary of thesis.

Judith Thompson has the ability to make a person come instantly into touch with the evil and the possible virtues of people. She sinks these ideas into the unconscious and the conscious mind through a dream-like atmosphere and the use of a poetic, mesmerizing language that is at once confusing and unavoidable. It

is in reaching the collective unconscious that
her plays become so powerful. The inner-
child, it would seem, is the rendezvous point
of good and evil; its evil must be controlled
and its purity set free. The progression from
White Biting Dog to Lion in the Streets shows

Strong ending looks to a positive interpretation.

Thompson's growing ability to control
atmosphere and language and to lead the
audience to the idea of grace. The confusion
within her plays gives way to an exciting and
positive experience.

Works Cited

Documentation.

Chung, Kathy. "Emotions and Facts." Canadian
    Literature 141 (1994): 132-34.
Tomc, Sandra. "Revisions of Probability: An
    Interview with Judith Thompson."
    Canadian Theatre Review 59 (1989): 18-23.
Thompson, Judith. White Biting Dog. Toronto:
    Playwrights Canada, 1984.
---. Lion in the Streets. Toronto: Coach
    House, 1992.
Wachtel, Eleanor. "An Interview with Judith
    Thompson." Brick 41 (1991): 37-41.

TYPES OF PLAYS

Most of the world's great plays written before the twentieth century may be
regarded as one of two kinds: TRAGEDY or COMEDY. Roughly speaking, tragedy
dramatizes the conflict between the vitality of the single life and the laws or
limits of life. The TRAGIC HERO reaches a height, going beyond the experience
of others but at the cost of his or her life. Comedy dramatizes the vitality of
the laws of social life. In comedy, the good life is seen to reside in the shed-
ding of an individualism that isolates, in favour of a union with a genial and
enlightened society. These points must be amplified a bit before we go on to
the point that, of course, any important play does much more than can be put
into such crude formulas.

Tragedy

Tragic heroes usually go beyond the standards to which reasonable people
adhere; they do some fearful deed that ultimately destroys them. This deed

is often said to be an act of **HUBRIS**, a Greek word meaning something like "overweening pride." It may involve, for instance, violating a taboo, such as that against incest, or taking life. But if the hubristic act ultimately destroys the man or woman who performs it, it also shows that person (paradoxically) to be in some way more fully a living being—whether by heroic action or by capacity for enduring suffering—than the other characters in the play. Othello kills Desdemona, Lear gives away his crown and banishes his one loving daughter; but both of these men seem to live more fully than the other characters in the plays. For one thing, they experience a kind of anguish unknown to those who surround them and who outlive them. (If the hero does not die, he or she usually is left in some deathlike state, as is the blind Oedipus in *Oedipus the King*.)

In tragedy, we see humanity pushed by agony and grief to an extreme. This purgation of emotion is called **CATHARSIS** (purgation). After the tragic figure departs the stage, we are left in a world of smaller people. The closing lines of almost any of Shakespeare's tragedies may be used to illustrate the point. *King Lear,* for example, ends thus:

> The oldest hath bore the most: we that are young
> Shall never see so much, nor live so long.

What has just been said may be true of many tragedies, but it certainly is not true of all. You might consider whether the points just made are illustrated in your play. Is the hero guilty of hubris? Does the hero seem a greater person than the others in the play? An essay examining such questions probably requires not only a character sketch but also some comparison with other characters. Tragedy commonly involves irony of two sorts: unconsciously ironic deeds and unconsciously ironic speeches. Ironic deeds have some consequence more or less the reverse of what the doer intends.

Macbeth thinks that by killing Duncan he will gain happiness, but he finds that his deed brings him sleepless nights. Brutus thinks that by killing Caesar he will bring liberty to Rome, but he brings tyranny. In an unconsciously **IRONIC SPEECH**, the speaker's words mean one thing to him or her but something more significant to the audience, as do all of Oedipus' speeches. [1]

When Oedipus speaks of suffering, or taking on the sins of his people, we are aware—as he is not—that his fate is to do precisely that. Sophocles' use of ironic deeds and speeches is so pervasive, especially in *Oedipus the King*, that **SOPHOCLEAN IRONY** has become a critical term.

In the *Poetics*, Aristotle named the moment when the deed backfires or has a reverse effect (such as Macbeth's ultimately tragic effort to gain happiness), as a **PERIPETEIA** or a **REVERSAL**.

---

[1] **DRAMATIC IRONY** (ironic deeds or happenings, and unconsciously ironic speeches) must be distinguished from **VERBAL IRONY**, which is produced when the speaker is conscious that his or her words mean something different from what they say. In *Macbeth*, Lennox says: "The gracious Duncan / Was pitied of Macbeth. Marry, he was dead! / And the right valiant Banquo walked too late. / [. . .] / Men must not walk too late." He *says* nothing about Macbeth having killed Duncan and Banquo, but he *means* that Macbeth has killed them.

Aristotle's *Poetics*, by the way, has influenced all drama criticism in the West and most of the terms we use about tragedy come from this book. Two cautions are needed, however: First, Aristotle did not set out to "define" theatre, but to record what was happening in the Greek theatre of his day and, second, contemporary criticism of Aristotle's opinions in the *Poetics* and elsewhere is opening up the accepted definitions of theatre to new interpretations.

When a character comes to perceive what has happened (Macbeth: "I have lived long enough: my way of life / Is fall'n into the sere, the yellow leaf"), he experiences what Aristotle termed an ANAGNORISIS, or **RECOGNITION**. Strictly speaking, for Aristotle, the recognition was a matter of literal identification: for example, that Oedipus was the son of a man he killed. In Macbeth, the recognition in this sense is that Macduff, "from his mother's womb / Untimely ripped," is the man who fits the prophecy that Macbeth can be conquered only by someone not "of woman born."

In his analysis of drama, Aristotle says that the tragic HERO comes to grief through his HAMARTIA, a term sometimes translated as **TRAGIC FLAW** but perhaps better translated as TRAGIC ERROR. Thus, it is a great error for Othello to trust Iago and to strangle Desdemona, for Lear to give away his kingdom, and for Macbeth to decide to help fulfil the prophecies. If we hold to the translation "flaw," we begin to hunt for a fault in their characters; and we say, for instance, that Othello is gullible, Lear self-indulgent, or Macbeth ambitious. In doing this, we may overlook their grandeur or other nuances of character that help to form their doom. Perhaps that is one reason why classic tragedy is less often written today and often seems too uncomplicated in its treatment of character. Another may be that grand tragedy depends upon absolutes (good and evil; greed and selflessness) and many people today do not accept such absolutes, nor that a character is unfailingly drawn to one side of such a binary.

Writing about Tragedy

When writing about tragedy, probably the commonest essay topic is on the tragic hero. Too often the hero is judged mechanically: He or she must be noble, must have a flaw, must do a fearful deed, must recognize the flaw, must die. The previous paragraph cautions you to look beyond such a formula. An essay that seeks to determine whether a character is a tragic character ought at its outset to make clear its conception of tragedy and the degree of rigidity, or flexibility, with which it will interpret some or all of its categories. For example, it may indicate that although nobility is a *sine qua non*, nobility is not equivalent to high rank. Any figure with certain mental or spiritual characteristics may, in such a view, be an acceptable TRAGIC HERO.

An essay closely related to the sort we have been talking about measures a character by some well-known theory of tragedy. For example, one can measure Sgt. Walsh, in Sharon Pollock's *Walsh*, against Aristotle's remarks on tragedy. The organization of such an essay is usually not a problem: Isolate the relevant aspects of the theoretical statement, and then examine the character to see if, point by point, he illustrates them. But remember that even if Walsh fulfils Aristotle's idea of a tragic figure, you need not accept him as tragic; conversely, if he does not fulfil Aristotle's idea, you need not deny him tragic status. Aristotle may be wrong.

Comedy

Although a comedy ought to be amusing, the plays that are called comedies are not just collections of jokes. Rather, they are works that are entertaining throughout and that end happily, usually by returning the world of the play to the set of accepted norms that govern the society of the spectators. In this way, comedy serves to reiterate the values of the society even though it begins by apparently toppling them.

At the beginning of a comedy we find banished dukes, unhappy lovers, crabby parents, jealous husbands, and harsh laws; but at the end we usually have a unified and genial society, often symbolized by a dance or marriage feast to which everyone, or almost everyone, is invited. Early in *A Midsummer Night's Dream,* for instance, we meet quarrelling young lovers and a father who demands that his daughter either marry a man she does not love or enter a convent. Such is the Athenian law. At the end of the play the lovers are properly matched, and the social classes are reinstated to everyone's satisfaction.

Speaking broadly, most comedies fall into one of two classes: SATIRIC COMEDY and ROMANTIC COMEDY. In satiric comedy the emphasis is on the obstructionists—the irate fathers, hard-headed businessmen, and other members of the Establishment who at the beginning of the play seem to hold all the cards, preventing joy from reigning. They are held up to ridicule because they are repressive monomaniacs enslaved to themselves, acting mechanistically instead of responding to the ups and downs of life. The outwitting of these obstructionists, usually by the younger generation, often provides the resolution of the plot. Jonson, Molière, and Shaw are in this tradition; their comedy, according to an ancient Roman formula, "chastens morals with ridicule"; that is, it reforms folly or vice by laughing at it. In romantic comedy (one thinks of Shakespeare's *Midsummer Night's Dream, As You Like It,* and *Twelfth Night*) the emphasis is on a pair or pairs of delightful people who engage our sympathies as they run their obstacle race to the altar. Obstructionists are found here too, but the emphasis is on festivity.

Writing about Comedy

Essays on comedy often examine the nature of the humour. Why is an irate father, in this context, funny? Or why is a young lover, again in this context, funny? Commonly, one will find that at least some of the humour is in the disproportionate nature of their activities (they get terribly excited) and in their inflexibility. The following is a skeleton of a possible essay on why Jaques in *As You Like It* is amusing:

> Jaques is insistently melancholy. In the Eden-like Forest of Arden, he sees only the dark side of things.

> His monomania, however, is harmless to himself and to others; because it causes us no pain, it may entertain us.

Indeed, we begin to look forward to his melancholy speeches. We delight in hearing him fulfill our expectations by wittily finding gloom where others find mirth.

We are delighted, too, to learn that this chastiser of others has in fact been guilty of the sort of behavior he chastises.

At the end of the play, when four couples are wed, the inflexible Jaques insists on standing apart from the general rejoicing.

Such might be the gist of an essay. It needs to be supported with details, and it can be enriched, for example, by a comparison between Jaques's sort of jesting and Touchstone's; but it is at least a promising draft of an outline.

In writing about comedy, you may be concerned with the function of one scene or character, but whatever your topic, you may find it helpful to begin by trying to decide whether the play is primarily romantic or primarily satiric (or something else). One way of getting at this is to ask yourself to what degree you sympathize with the characters. Do you laugh *with* them, sympathetically, or do you laugh *at* them, regarding them as at least somewhat contemptible?

Tragicomedy

The term **TRAGICOMEDY** has been used to denote (1) plays that seem tragic until the happy ending, (2) plays that combine tragic and comic scenes, and (3) plays that combine the anguish of tragedy with the improbable situations and unheroic characters and funny dialogue of comedy. This last sort of TRAGICOMEDY (also called BLACK COMEDY) has attracted most of the best dramatists of our time—for example, Beckett, Pinter, and Ionesco. They are the dramatists of the ABSURD in two senses: the irrational and the ridiculous. These writers differ from one another and from play to play, but they all are preoccupied with the loneliness of people in a world without the certainties afforded by God or by optimistic rationalism. This loneliness is heightened by a sense of impotence derived partly from an awareness of our inability to communicate in a society that has made language meaningless, and partly from an awareness of the precariousness of our existence.

The result of developments in thought by people such as Darwin, Marx, and Freud seems to be that a "tragic sense" in the twentieth century commonly meant a despairing or deeply uncertain view, something very different from what it meant in Greece and in Elizabethan England. This uncertainty is not merely about the cosmos or even about character or identity. In 1888, in the preface to *Miss Julie*, Strindberg called attention to the new sense of the instability of character:

> I have made the people in my play fairly "characterless." The middle-class conception of a fixed character was transferred to the stage, where the middle class has always ruled. A character there came to mean an actor who was always one and the same, always drunk, always comic or always melancholy, and who needed to be characterized only by some physical defect such as a club foot, a wooden leg, or a red nose, or by the repetition of some [. . .] phrase [. . .]. Since the persons in my play are

modern characters, living in a transitional era more hurried and hysterical than the previous one at least, I have depicted them as more unstable, as torn and divided, a mixture of the old and the new.

Along with a sense of characterlessness, the drama (and the underground film and novel) developed a sense of plotlessness or, at least, rejected the fundamental untruthfulness of the traditional plot that moved by cause and effect. Ionesco, for example, has said that a play should be able to stop at any point; it ends only because—as in life—the audience at last has to go home to bed. Moreover, Ionesco has allowed directors to make heavy cuts, and he has suggested that endings other than those he wrote are possibilities. Many **POSTMODERN** plays allow provisional interpretations or alternate endings.

The "tragic sense" of the twentieth century seems to be in flux again as we move into a new century. Postmodern plays (and other texts) mix comedy and tragedy even more casually than is done in TRAGICOMEDY, but not always with the same Modernist despair. Comedies are often sociological statements that highlight conditions some might call tragic; tragedies present serious dilemmas but often, today, poke fun at our reaction to what seems tragic. A kind of emptiness, often accompanied by violence, empties out many plays of any direct statement you could call either tragic or comic.

Every play is different from every other play; each is a unique and detailed statement, and the foregoing paragraphs give only the broadest outlines. The analyst's job is to try to study the differences, as well as the similarities, in an effort (in Henry James's words) "to appreciate, to appropriate, to take intellectual possession, to establish in fine a relation with the criticized thing and make it one's own."

ASPECTS OF DRAMA

Theme

If we have perceived the work properly, we ought to be able to formulate its THEME, its underlying idea, its moral attitudes, its view of life. Some critics, it is true, have argued that the concept of theme is meaningless. They hold that *Macbeth*, for example, gives us only an extremely detailed history of one imaginary man. In this view, *Macbeth* says nothing to you or me; it only says what happened to some imaginary man. Even *Julius Caesar* says nothing about the historical Julius Caesar or about the nature of Roman politics. On this we can agree; no one would offer Shakespeare's play as evidence of what the historical Caesar said or did. But surely the view that the concept of theme is meaningless and that a work tells us only about imaginary creatures is a desperate one. We *can* say that we see in *Julius Caesar* the fall of power or (if we are thinking of Brutus) the vulnerability of idealism.

We must, however, avoid the danger of equating the play with the theme that we sense underlies it. If, for example, we say that *Rhinoceros* is "an attack on collective hysteria and the epidemics that lurk beneath the surface of reason" (as Ionesco himself said of his play), we do not believe that our statement of the theme is the equivalent of the play itself. We recognize that the play presents the theme with such detail that our statement is only a wedge to help us enter into the play, so that we may more fully appropriate it. And we realize that more than one theme may be found in most plays. And we realize that our interpretation of theme (as well as the author's) is subject to those factors that have moulded us within a particular society and that allow us to see in certain ways.

Some critics (influenced by Aristotle's statement that a drama is an imitation of an action) use *action* in a sense equivalent to theme. In this sense, the action is the underlying happening—the inner happening. So, for example, the action illuminates "the enlightenment of someone" or "the coming of unhappiness" or "the finding of the self by self-surrender." One might say that the theme of *Macbeth,* for example, is embodied in some words that Macbeth himself utters: "Blood will have blood." Of course, this is not to say that these words and no other words embody the theme or the action. Critics such as Francis Fergusson, who are influenced by Aristotle's *Poetics,* assume that the dramatist conceives of an action and then imitates it or sets it forth by means of first a plot and characters and then by means of language, GESTURE, and perhaps spectacle and music. When the Greek comic dramatist Menander told a friend he had finished his play and now had only to write it, he must have meant that he had the action or the theme firmly in mind and had worked out the plot and the requisite characters. All that remained was to set down the words.

Plot and Meaning

PLOT is variously defined sometimes as equivalent to "story" (in this sense a synopsis of *Romeo and Juliet* has the same plot as *Romeo and Juliet*) but more often, and more usefully, as the dramatist's particular arrangement of the story. In Chapter 10, we introduced the formalist terms for these two different ways of relating the story. In drama, the distinction is particularly important since the arrangement of the story (the *sjuzet*) is often quite out of sequence, quite "theatrically" designed, and the audience must extract the set of events (the *fabula*) from what is performed before it. The spectators may or may not be aware that they are creating this *fabula* in relation to their own ways of knowing who they are and the PERFORMATIVITY by which they construct themselves. This sort of analysis, which is now very common in drama criticism, explores the SPECTATORIAL EXPERIENCE, the interaction between watching and participating, both off-stage as well as on. (An extreme example is the carnival, where, as David Edgar noted in 1988, the spectator need only step off the pavement to become part of the spectacle. The same experience is always true in theatre, though it is less physical in a proscenium auditorium. It is concerned with the roles of subject and object and interrogates the role of the viewer—who owns the GAZE—in creating the object(s) seen on stage.) The question of whether a play is simply an aesthetic experience or always tells a story is currently under discussion among critics who argue in both directions. Speaking of dance, Janet Wolff says that the spectators do not simply enjoy an aesthetic spectacle, for the true experience of art involves the understanding of meaning. Indeed this is not merely a precept to be followed, but necessarily true since perception itself always includes meaning.

—Janet Wolff, *Hermeneutic Philosophy and the Sociology of Art* (London, 1975) 109.

This seems to be very true in drama. Consider, for example, the opening scene of Thompson's *Lion in the Streets*. Isobel begins with important exposition, but she also tells us that what we are viewing is a "pickshur." Her dialect establishes character, but it also tells the audience what to expect. As she says, "You know me very hard." This diction error (she means "you know me very well," of course) not only tells us about her command of English— part of plot and characterization—but warns that the action we are about to see is going to be hard, rough. It is also going to make us "know" her in a way we don't yet. Isobel tells the viewers not to be afraid, which reminds us again that we are watching a play and, at the same time, foreshadows harsh upcoming scenes that might well bother us. Each viewer's personal reaction to children, to new immigrants, to the language, and to the theatre itself— whether one wants to be entertained in a fantasy world or to participate in an intellectual debate that one knows to be an artistic contrivance—conditions how the viewer responds to Isobel's speech. Even the degree of familiarity with theatre convention (like the appearance of a ghost, such as Hamlet's Father, in Act 1) governs how a viewer "reads" Isobel's speech. A play like this, which is **METADRAMATIC**, destroys plot on one hand by referring to itself *as a play,* but on the other hand helps the audience to construct the plot on a deeper level, by including the viewer's own perceptions and sense of identity. It is a good example of how PLOT and MEANING are interwoven.

Handbooks on the drama often suggest that a plot (arrangement of happenings) should have a RISING ACTION, a CLIMAX, and a FALLING ACTION. This sort of plot may be diagrammed as a pyramid: The tension rises through complications or crises to a climax, at which point the climax is the apex, and the tension allegedly slackens as we witness the DÉNOUEMENT (unknotting). (This is Freytag's Pyramid, discussed in Chapter 10.) Many playwrights have used a structure like this. No law, however, demands such a structure, and a hunt for the pyramid usually causes the hunter to overlook all the crises but the middle one. William Butler Yeats once suggestively diagrammed a good plot not as a pyramid but as a line moving diagonally upward, punctuated by several crises. The writer can also use **FLASHBACK**. It has been said that in Beckett's *Waiting for Godot,* "nothing happens, twice." Perhaps it is sufficient to say that a good plot has its moments of *tension* followed by *release,* but that the location of these will vary with the play. They are the product of conflict, but not all conflict produces tension; there is conflict but little tension in a hockey game when the home team is ahead 10–0, two minutes remain on the clock, and the visiting team has four men in the penalty box.

Regardless of how a plot is diagrammed, the EXPOSITION is the part that tells the audience what it has to know about the past, the ANTECEDENT ACTION. The mother in *Sticks and Stones* (part of James Reaney's trilogy, *The Donnellys*) who tells her son that those who wouldn't join a secret society in Ireland in 1844 are still being persecuted in Ontario in 1867 is giving the audience the exposition needed to follow this historical plot. The exposition in Shakespeare's *Tempest* is almost ruthlessly direct: Prospero tells his naïve daughter, "I should inform thee farther," and for about 150 lines he proceeds to tell her why she is on an almost uninhabited island. The Elizabethans (and the Greeks) sometimes tossed out all pretence at dialogue and began with a PROLOGUE, like the one spoken by the Chorus at the opening of *Romeo and Juliet:*

> Two households, both alike in dignity
>   In fair Verona, where we lay our scene,
> From ancient grudge break to new mutiny,
>   Where civil blood makes civil hands unclean.
> From forth the fatal loins of these two foes
>   A pair of star-crossed lovers take their life [. . .].

Sharon Pollock importantly uses a prologue in *Walsh*, as does George F. Walker in *Zastrozzi*, but, today, the exposition is often revealed in small scenes or remarks that extend far into the play.

Exposition can do much more than simply inform the audience about events. It can give us an understanding of the characters who themselves are talking about other characters, it can evoke a MOOD, and it can generate tension. When we summarize the opening act and treat it as "mere exposition," we are probably losing what is, in fact, dramatic in it. The first scene of *Walsh*, for example, does not exist merely to tell the audience certain facts; it rounds out the character of Sgt. Walsh and it prefigures his moral decline.

In fact, exposition usually includes FORESHADOWING of this kind. Details given in the exposition, which we may at first take as mere background, often turn out to be highly relevant to later developments. For instance, in the very short first scene of *Macbeth* the Witches introduce the name of Macbeth, but in such phrases as "fair is foul" and "when the battle's lost and won" they also give glimpses of what will happen. Similarly, during the exposition in the second scene we learn that Macbeth has loyally defeated Cawdor, who betrayed King Duncan, and Macbeth has been given Cawdor's title. Later we will find that, like Cawdor, Macbeth betrays Duncan; that is, in giving us the background about Cawdor, the exposition is also telling us something about what will happen to Macbeth—though we don't realize it when we first see or read the play.

Writing about Plot
In writing about an aspect of plot, you may want to consider one of the following topics:

1. Is the plot improbable? If so, is the play weaker or stronger?
2. Does a scene that might at first glance seem unimportant or even irrelevant serve an important function?
3. If certain actions that could be shown onstage take place *offstage*, what is the reason? In *Macbeth*, for instance, why do you suppose the murder

of Duncan takes place offstage, whereas Banquo and Macduff's family are murdered onstage? Why might Shakespeare have preferred not to show us the murder of Duncan? What has he gained? (A good way to approach this sort of question is to think of what your own reaction would be if the action were shown onstage.)

4. If the play has several conflicts—for example, between pairs of lovers or between parents and their children and also between the parents themselves—how are these conflicts related? Are they parallel? Or contrasting?

5. Does the arrangement of scenes have a structure? For instance, do the scenes depict a rise and then a fall? Where is the actual climax? Is there more than one?

6. Does the plot seem satisfactorily concluded? Any loose threads? If so, is the apparent lack of a complete resolution a weakness or strength in the play?

7. Does the play exhibit METADRAMATIC elements? That is, does it refer to itself, or make obvious how its effects work, or play with illusion, showing that it is only make-believe? If so, does this rupture of illusion help the point of the play?

An analysis of plot, then, will consider the arrangement of the episodes and the effect of juxtapositions, as well as the overall story. A useful essay may be written on the function of one scene. Such an essay may point out, for example, that the long, comparatively slow scene (4.3) in *Macbeth*, in which Malcolm, Macduff, an English doctor, and Ross converse near the palace of the King of England, is not so much a leisurely digression as may at first be thought. After reading it closely, you may decide that the scene has several functions. For example, it serves to indicate the following:

1. The forces that will eventually overthrow Macbeth are gathering.
2. Even good men must tell lies during Macbeth's reign.
3. Macbeth has the vile qualities that the virtuous Malcolm pretends to have.
4. Macbeth has failed—as the King of England has not—to be a source of health for the realm.

Once you have come to such conclusions (probably by means of brainstorming and listing), the construction of an essay on the function of a scene is usually fairly simple: An introductory paragraph announces the general topic and thesis—an apparently unnecessary scene will be shown to be functional—and the rest of the essay demonstrates the functions, usually in climactic order if some of the functions are more important than others.

How might you organize such an essay? If you think all of the functions are equally important, perhaps you will organize the material from the most obvious to the least obvious, thereby keeping the reader's attention to the end. If, on the other hand, you believe that although justifications for the scene can be imagined, the scene is nevertheless unsuccessful, say so; announce your view early, consider the alleged functions one by one, and explain your reasons for finding them unconvincing as you take up each point.

Sometimes an analysis of the plot will examine the relationships between the several stories in a play: *A Midsummer Night's Dream* has supernatural lovers, mature royal lovers, young Athenian lovers, a bumpkin who briefly becomes the lover of the fairy queen, and a play (put on by buffoons) about legendary lovers. How these are held together and how they help define each other and the total play are matters that concern anyone looking at the plot. Richard Moulton suggested in 1893 that Shakespeare's subplots "have the effect of assisting the main stories, smoothing away their difficulties and making their prominent points yet more prominent." Moulton demonstrates his thesis at some length, but a very brief extract from his discussion of the Jessica–Lorenzo story in *The Merchant of Venice* may be enough to suggest the method. The main story concerns Shylock and his rivals, Antonio, Bassanio, and Portia. Shylock's daughter, Jessica, is not needed for the narrative purpose of the main story. Why, then, did Shakespeare include her? (**Remember**: When something puzzles you, you have an essay topic at hand.) Here is part of Moulton's answer:

> A Shylock painted without a tender side at all would be repulsive [. . .] and yet it appears how this tenderness has grown hard and rotten with the general debasement of his soul by avarice, until, in his ravings over his loss, his ducats and his daughter are ranked as equally dear.
>
> I would my daughter were dead at my foot, and the jewels in her ear! Would she were hearsed at my foot, and the ducats in her coffin!
>
> For all this we feel that he is hardly used in losing her. Paternal feeling may take a gross form, but it is paternal feeling none the less, and cannot be denied our sympathy; bereavement is a common ground upon which not only high and low, but even the pure and the outcast, are drawn together. Thus Jessica at home makes us hate Shylock; with Jessica lost we cannot help pitying him.
>
> —*Shakespeare as a Dramatic Artist* (Oxford, 1893) 79.

Characterization and Motivation

CHARACTERIZATION, or personality, is defined most obviously in drama (as in fiction), by what the characters do (a stage direction tells us that "Hedda paces up and down, clenching her fists"), by what they say (she asks her husband to draw the curtains), by what others say about them, and by the setting in which they move. But in theatre, character is also established by a range of gestures, by body positions, by voice inflection, costume, and so on. In fact, it is dangerous to rely on **STAGE DIRECTIONS** since every performance of a play is restaged and may or may not resemble other productions or the printed text. Do not read stage directions as if they were descriptions in fiction: They are merely guidelines in production. In current performance analysis, critics are very wary indeed of stage directions. If you are writing about a play you haven't seen, you might try to watch a video or film version in order to determine how the characters look and act (remembering that these will use the conventions of each medium and will not exactly resemble a stage production). If you can't see a performance, you must use the stage directions, but also try to bring the play to life in your mind—and if your staging does not obey the directions, use your own version, but defend it.

The characters are also defined in part by other characters whom they resemble to some degree. Remember that when characters appear like other characters or types they are often ICONIC or SYMBOLIC. You will want to determine whether they are "real" people or simply fulfilling established roles. In his wordless play, *The Overcoat*, Morris Panych picks up types from Gogol's short story, but invests some with subtle personal traits, making them "real" persons in the fiction who act with and against representative types who are somehow "unreal" in the fiction. Hamlet, Laertes, and Fortinbras have each lost their fathers— they are all examples of a type of young man—but Hamlet spares the praying King Claudius, whereas Laertes, seeking vengeance on Hamlet for murdering Laertes' father, says he would cut Hamlet's throat in church; Hamlet meditates about the nature of action, but Fortinbras leads the Norwegians in a military campaign and ultimately acquires Denmark. Here is Kenneth Muir commenting briefly on the way Laertes helps us to see Hamlet more precisely. (Notice how Muir first offers a generalization, then supports it with details, and finally, drawing a conclusion from the details he has just presented, offers an even more important generalization that effectively closes his paragraph.)

> In spite of Hamlet's description of him as "a very noble youth," there is a coarseness of fibre in Laertes which is revealed throughout the play. He has the stock responses of a man of his time and position. He gives his sister copy-book advice; he [leaves her to go] to Paris [. . .] and after his father's death and again at his sister's grave he shows by the ostentation and "bravery of his grief" that he pretends more than he really feels. He has no difficulty in raising a successful rebellion against Claudius, which suggests that the more popular prince could have done the same. Laertes, indeed, acts more or less in the way that many critics profess to think Hamlet ought to act; and his function in the play is to show precisely the opposite. Although Hamlet himself may envy Laertes' capacity for ruthless action we ought surely to prefer Hamlet's craven scruples.

> —*Shakespeare: The Great Tragedies* (London, 1961) 12–13.

Muir has not exhausted the topic in this paragraph. If you are familiar with *Hamlet*, you may want to think about writing an entire essay comparing Hamlet with Laertes.

Other plays provide examples of such FOILS or characters who set one another off. Macbeth and Banquo both hear prophecies, but they act and react differently; Sue and Lily are both in love with Bill in *Lion in the Streets*, but their responses to him are very different. In *Waiting for Godot*, the two tramps Didi and Gogo are contrasted with Pozzo and his slave Lucky, the former two suggesting (roughly) the contemplative life, the latter two the practical or active (and, it turns out, mistaken) life.

Any analysis of a character, then, will probably have to take into account the other characters that help show what he or she is, that help set forth his or her MOTIVATION (grounds for action, inner drives, goals). In Ibsen's *Doll's House*, Dr. Rank plays a part in helping define Nora:

This is not Rank's play, it is Nora's. Rank is a minor character—but he plays a vital dramatic role. His function is to act as the physical embodiment, visible on the stage, of Nora's moral situation as she sees it. Nora is almost hysterical with terror at the thought of her situation—almost, but it is part of her character that with great heroism she keeps her fears secret to herself; and it is because of her reticence that Rank is dramatically necessary, to symbolize the horror she will not talk about. Nora feels, and we feel, the full awfulness of Rank's illness, and she transfers to herself the same feeling about the moral corruption which she imagines herself to carry. Nora sees herself, and we see her seeing herself (with our judgment), as suffering from a moral disease as mortal, as irremediable as Rank's disease, a disease that creeps on to a fatal climax. This is the foe that Nora is fighting so courageously.

> —John Northam, "Ibsen's Search for the Hero," *Ibsen*, ed. Rolf Fjelde
> (Englewood Cliffs, NJ, 1965) 103.

Costumes, Gestures, and Settings

Characters on stage physically and thematically "point" to other characters, and that helps build character (and theme). Critics talk about **DEIXIS**, a Greek word with the same root as "index finger," to discuss this "pointing out" or "pointing to." Certain gaits or costumes or postures, then, **INDEX** characters (the spastic movements of the paraplegic characters in David Freeman's *Creeps;* Hamlet's "inky cloak," or the corset and garter belt of the prostitute in Brad Fraser's *Unidentified Human Remains and the True Nature of Love;* the cocky stance of the "greasy, seedy and potentially violent" ghost, Screamin' John McGee, in John Gray's *Rock and Roll*). The text of a play includes the costumes that the characters wear, the GESTURES that the characters make, and the SETTINGS in which the characters move. As Ezra Pound says, "The medium of drama is not words, but persons moving about on a stage using words." **SEMIOTIC** criticism is especially interested in analyzing the words and their relationship to the non-verbal SIGNS.

Let's begin with COSTUME, specifically with Nora Helmer's changes of costume in Ibsen's *A Doll's House.* In the first act, Nora wears ordinary clothing, but in the middle of the second act she puts on "a long, many-coloured shawl" when she frantically rehearses her tarantella. The shawl is supposed to be appropriate to the Italian dance, but surely its multitude of colours also helps express Nora's conflicting emotions, her near hysteria, expressed, too, in the fact that "her hair comes loose and falls down over her shoulders," but "she doesn't notice." The shawl and her dishevelled hair, then, *speak* to us as clearly as the dialogue does.

In the middle of the third act, after the party and just before the showdown, Nora appears in her "Italian costume," and her husband, Torvald, wears "evening dress" under an open black cloak. She is dressed for a masquerade (her whole life has been a masquerade, it turns out), and Torvald's formal suit and black cloak help express his stiffness and the blight that has forced her to present a false front throughout their years of marriage. A little later, after Nora sees that she never really has known her husband for the selfish creature he is, she leaves the stage, and when she returns she is "in an everyday dress." The pretence is over. She is no longer Torvald's "doll." When she finally leaves the stage—leaving the house—she "wraps her shawl around her." This is not the "many-coloured shawl" she used in rehearsing the dance, but the "big, black shawl" she wears when she returns from the dance. The blackness of this shawl helps express the death of her old way of life; Nora is now aware that life is not child's play.

Ibsen did not invent the use of costumes as dramatic language; it goes back to the beginnings of drama, and one has only to think of Lear tearing off his clothing or of the fresh clothing in which Lear is garbed after his madness in order to see how eloquently costumes can speak. In Panych's *The Overcoat*, of course, the eponymous costume worn by The Man (who has almost no personality without it) entirely creates his character and finally takes on a stage life of its own—dancing around on its coat rack.

To this may be added the matter of disguises—for example, Edgar's disguise in *King Lear*—which are removed near the end of plays, when the truth is finally revealed and the characters can be fully themselves. In short, the removal of disguises *says* something. All the cross-dressing comedies of Shakespeare (such as *Twelfth Night* and *As You Like It*) rely for their comic resolution on this moment of costume disclosure.

GESTURES, too, are a part of the language of drama. Helmer "playfully pulls [Nora's] ear," showing his affection—and his domineering condescension; Nora claps her hands; Mrs. Linde (an old friend of Nora's) "tries to read but seems unable to concentrate," and so forth. All such gestures clearly and naturally convey states of mind. One of the most delightful and revealing gestures in Ibsen's play occurs when, in the third act, Helmer demonstrates to Mrs. Linde the ugliness of knitting ("Look here: arms pressed close to the sides") and the elegance of embroidering ("[. . .] with your right [hand] you move the needle like this—in an easy, elongated arc"). None of his absurd remarks throughout the play is quite so revealing of his absurdity as this silly demonstration.

Some gestures or stage directions that imply gestures are a bit more complex. For example, when Nora "walks cautiously over to the door to the study and listens," this direction conveys Nora's fear that her husband may detect her foibles—or even her crime. We read this stage direction almost at the start of the play, when we do not yet know who is who or what is what, but we do know from this gesture alone that Nora is not at ease even in her own home. Similarly, when Nora "wildly" dances during her rehearsal in the second act, the action indicates the terrible agitation in her mind. One other, quieter example: In Act 3, when the dying Dr. Rank for the last time visits Nora in order to gain comfort, she lights his cigar, and a moment later Rank replies—these are his last words—"And thanks for the light." Thus, we not only hear words about a cigar, but we *see* an act of friendship, a flash of light in this oppressive household.

Gesture may be interpreted even more broadly: The mere fact that a character enters, leaves, or does not enter may be highly significant. John Russell Brown comments on the actions and the absence of certain words that in *Hamlet* convey the growing separation between King Claudius and his wife, Gertrude:

Their first appearance together with a public celebration of marriage is a large and simple visual effect, and Gertrude's close concern for her son suggests a simple, and perhaps unremarkable modification [. . .]. But Claudius enters without Gertrude for his "Prayer Scene" (3.3) and, for the first time, Gertrude enters without him for the Closet Scene (3.4) and is left alone, again for the first time, when Polonius hides behind the arras. Thereafter earlier accord is revalued by an increasing separation, often poignantly silent, and unexpected. When Claudius calls Gertrude to leave with him after Hamlet has dragged off Polonius' body, she makes no reply; twice more he urges her and she is still silent. But he does not remonstrate or question; rather he speaks of his own immediate concerns and, far from supporting her with assurances, becomes more aware of his own fears:

> O, come away!
> My soul is full of discord and dismay.   (5.1.44–45)

Emotion has been so heightened that it is remarkable that they leave together without further words. The audience has been aware of a new distance between Gertrude and Claudius, of her immobility and silence, and of his self-concern, haste and insistence.

—*Shakespeare's Plays in Performance* (New York, 1967) 139.

Sometimes the dramatist helps us interpret the gestures: Shaw and Michael Cook, for example, give notably full stage directions. Detailed stage directions, however, are rarely seen before the middle of the nineteenth century. **Remember:** Do not assume that stage directions will always be used in performance or that your mental performance is less valid than the ideal performance the notes suggest.

Settings have changed through theatre history. Drama of the nineteenth and early twentieth centuries (for example, the plays of Ibsen or Chekhov) is often thought to be "realistic," but even a realistic playwright or stage designer selects his or her materials.

We should distinguish between REALISM and **NATURALISM**. In simple terms, realism refers to an issue or theme, and naturalism to the display of the inner workings of a real thing. Naturalistic sets, in the theatre, carefully reproduce the exact workings of real places—with running water in sinks and stoves that heat up and boil kettles. It is possible to present a realistic theme in a non-naturalistic setting (think of early *Star Trek* episodes), but a naturalistic setting will almost always present a drama with a realistic theme (think of French's four Mercer plays, in which family stress is played out in an exactly reproduced family home). Ibsen often created meticulous stage directions to recreate the heavy nineteenth-century drawing room with its heavy draperies and bulky furniture: such naturalistic settings help convey his vision of a bourgeois world that oppresses any individual who struggles to affirm other values.

Apparently naturalistic sets can, then, serve other dramatic and symbolic purposes. In the setting of *Hedda Gabler,* for example, Ibsen uses two suggestive details as more than mere background: Early in the play Hedda is distressed by the sunlight that shines through the opened French doors, a detail that we later see helps reveal her fear of the processes of nature. More evident and more pervasive is her tendency, when she cannot cope with her present situation, to move to the inner room, at the rear of the stage, in which hangs a picture of her late father. In theatre, non-verbal devices are every bit as important as verbal ones or the figures and **TROPES** of fiction and poetry. Here is Ibsen on such theatrical devices:

> I can do quite a lot by manipulating the prosaic details of my plays so that they become theatrical metaphors and come to mean more than what they are; I have used costume in this way, lighting, scenery, landscape, weather; I have used trivial every-day things like inky fingers and candles; and I have used living figures as symbols of spiritual forces that act upon the hero. Perhaps these things could be brought into the context of a modern realistic play to help me to portray the modern hero and the tragic conflict which I now understand so well.

> —Qtd. in John Northam. "Ibsen's Search for the Hero." *Ibsen*, ed. Rolf Fjelde (Englewood Cliffs, NJ, 1965) 99.

Twentieth-century dramatists are often explicit about the symbolic qualities of the setting. Here is an example from Michael Cook's *Jacob's Wake*. Only a part of the long initial stage direction is given here.

> The play can be staged in a variety of ways. The most obvious representation is one of total realism [. . .] An acceptable alternative would be a stark, skeleton-ized set. The levels would have to remain essentially the same, but a structure as white as bone [. . .] [would be needed, with] only the ribs poking towards an empty sky [. . .] [to] free the director for an existential interpretation of the play (9).

A second example is part of Bryan MacDonald's description of the destruction of the set in the final moments of *Whale Riding Weather*. MacDonald so feels the nature of his one-room set to be symbolic that his directions throughout the play form a kind of poetic complement to the dialogue:

> Furniture slides.
> The pen collapses.
> The plaster on the walls
> begins to crack
> The lights fade into lapis blue
> And emerald green: flashes
> fragments of light
> like that created
> when too much pressure
> is applied to closed eyelids (126).

Material such as this cannot be skimmed. These directions and the settings they describe are symbols that help give the plays their meaning. An essay might examine in detail the degree to which the setting contributes to the theme of the play. Take, for example, Cook's setting. The two-level construction is the most important aspect, but an essayist might also point out the "stiff, formal photographs" of the Skipper and his wife—she, "sad and beautiful"; he, with the "walrus moustache of the male"—which dominate the walls. Important, too, is the "illuminated prayer with a sorrowing Christ" which announces the family's Roman Catholic religion but also the notion of pain and sacrifice. An essayist might notice how poor the plain furniture is and yet how it captures a kind of plain, hard-working lifestyle. It would be important to mention Cook's insistence that there "should be a sense of confining, of a claustrophobic intensity"; it is this constriction that leads to the play's symbolic conclusion.

Because Shakespeare's plays were performed in broad daylight on a stage that (compared with Ibsen's, Cook's, and MacDonald's) made little use of scenery, he had to use language to manufacture his settings. But the attentive ear or the mind's eye responds to these settings, too. Early in *King Lear*, when Lear reigns, we hear that we are in a country "With plenteous rivers, and wide-skirted meads"; later, when Lear is stripped of his power, we are in a place where "For many miles about / There's scarce a bush." Radio drama was extremely popular in Canada until the arrival of television, and Canadian radio plays form an important part of our theatre history. These plays, of course, rely on language to create mental settings.

In any case, a director must provide some sort of setting—even if only a bare stage—and this setting will be part of the play. Thompson's *Lion in the Streets*, with which we began this chapter, uses a simultaneous set where a number of acting areas help the flow of the "daisy chain" structure and also suggest the dream-like quality of Isobel's quest for grace. The set helps to disrupt the audience's attempt to see a safe, fictional world. It forces the spectators to construct the world of Isobel's memories—all in a day and out of time—and, by doing so, forces them also to see something of their own lives in the types on stage. The ending, in which Isobel ascends to heaven, could have been shown in an elaborate effect. By calling, instead, for a simple symbolic gesture to signify Isobel's DISCOVERY of grace, Thompson requires the spectators to create for themselves a picture of forgiveness and a place of heavenly peace. She refuses to provide easy CLOSURE, making the audience take home the set—and the play—in their minds and replay it. In a review of a production, or an essay of performance analysis, you will almost surely want to pay some attention to the function of the setting.

CONVENTIONS

Artists and their audience have some tacit—even unconscious—agreements. When we watch a motion picture and see an image dissolve and then reappear, we understand that some time has passed. Such a device, unrealistic but widely accepted, is a CONVENTION. In the theatre, we sometimes see on the stage a room, realistic in all details except that it lacks a **FOURTH WALL** preventing our view. We do not regret the missing wall, and, indeed, we are scarcely aware that we have entered into an agreement to pretend that this strange room is an ordinary room with the usual number of walls. Sometimes the characters in a play speak verse, or rap, although outside the theatre no human beings speak verse or rap for more than a few moments. Again we accept the device because it allows the author to make a play. In *Hamlet*, the characters are understood to be speaking Danish, in *Julius Caesar*, Latin, in *A Midsummer Night's Dream*, Greek, yet they all speak English for our benefit. (This illusion is broken on purpose in bilingual plays, such as David Fennario's *Balconville* and Rick Salutin's *Les Canadiens*, in which characters are meant to be actually speaking English or French or both, and in Tomson Highway's and Drew Hayden Taylor's plays, in which characters speak Cree and Ojibway without translation.)

Two other conventions are especially common in older drama: the SOLILOQUY and the ASIDE. In the former, although a solitary character speaks his or her thoughts aloud, we do not judge him or her to be a lunatic; in the latter, a character speaks in the presence of others but is understood not to be heard by them, or to be heard only by those to whom he or she directs those words. The soliloquy and the aside strike us as artificial—and they are. But they so strike us only because they are no longer customary. Because we are accustomed to it, we are not bothered by the artificiality of music accompanying dialogue in a film. The conventions of the modern theatre are equally artificial but are so customary that we do not notice them. For example, we have substituted the voice-over, or projected images, or telephone conversations, or TV programmes in the background as versions of the soliloquy and aside. Some plays, such as Fraser's *Unidentified Human Remains and the True Nature of Love*, use such devices as a "secondary score" of voices, songs, ghost stories, and action that play across the main action, in the same way as the classic Chorus or a repeated aside. The Elizabethans, who saw a play acted without a break, would probably find strange our assumption that, when we return to the auditorium after a fifteen-minute intermission, the ensuing action may be supposed to follow immediately the action before the intermission. (Plays such as Pinter's *The Birthday Party*, in which the action has continued while we were out in the lobby, are very disconcerting for most audiences.) The theatre is a place of illusion and participation; like all those who have watched drama over the centuries, we agree to these conventions in order to act out the drama together. Although many modern plays break these illusions on purpose, the theatre, as a form, relies on this WILLING SUSPENSION OF DISBELIEF.

📖 Suggestions for Further Reading

Among useful reference works are: Stanley Hochman, ed., *McGraw-Hill Encyclopedia of World Drama*, 5 vols., 2nd ed. (1984); Phyllis Hartnoll, ed., *The Oxford Companion to the Theatre*, 4th ed. (1983); Martin Banham, ed., *Cambridge Guide to World Theatre* (1995); Myron Matlaw, *Modern World Drama: An Encyclopedia* (1972); Daniel Gerould, ed., *Theatre, Theory, Theatre: The Major Critical Texts from Aristotle and Zeami to Soyinka and Havel* (2000); Eugene Benson and L. W. Conolly, eds., *The Oxford Companion to Canadian Theatre* (1989); Eugene Benson and L. W. Conolly, eds., *English-Canadian Theatre* (1987); L. W. Conolly, ed., *Canadian Drama and the Critics* (1987); Ric Knowles, *The Theatre of Form and the Production of Meaning: Contemporary Canadian Dramaturgies* (1999).

Two useful introductions to the nature of drama are Eric Bentley, *The Life of the Drama* (1964), and J. L. Styan, *The Elements of Drama* (1969), and J. L. Styan. *The English Stage: A History of Drama and* Performance (1996). A collection of plays with particularly useful introductions is W. B. Worthen, ed., *The HBJ Anthology of Drama* (2000).

More specialized studies are: Eric Bentley, *The Playwright as Thinker* (1946); C. W. E. Bigsby, *A Critical Introduction to Twentieth-Century American Drama*, 3 vols. (1982–85); Sue-Ellen Case, *Feminism and the Theatre* (1984); Susan Bennett, *Theatre Audiences: A Theory of Production and Reception* (1990); Keir Elam, *The Semiotics of Theatre and Drama* (1980); Marvin Carlson, *Theatre Semiotics: Signs of Life* (1990); Robert Wallace, *Producing Marginality: Theatre and Criticism in Canada* (1990); Marvin Carlson, *Theories of the Theatre: A Historical and Critical Survey from the Greeks to the Present* (1993); Mary Jane Miller, *Turn Up the Contrast: CBC Television Drama Since 1952* (1987); Alan Filewod, *Collective Encounters: Documentary Theatre in English Canada* (1987); Anton Wagner, ed., *Contemporary Canadian Theatre: New World Visions, a Collection of Essays Prepared by the Canadian Theatre Critics Association* (1985); Edward Buller, *Indigenous Performing and Ceremonial Arts in Canada, A Bibliography* (1976).

A quarterly journal, *Modern Drama*, publishes articles on Canadian, American, and English drama from 1850 to the present. It also includes an annual bibliography of studies of this material. *Theatre Journal* is an important journal of contemporary criticism; *Canadian Theatre Review* is a journal that mixes academic articles with essays from theatre professionals; it provides an excellent overview of what is current in the country. The journals *Theatre Research in Canada/Recherches Théâtrales au Canada*, and *Essays in Theatre/Études Théâtrales* publish articles on Canadian and world literature. *Theatre Research International* publishes essays from theatre scholars around the world.

✓ A Checklist: Getting Ideas for Writing about Drama

The following questions may help you to formulate ideas for an essay on a play.

Plot and Conflict
✓ Does the exposition introduce elements that will be ironically fulfilled?
✓ During the exposition do you perceive things differently from the way the characters perceive them?
✓ Are certain happenings or situations recurrent? If so, what significance do you attach to them?
✓ If there is more than one plot, do the plots seem to you to be related? Is one plot clearly the main plot and another plot a sort of subplot, a minor variation on the theme?

✓ Take one scene of special interest and indicate the structure, for example from stability at the beginning to the introduction of an instability, and then to a new sort of stability or resolution.

✓ Do any scenes strike you as irrelevant?

✓ Are certain scenes so strongly foreshadowed that you anticipated them? If so, did the happenings in these scenes merely fulfill your expectations, or did they also in some way surprise you?

✓ What kinds of conflict are there? One character against another, one group against another, one part of a personality against another part in the same person?

✓ How is the conflict resolved? By an unambiguous triumph of one side or by a triumph that is also in some degree a loss for the triumphant side? Do you find the resolution satisfying, or unsettling, or what? Why?

Character

✓ What are the traits of the chosen character?

✓ A dramatic character is not likely to be thoroughly realistic, a copy of someone we might know. Still, we can ask if the character is consistent and coherent. We can also ask if the character is complex or is, on the other hand, a rather simple representative of some human type. Is the character a false icon, say, of a gender stereotype? If so, is the author using the stereotype to a purpose, perhaps in a subversive manner?

✓ How is the character defined? Consider what the character says and does and what others say about him or her and do to him or her. Also consider other characters who more or less resemble the character in question, because the similarities—and the differences—may be significant.

✓ How trustworthy are the characters when they characterize themselves? When they characterize others?

✓ Do characters change as the play goes on, or do we simply know them better at the end? If characters change, why do they change?

✓ What do you make of the minor characters? Are they merely necessary to the plot, or are they foils to other characters? Or do they serve some other functions?

✓ If a character is tragic, does the tragedy seem to proceed from a moral flaw, from an intellectual error, from the malice of others, from sheer chance, or from some combination of these?

✓ What are the character's goals? To what degree do you sympathize with them? If a character is comic, do you laugh with or at the character?

✓ Do you think the characters are adequately motivated?

✓ Is a given character so meditative that you feel he or she is engaged less in a dialogue with others than in a dialogue with the self? If so, do you feel that this character is in large degree a spokesperson for the author, commenting not only on the world of the play but also on the outside world? If so, does the character cease to seem real within the world of the play? Is the character meant to be real?

Nonverbal Language

✓ If the playwright does not provide full stage directions, try to imagine for a least one scene what gestures and tones might accompany each speech. (The first scene is usually a good one to try your hand at.)

✓ What nonverbal signs is the author using? How do the characters "point" to one another? How is music or sound used? Lighting? Effects? What do the actors' bodies signify?

✓ What do you make of the setting? Does it help reveal character? Do changes of scene strike you as symbolic? If so, symbolic of what? What stage signs does the set provide for the spectator to "read"?

The Play on Film

✓ If the play has been turned into a film, what has been added? What has been omitted? Why? Are the conventions of film taking over from the original conventions of the stage? Is the camera a member of the cast or a silent narrator?

✓ Has the film medium been used to advantage—for example, in focusing attention through close-ups or reaction shots? Or do some of the inventions—for example, outdoor scenes that were not possible in the play—seem mere busywork, distracting from the urgency or the conflict or the unity of the play?

✓ Have the meanings written on the actors' bodies changed now that they are close-up, or enlarged? Have social constructions typical of movie-making changed the bodies into something different from the playwright's intention?

12

Writing about Poetry

Learning Objectives

When you've read this chapter, you should be able to

➢ differentiate the poet from the persona and write about this distinction;

➢ respond to figurative language;

➢ notice imagery and symbolism;

➢ analyze the structure of a poem;

➢ explicate a poem;

➢ use the technical terms of versification; and

➢ write about aspects of prosody, including metrics.

THE SPEAKER AND THE POET

The SPEAKER or VOICE or MASK or PERSONA (Latin for *mask*) that speaks a poem is not usually identical with the poet who writes it. The author assumes a role, or counterfeits the speech of a person in a particular situation. Robert Browning, for instance, in "My Last Duchess" (1842) invented a Renaissance duke who, in his palace, talks, in a DRAMATIC MONOLOGUE, about his first wife and his art collection with an emissary from a count who is negotiating to offer his daughter in marriage to the duke.

In reading a poem, an important question to ask yourself is this: Who is speaking? If an audience and a setting are suggested, keep them in mind, too, although these are not always indicated in a poem. For instance, Phyllis Webb's "And in Our Time" is the utterance of an impassioned lover, but we need not assume that the beloved is actually in the presence of the lover. The poem apparently represents a state of mind—a sort of talking to one-self—rather than an address to another person.

AND IN OUR TIME
Phyllis Webb

A world flew in my mouth with our first kiss
and its wings were dipped in all the flavours of grief,
Oh, my darling, tell me, what can love mean in such a world,
and what can we or any lovers hold in this immensity
of hate and broken things?
Now it is down, down, that's where your kiss travels me,
and, as a world tumbling shocks the theories of spheres,
so this love is like falling glass shaking with stars
the air which tomorrow, or even today, will be
a slow, terrible movement of scars.

Clearly, the speaker is someone passionately in love. The following questions invite you to look more closely at how the speaker of "And in Our Time" is characterized.

Questions to Stimulate Ideas about "And in Our Time"
This chapter, near the end, will list many questions that you may ask yourself in order to get ideas for writing about any poem. Here, however, are a few questions about this particular poem, to help you to think about it.

1. How does this poem communicate the speaker's state of mind? For example, in line 6, what—beyond the meaning of the words—is communicated by the repetition of "down"? In line 3, what is the tone of "Oh, my darling"? (TONE means something like emotional colouring, as for instance when one speaks of a "sinister tone," a "bitter tone," or an "eager tone.")
2. PARAPHRASE (put into your own words) the first section of the poem, the first five lines. What does this stanza communicate about the speaker's love for the beloved? Compare your paraphrase and the original. What does the original imagery (the picture of a world flying into a mouth in line 1; the "taste" of that world in line 2) communicate?
3. PARAPHRASE the second part of the poem. How did you express the verb use in the construction, "your kiss travels me," in your version? If you had trouble fitting it in, do you think the poem would be better off without it? If not, why not? Was your version much longer at this point, trying to capture a complex idea?

The voice speaking a poem, however, often does have the ring of the author's own voice, and to make a distinction between speaker and author may at times seem perverse. In fact, some poetry (especially contemporary poetry) is highly autobiographical. Still, even in autobiographical poems it may be convenient to distinguish between author and speaker. The speaker of a given poem is, let's say, the American poet Sylvia Plath in her role as parent, or Sylvia Plath in her role as daughter, not simply Sylvia Plath the poet.

The Language of Poetry: Diction and Tone

How is a VOICE or MASK or PERSONA created? From the whole of language, the author consciously or unconsciously selects certain words and grammatical constructions; this selection constitutes the persona's DICTION. It is, then, partly by the diction that we come to know the speaker of a poem. Just as in life there is a difference between people who speak of a *belly button,* a *navel,* and an *umbilicus,* so in poetry there is a difference between speakers who use one word rather than another. Of course, it is also possible that all three of these words are part of a given speaker's vocabulary, but the speaker's choice among the three would depend on the situation; that is, in addressing a child, the speaker would probably use the word *belly-button* (or even *tummy-button);* in addressing an adult other than a family member or close friend, the speaker might be more likely to use *navel;* and if the speaker is a physician addressing an audience of physicians, he or she might be most likely to use *umbilicus.* This is only to say that the dramatic situation in which one finds oneself helps define oneself, helps establish the particular role that one is playing.

Some words are used in virtually all poems: *I, see, and,* and the like. Still, the grammatical constructions in which they appear may help define the speaker. In Webb's "And in Our Time," for instance, such expressions as "the theories of spheres" (referring to the medieval cosmology) or "immensity of hate" indicate an educated speaker. The syntax of "the air which tomorrow, or even today, will be" indicates a precise individual.

Speakers have attitudes toward themselves, their subjects, and their audiences, and, consciously or unconsciously, they choose their words, pitch, and modulation accordingly; all these add up to their tone. In written literature, tone must be detected without the aid of the ear, although it's a good idea to read poetry aloud, trying to find the appropriate tone of voice. The reader must understand by the selection and sequence of words the way the words are meant to be heard—playfully, angrily, confidentially, ironically, or whatever. The reader must catch what Frost calls "the speaking tone of voice somehow entangled in the words and fastened to the page for the ear of the imagination."

Writing about the Speaker:
Margaret Atwood's "This is a Photograph of Me"

Suppose we try to establish "by whom, where, and when" Atwood's poem is spoken. We may not be able to answer all three questions in great detail, but let's see what the poem suggests. As you read it, you'll notice—alerted by the parentheses—that the poem has *two* speakers, one of whom is a narrator: The poem is a tiny drama. Thus, the parenthesis at the beginning of line 15 signals to us that the first speech is finished.

THIS IS A PHOTOGRAPH OF ME
Margaret Atwood

It was taken some time ago.
At first it seems to be
a smeared
print: blurred lines and grey flecks
blended with the paper;   5
then, as you scan
it, you see in the left-hand corner
a thing that is like a branch: part of a tree
(balsam or spruce) emerging
and, to the right, halfway up   10
what ought to be a gentle
slope, a small frame house.

In the background there is a lake,
and beyond that, some low hills.

(The photography was taken   15
the day after I drowned.

I am in the lake, in the centre
of the picture, just under the surface.

It is difficult to say where
precisely, or to say   20
how large or small I am:
the effect of water
on light is a distortion

but if you look long enough,
eventually   25
you will be able to see me.)

Suppose we ask: Who are these two speakers? What is their relationship? Is the voice of the drowned person also the voice of the narrator? If so, why is the last part marked off? Or is the first part narrated quite dispassionately while the second part is the cry of the dead person? Does the title influence your opinion by using the pronoun "me"? Probably these questions cannot be answered with absolute certainty, but some answers are more probable than others. For instance, the pronoun "I" in lines 16, 17, and 21 seem to echo the "me" of the title and argue for one voice. Yet the title need not—usually should not—be read as part of the text, so it may be the poet is intentionally leading the reader toward one conclusion and then altering the point of view.

Let's put the questions (even if they may turn out to be unanswerable) into a more specific form.

Questions

1. A narrator speaks lines 1–14. A persona, "I," speaks lines 15–26. Are you sure these are the voices of two people?
2. Who is the "you" in lines 6, 24, and 26? Is it the reader? Are you sure? Could it be the "I" of line 16? If so, how do lines 24 and 26 make sense?
3. Is the parenthesis "(balsam or spruce)" in line 9 simply a grammatical structure or is it actually the first time you hear the parenthetical voice of the "I"? Why—then—does "I" interrupt with this detail?
4. How would you characterize the tone of lines 6–14? Of the last three lines of the poem?

If you haven't jotted down your responses, consider doing so before reading what follows.

Journal Entries

Given questions somewhat like these, students were asked whether they could identify the speakers and then to add whatever they wished to say. One student recorded the following thoughts:

```
I think this is two voices.  The narrator just tells us
about this photograph he found.  The title fools you or
foreshadows the switch in speaker.  Maybe that's the
reason for it--to set us up for the change, but to delay
it.  Anyway, the photo is old and smeared and the
narrator just talks about it like a scientist or
historian.  It doesn't mean anything to him.  But to the
other voice it is really important.  It is a record of
her drowning.  (I think it's a woman who drowned and a
man who found the photo.  He isn't very concerned about
emotions, just about exact details, but she is emotional
about it.  After all, she died!)  On the other hand, she
is pretty careful about details, too, like "the effect
of water on light is a distortion."  Does that mean the
other voice is coming back in?  But she says it is
"difficult" to be precise and the other voice is very
precise.  So this is a second voice.  She is quite
bitter, I think.  People haven't seen her in life, I
bet, just like they can't see her in death.  You have to
look hard.  "Eventually" on a line by itself like that
seems to say that she must wait and wait for people to
see her.  The guy looking at the photo certainly won't
see her quickly because he's too interested in his own
```

description. Maybe that's why he pauses to identify the
kind of tree. Or maybe she is mocking him. I'm not
sure if this bit is her voice. I don't think she would
interrupt. Maybe that's why no one sees her, because
she's too quiet and passive. Speaking inside a ( ) is
pretty passive. Maybe she should speak out.

Another student thought only one voice was speaking to the reader:

As the poem goes on, we learn that "I" drowned at a spot
in the lake seen in the picture, but it starts by
telling us details about the photo itself. The title is
important because it tells the reader before you start
what the photograph is about. There's never any
suspense. That makes it weirder when we learn that the
"I" died the day before the photo was taken. Obviously
he isn't really in this snapshot, just the place he
died. So why say it is a photograph of "me"? I think
the speaker is saying that just as the photo is
"blurred" and "blended with the paper," so our lives are
blurry and can't be "precisely" seen. The guy who died
is still trying to be precise but realizes there is an
optical distortion. He says if we look carefully enough
at the photo we'll see details of the branches and
houses and stuff and that will also let us see the
actual details of his life. It's neat how Atwood makes
you realize that a photo isn't just a record of actual
objects, but has a three-dimensional quality. Secrets
might be in the "grey flecks" that seem to blend. You
have to "scan" a life like that, too. Most of us just
see how someone looks or what they wear but that is all
distorted. The photos we take of other people, even
when we just look at them (like with camera eyes), won't
reveal anything unless we look hard. Then,
"eventually," they will. That's why I think it is one
voice, saying he has been faulty like everyone else at
seeing properly. The voice in line 9 is like an inner
voice that has learned through death how to see better.
Now it speaks to itself and makes the camera eye look
more carefully. Tell me exactly what kind of tree.
What "ought" that blurred line be? Maybe only when it's
too late can we realize how to "read" a picture of
another person or even of ourselves. After we're dead.
And take the time to do it right. Our eyes don't tell
us enough about ourselves. I think the word play on
"eye" and "I" would make a good essay about this idea.

A Brief Exercise

1. Evaluate one of these two journal entries by students. Do you think the comments are convincing, plausible, or weak, and *why* do you think so? Can you offer additional supporting evidence, or counterevidence?

2. Two small questions: Why do you think Atwood broke line 3 after "smeared" rather than letting it be a modifier of "print" in line 4? Second, in lines 17–18, Atwood has the speaker say, "I am [. . .] in the centre / of the picture." Why is the speaker in the centre? Given that we can't see the speaker, should he or she be in one corner, rather out of view? What is achieved by having the invisible speaker dead centre (as it were)?

FIGURATIVE LANGUAGE

It is, of course, an exaggeration to say, as the American poet Robert Frost has said, that "Poetry provides the one permissible way of saying one thing and meaning another." Poets do, however, often use figurative language—saying one thing in terms of something else. Words have their literal meanings, but they can also be used so that something other than the literal meaning is implied. "My love is a rose" is, literally, nonsense, for a person is not a five-petaled, many-stamened plant with a spiny stem. But the suggestions of rose (at least for Robert Burns, the Scottish poet who compared his beloved to a rose in the line, "My Love is like a red, red rose") include "delicate beauty," "soft," and "perfumed," and, thus, the word *rose* can be meaningfully applied—figuratively rather than literally—to "my love." The beloved is fragrant, with skin that is perhaps like a rose in texture and (in some measure) colour and, like a rose, the beloved will not keep such beauty long. The poet has communicated his perception very precisely.

People who write about poetry have found it convenient to name the various kinds of figurative language. Just as the student of geology employs such special terms as *kames* and *eskers*, the student of literature employs special terms to name things as accurately as possible. The following paragraphs discuss the most common terms.

In a SIMILE, items from different classes are explicitly compared by a connective such as *like*, *as*, or *than*, or by a verb such as *appears* or *seems*. (If the objects compared are from the same class, for example, "Geographically, Vancouver is like Hong Kong," no simile is present.)

> This land like a mirror turns you inward
> —*Gwendolyn MacEwen*

> [. . .] winter pears, green and hard as ovaries
> —*Marilyn Bowering*

> All of our thoughts will be fairer than doves.
> —*Elizabeth Bishop*

> Seems he a dove? His feathers are but borrowed.
> —*Shakespeare*

A **METAPHOR** asserts the identity, without a connective such as *like* or a verb such as *appears,* of terms that are literally incompatible.

> then air is kisses, kisses
> —*P. K. Page*

> The rushing river of cars
> makes you a stillness. . . .
> —*Margaret Avison*

> I write because I can't sing
> I am the book exiled
> —*Lola Lemire Tostevin*

In the following poem, Keats's excitement on reading Chapman's sixteenth-century translation of the Greek poet Homer is communicated first through a metaphor and then through a simile.

ON FIRST LOOKING INTO CHAPMAN'S HOMER
John Keats (1795–1821)

Much have I traveled in the realms of gold,		
And many goodly states and kingdoms seen;		
Round many western islands have I been		
Which bards in fealty° to Apollo hold.	*loyalty*	4
Oft of one wide expanse had I been told,		
That deep-browed Homer ruled as his demesne:°	*property*	
Yet did I never breathe its pure serene°	*vast expanse*	
Till I heard Chapman speak out loud and bold:		8
Then felt I like some watcher of the skies		
When a new planet swims into his ken;		
Or like stout Cortez when with eagle eyes		
He stared at the Pacific—and all his men		12
Looked at each other with a wild surmise—		
Silent, upon a peak in Darien.°	*in Central America*	

We might pause for a moment to take a closer look at Keats's poem. If you write an essay on the figurative language in this sonnet, you will probably discuss the figure involved in asserting that reading is a sort of travelling (it brings us to unfamiliar worlds) and especially that reading brings us to realms of gold. Presumably, the experience of reading is valuable. "Realms of gold" not only continues and modifies the idea of reading as travel, but in its evocation of El Dorado (an imaginary country in South America, thought to be rich in gold and, therefore, the object of search by Spanish explorers of the Renaissance) it introduces a suggestion of the Renaissance appropriate to a poem about a Renaissance translation of Homer. The figure of travelling is amplified in the next few lines, which assert that the "goodly states and king-doms" and "western islands" are ruled by poets who owe allegiance to a higher authority, Apollo.

The beginning of the second sentence (line 5) enlarges this already spacious area with its reference to "one wide expanse," and the ruler of this area (unlike the other rulers) is given the dignity of being named. He is Homer, "deep-browed"—"deep" suggesting not only his high or perhaps furrowed forehead, but the profundity of the thoughts behind the forehead. The speaker continues the idea of books as remote places, but now he also seems to think of this place as more than a rich area; instead of merely saying that until he read Chapman's translation he had not "seen" it (as in line 2) or "been" there (line 3), he says he never breathed its air; that is, the preciousness is not material but ethereal, not gold but something far more exhilarating and essential.

This reference to air leads easily to the next dominant image, that of the explorer of the illimitable skies (so vast is Homer's world) rather than of the land and sea. But the explorer of the skies is conceived as watching an *oceanic* sky. In hindsight we can see that the link was perhaps forged earlier in line 7, with "serene" (a vast expanse of air *or* water); in any case, there is an unforgettable rightness in the description of the suddenly discovered planet as something that seems to "swim" into one's ken.

After this climactic discovery, we return to the Renaissance Spanish explorers (though, in fact, Balboa, and not Cortez, reached the Pacific) by means of a simile that compares the speaker's rapture with Cortez's as he gazed at the expanse before him. The writer of an essay on the figurative language in a poem should, in short, try to call attention to the aptness (or ineptness) of the figures and to the connecting threads that make a meaningful pattern.

Some Important Figures of Speech

Two types of metaphor deserve special mention: **SYNECDOCHE** and **METONYMY**. This is particularly the case in contemporary Canadian poetry, where simile and metaphor are more and more giving way to metonymy. Many poets feel that metaphors create false comparisons by suggesting links between phenomena where no linkage honestly exists. Such contrived comparisons may be part of a CONSTRUCTIONIST METANARRATIVE (see Chapter 8). Very often similes and even metaphors join notions we have been taught to connect, but which may actually each be part of a larger, unexplained whole. As Pat Lowther says in her poem "Coast Range,"

> The land is what's left
> after the failure
> of every kind of metaphor.

SYNECHDOCHE is the name for a figure in which the whole is replaced by the part, or the part by the whole. For example, "bread," in "Give us this day our daily bread," replaces all sorts of food. The "agonized Y" which "initials their faith" in A. M. Klein's "Political Meeting" stands for the whole crucifix as well as the question "why."

In METONYMY, something is named that replaces something closely related to it. For example, James Shirley names certain objects ("Scepter and crown," and "scythe and spade"), using them to replace social classes (powerful people, and poor people) to which the objects are related:

Scepter and crown must tumble down
And in the dust be equal made
With the poor crooked scythe and spade.

PERSONIFICATION is the attribution of human feelings or characteristics to abstractions or to inanimate objects.

Just north of town
the mountains start to talk
                —*Pat Lowther*

. . . and in the darkness rises
The body-odour of race.
                —*A. M. Klein*

Hope, thou bold taster of delight.
                —*Richard Crashaw*

Crashaw's personification, "Hope, thou bold taster of delight," is also an example of the figure called **APOSTROPHE**, an address to a person or thing not literally listening. Wordsworth begins a sonnet by apostrophizing Milton:

Milton, thou shouldst be living at this hour

and Bliss Carmen apostrophizes the "Spirit of things unseen":

Be thou my aspiration
Consuming and serene

Connotation and Denotation

What conclusions can we draw about figurative language?

First, figurative language, with its literally incompatible terms, forces the reader to attend to the **CONNOTATIONS** (suggestions, associations) rather than to the **DENOTATIONS** (dictionary definitions) of one of the terms.

Second, although figurative language is said to differ from ordinary discourse, it is found in ordinary discourse, as well as in literature. "It rained cats and dogs," "War is hell," "Don't be an ass," "Mr. Know-it-all," and other tired figures are part of our daily utterances. But through repeated use, these, and most of the figures we use, have lost whatever impact they once had and are only a shade removed from expressions that, though once figurative, have become literal: the *eye* of a needle, a *branch* office, the *face* of a clock.

Third, good figurative language is usually concrete, condensed, and interesting. The *concreteness* lends precision and vividness; when Keats writes that he felt "like some watcher of the skies / When a new planet swims into his ken," he characterizes his feelings more sharply than if he had said, "I felt excited." Through his brief life, Keats made astonishing progress at learning to create exact figures rather than vague ones. A comparison of his earlier and later poems, separated by only a few years, makes this clear. His simile isolates for us a precise kind of excitement, and the personification of "swims" vividly brings up the oceanic aspect of the sky. The effect of the second of these three qualities, *condensation*, can be seen by attempting to paraphrase some of the figures. A paraphrase will commonly use more words than the original, and it will have less impact—as the gradual coming of night usually has less impact on us than a sudden darkening of the sky, or as a prolonged push has less impact than a sudden blow. The third quality, *interest*, is largely dependent on the previous two; the successful figure often makes us open our eyes wider and take notice. Keats's "deep-browed Homer" arouses our interest in Homer as "thoughtful Homer" or "meditative Homer" does not. Similarly, when W. B. Yeats says

> An aged man is but a paltry thing,
> A tattered coat upon a stick, unless
> Soul clap its hands and sing, and louder sing
> For every tatter in its mortal dress,

the metaphoric identification of an old man with a scarecrow jolts us out of all our usual unthinking attitudes about old men as kind, happy folk who are content to have passed from youth into age.

Preparing to Write about Figurative Language

As you prepare to write about figurative language, consider

1. the areas from which the images are drawn (for instance, myth, religion, science, commerce, nature);
2. the kinds of images (for instance, similes, metaphors, overstatements, understatements);
3. any shifts from one type of imagery to another (for instance, from similes to metaphors, metaphor to metonymy, or from abundant figures of speech to literal speech) and the effects that the shifts arouse in you; and
4. the location of the images (perhaps they are concentrated at the beginning of the poem or in the middle or at the end) and if parts of the poem are richer in images than other parts, consider their effect on you.

If you underline or highlight images in your text or in a copy of the poem that you have photocopied, you'll probably be able to see **IMAGE PATTERNS**, and you can indicate the connections by drawing arrows or perhaps by making lists of related images. Thinking about these patterns, you will find ideas arising about some of the ways in which the poem makes its effect. With a little luck, you will be able to formulate a tentative thesis for your essay, though as you continue to work—say, as you write a first draft—you will probably find yourself modifying the thesis in the light of additional thoughts that come to you while you are putting words onto paper.

Imagery and Symbolism

When we read *rose,* we may call to mind a picture of a rose, or perhaps we are reminded of the odour or texture of a rose. Whatever in a poem appeals to any of our senses (sight, smell, taste, sound, touch—including sensations like heat and cold) is an image. In short, images are the sensory content of a work, whether literal or figurative. When a poet says "My rose" and is speaking about a rose, we have no figure of speech—though we still have an image. If, however, "My rose" is a shortened form of "My love is a rose," some would say that the poet is using a metaphor; but others would say that because the first term ("My love is") is omitted, the rose is a symbol. A poem about the transience of a rose might compel the reader to feel that the transience of female beauty is the larger theme even though it is never explicitly stated, because a rose has been associated in Western symbolism with the female; it is a YONIC symbol as opposed to a PHALLIC symbol.

Some symbols are conventional symbols—people have agreed to accept them as standing for something other than their literal meanings: A Western poem about a cross would probably be about Christianity; similarly, the desert is generally seen as a symbol of emptiness as well as aridity and—as we've been discussing—the rose has long been a symbol for love as well as for the woman. In Virginia Woolf's novel *Mrs. Dalloway,* the husband communicates his love by proffering this conventional symbol: "He was holding out flowers—roses, red and white roses. (But he could not bring himself to say he loved her; not in so many words.)" Later in the novel, he thinks of his wife and, immediately, again buys her a bouquet of flowers. Objects that are not conventional symbols, however, may also give rise to rich, multiple, indefinable associations. The following poem uses the traditional symbol of the rose, but in a non-traditional way.

THE SICK ROSE
William Blake (1757–1827)

O rose, thou art sick!
The invisible worm
That flies in the night,
In the howling storm,
Has found out thy bed
Of crimson joy,
And his dark secret love
Does thy life destroy.

A reader might perhaps argue that the worm is invisible (line 2) merely because it is hidden within the rose, but an "invisible worm / That flies in the night" is more than a long, slender, soft-bodied, creeping animal; and a rose that has, or is, a "bed / Of crimson joy" is more than a gardener's rose. Blake's worm and rose suggest things beyond themselves—a stranger, more vibrant world than the world we are usually aware of. They are, in short, symbolic, though readers will doubtless differ in their interpretations. Perhaps we find ourselves half thinking, for example, that the worm is male, the rose female, and that the poem is about the violation of virginity. Or that the poem is about the destruction of beauty: Woman's beauty, rooted in joy, is destroyed by a power that feeds on her. But these interpretations are not fully satisfying: The poem presents a worm and a rose, and yet it is not merely about a worm and a rose. These objects resonate, stimulating our thoughts toward something else, but the something else is elusive. This is not to say, however, that symbols mean whatever any reader says they mean. A reader could scarcely support an interpretation arguing that the poem is about the need to love all aspects of nature. All interpretations are not equally valid; it's the writer's job to offer a reasonably persuasive interpretation.

A symbol, then, is an image so loaded with significance that it is not simply literal, and it does not simply stand for something else; it is both itself *and* something else that it richly suggests, a kind of manifestation of something too complex or too elusive to be otherwise revealed. Blake's poem is about a blighted rose and at the same time about much more. In a symbol, as Thomas Carlyle wrote, "the Infinite is made to blend with the Finite, to stand visible, and as it were, attainable there."

STRUCTURE

The arrangement of the parts, the organization of the entire poem, is its structure. Sometimes a poem is divided into blocks of, say, four lines each, but even if the poem is printed as a solid block, it probably has some principle of organization—for example, from sorrow in the first two lines to joy in the next two, or from a question in the first three lines to an answer in the last line.

Consider this short poem by an English poet of the seventeenth century.

UPON JULIA'S CLOTHES
Robert Herrick (1591–1674)

Whenas° in silks my Julia goes,   *whenever*
Then, then (methinks) how sweetly flows
That liquefaction of her clothes.
Next, when I cast mine eyes, and see
That brave° vibration, each way free,   *splendid*
O, how that glittering taketh me.

Annotating and Thinking about a Poem

One student began thinking about this poem by photocopying it, double-spaced, and by making the following notes on her copy. (To give yourself room to make annotations, it is sometimes worth the effort to copy out a short poem with double or triple spacing—though it is certainly quicker to mark up a photocopy or your own text.)

Upon Julia's Clothes

Whenas in silks my Julia goes, —— *cool tone?*
Then, then (methinks) how sweetly flows
That liquefaction of her clothes.

Next, when I cast mine eyes, and see
That brave vibration, each way <u>free</u>,
O, how that glittering taketh me. *free to do what?*
                                    free from what?

"Then, then" -)
more excited?
almost at a
loss for words?
3
3
— emotional?

The student developed further ideas by thinking about several of the questions that, at the end of this chapter, we suggest you ask yourself while rereading a poem. Among the questions are these:

Does the poem proceed in a straightforward way, or at some point or points does the speaker reverse course, altering his or her tone or perception?
What is the effect on you of the form?

With such questions in mind, the student was stimulated to see if Herrick's poem has some sort of reversal or change and, if so, how it is related to the structure. After rereading the poem several times, thinking about it in the light of these questions and perhaps others that came to mind, she produced the following notes:

Two stanzas, each of three lines, with the same
  structure
Basic structure of 1st stanza: When X (one line), then Y
  (two lines)
Basic structure of second stanza: Next (one line), then
  Z (two lines)

When she marked the text after reading the poem a few times, she noticed that the last line—an exclamation of delight ("O, how that glittering taketh me")—is much more personal than the rest of the poem. A little further thought enabled her to refine this last perception:

Although the pattern of stanzas is repeated, the somewhat
analytic, detached tone of the beginning ("Whenas,"
"Then," "Next") changes to an open, enthusiastic
confession of delight in what the poet sees.

Further thinking led to this:

Although the title is "Upon Julia's Clothes," and the
first five lines describe Julia's silken dress, the poem
finally is not only about Julia's clothing but about the

```
effect of Julia (moving in silk that liquefies or seems
to become a liquid) on the poet.
```

This is a nice observation, but when the student looked again at the poem the next day and started to write about it, she found that she was able to refine her observation.

```
Even at the beginning, the speaker is not entirely
detached, for he speaks of "my Julia."
```

In writing about Herrick's "Upon Julia's Clothes," the student tells us the thoughts did not come quickly or neatly. After two or three thoughts, she started to write. Only after drafting a paragraph and rereading the poem did she notice that the personal element appears not only in the last line ("taketh *me*") but even in the first line ("*my* Julia"). In short, for almost all of us, the only way to get to a good final essay is to read, to think, to jot down ideas, to write a draft, and to revise and revise again. Having gone through such processes, the student came up with the following excellent essay.

By the way, the student did not hit on the final version of her title ("Herrick's Julia, Julia's Herrick") until shortly before she typed her final version. Her preliminary title was

```
        Structure and Personality in
      Herrick's "Upon Julia's Clothing"
```

That's a bit heavy-handed but at least it is focused, as opposed to such an uninformative title as "On a Poem by Herrick." She soon revised her tentative title to

```
    Julia, Julia's Clothing, and Julia's Poet
```

That's quite a good title: It is neat, and it is appropriate since it moves (as the poem and the essay do) from Julia and her clothing to the poet himself. Of course, this title doesn't tell the reader exactly what the essay will be about, but it does stimulate the reader's interest. The essayist's final title, however, is even better. Again, it is neat (the balanced structure, and structure is part of the student's topic), and it moves (as the poem itself moves) from Julia to the poet.

The Finished Essay

```
Anna West
English 201
14 February 2003

        Herrick's Julia, Julia's Herrick

    Robert Herrick's "Upon Julia's Clothes" begins as a
description of Julia's clothing and ends as an
```

expression of the poet's response not just to Julia's
clothing but to Julia herself. Despite the apparently
objective or detached tone of the first stanza and the
first two lines of the second stanza, the poem finally
conveys a strong sense of the speaker's excitement.

The first stanza seems to say, "Whenas" X (one
line), "Then" Y (two lines). The second stanza repeats
this basic structure of one line of assertion and two
lines describing the consequence: "Next" (one line),
"then" (two lines). But the logic or coolness of
"Whenas," "Then," and "Next," and of such rather
scientific language as "liquefaction" (a more technical-
sounding word than "melting") and "vibration" is
undercut by the breathlessness or excitement of "Then,
then" (that is very different from a simple "Then"). It
is also worth mentioning that although there is a
personal rather than a fully detached note even in the
first line, in "my Julia," this expression scarcely
reveals much feeling. In fact, it reveals a touch of
male chauvinism, a suggestion that the woman is a
possession of the speaker's. Not until the last line
does the speaker reveal that, far from Julia being his
possession, he is possessed by Julia, overwhelmed by
her: "O, how that glittering taketh me." If he begins
coolly, objectively, and somewhat complacently, and uses
a structure that suggests a somewhat detached mind, in
the exclamatory "O" he nevertheless at last confesses
that he is enraptured by Julia. In this moment, the
poem becomes personal, subjective and moving.

Other things, of course, might be said about this poem. For instance,
the writer says nothing about the changes in the metre and their possible
value in the poem. Nor does she say anything about the sounds of any of the
words (she might have commented on the long vowels in "sweetly flows"
and shown how the effect would have been different if instead of "sweetly
flows" Herrick had written "swiftly flits"), but such topics might be material
for another essay. You can't say everything about a text in one essay.
Furthermore, another reader might have found the poem less charming—even
offensive in its exclusive concern with Julia's appearance and the sexuality
of her "liquefaction." Still, this essay is, in itself, an interesting and perceptive
discussion of the way the poet used a repeated structure to set forth a minia-
ture drama in which observation is, at the end, replaced by emotion.

Some Kinds of Structure

Although every poem has its own structure, if we stand back from a given poem we may see that the structure is one of three common sorts: repetitive, narrative, or logical.

Repetitive Structure

REPETITIVE STRUCTURE is especially common in lyrics that are sung, where a single state of mind is repeated from stanza to stanza so that the stanzas are pretty much interchangeable. As we read through "Auld Lang Syne," for instance, we get reaffirmation rather than progression. Other repetitions, however, move the meaning of the poem forward, or emphasize a key point. In these cases the stanzas are not interchangeable, and the repetition builds meaning.

Narrative Structure

In a poem with a NARRATIVE STRUCTURE, there is a sense of advance. (Note: we are not talking about "narrative poems," poems that tell a story—such as *The Odyssey* or "The St. Lawrence and the Saguenay," by Charles Sangster—but about a kind of lyric poem such as Archibald Lampman's "A Summer Dream"). Blake's "The Sick Rose," discussed earlier, is an example. What comes later in the poem could not come earlier. The poem seems to get somewhere, to settle down to an end. A lyric in which the speaker at first grieves and then derives some comfort from the thought that at least he was once in love similarly has a narrative structure. Here is a short poem with a narrative structure.

A SLUMBER DID MY SPIRIT SEAL
William Wordsworth (1770–1850)

A slumber did my spirit seal;
I had no human fears:
She seemed a thing that could not feel
The touch of earthly years.

No motion has she now, no force;
She neither hears nor sees;
Rolled round in earth's diurnal° course,   *daily*
With rocks, and stones, and trees.

If this poem is a sort of narrative of the speaker's change in perceptions, exactly what are the perceptions? Is the idea, as some readers have argued, "I thought she seemed immortal, but now I am appalled that she is reduced to mere earthly matter"? Or is it, as other readers have argued, "I knew a woman who seemed more than earthly; now I see, pantheistically, that in her death she is part of the grandness of nature"? According to the first of these views, there is a chilling irony in the fact that the woman who in the first stanza seemed exempt from "The touch of earthly years" is, in the second stanza, laid in earth, with no motion of her own. She is as inert as the "rocks, and stones, and trees." In this view, the poem moves from a romantic state of mind to a report of facts, and the facts imply an abrupt understanding of the brutality of death. But according to the second view, the woman participates (with natural objects) in the grand motion of "earth's diurnal course." In further support of this second view it can be argued that Wordsworth is known to have held pantheistic beliefs and that the Latinism, *diurnal*—the longest word and the only unusual word in the poem—adds dignity, especially in a line noted for melodiousness: "*Rolled round in earth's diurnal course.*" Perhaps one can even push this view further and say that the second stanza does not offer a sharp contrast to the first but deepens it by revealing a mature and satisfying view of the woman's true immortality, an immortality perceived only naïvely in the first stanza.

Possibly the poem is of indeterminate meaning, and the disagreement cannot be settled, but you might spend a moment thinking about which of these views you prefer, and why. Or do you accept all of them? Or do you hold an entirely different view?

Logical Structure

The third kind of structure commonly found is LOGICAL STRUCTURE. The speaker argues a case and comes to some sort of conclusion. Probably the most famous example of a poem that moves to a resolution through an argument is Andrew Marvell's "To His Coy Mistress." The speaker begins, "Had we but world enough, and time" (that is, "if we had"), and for 20 lines he sets forth what he might do. At the twenty-first line he says, "But," and he indicates that the preceding 20 lines, in the conditional, are not a description of a real condition. The real condition (as he sees it) is that Time oppresses us, and he sets this idea forth in lines 21–32. In line 33 he begins his conclusion, "Now therefore," clinching it in line 45 with "Thus." Here is another example of a poem with a logical structure.

THE FLEA
John Donne (1572?–1631)

Mark but this flea, and mark in this
How little that which thou deniest me is:
It sucked me first, and now sucks thee,
And in this flea our two bloods mingled be.
Thou knowest that this cannot be said   5
A sin, nor shame, nor loss of maidenhead;
    Yet this enjoys before it woo,
    And pampered swells with one blood made of two,
    And this, alas, is more than we would do.

O stay! Three lives in one flea spare,   10
Where we almost, yea, more than married are;
This flea is you and I, and this
Our marriage bed and marriage temple is.
Though parents grudge, and you, we're met
And cloistered in these living walls of jet.   15
　　Though use° make you apt to kill me,   *custom*
　　Let not to that, self-murder added be,
　　And sacrilege, three sins in killing three.

Cruel and sudden! Hast thou since
Purpled thy nail in blood of innocence?   20
Wherein could this flea guilty be,
Except in that drop which it sucked from thee?
Yet thou triumph'st and saist that thou
Find'st not thyself, nor me, the weaker now.
　　'Tis true. Then learn how false fears be;   25
　　Just so much honor, when thou yield'st to me,
　　Will waste, as this flea's death took life from thee.

The speaker is a lover who begins by assuring his mistress that sexual inter-
course is of no more serious consequence than a fleabite. Between the first
and second stanzas, the woman has apparently threatened to kill the flea,
moving the lover to exclaim in line 10, "O stay! Three lives in one flea spare."
In this second stanza he reverses his argument, now insisting on the importance of the flea, arguing that since it has bitten both man and woman it
holds some of their lives, as well as its own. The speaker uses religious images
to strengthen his case. Unpersuaded of its importance, the woman kills the flea
between the second and third stanzas; and the speaker uses her action to
reinforce his initial position when he says, beginning in line 25, that the death
of the flea has no serious consequences and her yielding to him will have no
worse consequences.

Verbal Irony

Among the commonest devices in poems with logical structure (although
this device is employed elsewhere, too) is VERBAL IRONY. The speaker's words
mean more or less the opposite of what they seem to say. Sometimes it takes
the form of UNDERSTATEMENT, or MEIOSIS, as when Andrew Marvell's speaker
remarks with cautious wryness, "The grave's a fine and private place, / But
none, I think, do there embrace," or when F. R. Scott sums up his 37-line
attack on Prime Minister Mackenzie King in "W.L.M.K" by saying simply,
"He blunted us." Sometimes it takes the form of overstatement, or
HYPERBOLE, as when Donne's speaker says that in the flea he and the lady are
"more than married." Speaking broadly, intensely emotional contemporary
poems often use irony to undercut—and thus make acceptable—the emotion.

Paradox

Another common device in poems with a logical structure is **PARADOX**: the assertion of an apparent contradiction, as in "This flea is you and I." (Of course, this statement is metaphoric so what would be a paradox in the real world is not necessarily paradoxical in the figurative world.) But again it must be emphasized that irony and paradox are not limited to poems with a logical structure. In Webb's "Non Linear" poem, discussed in Chapter 5, for instance, there is a paradox in the fact that while the speaker has given up complaining—which is an occasion for joy—no one seems to notice, evoking a kind of sadness.

EXPLICATION

In Chapter 6, which included a discussion of Patrick Lane's "The Children of Bogota," we saw that an explication is a line-by-line commentary on what is going on in a text. (*Explication* literally means "unfolding," or "spreading out.") Although your explication will for the most part move steadily from the beginning to the end of the selection, try to avoid simply listing: "In line one [. . .], In the second line [. . .], In the third line [. . .],"; that is, don't hesitate to write such things as "The poem begins [. . .]. In the next line [. . .]. The speaker immediately adds [. . .]. She then introduces [. . .]. The next stanza begins by saying [. . .]." And of course you may discuss the second line before the first if that seems the best way of handling the passage. It is rarely a good idea to write about any text in strict chronological order: It tends to create plot summary rather than explication (or analysis).

An explication is not concerned with the writer's life or times, and it is not a paraphrase (a rewording)—though it may include paraphrase if a passage in the original seems unclear, perhaps because of an unusual word or an unfamiliar expression. On the whole, however, an explication goes beyond paraphrase, seeking to make explicit what the reader perceives as implicit in the work. To this end it calls attention, as it proceeds, to the implications of words, especially of their tone (repetitions, shifts in levels of diction, for instance from colloquial to formal language, or from ordinary language to technical language); figures of speech; length of lines (since an exceptionally short or exceptionally long sentence conveys a particular effect); sound effects, such as **ALLITERATION** and RHYME; and structure (for instance, a question in one stanza, and the answer in the next, or a generalization and then a particularization, or a contrast of some sort).

To repeat, in short, an explication makes *explicit* what is implicit, especially in the words. It sets forth the reader's sense of the precise meaning of the work, word by word, or phrase by phrase, or line by line.

A Sample Explication of Yeats's "The Balloon of the Mind"

Read this short poem (published in 1917) by the Irish poet William Butler Yeats (1865–1939). The "balloon" in the poem is a dirigible, a blimp, a hot air ship. These early flying machines appeared during World War I, when Yeats was writing.

THE BALLOON OF THE MIND
William Butler Yeats

Hands, do what you're bid:
Bring the balloon of the mind
That bellies and drags in the wind
Into its narrow shed.

Annotations and Journal Entries

A student began thinking about the poem by copying it, double-spaced. Then she jotted down her first thoughts.

> *sounds abrupt*
>
> Hands, do what you're bid:
> Bring the balloon of the mind
> That bellies and drags in the wind
> Into its narrow shed.
>
> *balloon imagined by the mind? Or a mind like a balloon?*
>
> *no real rhymes? line seems to drag it's so long!*

Later, she wrote some notes in a journal. (You can always simply think these ideas out carefully, but jotting them down helps you to frame them, and to remember them when you later come to write, so a journal system is often a good technique.)

```
I'm still puzzled about the meaning of the words, "The
balloon of the mind."  Does "balloon of the mind" mean a
balloon that belongs to the mind, sort of like "a disease
of the heart"?  If so, it means a balloon that the mind
has, a balloon that the mind possesses, I guess by
imagining it.  Or does it mean that the mind is like a
balloon, as when you say "he's a pig of a man," meaning
he is like a pig, he is a pig?  Can it mean both?  What's
a balloon that the mind imagines?  Something like dreams
of fame, wealth?  Fantasies of love?

     Is Yeats saying that the "hands" have to work hard
to make dreams a reality?  Maybe.  But maybe the idea
really is that the mind is like a balloon--hard to keep
under control, floating around.  Very hard to keep the
mind on the job.  If the mind is like a balloon, it's
hard to get it into the "shed"--the hangar.  Part of the
problem is that this kind of dirigible is so old-
fashioned that I don't know how they flew or were
launched.  I should check these airships out on the web.
```

"Bellies." Is there such a verb? In this poem it seems to mean something like "puffs out" or "flops around in the wind." Just checked The Gage Canadian Dictionary, and it says "belly" can be a verb, "to swell out," "to bulge." Well, you learn something every day.

A later entry:

OK; I think the poem is about a writer trying to keep his balloon-like mind under control, trying to keep it working at the job of writing something, maybe writing something with the "clarity, unity, and coherence" I keep hearing about in this course.

Here is the student's final version of the explication.

Yeats's "Balloon of the Mind" is about writing poetry, specifically about the difficulty of getting one's floating thoughts down in lines on the page. The first line, a short, stern, heavily stressed command to the speaker's hands, perhaps implies by its severe or impatient tone that these hands will be disobedient or inept or careless if not watched closely: the poor bumbling body so often fails to achieve the goals of the mind. The bluntness of the command in the first line is emphasized by the fact that all the subsequent lines have more syllables. Furthermore, the first line is a grammatically complete sentence, whereas the thought of line 2 spills over into the next lines, implying the difficulty of fitting ideas into confining spaces, that is, of getting one's thoughts into order, especially into a coherent poem.

Lines 2 and 3 amplify the metaphor already stated in the title (the product of the mind is an airy but unwieldy balloon) and they also contain a second command, "Bring." Alliteration ties this command "Bring" to the earlier "bid"; it also ties both of these verbs to their object, "balloon" and to the verb that most effectively describes the balloon, "bellies." In comparison with the abrupt first line of the poem, lines 2 and 3 themselves seem almost swollen, bellying and dragging, an effect aided by using adjacent unstressed syllables ("of the," "[bell]ies and," "in the") and by using an eye rhyme ("mind" and "wind") rather than an exact rhyme. And then comes the short last line: almost

```
before we could expect it, the cumbersome balloon--here
the idea that is to be packed into the stanza--is
successfully lodged in its "narrow shed."  Aside from
the relatively colourless "into," the only words of more
than one syllable in the poem are "balloon," "bellies,"
and "narrow," and all three emphasize the difficulty of
the task.  But after "narrow"--the word itself almost
looks long and narrow, in this context like a hangar--we
get the simplicity of the monosyllable "shed."  The
difficult job is done, the thought is safely packed
away, the poem is completed--but again with an off rhyme
("bid" and "shed"), for neatness can go only so far when
hands and mind and a balloon are involved.
```

VERSIFICATION AND RHYTHM: A GLOSSARY FOR REFERENCE

The technical vocabulary of **PROSODY** (the study of the principles of verse structure, including METRE, RHYME and other sound effects, and stanzaic patterns) is large. An understanding of these terms will not turn anyone into a poet, but it will enable you to write about some aspects of poetry more efficiently. The following are the chief terms of prosody.

Metre

Most poetry written in English has a pattern of stressed (accented) sounds, and this pattern is the metre (from the Greek word for "measure"). Strictly speaking, we really should not talk of "unstressed" or "unaccented" syllables, since to utter a syllable—however lightly—is to give it some stress. It is really a matter of *relative* stress, but the fact is that "unstressed" or "unaccented" are part of the established terminology of versification.

In a line of poetry, the **FOOT** is the basic unit of measurement. It is on rare occasions a single stressed syllable; generally a foot consists of two or three syllables, one of which is stressed. The repetition of feet, then, produces a pattern of stresses throughout the poem.

Two cautions:

1. A poem will seldom contain only one kind of foot throughout; significant variations usually occur, but one kind of foot is dominant.

2. In reading a poem, one chiefly pays attention to the sense, not to a presupposed metrical pattern. By paying attention to the sense, one often finds (reading aloud is a great help) that the stress falls on a word that according to the metrical pattern would be unstressed. Or, a word that according to the pattern would be stressed may be seen to be unstressed. Furthermore, by reading for sense, one finds that not all stresses are equally heavy; some are almost as light as unstressed syllables, and some

have a hovering stress; that is, the stress is equally distributed over two adjacent syllables. To repeat: One reads for sense, allowing the syntax to help indicate the stresses.

Metrical Feet

The most common feet in English poetry are the six that follow:

IAMB (adjective: **IAMBIC**): one unstressed syllable followed by one stressed syllable. The iamb, said to be the most common pattern in English speech, is surely the most common in English poetry. The following example has four iambic feet:

My heart is like a sing -ing bird
> —*Christina Rossetti*

TROCHEE (**TROCHAIC**): one stressed syllable followed by one unstressed:

We were very tired, we were very merry
> —*Edna St. Vincent Millay*

ANAPEST (**ANAPESTIC**): two unstressed syllables followed by one stressed:

There are man -y who say that a dog has his day
> —*Dylan Thomas*

DACTYL (**DACTYLIC**): one stressed syllable followed by two unstressed. This trisyllabic foot, like the anapest, is common in light verse or verse suggesting joy, but its use is not limited to such material. Janice Kulyk Keefer's "Perceptual Elegy" begins:

Out a bare window I

SPONDEE (**SPONDAIC**): two stressed syllables; most often used as a substitute for an iamb or trochee:

Nobody stuffs the world in at your eyes
> —*Margaret Avison from* "Snow"

PYRRHIC: two unstressed syllables; it is often not considered a legitimate foot in English.

Metrical Lines

A metrical line consists of one or more feet and is named for the number of feet in it. The following names are used:

MONOMETRE: one foot	**PENTAMETRE**: five feet
DIMETRE: two feet	**HEXAMETRE** (**ALEXANDRINE**): six feet
TRIMETRE: three feet	**HEPTAMETRE**: seven feet
TETRAMETRE: four feet	

A line is scanned for the kind and number of feet in it, and the **SCANSION** tells you if it is, say, trochaic pentametre (five trochees):

Wíld wǐth rúshǐng dréams ǎnd déep wǐth sádněss!
> —*Duncan Campbell Scott* from "Rapids at Night"

Or, in another example, iambic tetrametre:

Thěy áre nǒt flésh, thěy áre nǒt bóne
> —*Archibald Lampman* from "The City at the End of Things"

A line ending with a stress has a **STRONG ENDING**; a line ending with an extra unstressed syllable has a **WEAK ENDING**. (***Note***: these terms used to be "masculine" and "feminine" endings and you may see these terms in older commentaries. The older terms are rarely used in Canada.) The **CAESURA** (sometimes indicated by the symbol //) is a slight pause within the line which does not affect the metrical count. It need not be indicated by punctuation as it is not in Earle Birney's "Anglosaxon Street":

Dawn drizzle ended	dampness steams from
blotching brick and	blank plasterwaste
Faded housepatterns	hoary and finicky
unfold stuttering	stick like a phonograph

Much contemporary poetry includes irregular caesura made visible by spacing on the page. Consider, for example, Robert Kroetsch's "Collected Poem":

The world is   always
ending.

When you get to the
beginning   stop.

An **END-STOPPED LINE** concludes with a distinct syntactical pause, but a **RUN-ON LINE** has its sense carried over into the next line without syntactical pause. (The running-on of a line is called **ENJAMBMENT**.) In the following passage, only the first is a run-on line:

Yet if we look more closely we shall find
Most have the seeds of judgment in their mind:
Nature affords at least a glimmering light;
The lines, though touched but faintly, are drawn right.
> —*Alexander Pope*

Rhythm

RHYTHM (most simply, in English poetry, STRESSES at regular intervals) has a power of its own. A highly pronounced rhythm is common in such forms of poetry as charms, yells at sports events (like The Wave), and lullabies; all of them aim to induce a special effect magically. It is not surprising that *carmen*, the Latin word for poem or song, is also the Latin word for charm and the word from which our word *charm* is derived.

In much poetry, rhythm is only half heard, but its presence is suggested by the way poetry is printed. Prose (from Latin *prorsus,* "forward," "straight on") keeps running across the paper until the right-hand margin is reached; then, merely because the paper has given out, the writer or printer starts again at the left, with a small letter. (This is very obvious with word-wrap in word processing.) But verse (Latin *versus,* "a turning") often ends well short of the right-hand margin. The next line begins at the left—sometimes with a capital, but less often so today—not because paper has run out but because the rhythmic pattern begins again. Lines of poetry are continually reminding us that they have a pattern.

Note that a mechanical, unvarying rhythm may be good to put the baby to sleep, but it can be deadly to readers who want to stay awake. Poets vary their rhythm according to their purposes; they ought not to be so regular that they are (in W. H. Auden's words) "accentual pests." In competent hands, rhythm contributes to meaning; it says something. Ezra Pound has a relevant comment: "Rhythm *must* have meaning. It can't be merely a careless dash off, with no grip and no real hold to the words and sense, a tumty tum tumty tum tum ta."

Consider this description of Hell from John Milton's *Paradise Lost* (stressed syllables are marked by ´, unstressed syllables by ˘):

> Rocks, caves, lakes, fens, bogs, dens, and shades of death

The normal line in *Paradise Lost* is written in iambic feet—alternate unstressed and stressed syllables—but in this line Milton immediately follows one heavy stress with another, helping communicate the "meaning"—the oppressive monotony of Hell. As a second example, consider the function of the rhythm in two lines by Alexander Pope:

> When Ajax strives some rock's vast weight to throw
> The line too labours, and the words move slow.

The stressed syllables do not merely alternate with the unstressed ones; rather, the great weight of the rock is suggested by three consecutive stressed words, "rock's vast weight," and the great effort involved in moving it is suggested by another three consecutive stresses, "line too labours," and by yet another three, "words move slow." Note, also, the abundant pauses within the lines. In the first line, for example, unless one's speech is slovenly, one must pause at least slightly after "Ajax," "strives," "rock's," "vast," "weight," and "throw." The grating sounds in "Ajax" and "rock's" do their work, too, and so do the explosive *t*s. When Pope wishes to suggest lightness, he reverses his procedure, and he groups *un*stressed syllables:

> Not so, when swift Camilla scours the plain,
> Flies o'er th' unbending corn, and skims along the main.

This last line has 12 syllables and is, thus, longer than the line about Ajax, but the addition of *along* helps communicate lightness and swiftness because in this line (it can be argued) neither syllable of *along* is strongly stressed. If *along* is omitted, the line still makes grammatical sense and becomes more regular, but it also becomes less imitative of lightness.

The very regularity of a line may be meaningful, too. Shakespeare begins a sonnet thus:

When I do count the clock that tells the time.

This line about a mechanism runs with appropriate regularity. (It is worth noting, too, that "count the *c*lock" and "*t*ells the *t*ime" emphasize the regularity by the repetition of sounds and syntax.) But notice what Shakespeare does in the middle of the next line:

And see the brave day sunk in hideous night.

As we've seen, metre produces rhythm—recurrences at equal intervals—but rhythm (from a Greek word meaning "flow") is usually applied to larger units than feet. Often it depends most obviously on pauses. Thus, a poem with run-on lines will have a different rhythm from a poem with end-stopped lines, even though both are in the same metre. And prose, though it is unmetrical, may have rhythm, too.

In addition to being affected by syntactical pause, rhythm is affected by pauses attributable to consonant clusters and to the length of words. Polysyllabic words establish a different rhythm from monosyllabic words, even in metrically identical lines. One may say, then, that rhythm is altered by shifts in metre, syntax, and the length and ease of pronunciation. Even with no such shift, even if a line is repeated verbatim, a reader may sense a change in rhythm. The rhythm of the final line of a poem, for example, may well differ from that of the line before. Repeated lines may have different rhythms even though in other respects the lines are identical, as in D. C. Scott's "The Forsaken," in which each section ends with the clause "Then she had rest." The rhythm assists a change in tone in the second, final use of the line where one senses that the words ought to be spoken, say, more slowly and with more stress on "rest."

Patterns of Sound

Though rhythm is basic to poetry, rhyme—the repetition of the identical or similar stressed sound or sounds—is not. Rhyme is, presumably, pleasant in itself; it suggests order; and it also may be related to meaning, for it brings two words sharply together, often implying a relationship, as in the now trite *dove* and *love* or in the more imaginative *throne* and *alone*, or *rap* and *trap*.

PERFECT OR EXACT RHYME: differing consonant sounds are followed by identical stressed vowel sounds, and any further following sounds are also identical (*row—toe; meet—fleet; buffer—rougher*). Notice that perfect rhyme involves identity of sound, not of spelling. *Fix* and *sticks*, like *buffer* and *rougher,* are perfect rhymes.

HALF-RHYME (or off-rhyme): only the final consonant sounds of the words are identical; the stressed vowel sounds, as well as the initial consonant sounds, if any, differ (*soul—oil; mirth—forth; trolley—bully*).

EYE-RHYME: the sounds do not in fact rhyme, but the words look as though they would rhyme (*cough—bough*). This pattern is effective when you read a poem, not when you hear one.

STRONG RHYME: the final syllables are stressed and, after their differing initial consonant sounds, are identical in sound (*stark—mark; support—retort*). (Formerly called masculine rhyme.)

WEAK RHYME (or double rhyme): stressed rhyming syllables are followed by identical unstressed syllables (*revival—arrival; flatter—matter*). (Formerly called feminine rhyme.) Triple rhyme is a kind of weak rhyme in which identical stressed vowel sounds are followed by two identical unstressed syllables (*machinery—scenery; tenderly—slenderly*).

END RHYME (or terminal rhyme): the rhyming words occur at the ends of the lines.

INTERNAL RHYME: at least one of the rhyming words occurs within the line (Oscar Wilde's "Each narrow *cell* in which we *dwell*").

ALLITERATION: sometimes defined as the repetition of initial sounds ("All the *a*wful *a*uguries" or "Bring me my *b*ow of *b*urning gold"), and sometimes as the prominent repetition of a consonant ("*a*fter li*f*e's *f*it*f*ul *f*ever").

ASSONANCE: the repetition, in proximate words, of identical vowel sounds preceded and followed by differing consonant sounds. Whereas *tide* and *hide* are rhymes, *tide* and *mine* are assonantal.

CONSONANCE: the repetition of identical consonant sounds and differing vowel sounds in words in proximity (*fail—feel; rough—roof; pitter—patter*). Sometimes, consonance is more loosely defined merely as the repetition of a consonant (*fail—peel*).

ONOMATOPOEIA: the use of words that imitate sounds, such as *hiss* and *buzz*. (Consider the effect of " [. . .] and the hiss / cease not [. . .]." in Lampman's "The City at the End of Things.") A common mistaken tendency is to see onomatopoeia everywhere—for example, in *thunder* and *horror*. Many words sometimes thought to be onomatopoeic are not clearly imitative of the thing they refer to; they merely contain some sounds that, when we know what the word means, seem to have some resemblance to the thing they denote. Tennyson's lines from "Come Down, O Maid" are famously onomatopoeic: "The moan of doves in immemorial elms / And murmuring of innumerable bees." Consider this example, again from Lampman's "The City at the End of Things." Does this excerpt contain true onomatopoeia or merely suggestive words? Or does the example provide both?

And all the while an awful sound
Keeps roaring on continually,
And crashes in the ceaseless round
Of a gigantic harmony.

Stanzaic Patterns

Lines of poetry are commonly arranged into a rhythmical unit called a STANZA (from an Italian word meaning "room" or "stopping-place"). Usually, all the stanzas in a poem have the same rhyme pattern. A stanza is sometimes called a VERSE, though *verse* also (and correctly) means a single line of poetry. (In discussing stanzas, rhymes are indicated by identical letters. Thus, *a b a b* indicates that the first and third lines rhyme with each other, while the second and fourth lines are linked by a different rhyme. An unrhymed line is denoted by *x*.) Common stanzaic forms in English poetry are the following:

   COUPLET: a stanza of two lines, usually, but not necessarily, with end-rhymes. *Couplet* is also used for a pair of rhyming lines. The OCTOSYLLABIC COUPLET is iambic or trochaic tetrametre:

> Had we but world enough, and time,
> This coyness, lady, were no crime.
> —*Andrew Marvell*

   HEROIC COUPLET: a rhyming couplet of iambic pentametre, often "closed," that is, containing a complete thought, with a fairly heavy pause at the end of the first line and a still heavier one at the end of the second. Commonly, a parallel or an *antithesis* (contrast) is found within a line or between the two lines. It is called heroic because in England, especially in the eighteenth century, it was much used for heroic (epic) poems.

> Some foreign writers, some our own despise;
> The ancients only, or the moderns, prize.
> —*Alexander Pope*

   TRIPLET (or TERCET): a three-line stanza, usually with one rhyme. Here's an example which is now familiar to you:

> Whenas in silks my Julia goes
> Then, then (methinks) how sweetly flows
> That liquefaction of her clothes.
> —*Robert Herrick*

   QUATRAIN: a four-line stanza, rhymed or unrhymed. The heroic (or elegiac) quatrain is iambic pentametre, rhyming *a b a b*.
   SONNET: a 14-line poem, predominantly in iambic pentametre. The rhyme is usually according to one of the two following schemes. The PETRARCHAN (or ITALIAN) SONNET has two divisions: the first 8 lines (rhyming *a b b a a b b a*) are the OCTAVE; the last 6 (rhyming *c d c d c d,* or a variant) are the SESTET. Keats's "On First Looking into Chapman's Homer" (page 212) is a Petrarchan sonnet as is Lampman's, "A Summer Dream," mentioned earlier. The second kind of sonnet, the SHAKESPEAREAN (or ENGLISH) SONNET, is arranged usually into three quatrains and a couplet, rhyming *a b a b c d c d e f e f g g*. Lampman's "A Summer Evening" is a Shakespearean sonnet. Many sonnets have a marked correspondence between the rhyme scheme and the development of the thought. Thus, a Petrarchan sonnet may state a

generalization in the octave and a specific example in the sestet. Or a Shakespearean sonnet may give three examples—one in each quatrain—and draw a conclusion in the couplet. Very often the Shakespearean sonnet also divides, subtly, into octave and sestet, the first two quatrains forming one thought—but this need not be so.

Blank Verse and Free Verse

A good deal of English poetry is unrhymed, much of it in **BLANK VERSE**, that is, unrhymed iambic pentametre. Introduced into English poetry by Surrey in the middle of the sixteenth century, late in the century it became the standard medium (especially in the hands of Marlowe and Shakespeare) of English drama. A passage of blank verse that has a rhetorical unity is sometimes called a verse paragraph.

The second kind of unrhymed poetry fairly common in English, especially in the twentieth century, is **FREE VERSE** (or *VERS LIBRE*): rhythmical lines varying in length, adhering to no fixed metrical pattern, and usually unrhymed. The pattern is often largely based on repetition and parallel grammatical structure. Here is a sample of free verse. It is an excerpt from F. R. Scott's "Laurentian Shield":

> Hidden in wonder and snow, or sudden with summer
> This land stares at the sun in a huge silence
> Endlessly repeating something we cannot hear.
> Inarticulate, arctic,
> Not written on by history, empty as paper,   5
> It leans away from the world with songs in its lakes
> Older than love, and lost in the miles.

What can be said about the rhythmic structure of this poem? Rhymes are absent, and the lines vary greatly in the number of syllables, ranging from 7 (the fourth line) to 13 (the first line) and, in fact, to 16 (in line 27, not reproduced here), but when we read the poem we sense a rhythmic structure. The first three lines obviously hang together, each dealing with the silence of the land. We may notice, too, that each of these three lines has approximately the same number of syllables (the numbers are 13, 11, 12); this similarity in length, leading to and highlighting the short fourth line, is a kind of pattern. Long lines lead to short lines—such as "cabin syllables"—throughout the poem.

A division occurs when Scott inserts a quotation from an essay by Stephen Spender in *The Making of a Poem* (1955). This prose interruption both sums up the silent search for a tongue in which to speak the land—in the first section—and lays a foundation for the discussion of what kind of language is appropriate for Canada in the second section: "Cabin syllables/ Nouns of settlement / [. . .] / a language of life." The pause which the prose line creates (and the fact that it is printed in italics) marks a division and, as a result, the next section develops a new rhythm.

The next three lines each have 5 syllables, then the number of syllables grows: 7, 10. The pattern continues: 11 syllables, 14, and so on. From the "pre-words" of line 14 to the words of "full culture" in the longest line (27), the poem's rhythm builds as the land becomes more and more articulate.

The effect of naturalness in the speech rhythm of the penultimate line— "Will come, presently, tomorrow"—gives the sense of the speaker thinking aloud, being more precise as he or she thinks through how the future "speech" of the land will develop. Of course, this final effect of naturalness is part of a carefully constructed pattern in which rhythmic structure is part of meaning. Though at first glance free verse may appear unrestrained, as T. S. Eliot (a practitioner) said, "No *vers* is *libre* for the man who wants to do a good job"—or for the woman who wants to do a good job.

In recent years, poets who write what earlier would have been called "free verse" have characterized their writing as **OPEN FORM**. Such poets as the Americans Charles Olson, Robert Duncan, and Denise Levertov and the Canadian "Tish" poets and others reject the "closed form" of the traditional, highly patterned poem, preferring instead a form that seems spontaneous or exploratory. Olson's interest was in "composition by field"—that is, a poetics of the breath. To some readers, the unit seems to be the phrase or the line rather than the group of lines; it is, in fact, a set of words bounded by breath. Denise Levertov insists that the true writer of open-form poetry must have a "form sense"; she compares such a writer to "a sort of helicopter scout flying over the field of the poem, taking aerial photos and reporting on the state of the forest and its creatures [. . .]."[1] The "Tish" group of poets were influenced by Olson; they include George Bowering, Fred Wah, Frank Davey, Jamie Reid, and Daphne Marlatt. Although not part of the "Tish" group, bill bissett also works in this way. Marlatt has recently rethought Olson's theory of the breath as a compositional principle, converting it to her own sense of the word as an extension of her *female* body. (See the discussion of *écriture féminine*.)

All of these approaches to POETIC LINE, RHYTHM, RHYME, and BREATH demonstrate the ongoing attempt by poets to link *what* they say to *how* they say it. An understanding of form is essential to an understanding of poetry, yet, as Levertov says, "Form is never more than a *revelation* of content."

PREPARING TO WRITE ABOUT PROSODY

- Once you have decided to write about verse structure (whether metre, rhyme, or other sound pattern), write out a copy of the poem, photocopy it several times to give yourself a text upon which to work or—if you can scan it into your word processor—triple space it so you have plenty of room to work.

- Number the lines.

- Read the poem several times aloud, reading for sense and not imposing a false metre.

[1] "Some Notes on Organic Form," *The Poetics of the New American Poetry*, ed. Donald M. Allen, and Warren Tallman (New York, 1973) 316–17.

- Mark the stresses.

- Make marginal notes of any irregularities.

- Circle words that seem connected (by alliteration, or assonance, for example) and consider if this pattern is meaningful.

- Mark the rhyme scheme and make marginal notes of any imperfect rhymes. (Be careful of pronunciation in earlier poetry. In the eighteenth century, for example, line and join (pronounced jine) were perfect rhymes.)

- Prepare a tentative essay plan. Remember that your plan may change as you prepare a second draft. You may find that you want to focus on another pattern, or add a second grouping to the pattern which first interested you.

SAMPLE ESSAY ON METRICS: "SOUND AND SENSE IN HOUSMAN'S 'EIGHT O'CLOCK'"

Once you have decided to write about some aspect of versification, write your own copy of the poem, double-spaced or even triple-spaced, providing plenty of space to mark the stresses, indicate pauses, and annotate in any other way that strikes you. At this stage, it's probably best to use pencil for your scansion, since on rereading the poem you may revise some of your views, and you can simply erase and revise.

Here is an excellent analysis by a student. Notice that he quotes the poem and indicates the metrical pattern and that he proceeds chiefly by explaining the effect of the variations or departures from the norm in the order in which they occur.

Notice, too, that although it is usually a good idea to announce your thesis early—that is, in the first paragraph—this writer does *not* say, "This paper will show that Housman effectively uses rhythm to support his ideas." It's sufficient that the writer announces his topic in the title and again, in slightly different words, in the first sentence (the paper will "analyze the effects of sounds and rhythms in Housman's 'Eight O'Clock'"). We know where we will be going, and we read with perhaps even a bit of suspense, looking to see what the analysis will produce.

```
William Cott
English 303-02
Dr. S. Benet
20 March 2003
```

```
            Sound and Sense in Housman's "Eight O'Clock"
Before trying to analyze the effects of sounds and
rhythms in Housman's "Eight O'Clock," it will be useful
to quote the poem and to indicate which syllables are
```

stressed and which are unstressed. It must be
understood, however, that the following scansion is
relatively crude, because it falsely suggests that all
stressed syllables (marked ╱ are equally stressed, but
of course they are not: in reading the poem aloud, one
would stress some of them relatively heavily, and one
would stress others only a trifle more than the
unstressed syllables. It should be understood, too,
that in the discussion that follows the poem some other
possible scansions will be proposed.

> He stood,│and heard│the steeple
>   Sprinkle│the quar│ters on│the mor│ning town.
> One, two,│three, four,│to mar│ket-place│and people
>   It tossed│them down.
>
> Strapped, noosed,│nighing│his hour.
>   He stood│and coun│ted them│and cursed│his luck;
> And then│the clock│collec│ted in│the tower
>   Its strength,│and struck.

As the first line of the second stanza makes
especially clear, the poem is about a hanging at eight
o'clock, according to the title. Housman could have
written about the man's thoughts on the justice or
injustice of his fate, or about the reasons for the
execution, but he did not. Except for the second line
of the second stanza--"He stood and counted them and
cursed his luck"--he seems to tell us little about the
man's thoughts. But the poem is not merely a narrative
of an event; the sound effects in the poem help to
convey an idea as well as a story.

The first line establishes an iambic pattern. The
second line begins with a trochee ("Sprinkle"), not an
iamb, and later in the line possibly "on" should not be
stressed even though I marked it with a stress and made
it part of an iambic foot, but still the line is mainly
iambic. The poem so far is a fairly jingling description
of someone hearing the church clock chiming at each
quarter of the hour. Certainly, even though the second

line begins with a stress, there is nothing threatening
in "Sprinkle," a word in which we almost hear a tinkle.

But the second half of the first stanza surprises
us, and maybe even jolts us. In "One, two, three, four"
we get four consecutive heavy stresses. These stresses
are especially emphatic because there is a pause,
indicated by a comma, after each of them. Time is not
just passing to the chimes of a clock: this is a
countdown, and we sense that it may lead to something
significant. Moreover, the third line, which is longer
than the two previous lines, does not end with a pause.
This long line (eleven syllables) runs on into the next
line, almost as though once the countdown has begun
there is no stopping it. But then we do stop suddenly,
because the last line of the stanza has only four
syllables--far fewer than we would have expected. In
other words, this line stops unexpectedly because it has
only two feet. The first line had three feet, and the
second and third lines had five feet. Furthermore, this
short, final line of the stanza ends with a heavy stress
in contrast to the previous line, which ends with an
unstressed syllable, "péople." As we will see, the
sudden stopping at the end is a sort of preview of a
life cut short. Perhaps it is also a preview of a man
dropping through a trapdoor and then suddenly stopping
when the slack in the hangman's rope has been taken up.

In the first line of the second stanza the
situation is made clear, and it is also made emphatic by
three consecutive stresses: "Strapped, noosed, nighing
his hour." The pauses before each of these stresses make
the words especially emphatic. And though I have marked
the first two words of the next line "He stood,"
possibly "He" should be stressed too. In any case even
if "He" is not heavily stressed, it is certainly
stressed more than the other unstressed syllables,
"and," "-ed" (in "counted"), and "his." Similarly in
the third line of the stanza an effective reading might
even stress the first word as well as the second, thus:

"And then." And although normal speech would stress only the second syllable in "collected," in this poem the word appears after "clock," and so one must pause after the <u>k</u> sound in "clock" (one simply can't say "clock collected" without pausing briefly between the two words), and the effect is to put more than usual stress on the first syllable, almost turning it into "collected." And so this line really can reasonably be scanned like this:

And then the clock collected in the tower.

And again the third line of the stanza runs over into the fourth, propelling us onward. The final line surely begins with a stress, even though "Its" is not a word usually stressed, and so in the final line we begin with two strong stresses, "Its strength." This line, like the last line of the first stanza, is unusually short, and it too ends with a heavy stress. The total effect, then, of the last two lines of this stanza is of a clock striking, not just sprinkling music but forcefully and emphatically and decisively striking. The pause after "strength" is almost like the suspenseful pause of a man collecting his strength before he strikes a blow, and that is what the clock does:

And then the clock collected in the tower.
Its strength and struck.

If "clock collected" has in its <u>k</u> sounds a sort of ticktock effect, the clock at the end shows its force, for when it strikes the hour, the man dies.

I said near the beginning of this essay that Housman did not write about the man's thoughts about the justice or injustice of the sentence, and I think this is more or less true, but if we take into account the sound effects in the poem we can see that in part the poem is about the man's thoughts: he sees himself as the victim not only of his "luck" but of this machine, this ticking, unstoppable contraption that strikes not only the hours but a person's life.

📖 Suggestions for Further Reading

Alex Preminger and T. V. F. Brogan, eds., *The New Princeton Encyclopedia of Poetry and Poetics* (1993) is an indispensable reference work, with entries ranging from a few sentences to a number of pages on prosody, genres, critical approaches, schools, and so on. See also Ross Murfin and Supryia M. Ray, *The Bedford Glossary of Critical and Literary Terms* (1997).

On prosody see Paul Fussell, *Poetic Meter and Poetic Form,* rev. ed. (1997), and John Hollander, *Rhyme's Reason* 3rd. ed. (2001). Also consider Robert Pinsky, *The Sounds of Poetry: A Brief Guide* (1998).

For poets talking about their work, see *The Poet's Work: 29 Masters of 20th Century Poetry on the Origins and Practice of Their Art,* ed. Reginald Gibbons (1979). There are a number of videos showing American and Canadian poets reading and discussing their own work.

See also: Helen Vendler, *Part of Nature, Part of Us: Modern American Poets* (1980); and *The Music of What Happens: Poems, Poets, Critics* (1988); Peter Quartermain, *Disjunctive Poetics* (1992); Linda Hutcheon, *Splitting Images: Contemporary Canadian Ironies* (1991); Diana A. M. Relke, *Literary Mothers and Daughters: A Review of Twentieth Century Poetry by Canadian Women* (1987); Marjorie Perloff, *Poetic License* (1990).

✓ A Checklist: Getting Ideas for Writing about Poetry

If you are going to write about a fairly short poem, it's a good idea to copy out the poem, writing or typing it double-spaced. By writing it out you will be forced to notice details, down to the punctuation. After you have copied it, proofread it carefully. Catching an error—even the addition or omission of a comma—may help you to notice a detail in the original that you might otherwise have overlooked. And, once you have the poem written down with ample space between the lines, you have a worksheet with room for jottings.

A good essay is based on a genuine response to a poem; a response may be stimulated in part by first reading the poem aloud and then considering questions like these:

First Response

✓ What was your response to the poem on first reading?
✓ Did some parts please or displease you? Or puzzle you?
✓ After some study—perhaps checking the meaning of some words in the dictionary and reading the poem several times—did you modify your initial response to the parts and to the whole?

Speaker and Tone

✓ Who is the speaker? (Consider such issues as age, sex, personality, frame of mind, and tone of voice.)
✓ Is the speaker defined fairly precisely, or is the speaker simply a voice meditating?
✓ Does the speaker unconsciously reveal his or her personality and values?

✓ What is your attitude toward this speaker?

✓ Is the speaker reflecting on an earlier experience or attitude? If so, does he or she convey a sense of new awareness, such as regret for innocence lost?

Audience

✓ To whom is the speaker speaking?

✓ What is the situation (including time and place)? In some poems a listener is strongly implied, but in others there may be no audience other than the reader who "overhears" the speaker's meditation.

Structure and Form

✓ Does the poem proceed in a direct way, or at some points does the speaker reverse course, altering his or her tone or perceptions? If there is a shift, what do you make of it?

✓ Is the poem organized into parts? Is so, what are these parts—stanzas, for instance—and how does each develop from what precedes it?

✓ What is the effect of the form? Does the fact that the poem is organized into stanzas, or is written in blank verse matter to its meaning or effect? If the sense overflows the form, running from one part to the next, what effect is created?

Centre of Interest and Theme

✓ What is the poem about? Is the interest chiefly in a particular character or on a particular idea?

✓ Is the theme stated explicitly or implicitly? How might you state the theme in one sentence? What is lost by reducing the poem to a statement of a theme?

Diction

✓ How would you characterize the language?

✓ Do certain words have rich associations that relate to other words and help to define the speaker or the theme or both?

✓ What is the role of figurative language, if there is any? Does it help to define the speaker or the theme?

✓ What do you think is to be taken figuratively or symbolically, and what literally?

Sound Patterning

✓ What is the role of sound patterns, including repetition of sounds (for example, alliteration) and of entire words, and shifts in versification?

✓ If there are rhymes or half-rhymes or off-rhymes, what is their effect on you?

✓ If there are stresses or pauses, what do they communicate about the speaker's experience or thoughts? How do they affect you?

13

Writing about Film

Learning Objectives

When you've read this chapter, you should be able to

➤ see film as a medium with links to novels and drama, but with its own highly visual character.

Some literature classes study film. You may be asked to write about a film, or you may compare a film version of a text to the printed version. This brief chapter offers some definitions of indispensable technical terms, a few suggestions about topics, a sample essay by a student, and a list of questions that you may want to ask yourself as you begin to think about writing on a film.

THE CAMERA

An immediate reality in film criticism is the fact that film is more a matter of pictures than of words. The camera usually roves, giving us crowded streets, empty skies, rainy nights, or closeups of filled ashtrays and chipped coffee cups. A critic has aptly said that in Ingmar Bergman's *Smiles of a Summer Night* "the almost unbearably ornate crystal goblets, by their aspect and their positioning in the image, convey the oppressive luxuriousness of the diners' lives in purely and uniquely FILMIC terms." Cinema is primarily a visual medium.

Much Canadian film demonstrates this fact. Vast landscapes or harsh winter scenes dominate the action, which is often turned inward against the hard climate. Often little seems to happen—indeed, for some viewers Canadian films seem static—but, in fact, the camera is busy, interrogating the setting and exposing connections between the characters and their environment. Such is the case, for example, in Atom Egoyan's *The Adjuster,* where the camera returns again and again to a bleak undeveloped subdivision site which becomes a dominating symbol of the characters' lives and the adjuster's moral emptiness. It is true also in Jean-Claude Lauzon's *Un Zoo, la Nuit (Night Zoo)* where the PROTAGONIST is seen surrounded by high tech stereo equipment and telephone answering machines that seem to have more life than he does.

In short, the speaker in a film does not usually dominate. When a character speaks, the camera often gives us a *reaction shot,* focusing not on the speaker but on the face or gestures of a character who is affected by the speech, thus giving the spectator a visual interpretation of the words. Even when the camera does focus on the speaker, it is likely to offer an interpretation. An extreme example is a scene from *Brief Encounter:* A gossip is talking, and the camera gives us a close-up of her jabbering mouth, which monstrously fills the screen.

In many ways, film is more like a novel than a play, the action being presented not directly by actors but by a camera, which, like a novelist's point of view, comments on the story while telling it. A novelist may, like a dramatist, convey information about a character through dialogue and gesture but may also simply tell us about the character's state of mind. Similarly, a filmmaker may use the camera to inform us about unspoken thought.

The medium, as everyone knows, is part of the message, an idea that the Canadian media theorist Marshall McLuhan popularized. Lord Laurence Olivier made Shakespeare's *Henry V* in colour, but *Hamlet* in black and white because these media say different things. Peter Brook's film of *King Lear* is also in black and white, with an emphasis on an icy whiteness that catches the play's spirit of old age and desolation; a *Lear* in colour might have an opulence that would work against the lovelessness and desolation of much of the play. Richard Brooks's *In Cold Blood,* also in black and white, tried to look like a documentary. This documentary quality is very prevalent in early Canadian film, much of which is shot to appear as reportage even when it is in colour. Indeed, the term **DOCUMENTARY** was coined by John Grierson in his early work at the National Film Board. Similarly, although most contemporary films are made in colour, Todd Haynes made parts of *Poison* (1991) in black and white, to evoke the grainy "B movie" horror films of the 1950s, and parts in lurid Technicolor to exaggerate the Romantic films of that decade.

Of course, a filmmaker, though resembling a novelist in offering pervasive indirect comment, is not a novelist any more than he or she is a playwright or director of a play; the medium has its own techniques, and the filmmaker works with them. These choices are sometimes purely artistic, but often involve specific use of the technical apparatus of the medium. For example, the kind of lens used can help determine what the viewer sees. In *The Graduate,* Benjamin runs toward the camera (he is trying to reach a church before his girl marries another man), but he seems to make no progress because a telephoto lens was used and thus his size does not increase as it normally would. The lens helps communicate his desperate sense of frustration. Conversely, a wide-angle lens makes a character approach the camera with menacing rapidity; he quickly looms into the foreground. There are, of course, many such techniques available to the director.

POSTSTRUCTURAL CRITICISM
AND THE CINEMATIC GAZE

Film criticism in the past 20 years has changed radically. Important film journals, such as *Screen* and *Cahiers du Cinéma*, review film using the poststructuralist theories discussed in Chapter 8. PSYCHOLOGICAL CRITICISM, especially Lacanian criticism, is appropriate for cinema in which human identity is observed, mirrored, and seen to fade. Political criticisms, especially MARXIST approaches, show cinema to be part of the larger structures by which society forms, explains, and regulates itself. The major debate over authorship is particularly fraught in film criticism, where the role of the viewer in interpreting what is seen is central. FEMINIST CRITICISM has been especially interested in film, and it is as a result of feminist discourse that film criticism generally has opened up.

Feminist critics argue that film has been a major force of the patriarchy, creating images of women (and men) that construct gender and subordinate women. Perhaps most important in this context is the important notion of the GAZE. Since the viewer watches without actually being present (and without the same level of imaginative participation that is seen in drama spectatorship), the relationship of the viewer as subject to the character on the screen as object is full of important implications. Theorists suggest that our love of watching (scopophilia) makes the viewing erotic (at least on the deepest psychological level), which further complicates the viewing of, say, female movie stars by male watchers. A number of critics have used the term the *male gaze*, which, it is asserted, reduces the object of its vision to a position of non-male object. Female screenwriters and directors are attempting to find new ways to use film to explore women's and men's bodies, women's place in society, and female language without subscribing to the traditional voyeuristic objectification which, it is argued, has been typical of film since its outset. Many of the issues here are very complex and require extensive reading in psychology, feminist theory, and film methodology. For an excellent, detailed overview of recent trends in film criticism, see Robert Lapsley and Michael Westlake, *Film Theory: An Introduction* (1988).

EDITING

A film, no less than a poem or a play, is something made, and it is not made by simply exposing some footage. Shots—often taken at widely separated times and places—must be appropriately joined. For example, we see a man look off to the right, and then we get a shot of what he is looking at and then a shot of his reaction. Until the shots are assembled, we don't have a film— we merely have the footage. V. I. Pudovkin put it this way: "The film is not *shot*, but built, built up from the separate strips of celluloid that are its raw material." This building-up is the process of editing.

More than a story can be told, of course; something of the appropriate emotion can be communicated by juxtaposing, say, a medium-long shot of a group of impassively advancing muggers against a close-up of a single terri-fied victim. Similarly, emotion can be communicated by the duration of the shots (quick shots suggest haste; prolonged shots suggest slowness) and by the lighting (progressively darker shots can suggest melancholy; progressively lighter shots can suggest hope or joy).

The Russian theorists of film called this process of building by quick cuts MONTAGE. The theory held that shots, when placed together, add up to more than the sum of the parts. Montage, for them, was what made a film a work of art and not a mere replica of reality. American writers commonly use the term merely to denote quick cutting, and French writers use it merely in the sense of cutting. Today, some people oppose extensive editing, arguing that the viewer should be allowed to react with less direction. Even when the director steps back from suggesting interpretation, however, the art form *itself* is an agent of construction.

THEME

It is time now to point out an obvious fact: Mastery of technique, though necessary to good filmmaking, will not in itself make a good film. A good film is not a bag of cinematic devices but the embodiment, through cinematic devices, of a vision, an underlying theme. What is this theme or vision? It is a filmmaker's perception of some aspect of existence that he or she thinks is worthy of our interest. Normally, this perception involves characters and a plot. Though recent North American films, relying heavily on colour, music, quick cutting, and the wide screen, have tended to emphasize emotional experi-ence and de-emphasize narrative, still most of the best cinema is concerned with what people do: with character and plot.

Some critics have argued that the concept of theme is meaningless: A film is only a detailed presentation of certain imaginary people in imaginary situations, not a statement about an aspect of life. Susan Sontag, in a chal-lenging essay in *Against Interpretation*, argues that our tendency to seek a meaning in what we perceive is a manifestation of a desire to control the work of art by reducing its rich particulars to manageable categories. Sontag's view is worth considering, but as we said in Chapter 11, quoting Janet Wolff, "the true experience of art involves the understanding of meaning" (191). When we watch a film we enjoy an aesthetic experience with its own criteria, but we also see characters and events that have wider meaning. These mean-ings, however, are neither more universal than other events we observe nor necessarily more significant. The new critics of film open up our under-standing of how film has become part of the SIGNIFYING PRACTICES by which we regulate our lives. It is, contemporary theorists argue, important that we are aware of how those narrative elements in a film which seem to point to universal types or truths are, themselves, part of larger social metanarratives. When we read a novel, or see a happening on the stage or screen, we inevitably feel—if only because we've been asked to give the event an hour or more of our time—that it is offered to us as noteworthy, an example not of what *happened* (it didn't happen; it's fictional) but an example of what *happens*. Contemporary film critics suggest we must resist the tendency always to extrapolate categories and classes from individual fictive representations. Sometimes a character can speak for a category of people, but usually a careful reader or viewer will see some aspects of character that a fictional person may share with others and some aspects that are unique to that particular fictional being. Making wide generalizations is never a good idea.

Sometimes we sense that a film has an arguable thesis. Stanley Kubrick, for example, has said that *A Clockwork Orange* "warns against the new psychedelic fascism—the eye-popping, multimedia, quadrasonic, drug-oriented conditioning of human beings by other human beings—which many believe will usher in the forfeiture of human citizenship and the beginning of zombiedom." A filmmaker, however, need not argue a thesis that is subject to verification. It is enough if he or she sees in the human experience something worth our contemplation and embodies it on film. Contemporary film— and certainly current film criticism—asks only that this "looking" be self-conscious, that viewers be aware that they are looking at a construction in art (in light, in the case of film) and not believe that they are looking at a fundamental reality.

GETTING READY TO WRITE

Probably an essay on a film will not be primarily about the use of establishing shots or of wipes or of any such matters, but rather it will be about some of the reasons why a particular film pleases or displeases, succeeds or fails, seems significant or insignificant, and in discussing these large matters it is sometimes necessary (or at least economical) to use the commonest technical terms.

Writing an essay about a new film—one not yet available for study on video—presents difficulties not encountered in writing about stories, plays, and poems. Because we experience film in a darkened room, we cannot easily take notes, and because the film may be shown only once, we cannot always take another look at passages that puzzle us. But some brief notes can be taken even in the dark; it is best to amplify them as soon as light is available, while you still know what the scrawls mean. If you can see the film more than once, do so; if it is available on video, rent it and watch it more than once and, of course, if the script has been published, study it. Draft your paper as soon as possible after your first viewing, and then see the film again. You can sometimes check hazy memories of certain scenes and techniques with fellow viewers. But even with multiple viewings and the aid of friends, it is almost impossible to get all the details right. Formal papers or books on film use sophisticated editing machines to pinpoint scenes, or even frames, and cite these, allowing for very specific comments. Student essays can rarely match this level of documentation; try your best to indicate clearly where in the film your point is illustrated and try very hard to get your facts correct.

A SAMPLE ESSAY ON VISUAL SYMBOLS: "A JAPANESE *MACBETH* "

Printed here is a student's essay on a film. Because it is on a version of *Macbeth*, it is in some degree a comparison between a film and a play, but it does not keep shifting back and forth and does not make the obvious point that many differences are found. Rather, it fairly quickly announces that it will be concerned with one kind of difference—the use of visual symbols that the camera can render effectively—and it then examines four such symbols.

The writer of this essay has done more than work out an acceptable organization; she has some perceptions to offer, and she has found the right details and provided neat transitions so that the reader can move through the essay with pleasure.

Bud Lockwood
English 242-02
Dr. H. Brockly

A Japanese Macbeth

Essayist's general position, and implicit thesis, is clear from the start.

A Japanese movie-version of Macbeth sounds like a bad idea--until one sees Kurosawa's film, Throne of Blood, in which Toshiro Mifune plays Washizu, the equivalent of Macbeth. It is a satisfying film largely because it is not merely a filmed version of a play, but rather it is a freely re-created version that is designed for the camera. The very fact that it is in Japanese is probably a great help to Westerners. If it were in English, we would be upset at the way some speeches are cut, but because it is in Japanese, we do not compare the words to Shakespeare's, and we concentrate on the visual aspects of the film.

As the paragraph proceeds, it zooms in on the topic.

There are several differences in the plots of the two works. Among the alterations are such things as these: Shakespeare's three witches are reduced to one; Lady Washizu has a

Essayist tells us exactly what will be covered in the rest of the essay.

miscarriage; Washizu is killed by his own troops and not by Macduff. But this paper will discuss another sort of change, the introduction of visual symbols, which the camera is adept at rendering, and which play an important part in the film. The four chief visual symbols are the fog, the castle, the forest, and the horses.

Transition (through repetition of part of previous sentence) and helpful forecast.

Analysis, not mere plot telling.

The fog, the castle, and the forest, though highly effective, can be dealt with rather briefly. When the film begins we get a slow panoramic view of the ruined castle seen through the fog. The film ends with a similar panoramic view. These two scenes end with a dissolve, though almost all of the other scenes end abruptly with sharp cuts, and so the effect is that of lingering sorrow at the transience of human creations, and awe at the permanence of the mysterious natural world, whose mist slowly drifts across what once was a mighty castle built by a great chief. The castle itself, when we come to see it in its original condition, is not a particularly graceful Japanese building. Rather, it is a low, strong building, appropriate for an energetic warrior. The interior scenes show low, oppressive ceilings, with great exposed beams that almost seem to crush the people within the rooms. It represents man's achievement in the centre of the misty tangled forest of the mysterious world, but it also

Thoughtful interpretation.

suggests, despite its strength, how stifling that achievement is, in comparison with the floating mists and endless woods. The woods, rainy and misty, consist of curiously gnarled trees and vines, and suggest a labyrinth that has entrapped man, even though for a while man thinks he is secure in his castle. Early in the film we see Washizu riding through the woods, in and out of mists, and behind a maze of twisted trees that periodically hide him from our sight. Maybe it is not too fanciful to suggest that the branches through which we glimpse him blindly riding in the fog are a sort of net that entangles him. The trees and the mist are the vast unfathomable universe; man can build his castle, can make his plans, but he cannot subdue nature for long. He cannot have his way forever; death will ultimately catch him, despite his strength. One later scene of the forest must be mentioned. Near the end of the film, when the forest moves (the soldiers are holding up leafy boughs to camouflage themselves), we get a spectacular shot; Shakespeare talks of the forest moving, but in the film we see it. Suddenly the forest seems to give a shudder and to be alive, crawling as though it is a vast horde of ants. Nature is seen to rise up against Washizu's crimes.

Further interpretation.

Essayist moves chronologically.

Summary leads, at the end of the paragraph, to interpretation.

Shakespeare's stage could do very little about such an effect as the fog, though his poetry can call it to mind, and it could do even less about the forest. Kurosawa did not feel bound to the text of the play: he made a movie, and he took advantage of the camera's ability to present impressive and significant scenic effects. Similarly, he made much use of horses, which, though mentioned in Shakespeare's play, could not be shown on the Elizabethan stage. In fact, in <u>Macbeth</u> Shakespeare more or less apologizes for the absence of horses when one murderer explains to the other that when horsemen approach the palace it is customary for them to leave their horses and to walk the rest of the way. But

The first half of this paragraph is a well-handled comparison.

A reminder of a point made earlier, but now developed at length.

the film gives us plenty of horses, not only at the start, when Washizu is galloping in the terrifying forest, but throughout the film, and they are used to suggest the terror of existence, and the evil passions in Washizu's heart. Shakespeare provided a hint. After King Duncan is murdered, Shakespeare tells us that Duncan's horses "Turned wild in nature, broke their stalls," and even that they ate each other (2.4.16-18). In the film, when Washizu and his wife plot the murder of their lord, we see the panic-stricken horses running around the courtyard of the castle--a sort of parallel to the scene of Washizu chaotically riding in and out of the fog near the beginning of the movie. The horses in the courtyard apparently have sensed man's villainous plots, or perhaps they are visual equivalents of the fierce emotions in the minds of Washizu and his wife. Later, when Washizu is planning to murder Miki (the equivalent of Banquo), we see Miki's white horse kicking at his attendants. Miki saddles the horse, preparing to ride into the hands of his assassins. Then Kurosawa cuts to a long shot of the courtyard at night, where Miki's attendants are nervously waiting for him to return. Then we hear the sound of a galloping horse, and suddenly the white horse comes running in, riderless. Yet another use of this motif is when we cut to a wild horse, after Washizu's wife has said that she is pregnant. In the film the wife has a miscarriage, and here again the horse is a visual symbol of the disorder engendered within her (the child would be the

Thoughtful generalization.

heir to the usurped throne), as the other horses were symbols for the disorder in her mind and in Macbeth's. All of these cuts to the horses are abrupt, contributing to the sense of violence that the unrestrained horses themselves embody. Moreover, almost the only close-ups in the film are some shots of horses, seen from a low angle, emphasizing their powerful, oppressive brutality.

Conclusion is chiefly a restatement but the last sentence gives it an interesting twist.

Throne of Blood is not Shakespeare's Macbeth--but even a filmed version of a staged version of the play would not be Shakespeare's Macbeth either, for the effect of a film is simply not identical with the effect of a play with live actors on the stage. But Throne of Blood is a fine translation of Macbeth into an approximate equivalent. Despite its lack of faithfulness to the literal text, it is in a higher way faithful. It is a work of art, like its original.

📖 Suggestions for Further Reading

For quick reference, see Ephraim Katz, *The Film Encyclopedia* (1980); and Leslie Halliwell, *The Filmgoer's Companion,* 9th ed. (1988). For somewhat fuller discussions of directors, see Richard Roud, ed., *Cinema: A Critical Dictionary: The Major Film-Makers,* 2 vols. (1980).

Good introductory books include Gerald Mast, *A Short History of the Movies,* 5th ed., rev. Bruce F. Kawin (1992); Leo Braudy, *The World in a Frame* (1984); Bruce F. Kawin, *How Movies Work* (1992); Thomas Sobchack and Vivian C. Sobchack, *An Introduction to Film,* 2nd ed. (1987); David Bordwell, *Making Meaning: Inference and Rhetoric in the Interpretation of Cinema* (1989); Edward R. Branigan, *Point of View in Cinema* (1984); Timothy Corrigan, *A Short Guide to Writing about Film* (1989).

For theory, see Robert Lapsley and Michael Westlake, *Film Theory: An Introduction* (1988); Gerald Mast, Marshall Cohen, and Leo Braudy, eds., *Film Theory and Criticism,* 4th ed. (1992). For a highly influential feminist study, see Laura Mulvey, *Visual and Other Pleasures* (1989).

For studies of Canadian film, see Gary Evans, *In the National Interest: A Chronicle of the National Film Board of Canada from 1949–1989* (1991); Joyce Nelson, *The Colonized Eye: Rethinking the Grierson Legend* (1988); Debbie Green, ed., *Guide to the Collection of the Film Library of the Canadian Film Institute* (1984); Jean T. Guenette and Jacques Gagone, *Inventory of the Collections of the National Film, Television and Sound Archives* (1983).

PART 4

Inside:
A Grammar Sketch,
Style, Format, and
Special Assignments

14

Grammar, Syntax, Style, and Format

Learning Objectives

When you've read this chapter, you should be able to

➢ recall basic elements of grammar and syntax;

➢ know how to avoid common expression errors;

➢ control elements of style such as diction, variation, and sound patterns;

➢ write effective sentences;

➢ write unified and coherent paragraphs;

➢ write emphatically;

➢ produce a correctly formed manuscript;

➢ use ellipsis and additions when quoting;

➢ set down quotations and quote lines of poetry;

➢ place commas, periods, and question marks correctly when using quotations; and

➢ indicate the published status of a title by using quotation marks, italics, or neither.

A VERY BRIEF REVIEW OF GRAMMAR AND SYNTAX

Grammar versus Syntax

Most people think that composition problems arise only from faulty GRAMMAR. In fact, in English, many sentences are confusing or incorrect in meaning—or just plain ugly—because of errors in SYNTAX rather than errors of grammar.

Syntax is the order of words in a sentence. In the most general case (in the ACTIVE VOICE), an English sentence looks like this:

subject	predicate

noun or noun substitute	verb or verb phrase + object or completion

The goal of good writing is to help the reader to discern these two fundamental elements. All other aspects of writing correct sentences flow from knowing the subject and the verb. In complex sentences—which we'll define in a moment—more than one subject and verb will appear. In these sentences, it becomes even more important to identify subjects and verbs, and to determine the most important of each of these: the *subject of the sentence* and the *principal verb*. Awkward syntax can twist sections of the sentence so that it becomes less clear exactly what the subject of the sentence is, or how it is modified, or what it is trying to accomplish. "Plain English" aims to place modifications and subordinations carefully within a simple syntax that renders the sentence's meaning crystal clear. (Don't take "simple" to mean "simple-minded." Very complex thought requires the clearest statement if your reader is to understand it.)

Grammar is a set of rules of common usage that helps to make clear to the reader exactly what any given "piece" of the sentence—a word, a phrase, or a clause—is doing. Grammar can vary depending on the purpose of your writing and your audience (see Chapter 1.) The way you speak to friends at a hockey game is not the way you write a business proposal or a literary analysis. In order for people to communicate effectively, therefore, literate people have agreed, over time, to a Standard Grammar (what was once called "The Queen's English"), which can be used in most cases and when the audience is unknown. This is the kind of grammar you might have learned in school and which you will need to employ in writing at the college and university level.

Grammar is a large subject and is not the purpose of this book. But the following set of definitions and ways to avoid common errors can be used as a concise checklist as you write. If you want to study grammar in more detail, turn to a grammar text or composition handbook—there are many in your institution's library or Writing Centre. In the examples on the next page, subjects are underlined once, verbs, twice, and objects or completions, three times. You might benefit from underlining these parts of speech in any sentence that seems awkward or that you think might contain errors. If you can identify the parts, you can more easily fit them together into pleasing syntax by means of correct grammar.

Some Definitions

NOUNS name things, including concepts.

PRONOUNS take the place of nouns; some are personal (*I, you, she, he, one, we, they*); some are relative (*who, which, that, whoever*). The pronoun *it* is personal, though it can sometimes refer back to an inanimate thing.

ANTECEDENTS are the nouns or noun substitutes to which a pronoun later refers (*The* woman *took* her *book back to the library;* Education *has* its *costs*).

ADJECTIVES modify nouns or pronouns; they can be words, phrases, or clauses.

ADVERBS modify verbs, adjectives, or other adverbs; they can be words, phrases, or clauses.

VERBS express an action or a state of being; they can be words or phrases (*may have given*).

Verbs can be:

> TRANSITIVE, if the verb directly passes action from the noun to an object: *Canadians often* send peacekeepers *abroad.*

> INTRANSITIVE, when the verb itself completes the sentence and no object or other completion is needed: *Snow* falls.

> LINKING, when the completion after the verb somehow describes the meaning of the noun, rather than showing that noun doing an independent action: *The* Rockies are mountains.

VERBALS are forms in which a word that is usually a verb acts as another part of speech; a verbal, therefore, cannot act as a true verb (and is sometimes called a NON-FINITE VERB). Any string that contains a verbal and no true verb, no FINITE VERB, will be a SENTENCE FRAGMENT.

Verbals can be:

> INFINITIVES, which are the basic form of the verb (to eat, to run): These can act as nouns (To sleep *next to an elephant* is *not* easy.); adjectives (*The* need *to exercise* increases *as one's stress levels increase.*); or adverbs Global warming makes *the weather difficult to predict.*)

> PARTICIPLES, when the word or phrase acts as an adjective: Living within North America, *Canadians* are subject *to American economic hegemony.* ("Living within North America" modifies "Canadians.")

> GERUNDS, when the word or phrase acts as a noun: Drinking *coffee* has become *increasingly* popular.

Verbals exist in the present tense and the past tense. In the present tense, both participles and gerunds take the ending *-ing*. No finite verb takes this ending. If you write *-ing*, you have just created a noun or adjective form, but you have not created a verb; so unless you have a true verb elsewhere in the string, it is not a full sentence. A string with only an -*ing* verbal is a sentence fragment, as, for example: *Writing a difficult task.* In the past tense, verbals are harder to recognize. They often end in -*d* or -*ed*, but some are irregular (like *begun*) and many end in -*en* (*eaten*). When you create a verbal in the past tense, you still need a finite verb elsewhere in the sentence, or you will have created a fragment.

PREPOSITIONS show connections between nouns or pronouns and other words; most often, they serve as adjectives or adverbs, showing relationships (often in space and time): *on, in, at, about, for, with, of,* etc. Prepositions can be words or phrases (*They decided to travel to New York* in spite of *the poor exchange on the dollar.*).

CONJUNCTIONS link words and clauses. (See COMPOUND SENTENCES, on the next page.)

PHRASES are sets of related words.

> Verb phrases are made up of the verb and auxiliary or helping words like *do, did, does, can, would, could, should, will, must,* and *others.* Example: Careful editing can help you improve your writing.

CLAUSES are sets of related words that contain a noun and a verb. They can be INDEPENDENT (or MAIN) CLAUSES, which can stand alone, or DEPENDENT (or SUBORDINATE) CLAUSES, which must be attached to an independent clause. If you allow a dependent (subordinate) clause to stand alone, you have created a sentence fragment.

Tense

Tense is a very complex matter in English. People learning the language as adults have considerable trouble with the preoccupation in English discourse with exact placement in time (and space). The subject is simply too large for this text, and you should consult a good grammar text. Here is a sketch of the sequences: a verb action moves forward from the completed PAST tense (usually shown by -*ed* but sometimes irregular) through a series of perfect and progressive tenses, each of which moves the action more exactly toward the PRESENT and then forward through a parallel series of placements to the eventual FUTURE, marked by the auxiliary *will.* As the verb moves, auxiliary verbs (forms of *to be* and *to have*) are attached to pinpoint its location in the continuum of time. So, a chart for the verb *to eat* might look like this:

past	past perfect	present perfect	present	future perfect	future
ate	had eaten	has eaten have eaten	eats	will have eaten	will eat

Past Perfect Progressive had been eating

Future Perfect Progressive have been eating

Types of Sentences

English sentences can be LOOSE (also called CUMULATIVE) or PERIODIC. In a loose sentence, elements can be rearranged and the verb can move around. Often, the main idea is laid out, and then modifications and amplifications provide additional information (*"Borders" is a short story that tells of a First Nations mother's pride in the face of governmental regulations and non-Native attitudes, as seen from the point of view of her young son, himself caught up in the cultural tension between his heritage and the media-controlled world in which he lives.*). As you can see, this sentence accumulates information as it goes along.

In a periodic sentence, the main clause comes at the end, before the period. (*By showing the mother's intransigence, the governmental regulations against which First Nations people must fight, and the ultimate capitulation of that bureaucracy in the face of media challenge, "Borders" teaches something about Native pride.*) A periodic sentence has stylistic uses because it delays the most important information to the end of the sentence, raising readers' expectations. (Note the use of the plural possessive in the preceding sentence).

English sentences can be SIMPLE, COMPOUND, OR COMPLEX, or can combine the latter two:

A SIMPLE sentence is at least a verb with an understood subject (*Run!*) but usually consists of a single main clause with no subordinate clauses (*The mother spoke.*).

A COMPOUND sentence is composed of two or more clauses that can stand as independent sentences but that are connected with a COORDINATING CONJUNCTION (*for, and, nor, but, or, yet, so*) or with a CORRELATIVE CONJUNCTION (such as *not only* or *but also*) or with a CONJUNCTIVE ADVERB (such as *also* or *however*) or with a colon, a semicolon, or (rarely) a comma. We'll talk about the comma splice in a moment. (A mnemonic that will help you to remember the coordinating conjunctions is the nonsense word FANBOYS. This acronym is a memory tag that reminds you that there are only seven such words in the language.)

A COMPLEX sentence is an independent clause and one or more dependent (subordinate) clauses.

A COMPOUND-COMPLEX SENTENCE consists of at least two independent clauses correctly joined and at least one other dependent clause correctly attached. As your subject matter becomes more complex, your sentences will become more complex, but remember that a mix of all types gives pleasing variety and that simple and compound sentences often assist a reader's understanding.

Voice

Sentences can be written in the ACTIVE or PASSIVE VOICE. The typical sentence pattern (diagrammed above) is active. In the active sentence, the subject performs the action of the verb (*The men pulled the ring in the bear's nose*). In the passive sentence, the object moves to the position of the subject (*The ring in the bear's nose was pulled by the men*) and is acted upon by the subject. Most contemporary writers use the active voice. The passive voice requires the reader to perform two cognitive actions rather than one in order to understand the meaning: the reader must "turn around" the sentence. This type of sentence is, therefore, harder to control and harder to understand. Student writers often like to use the passive as it sounds somehow more "formal" or "fancy"—and it does generate more words! The passive voice, however, is liable to cause you grammar troubles, so we urge you to use the active voice. (In the section on style, below, we discuss the deliberate use of the passive voice for effect.)

Mood

The attitude in which we write can change. Sometimes we are merely giving information or asking a question; we are then in the INDICATIVE mood (*The bear would prefer to be in his mountain home. Why did the two men take him away?*).

Sometimes we are giving a command, or giving direction; this is termed the IMPERATIVE mood (*Don't apply North American values to the "spare men of Kashmir" in Birney's poem*).

Sometimes—and this is the most difficult mood—we are speaking in a state of conjecture, desire, prayer, suggestion, or we are raising a notion that is hypothetical or imaginary. In this register of discourse, we are in the SUBJUNCTIVE mood and this mood has specific verb forms. You should consult a grammar text, which will explain all the aspects of the subjunctive, but here is a brief comment.

The verb most commonly altered in this mood is the verb *to be*. In expressions of doubt or imagination, the normal conjugation changes as, for example: *If I were to win the lottery, I would travel around the world.* (Not *if I was to win*). By the way, this example is also the CONDITIONAL tense, which often looks like the subjunctive. A common error, especially in the conditional, is to reverse the "if" proposition and the indicative response and to incorrectly use the auxiliary *would* to do so. **Incorrect:** *If I would have won the lottery, I would travel around the world.* Remember that the helper *would* appears in the indicative response to a subjunctive or conditional proposition and that this response is in the main clause.

All verbs revert to their plain form in the subjunctive: *The mother asked that her son accept Native mythology.* In the indicative mood, the conjugation would be *Her son accepts*.

Some expressions always use the subjunctive: *Be that as it may; Long live the Queen; Be damned*, and so on.

Case (and Who/Whom, We/Us)

Two pronouns, *who* and *whom*, seem to cause confusion, and they remind us that CASE is an important point of grammar. Remember that *who* is in the SUBJECTIVE CASE (that is, it is the subject) and *whom* is in the OBJECTIVE CASE. In the POSSESSIVE CASE, the form is *whose*. Hence:

> *The monk* to whom *the mason spoke traded clothes with him*

In this example, the pronoun is the object of the preposition *to*. Here is another example, where the pronoun is the subject of the sentence:

> Who *is going to the party?*

And, finally, consider this sentence where the pronoun is possessive:

> Whose *car is this?*

Other pronouns cause similar problems. Always test yourself for case when you are using pronouns such as *he/him/his; she/her/hers; we/us/our(s)*. One test is to substitute *he/him* (or *she/her*) and see if you can "hear" the correct version. In compound constructions, break the sentence and consider the appropriate pronoun case for each half. (It should be the same case for each part of the compound.) Then put the sentence back together, preserving the correct pronoun:

> *(She, Her) and (We, Us) went to a lecture by Suzuki.* (subjective case)
>
> *Suzuki's comments on damage to the ecology made sense to (she, her) and (we, us).* (objective case)
>
> *She went to the lecture [. . .]. // We went to the lecture [. . .].*
>
> *Suzuki's comments [. . .] made sense to her. // Suzuki's comments [. . .] made sense to us.*

Therefore:

> *She and we went to the lecture.*
>
> *Suzuki's comments on damage to the ecology made sense to her and us.*

Comma Use

Because of its loose syntax, English depends upon proper comma use. Commas do not indicate places to breathe or pause: they have very specific grammatical uses. Commas *set off* items and *separate* items. Consult a grammar text for the complete rules of comma use.

Commas that set off

Here, in a sketch, is a way of thinking about commas used to set off:

In the active sentence pattern above, we seek to identify the subject, its verb, and any completion. Anything that intrudes between these basic elements needs to be marked off, unless it is essential or RESTRICTIVE information. Consider this string:

Students who are lazy fail.

What is the subject? It might be "students": *Students fail.* The clause "who are lazy" is extra, non-essential, or NON-RESTRICTIVE information. Such a sentence tells us that all students fail, and, by the way, all students are also lazy. If you do mean this libelous statement, you would mark off the clause that intrudes between the subject and the verb:

Students, who are lazy, fail.

But this is not likely the intended meaning. Not all students fail, and certainly not all students are lazy (you aren't if you're reading this book). The true subject is likely *Students who are lazy* (which might also be written *lazy students*). These students fail. If this is the intention, then the clause is RESTRICTIVE—it provides essential information. In this case, no commas are needed:

Students who are lazy fail.

Any other comma placement is incorrect. If you put a comma after "lazy," as many are tempted to do, you are actually placing a comma between the subject, *Students who are lazy,* and its verb, *fail.* There is never a comma between a subject and its verb because, as we said above, the purpose of the comma is to mark off intrusions between these linked elements.

If you can remember this notion of RESTRICTIVE and NON-RESTRICTIVE elements, you will generally place commas correctly. The trick is to ask yourself each time, "is this restrictive or not"? If it is a non-restrictive element (word, phrase, clause), it will likely need commas around it; if it is restrictive, it will likely need no comma(s).

This applies, for example, to introductory phrases and clauses: if they do not restrict meaning (and they usually don't), they need a comma: *Reading Birney's poem, the student felt great empathy with the "tranced" men of Kashmir.* The main idea is that the student felt empathy; the information that clarifies what stimulated this feeling is extra.

Commas, then, are used to set off non-restrictive elements, including parenthetical expressions, explanations, transitions, tags, interjections, and elements that contrast with one another.

Commas that separate
In this usage, commas appear before coordinating conjunctions (FANBOYS) to separate independent clauses. They also separate groups of three or more words, phrases, or clauses in a series—as they just did in this sentence. (Some people suggest omitting the final comma in a series, but it is generally a good idea to retain it for clarity.) Commas also mark off dates, addresses, and titles.

COMMON ERRORS OF COMPOSITION

Fragments

frag

Writing a string of words that is actually a phrase or a dependent (subordinate) clause and trying to make it stand alone creates a fragment. You need to supply a verb. Hence, *Hoping to enjoy a hamburger* is a fragment and needs both a subject and verb: *Hoping to enjoy a hamburger, the boy in King's story was dismayed to see his mother packing sandwiches for the trip.*

Fused sentences

fs

If you write two dependent clauses and "stick them together" with no indication that one has ended and the other has begun, you will have fused the two. Hence, *The young narrator in Joyce's story was disillusioned he found that infatuation leads to disappointment* is a fused sentence. You correct this error by dividing the two clauses or by one of the means we next discuss in the spliced sentence.

The Comma Splice

cs

This is one of the most common of grammar errors; it also seems to be a particular annoyance to Canadian readers. British writers more often allow the splice, or create the particular, balanced syntax which allows it, than do Canadian writers.

If you write two dependent clauses and, recognizing that each is a unit, separate them only by a comma, you will have created a **comma splice**. Hence, *The hangman is a social outcast, the woman who marries the hangman becomes doubly condemned.* is incorrect.

There are four ways to correct a comma splice:

1. Determine that you do want two independent clauses and separate them with a period: *The hangman is a social outcast. The woman who marries the hangman becomes doubly condemned.*
2. Determine that you do want two independent clauses and ask yourself if both parts are equally strong, or if one is more important than the other. If one is more important, connect the two with the appropriate coordinating conjunction (FANBOYS) so that the second clause amplifies the first: *The hangman is a social outcast, so the woman who marries the hangman becomes doubly condemned. The hangman is a social outcast and the woman who marries the hangman becomes doubly condemned.* Notice that each conjunction except "and" inflects the meaning of the subsequent clause; "and" merely joins without comment.

If you wish both parts to have equal strength and simply to work with or against each other, then substitute a punctuation mark for the conjunction. Usually, this is the SEMI-COLON. (The COLON and DASH can do the same job; see the note below to learn about the special emphasis that each of these marks adds to your meaning.) Thus, *The hangman is a social outcast; the woman who marries the hangman becomes doubly condemned.* The semi-colon creates a stark relationship; hence, you don't want to overuse it.

Many writers accidentally create a comma splice by using a CONJUNC-TIVE ADVERB instead of a coordinating conjunction (remember FANBOYS—only seven words qualify). These connectors are words and phrases like *hence, therefore, in consequence, for example, thus, however,* and some others. Let's put one in our example sentence and see the resulting grammar:

> *The hangman is a social outcast therefore the woman who marries the hangman becomes doubly condemned.*

This is a fused sentence. What is the word, *therefore,* actually doing here? It is an adverb that modifies how the woman becomes condemned. She is condemned *therefore*—as a result of her marriage. An adverb can be moved around in this loose sentence:

> *Therefore, the woman who marries the hangman becomes doubly condemned.*

> *The woman who marries the hangman becomes, therefore, doubly condemned.*

> *The woman who marries the hangman becomes doubly condemned, therefore.*

So, how can *therefore* be said to join the two parts? It needn't even appear at the juncture. In fact, it is part of the second independent clause and the sentence still needs to be joined. The conjunctive adverb is marked off from the rest of its sentence. The correct form for all such conjunctive situations, then, is:

> *The hangman is a social outcast; therefore, the woman who marries the hangman becomes doubly condemned.*

> *The hangman is a social outcast; thus, the woman who marries the hangman becomes doubly condemned.*

> *The hangman is a social outcast; in consequence, the woman who marries the hangman becomes doubly condemned.*

3. Determine that one clause is more important and the other is truly subordinate (or dependent upon the independent clause). In this case, add a subordinating conjunction (such as *because, although, as, as if, before, if, in order that, once, since, than, that, unless, until, when, whenever, where, whereas, wherever, while,* and others). The conjunction inflects the meaning of the dependent clause, regardless of the order in which these two elements appear. You may also use a relative pronoun (*which, that, what, who, whomever, whom, whomever, whatever*) in some cases. Hence,

> *The woman who marries the hangman becomes doubly condemned because the hangman is a social outcast.*

Because the hangman is a social outcast, the woman who marries him becomes doubly condemned.

The woman who marries the hangman becomes doubly condemned since the hangman is a social outcast.

Since the hangman is a social outcast, the woman who marries him becomes doubly condemned.

The woman who marries the hangman becomes doubly condemned when the hangman is a social outcast.

4. Recast the sentence entirely. Rewrite your ideas into another syntax.

Misplaced Modifiers   мм

In the loose syntax of English, words that amplify or explain other words, or "modify" them, can often be misplaced. Each modifier must attach carefully to the correct receiver of its extra information. Consider: *Healing is an important issue for First Nations Canadians in the twenty-first century which is both physical and spiritual.* Here, the clause "which is both physical and spiritual" seems to modify "century," but that is not the correct meaning. This modifier is misplaced. The revised version is, *Healing, which is both physical and spiritual, is an important issue for First Nations Canadians in the twenty-first century.*

Sometimes the misplacement is such that the modifier looks in both directions for something to correctly amplify. These errors are called SQUINTING MODIFIERS.

Dangling Modifiers   дм

These incorrect modifiers try to attach to an element that is actually missing from the sentence. We've already seen how participial phrases often cause this problem: *Travelling to an underdeveloped country, the privileges of Canadian life were appreciated.* Clearly, "privileges" aren't travelling; a human being is. So the revised version is: *Travelling to an underdeveloped country, he appreciated the privileges of Canadian life.* "Travelling" now modifies "he." Notice, by the way, that the PASSIVE VOICE often leads you to make this error. In the first version, the sentence calls out for, "were appreciated *by him*," though this addition would not correct the dangling modification. The corrected version is ACTIVE: *Travelling, he appreciated* [. . .].

Pronoun Reference (Pronoun Agreement)   ref

Pronouns cause a number of problems for writers. Unclear reference can create an ambiguous sentence or actually create false meaning. One type of confusion occurs when two or more nouns precede a pronoun; it can be unclear which one is the antecedent: *The mason told the monk that he would never escape from a prison with weak walls.* Is it the mason or the monk who would not escape? We know the answer if we've read Vigneault's story in Chapter 1, but the grammar here doesn't tell us. Revised: *The mason told the monk, "I would never escape from a prison with weak walls."*

Another confusion occurs when subordinate material comes between the antecedent and its pronoun: *Social inequality, which has declined over time but is nevertheless still one of the most potent of political factors, affected the sentence imposed on the woman in Atwood's story whose harsh sentence can probably be attributed, in part, to it.* This is an ugly sentence because it is very overloaded and the reader may well have trouble linking "it" back to "inequality." In fact, the writer may also become confused by the intrusion of the plural noun "factors" and incorrectly make the final pronoun "them," not "it." Simplify such a sentence and make the link easier and clearer: *The harsh sentence imposed on the woman in Atwood's story can probably be attributed, in part, to social inequality, which has declined over time but is still one of the most potent political factors.*

Pronouns like *it, that, this, which,* and *whom* also cause confusion. Try to replace such pronouns with nouns. Consider the example, *King shows the interrelationships among nationality, ethnicity, and membership in a global, media-defined community. It affects the mother's sense of self.* To what does "it" refer? If it is "interrelationships," then it should be "They affect." If it is one of these memberships (ethnicity?), say so. **Better:** *King shows the interrelationships among nationality, ethnicity, and membership in a global, media-defined community. The <u>relationship</u> between her sense of ethnicity and her sense of nationality <u>affects</u> the mother's sense of self.*

Shifts in Number, Tense, Voice, or Mood   *shift*

You must always make sure that related parts of your sentence agree. SHIFTS in NUMBER, TENSE, VOICE, or MOOD cause errors in understanding for your reader. While proofreading, make sure to pause over connected elements to ensure that you have agreement.

For many coming to English as a second language, number agreement is particularly tricky. There are several rules to learn; consult a grammar text. For our purposes, we'll remind you that the subject must agree with its verb, so this string is incorrect: *Trudeau, along with other politicians, seek to patriate the Constitution.* The modifier, "along with other politicians," does not alter the fact that the subject is Trudeau, which is a singular noun; the sentence is only about him. The correct version: *<u>Trudeau</u>, along with other politicians, <u>seeks</u> to patriate the Constitution.*

Be wary of COLLECTIVE NOUNS (*team, corporation, government, board, community,* etc.). These seem to be plural but are singular. Not *The team plan to win the semi-finals,* but *The <u>team</u> <u>plans</u> to win the semi-finals.*

Shifts in Person   *PV*

Don't shift from one person to another. Most of your writing will be in the third person (*he, she, it, one*)—though it need not always be in this person—so be careful not to shift, say, to the second person (*you*). The temptation arises from your natural desire to "talk to" your reader, but it can confuse or create foolish sentences. If, during a discussion of abortion, a male reader is told, "when you feel the baby in your womb [. . .]," the writer loses credibility.

Mixed Constructions   *mixed*

In a manner similar to shifts, MIXED CONSTRUCTIONS confuse readers. Make sure that your sentence doesn't start out in one grammar structure or meaning and then slide to another. Here is a mixed construction: *In "Propositions," Atwood shows various approaches to love can really upset someone if a relationship goes sour.* Notice these and correct them in your drafts. (You can also mix metaphors, and that should be avoided as well.)

Faulty Parallelism   *|| / llism*

When you write a sentence with a number of related elements, try to keep each parallel to the others; that is, keep elements with the same meaning in the same grammatical structure. Not parallel: *The mother experiences problems because the border guards are rigid, government red tape, and frontier security is increasing.* The revised version is a set of parallel nouns: *The mother experiences problems because of the <u>rigidity</u> of the border guards, government <u>red tape</u>, and increasing <u>security</u>.*

Coordinating conjunctions alert you to parallel conditions: *Global warming is causing reductions in river flows and restrictions on available water for farms. Politicians must propose immediate solutions or face the consequences of inaction.*

Notes on the Dash and the Hyphen

1. *A pair of dashes*—here is an example—is used to set off additional information. A pair of dashes is, in effect, like a pair of commas or like a pair of parentheses (just like the preceding commas, and the parentheses here), but the dashes are more emphatic—some people would say more breathless—and, therefore, they should be used sparingly. (A single dash can replace a colon or semi-colon, too, but always has this emphatic feeling, whatever its usage.)
2. *To indicate a dash*, type two hyphens without hitting the spacebar before, between, or after them. Notice that a hyphen (-) is shorter than a dash (—). Many word processors will autoformat these two hyphens into a continuous dash (—).
3. *Use the hyphen* to join words that are used as a single adjective, for example, a "six-volume work," "an out-of-date theory," or "a nineteenth-century author." Notice that the hyphen is neither preceded nor followed by a space.

Grammar Checkers and Other Electronic Aids

Modern word processors are equipped with increasingly sophisticated spell checkers and grammar checkers. They can be very helpful. But you need must be careful: unless you understand the basics of grammar yourself, you may easily accept a revision that actually spoils your already correct sentence. For example, in Chapter 8, you read the sentence,

> *Despite the emphasis on indeterminacy, deconstructionist interpretations share with Marxism the idea that authors are "socially constructed" from the "discourses of power" or "signifying practices" that surround them.*

The checker wants the declension of the verb "surround" changed to "surrounds," or it wants the pronoun "that" changed to "those." The first suggestion arises because the computer knows that the relative pronoun "that" is the subject of the verb "surround," but it doesn't correctly identify the antecedent of "that" as the plural noun "practices." In this case, "that" is not a singular subject (as in *that one surrounds the other*), but a plural subject: *practices surround them.* That is also why the computer offers the other correction—"those surround." It is now trying to find a way to create number agreement by changing to a plural subject for the plural verb.

This sentence is actually more grammatically complex. Let's work through it:

1. "Despite the emphasis on indeterminacy" is a non-restrictive introductory phrase, and that is why it is set off by the comma.
2. "deconstructionist interpretations share [. . .] the idea" provides the subject, verb, and object of the principal clause: the main subject ("interpretations"), main verb ("share"), and main object ("idea").
3. "that" simply introduces a dependent clause with its own plural subject, "authors."
4. "authors are 'socially constructed'" provides the secondary clause: subject ("authors"), verb ("are"), and completion ("constructed").
5. "from [. . .] 'discourses [. . .]" is an adverbial phrase showing the plural noun responsible for the construction.
6. "or" is a coordinating conjunction which here simply means "also called."
7. "signifying practices" is a second descriptor of the cause of construction. Notice that it further explains "discourses." Remember also the rule that says that when two nouns are separated by or, their verb takes on the number of the nearer noun. In this case, that is the plural noun "practices."
8. "that surround them" is an adverbial clause that modifies "discourses" or "practices" and shows how these forces "surround" the authors (antecedent of "them.") Here, "that" takes the place of the antecedent noun "practices," so it is plural and requires the plural verb "surround": "practices surround them."

As you can see, this is a fairly complex sentence. It is also the type of sentence you are writing, so you need to understand its grammar. You may not be able to assign all the names of the parts of speech—and that probably doesn't much matter—but you must be able to decode the sentence to see how each element is working with the next. You also see that the grammar checker can't parse this sentence and that it therefore makes incorrect suggestions. Ultimately, you must do your own editing.

In addition, apparently good corrections of grammar or usage can sometimes incorrectly alter the meaning or nuance of your sentence. Later in this chapter, you'll read: *Cut out all the deadwood, but in cutting it out, do not cut out supporting detail.* The grammar checker wants to change this sentence to, "Cut out the entire deadwood, but in cutting it out do not cut out supporting detail." While "entire deadwood" may be a better phrase than "all the deadwood" in some situations, it would be incorrect here. This sentence urges you to remove each and every bit of unnecessary diction one by one—a measure of number—but the checker's version urges you to remove the total mass of broken vegetation—a measure of volume. In other words, the checker has "read" the sentence within the meaning "to remove dead timber," while we meant it in the sense of a simile, as in "removing unnecessary words which are *as useless as* dead timber." Computer software can't yet interpret figurative language, so be very careful that you consider each suggestion before you accept it. This example also shows you how each aspect of your writing—the diction, grammar, and syntax—is important to the *exact* meaning.

When you are sure of your grammar and syntax—sure that your sentence is correct and clear—you will want to go further and ensure that your sentence is as powerful, economical, and beautiful as possible. These and other considerations comprise the art of style.

PRINCIPLES OF STYLE

Writing is hard work (Lewis Carroll's school in *Alice's Adventures in Wonderland* taught reeling and writhing), and there is no point fooling ourselves into believing that it is all a matter of inspiration. Evidence abounds that many of the poems, stories, plays, and essays that seem to flow so effortlessly as we read them were in fact the products of innumerable revisions. "Hard labour for life" was Conrad's view of his career as a writer. This labour for the most part is directed not to prettifying language but to improving one's thoughts and then getting the words that communicate these thoughts exactly.

The efforts are not guaranteed to pay off, but failure to expend effort is sure to result in writing that will strike the reader as confused. It won't do to comfort yourself with the thought that you have been misunderstood. You may know what you *meant to say*, but your reader is the judge of what indeed you *have said*.

Many books have been written on the elements of good writing, but the best way to learn to write is to generate ideas by such methods as annotating the text, listing, brainstorming, free writing, and making entries in a journal (see Chapter 2). Then, with some ideas at hand, you can write a first draft, which you will revise—perhaps in light of comments by your peers—and later will revise yet again, and again. After you hand your essay in, your instructor will annotate it. Study the annotations an experienced reader puts on your essay. In revising the annotated passages, you will learn what your weaknesses are. After drafting your next essay, put it aside for a day or so; when you reread it, preferably aloud, you may find much that bothers you. If the argument does not flow, check to see whether your organization is reasonable and whether you have made adequate transitions. Do not hesitate to delete interesting but irrelevant material that obscures the argument. Make the necessary revisions again and again if time permits. Revision is indispensable if you wish to avoid (in Maugham's words) "the impression of writing with the stub of a blunt pencil."

Still, a few principles can be briefly set forth here. On Dr. Johnson's belief that we do not so much need to be taught as to be reminded, these principles are brief imperatives rather than detailed instructions. They will not suppress your particular voice. Rather, they will get rid of static, enabling your voice to come through effectively. You have something to say, but you can say it only after your throat is cleared of "Well, what I meant was," and "It's sort of, like, you know." Your readers do *not* know; they are reading in order *to* know. The paragraphs that follow are attempts to help you let your individuality speak clearly.

Get the Right Word

Denotation
Be sure the word you choose has the right explicit meaning, or denotation. Don't say "tragic" when you mean "pathetic," "sarcastic" when you mean "ironic," "free verse" when you mean "blank verse," "disinterested" when you mean "uninterested."

Connotation
Be sure the word you choose has the right association or implication—that is, the right connotation. Here are three examples of words with the wrong connotations for their contexts: "The heroic spirit is not dead. It still *lurks* in the hearts of men." ("Lurks" suggests a furtiveness inappropriate to the heroic spirit. Something like "lives" or "dwells" is needed.) "Close study will *expose* the strength of Woolf's style." ("Reveal" would be better than "expose" here; "expose" suggests that some weakness will be brought to light, as in "Close study will expose the flimsiness of the motivation.") "Although Creon suffers, his suffering is not great enough to *relegate* him to the role of tragic hero. (In place of "relegate," we need something like "elevate" or "exalt.")

Concreteness
Catch the richness, complexity, and uniqueness of things. Do not write "Here one sees his lack of emotion" if you really mean "Here one sees his indifference" or "his iciness" or "his impartiality" or whatever the exact condition is. Instead of "The clown's part in *Othello* is very small," write "The clown appears in only two scenes in *Othello*" or "The clown in *Othello* speaks only 30 lines." ("Very," as in "very small" or "very big," is almost never the right word. A role is rarely "very big"; it "dominates" or "overshadows" or "is second only to [. . .].")

In addition to using the concrete word and the appropriate detail, use illustrative examples. Northrop Frye, writing about the perception of rhythm, illustrates his point:

Ideally, our literary education should begin, not with prose, but with such things as "this little pig went to market"—with verse rhythm reinforced by physical assault. The infant who gets bounced on somebody's knee to the rhythm of "Ride a cock horse" does not need a footnote telling him that Banbury Cross is twenty miles northeast of Oxford. He does not need the information that "cross" and "horse" make (at least in the pronunciation he is most likely to hear) not a rhyme but an assonance [. . .]. All he needs is to get bounced.

—*The Well-tempered Critic* (Bloomington, IN, 1963) 25.

Frye does not say that our literary education should begin with "simple rhymes" or with "verse popular with children." He says "with such things as 'this little pig went to market,'" and then he goes on to add "Ride a cock horse." We know exactly what he means. Notice, too, that we do not need a third example. Be detailed, but know when to stop.

Repetition and Variation

Although some repetitions—say, of words such as *surely* or *it is noteworthy*—reveal a tic that ought to be cured by revision, don't be afraid to repeat a word if it is the best word. The following paragraph repeats "cumulative," "women," "poets," and "voices":

If one were to follow Virginia Woolf's advice, one would read this anthology as a cumulative work, a single long poem created over one and a half centuries by woman poets writing in Canada. Behind the eclectic generation of contemporary women writers is a cumulative tradition of poets who might be thought of as facilitators, clearing a space for future voices. One of the pleasures of preparing this anthology has been to identify these, since many voices have disappeared. Another has been to trace the evolution in the concerns of women poets.

—Rosemary Sullivan, preface, *Poetry by Canadian Women* (Toronto, 1989) x.

Repetition, a device necessary for continuity and clarity, holds the paragraph together. Variations occur: "centuries" becomes "generation," and then "evolution." Similarly, "poets" becomes "writers," which in turn becomes "voices." Such substitutions, which neither confuse nor distract, keep the paragraph from sounding like a stuck CD.

Pronouns are handy substitutes, and they ought to be used, but other substitutes need not always be sought. An ungrounded fear of repetition often produces a vice known as *elegant variation:* Having mentioned "Borders," an essayist next speaks of "the previously mentioned work," then of "King's tale," and finally of "this work of our author." This vice is far worse than repetition; it strikes the reader as silly.

Pointless variation of this sort, however, is not to be confused with a variation that communicates additional useful information, such as "these many stories about Isobel's neighbours"; this variation is entirely legitimate, indeed necessary, for it furthers the discussion.

Notice in these lucid sentences by Helen Gardner the effective repetition of "end" and "beginning":

Othello has this in common with the tragedy of fortune, that the end in no way blots out from the imagination the glory of the beginning. But the end here does not merely by its darkness throw up into relief the brightness that was. On the contrary, beginning and end chime against each other. In both the value of life and love is affirmed.

—*The Noble Moor* (Oxford, 1956) 203.

The substitution of "conclusion" or "last scene" for the second "end" would be worse than pointless; it would destroy Gardner's point that there is *identity* or correspondence between beginning and end.

Do not repeat a word if it is being used in a different sense. Get a different word. Here are two examples of the fault: "This *image* presents the *image* of a beautiful rose." (The first "image" means "a literary device"; the second means "a picture.") "Caesar's *character* is complex. The comic *characters* too have some complexity." (The first "character" means "personality"; the second means "persons," "figures in the play.")

The Sound of Sense

Avoid awkward repetitions of sound, as in "The story is marked by a remarkable mystery," "The reason the season is Spring [. . .]," "Circe certainly [. . .]," "This is seen in the scene in which [. . .]." These irrelevant echoes call undue attention to the words and thus get in the way of the points you are making. But wordplay can be effective when it contributes to meaning. Gardner's statement that in the beginning and the end of *Othello* "the value of life and love is affirmed" makes effective use of the similarity in sound between "life" and "love." Her implication is that these two things that sound alike are indeed closely related, an idea that reinforces her contention that the beginning and the end of the play are in a way identical.

Write Effective Sentences

Economy

Say everything relevant, but say it in the fewest words possible. The wordy sentence

There are a few vague parts in the story that give it a mysterious quality.

may be written more economically as

A few vague parts in the story give it a mysterious quality.

Nothing has been lost by deleting "There are" and "that." Even more economical is

A few vague parts add mystery to the story.

The original version says nothing that the second version does not say, and says nothing that the third version—9 words against 15—does not say. If you find the right nouns and active verbs, you can often delete adjectives and adverbs.

272   GRAMMAR, SYNTAX, STYLE, AND FORMAT

(Compare "a mysterious quality" with "mystery.") Another example of wordiness is: "Sophocles's tragic play *Antigone* is mistitled because Creon is the actual tragic hero, and the play should be named for him." These 21 words can be reduced, with no loss of meaning, to 10 words: "Sophocles's *Antigone* is mistitled; Creon is actually the tragic hero."

Something is wrong with a sentence if you can delete words and not sense the loss. A chapter in a recent book on contemporary theatre begins:

> One of the principal and most persistent sources of error that tends to bedevil a considerable proportion of contemporary literary analysis is the assumption that the writer's creative process is a wholly conscious and purposive type of activity.

Well, there is something of interest here, but it comes along with a lot of hot air. Why that weaseling ("*tends* to bedevil," "a *considerable* proportion"), and why "type of activity" instead of "activity"? Those spluttering *p*'s ("principal and most persistent," "proportion," "process," "purposive") are a giveaway; the writer is letting off steam, not thinking. Pruned of the verbiage, what he says adds up to this:

> One of the chief errors bedeviling much contemporary criticism is the assumption that the writer's creative process is wholly conscious and purposive.

Some might call for an even tighter, more direct style:

> Much contemporary criticism suffers by assuming the writer is wholly conscious and purposeful during the creative process.

If the critic were to complain that this revision deprives the writing of style, might we not fairly reply that what the critic calls style is the display of insufficient thinking, a tangle of deadwood? Or pretentious diction, a showing-off?

Cut out all the deadwood, but in cutting it out, do not cut out supporting detail. Supporting detail is wordiness only when the details are so numerous and obvious that they offend the reader's intelligence.

The PASSIVE VOICE (wherein the subject is the object of the action) is a common source of wordiness. Do not say "This story was written by Fawcett"; instead, say "Fawcett wrote this story." The revision is one-third shorter, and it says everything that the longer version says. Sometimes, of course, the passive voice, although less vigorous, may be preferable to the active voice. Changing "The novel was received in silence" to "Readers neglected the novel" makes the readers' response more active than it was. The passive voice catches the passivity of the response. Furthermore, the revision makes "readers" the subject, but the true subject is (as in the original) the novel. Except in such conscious applications, however, you should avoid the passive voice.

Parallels
Use parallels to clarify relationships. Few of us are likely to compose such deathless parallels as "I came, I saw, I conquered," but we can see to it that coordinate expressions correspond in their grammatical form. A parallel such as "He liked to read and to write" (instead of "He liked reading and to write")

makes its point neatly. No such neatness appears in the sentence, "Virginia Woolf wrote novels, delightful letters, and penetrating stories." The reader is left wondering what value the novels have. If one of the items has a modifier, usually all should have modifiers. Notice how the omission of "the noble" in the following sentence would leave a distracting gap: "If the wicked Shylock cannot enter the fairy story world of Belmont, neither can the noble Antony."

Other examples of parallels are: "Scarlett longs to be free of her wheelchair and to meet the man she dreams of at night" (*not* "Scarlett longs to be free of her wheelchair and for the man she dreams of at night."); "He talked about metaphors, similes, and symbols" (*not* "He talked about metaphors, similes, and about symbols"). If you wish to emphasize the leisureliness of the talk, you might put it like this: "He talked about metaphors, about similes, and about symbols." The repetition of "about" in this version is not wordiness; because it emphasizes the leisureliness, it does some work in the sentence. Notice in the next example how Gardner's parallels ("in the," "in his," "in his," "in the") lend conviction:

> The significance of *Othello* is not to be found in the hero's nobility alone, in his capacity to know ecstasy, in his vision of the world, and in the terrible act to which he is driven by his anguish at the loss of that vision. It lies also in the fact that the vision was true.

> —*The Noble Moor* 205.

Subordination

Make sure that the less important element is subordinate to the more important. In the following example, the first clause, summarizing the writer's previous sentences, is a subordinate or dependent clause; the new material is made emphatic by being put into two independent clauses:

> As soon as the Irish Literary Theatre was assured of a nationalist backing, it started to dissociate itself from any political aim, and the long struggle with the public began.

The second and third clauses in this sentence, linked by "and," are coordinate—that is, of equal importance.

We have already discussed parallels ("I came, I saw, I conquered") and pointed out that parallel or coordinate elements should appear so in the sentence. The following line gives time and eternity equal treatment: "Time was against him; eternity was for him." The quotation is a *compound sentence*. (Refer back to the earlier section on grammar.) But a *complex sentence* does not give equal treatment to each clause; whatever is outside the independent clause is subordinate, less important. Consider this sentence:

> Aided by Miss Horniman's money, Yeats dreamed of a poetic drama.

The writer puts Yeats's dream in the independent clause, subordinating the relatively unimportant Miss Horniman. (Notice, by the way, that emphasis by subordination often works along with emphasis by position. Here, the independent clause comes *after* the subordinate clause; the writer appropriately put the more important material in the more emphatic position.)

Had the writer wished to give Miss Horniman more prominence, the passage might have run:

Yeats dreamed of a poetic drama, and Miss Horniman subsidized that dream.

Here Miss Horniman at least stands in an independent clause, linked to the previous independent clause by "and." The two clauses, and the two people, are now of approximately equal importance.

If the writer had wanted to emphasize Miss Horniman and to deemphasize Yeats, he might have written:

While Yeats dreamed of a poetic drama, Miss Horniman provided the money.

Here Yeats is reduced to the subordinate clause, and Miss Horniman is given the dignity of the only independent clause. (Again notice that the important point is also in the emphatic position, near the end of the sentence. A sentence is likely to sprawl if an independent clause comes first, followed by a long subordinate clause of lesser importance, such as the sentence you are now reading.)

In short, though simple sentences and compound sentences have their place, they make everything of equal importance. Since everything is not of equal importance, you must often write complex and compound-complex sentences, subordinating some things to other things.

Write Unified and Coherent Paragraphs

Unity

A unified paragraph is a group of sentences (rarely a single sentence) on a single idea. The idea may have several twists or subdivisions, but all the parts—the sentences—should form a whole that can be summarized in one sentence. A paragraph is, to put the matter a little differently, one of the major points supporting your thesis. If your essay is some 500 words long—less than two double-spaced pages—you probably will not break it down into more than four or five parts or paragraphs. (But you *should* break your essay down into paragraphs, that is, coherent blocks that give the reader a rest between them. One page of typing is about as long as you can go before the reader needs a slight break. Don't determine paragraph breaks by length, however. Begin a new paragraph whenever you change idea or slant.) A paper of 500 words with a dozen paragraphs is probably faulty not because it has too many ideas but because it has too few *developed* ideas. A short paragraph—especially one consisting of a single sentence—is usually anemic; such a paragraph may be acceptable when it summarizes a highly detailed previous paragraph or group of paragraphs, or when it serves as a transition between two complicated paragraphs, but usually summaries and transitions can begin the next paragraph.

Each paragraph has a unifying idea, which may appear as a TOPIC SENTENCE. Most commonly, the topic sentence is the first sentence, forecasting what is to come in the rest of the paragraph; or it may be the second sentence, following a transitional sentence. Less commonly, it is the last sentence, summarizing the points that the paragraph's earlier sentences have made. Least commonly—but thoroughly acceptable—the topic sentence may appear nowhere in the paragraph, in which case the paragraph has a TOPIC IDEA—an idea that holds the sentences together although it has not been explicitly stated. Whether explicit or implicit, an idea must unite the sentences of the paragraph. If your paragraph has only one or two sentences, the chances are that you have not adequately developed its idea. You probably have not provided sufficient details—perhaps including brief quotations—to support your topic sentence or your topic idea.

A paragraph can make several points, but the points must be related, and the nature of the relationship must be indicated so that the paragraph has a single unifying point. Here is a paragraph, unusually brief, that may seem to make two points but that, in fact, holds them together with a topic idea. The author is Edmund Wilson:

> James Joyce's *Ulysses* was an attempt to present directly the thoughts and feelings of a group of Dubliners through the whole course of a summer day. *Finnegans Wake* is a complementary attempt to render the dream fantasies and the half-unconscious sensations experienced by a single person in the course of a night's sleep.

—*The Wound and The Bow* (New York, 1947) 243.

Wilson's topic idea is that *Finnegans Wake* complements *Ulysses*. Notice that the sentence about *Finnegans Wake* concludes the paragraph. Not surprisingly, Wilson's essay is about this book, and the structure of the paragraph allows him to get into his subject.

The next example may seem to have more than one subject (Richardson and Fielding were contemporaries; they were alike in some ways; they were different in others), but again the paragraph is unified by a topic idea (although Richardson and Fielding were contemporaries and were alike in some ways, they differed in important ways):

> The names of Richardson and Fielding are always coupled in any discussion of the novel, and with good reason. They were contemporaries, writing in the same cultural climate (*Tom Jones* was published in 1719, a year after *Clarissa*). Both had genius and both were widely recognized immediately. Yet they are utterly different in their tastes and temperaments, and therefore in their visions of city and country, of men and women, and even of good and evil.

—Elizabeth Drew, *The Novel* (New York, 1963) 59.

This paragraph, like Edmund Wilson's, closes in on its subject.

The beginning and especially the end of a paragraph are usually the most emphatic parts. A beginning may offer a generalization that the rest of the paragraph supports. Or the early part may offer details, preparing for the generalization in the later part. Or the paragraph may move from cause to effect. Although no rule can cover all paragraphs (except that all must make a point in an orderly way), one can hardly go wrong in making the first sentence either a transition from the previous paragraph or a statement of the paragraph's topic. Here is a sentence that makes a transition and also states the topic: "Not only narrative poems but also meditative poems may have a kind of plot." This sentence gets the reader from plot in narrative poetry (which the writer has been talking about) to plot in meditative poetry (which the writer goes on to talk about).

Coherence

If a paragraph has not only UNITY but also a STRUCTURE, then it has coherence, its parts fit together. Make sure that each sentence is properly related to the preceding and the following sentences. One way of gaining coherence is by means of transitions—words such as *furthermore, on the other hand, moreover, however, but, for example, this tendency, in the next chapter,* and so on—but, of course, these transitions should not start every sentence. These words let the reader know how a sentence is related to the previous sentence, but while transitions must be explicit, it is more important that the argument proceed clearly. (***ESL hint:*** contemporary Canadian speakers of English do not use transitions as often as grammar books used in non-Canadian schools sometimes suggest. Be careful not to overuse transitional words, especially older-fashioned words, like *moreover* and *thus*.)

Introductory Paragraphs

Beginning a long section of one of his poems, Byron aptly wrote, "Nothing so difficult as a beginning." Clark Blaise, in an essay aptly titled, "To Begin, To Begin," suggests that "the most interesting thing about a story [. . .] is its beginning, its first paragraph, often its first sentence." Almost all writers—professionals as well as amateurs—find that the beginning paragraphs in their drafts are false starts. Don't worry too much about the opening paragraphs of your draft; you'll almost surely want to revise your opening later anyway, and when writing a first draft you merely need something—almost anything may do—to get you going. Though on rereading you will probably find that the first paragraph or two should be replaced, those opening words at least helped you break the ice.

In your finished paper, the opening cannot be mere throat clearing. It should be interesting and informative. Don't paraphrase your title ("Sex in *Beautiful Losers*") in your first sentence: "This essay will study the topic of sex in Leonard Cohen's novel *Beautiful Losers.*" The sentence contains no information about the topic here, at least none beyond the author's name, and no information about you, either—that is, no sense of your response to the topic, such as might be present in, say, "In Leonard Cohen's *Beautiful Losers* there are many sexual scenes which were shocking when the novel first appeared, but Cohen's real interest is in exploring the mysterious relationship of sex, love, and magic."

Often you can make use of a quotation, either from the work or from a critic. After all, if a short passage from the work caught your attention and set you thinking and stimulated you to develop a thesis, it may well provide a good beginning for your essay.

Remember: You cannot go wrong in stating your thesis in your opening paragraph, moving from a rather broad view to a narrower one. If you look at the sample essays in this book, you will see that most good opening paragraphs clearly indicate the writer's thesis. Here is an introductory paragraph, written by a student, on the ways in which Shakespeare manages in some degree to present Macbeth sympathetically:

> Near the end of <u>Macbeth</u>, Malcolm speaks of Macbeth as a "dead butcher" (5.8.69), and there is some--perhaps much--truth in this characterization. Macbeth is the hero of the play, but he is also the villain. And yet to call him a villain is too simple. Despite the fact that he murders his king, his friend Banquo, and even the utterly innocent Lady Macduff and her children, he engages our sympathy, largely because Shakespeare continually reminds us that Macbeth never (despite appearances) becomes a cold-blooded murderer. Macbeth's violence is felt not only by his victims but also by Macbeth himself; his deeds torture him, plaguing his mind. Despite all his villainy, he is a man with a conscience.

Concluding Paragraphs

With conclusions, as with introductions, try to say something interesting. It is not of the slightest interest to say "Thus we see [here the writer reminds of the title and the first paragraph]." And note that the hack phrase "In conclusion" actually produces a grammar mistake: "In conclusion, King shows that borders are political rather than human" suggests that King does this as the conclusion to his story, not that you are making this summation as the conclusion of your essay. The phrase almost always generates a misplaced modifier. Some justification may be made for a summary at the end of a long paper because the reader may have half-forgotten some of the ideas presented 30 pages earlier, but a paper that can be held easily in the mind needs something different. In fact, if your paper is short—say two or three pages—you may not need to summarize or to draw a conclusion. Just make sure that your last sentence is a good one and that the reader does not expect anything further.

If you do feel that a concluding paragraph (as opposed to a final paragraph) is appropriate or necessary, make sure that you do not merely echo what you have already said. A good concluding paragraph may round out the previous discussion, normally with a few sentences that summarize (without the obviousness of "We may now summarize"), but it may also draw an inference that has not previously been expressed. To draw such an inference is not to introduce a new idea—a concluding paragraph is hardly the place for a new idea—but is to see the previous material from a fresh perspective. A good concluding paragraph closes the issue while enriching it. Notice how the two examples that follow wrap things up and, at the same time, open out by suggesting a larger frame of reference.

The first example is the conclusion to Carole Gerson's "The Canon between the Wars: Fieldnotes of a Feminist Literary Archaeologist." In her discussion of the development of the Canadian canon, Gerson argues that the major historians and early critics of Canadian literature supported authors whose work fit their vision of the country. As a result, Gerson states, the "cultural canonizers" refused "to pay serious attention" to many women writers. At the end of the penultimate paragraph she quotes Phyllis Webb, who rethinks her early career and the role of F. R. Scott and A. J. M. Smith in documenting our literature. Working from the quotation, Gerson concludes:

> To restore the reputations of Phyllis Webb's predecessors and revalue their work, it is necessary to un-write the Smith/Scott history of Canadian literature. But it will take more than [...] anthologies [...] to undo the marginalization of women in the prevailing canon of Canadian writers from the first half of this century.

> —*Canadian Canons: Essays in Literary Value*, ed. Robert Lecker
> (Toronto: U of Toronto P, 1991) 56.

Notice that Gerson sums up her argument that women writers need to be recuperated ("to restore" and "revalue") in a firm sentence that urges the rewriting of history. Then she cautions that this will be a major job, pointing to work to be done. This conclusion suggests the next step of the argument (but doesn't begin a new essay!).

A second example of a concluding paragraph comes from Ric Knowles's essay, "Voices (off): Deconstructing the Modern English-Canadian Dramatic Canon," also in *Canadian Canons* (110–11). This paragraph is quite straightforward as summary, but note how well Knowles concentrates his 21-page argument into a succinct, dense paragraph. In fact, note that the whole paragraph is one long (correctly punctuated) sentence. In the final parallelism, Knowles heats up his summary and states his own position by calling (like Gerson) for radical action:

> The result of such a critical inquiry would be to amplify and encourage those marginalized but vibrant voices of "ex-centricity" that make theatre-going in Canada both exciting and disruptive, while introducing new theatrical forms and new ways of seeing; to provide places and positions from which non-generic spectators might experience and even enjoy theatre without surrendering their deviance from an implied hegemonic social norm; and finally to undermine the very will to consensus and drive towards identity that underly the concept of a developing Canadian theatrical repertoire and stable dramatic canon.

✓ A Checklist for Revising Paragraphs

✓ Does the paragraph say anything? Does it have substance?
✓ Does the paragraph have a topic sentence? If so, is it in the best place?
✓ If the paragraph doesn't have a topic sentence, might one improve the paragraph? Or does it have a clear topic idea?
✓ If the paragraph is an opening paragraph, is it interesting enough to attract and to hold a reader's attention? If it is a later paragraph, does it easily evolve out of the previous paragraph, and lead into the next paragraph?

✓ Does the paragraph contain some principle of development—for instance from cause to effect or from general to particular?

✓ Does each sentence clearly follow from the preceding sentence? Have you provided transitional words or cues to guide your reader? Would it be helpful to repeat certain key words, for clarity?

✓ What is the purpose of the paragraph? Do you want to summarize, or give an illustration, or concede a point? Is your purpose clear to your reader, and does the paragraph fulfill your purpose?

✓ If the paragraph is a closing paragraph, is it effective? Is it an unnecessary restatement of the obvious, or does it draw the sentences together into a cohesive unit?

Write Emphatically

All that has been said about getting the right word, about effective sentences, and about paragraphs is related to the matter of *emphasis*. When you write, be emphatic. But do not attempt to achieve emphasis by a *style* consisting *chiefly of italics* and *exclamation* marks!!! (Such devices attempt to reproduce spoken intonation and rarely belong in a written essay. In fact, be careful generally not to "chat" with your reader.) Do not rely on slang expressions such as "super important," "so significant," and "totally beautiful." The proper way to be emphatic is to find the right word, to use appropriate detail, to subordinate the lesser points, and to develop your ideas reasonably. The beginning and the end of a sentence (and of a paragraph) are emphatic positions; of these two positions, the end is usually the more emphatic. Here is a sentence that properly moves to an emphatic end (it is a *periodic* sentence, as you'll recall from the grammar section earlier in this chapter):

> Having been ill-treated by Hamlet and having lost her father, Ophelia goes mad.

If the halves are reversed, creating a *loose* sentence, it peters out:

> Ophelia goes mad because she has been ill-treated by Hamlet and she has lost her father.

Still, even this version is better than the shapeless:

> Having been ill-treated by Hamlet, Ophelia goes mad, partly too because she has lost her father.

The important point, that she goes mad, is dissipated by the lame addition of words about her father. In short, avoid anticlimaxes such as "Macbeth's deed is reprehensible and serious." Such mixed constructions creating awkward syntax and faulty diction are the most common errors in student papers these days. Try very hard to write clear, active, logical, parallel sentences; don't write as you think out the idea: craft the sentence when you know what you want to say and the order you want to use. Reread and revise: correct your grammar and syntax.

The advice to build emphasis needs a caution. Much of the writing you see is geared to advertising. ("Car X. The engine of a DEVIL—the body of a GOD.") Avoid this style. Be emphatic but courteous and sensible; do not shout.

REMARKS ABOUT MANUSCRIPT FORM

Basic Manuscript Form

Much of what follows is nothing more than common sense.

- Use good quality *8 1/2" x 11" (216 x 279 mm) paper*. Make a photocopy or print out a second copy, in case the instructor's copy goes astray.

- *Double-space*, and type on one side of the page. If you submit hand-written copy, use lined paper and write on one side of the page only in black or dark blue ink, on every other line.

- Use a *clear font*, large enough for your instructor to read easily, such as Arial 10 or 12 point, Helvetica 12 point, or Courier 10 or 12 point. Don't print in bold or light fonts. Remember that your instructor is reading many papers and legibility is important.

- Use *one-inch margins* on all sides.

- Within the top margin, put your last name and then (after hitting the space bar twice) the *page number* (in Arabic numerals), so that the number is flush with the right-hand margin. Like this: Name 2

  Put this information in a Header. Turn off any default Footer or the page numbering at the bottom of the page.

- On the first page, below the top margin and flush with the left-hand margin, put *your full name*, your *instructor's name*, the *course number* (including the section), and the *date*, one item per line, double-spaced.

- *Centre the title* of your essay. Remember that the title is important—it gives readers their first glimpse of your essay. *Create your own title*, one that reflects your topic or thesis. Often academic titles name the work and then, after a colon, give a catchy subtitle. This can also occur in the other order.

- *Capitalize the title* thus: Begin the first word of the title with a capital letter, and capitalize each subsequent word except articles (*a, an, the*), conjunctions (*for, and, nor, but, or, yet, so* and *if, when,* etc.), and prepositions (*in, on, with,* etc.). Notice that you do *not* enclose your title within quotation marks, and you do not underline it. If it includes the title of a story, *that title* is enclosed within quotation marks, or if it includes the title of a novel or play, *that title* is underlined to indicate italics (if your word processor can make italics, then use them). Your title has no period after it. Thus:

```
        Dreams and Reality in Joyce's "Araby"
```
and
```
    Lost in Time and Seeking Grace:  Isobel's Character
              in Lion in the Streets
```

- After writing your title, *double-space,* indent five spaces, and begin your first sentence.

- Unless your instructor tells you otherwise, *use a staple* to hold the pages together. (Do not use a stiff binder; it makes it difficult to turn pages.)

- Extensive revisions should have been made in your drafts, but minor *last-minute revisions* may be made—neatly—on the finished copy. Although you want your final paper to appear professional, it is much more important to turn in a correct manuscript than to turn in a "pretty" one. A last proofreading may catch some typographical errors, and you may notice some small weaknesses. You can make corrections using the following proofreader's symbols.

Changes in wording may be made by crossing through words and rewriting them:

```
                                      has
    The influence of Carmen and Roberts have greatly
    diminished.
```

Additions should be made above the line, with a caret below the line at the appropriate place:

```
                                          greatly
    The influence of Carmen and Roberts has diminished.
```

Transpositions of letters may be made thus:

```
    The influence of Carmen and Roberts has diminished
```

Deletions are indicated by a horizontal line through the word or words to be deleted. Delete a single letter by drawing a vertical or diagonal line through it; then indicate whether the letters on either side are to be closed up by drawing a connecting arc:

```
    The influence of Carmen and Roberts has greatly
    diminished.
```

Separation of words accidentally run together is indicated by a vertical line, *closure by* curved lines connecting the letters to be closed up:

```
    The influence of Carmen and Roberts has greatly
    diminished.
```

Paragraphing may be indicated by the symbol ¶ before the word that is to begin the new paragraph:

> The influence of Carmen and Roberts has greatly
> diminished.   ¶ In the mid-twentieth century, poets
> turned from lyrics of the wilderness to comments upon
> modern life.

Quotations and Quotation Marks

First, a word about the *point* of using quotations. Don't use quotations to pad the length of a paper. Rather, give quotations from the work you are discussing so that your readers will see the material you are discussing and (especially in a research paper) so that your readers will know what some of the chief interpretations are and what your responses to them are. Remember always to *use* the quotation. Work it into your own sentence if possible. Sometimes a longer quotation stands alone, but you must always comment upon it, work the idea in the quotation into the idea you are developing.

Note: The next few paragraphs do *not* discuss how to include citations of pages, a topic discussed in the next chapter under the heading "How to Document: Footnotes and Internal Parenthetical Citations."

Additional principles:

1. *Identify the speaker or writer of the quotation,* so that the reader is not left with a sense of uncertainty. Usually, in accordance with the principle of letting readers know where they are going, this identification precedes the quoted material, but occasionally it may follow the quotation, especially if it will provide something of a pleasant surprise.

2. If the quotation is part of your own sentence, be sure to fit the quotation grammatically and logically into your sentence.

> **Incorrect:** The narrator in King's "Borders" tells us
> that "I would have preferred lemon drops" (371) when he
> is given some peanut brittle by Mel.
> **Correct:** When Mel gives him a bag of peanut brittle,
> the narrator in King's "Borders" comments that he "would
> have preferred lemon drops [. . .]" (371).

3. *Indicate any omissions or additions.* The quotation must be exact. Any material that you add—even one or two words—must be enclosed within square brackets, thus:

> "When I was twelve, maybe thirteen, my mother announced
> that we were going to go to Salt Lake City [the Mormon
> capital of Utah] to visit my sister [. . .]" (364).

If you wish to omit material from within a quotation, indicate the ellipsis by three spaced periods inside square brackets. ("If you wish to omit material [. . .] indicate the ellipsis by three spaced periods inside square brackets.") If your sentence ends in an omission, indicate the ellipsis and then provide the period outside the brackets. ("If your sentence ends [. . .].") If your sentence ends and then a full sentence or more is left out, provide your period and then the ellipsis inside the brackets. ("If your sentence ends. [. . .]") Notice that the placement of the brackets within the four periods tells your reader exactly what has been omitted and where within your sentence's grammar. The following example is based on a quotation from the sentences immediately above this one:

```
The instructions say that "If you [ . . . ] omit material
from within a quotation, [you must] indicate the
ellipsis [ . . . ]." They also say that if your sentence
ends in an omission, add a closed-up period and then
three spaced periods. [ . . . ]"
```

Although text preceded "If you," ellipsis points are not needed to indicate the omission because "If you" began a sentence in the original. Initial and terminal omissions are indicated only when they are part of the sentence you are quoting. Even such omissions need not be indicated when the quoted material is obviously incomplete—as when it is a word or phrase.

When you provide a citation, as we'll point out later on in this chapter, you move the period outside the quotation mark to include the citation in your sentence. The same rule applies to an ellipsis. In such a case, you would have a sentence like the example below:

```
When Mel gives him a bag of peanut brittle, the
narrator in King's "Borders" comments that he "would
have preferred lemon drops [ . . . ]" (371).
```

4. *Distinguish between short and long quotations,* and treat each appropriately. SHORT QUOTATIONS (usually defined as fewer than five lines of typed prose or three lines of poetry) are enclosed within quotation marks and worked right into the text.

LONG (or SET DOWN) QUOTATIONS (more than four typed lines of prose or more than two lines of poetry), are shown by indenting the entire quotation ten spaces from the left margin. Usually, a long quotation is introduced by a clause ending with a colon—for instance, "Atwood brings the story up-to-date in a scene with contemporary women:" or "The mother's belief in the Native myths of Coyote is shown in the stories she tells: ". After typing your lead-in, type the quotation, indented and double-spaced as in the following example. Do not centre the quotation (an out-of-date style you'll still see in your reading.) Do not surround it with quotation marks.

The mother's belief in the native myths of Coyote is
shown in the stories she tells:

> We sat out under the stars that night, and my
> mother told me all sorts of stories. She was
> serious about it, too. She'd tell them slow,
> repeating parts as she went, as if she
> expected me to remember each one. (366)

If your short quotation is from a poem, be sure to follow the capitalization of the original, and use a slash mark (with a space before and after it) to indicate separate lines. Give the line numbers, if your source gives them, in parentheses, immediately after the closing quotation marks and before the closing punctuation, thus:

> In "The Bear on the Delhi Road," Earle Birney says that
> "it is no more joyous for them / in this hot dust to
> prance" (26-7), indicating that the Kashmir men are as
> oppressed as the bear.

5. *Commas and periods go inside the quotation marks when there is no citation.*

Here is a paraphrase of remarks by Ric Knowles from the essay cited earlier:

> A change in "critical inquiry," a new focus by those
> studying theatre in Canada, says Ric Knowles on p. 111,
> would invite more "ex-centricity" in playwrights and
> spectators. Such a move would dislodge the "will to
> consensus," the notion that there is one unified
> identity in the country.

Commas and periods go outside the quotation marks when there is a citation. If the quotation is immediately followed by material in parentheses or in square brackets, close the quotation, then give the parenthetic or bracketed material, and then put the comma or period:

> Raising the suspense, Vigneault tells us in the first
> sentence that the mason was repairing the wall "with
> surprising care"(3), and in the last sentence "that one
> feels something is bound to happen" (4).

> "Such a move would dislodge the 'will to consensus,' the
> notion that there is one unified identity in the
> country" (Knowles 111).

Semicolons, colons, and *dashes* go outside the closing quotation marks.

Question marks and *exclamation points* go inside if they are part of the quotation, outside if they are your own. In the following passage, again quoting Knowles's important essay, notice the difference in the position of the question marks. The first is part of the quotation, so it is enclosed within the quotation marks. The second question mark, however, is yours, so it comes after the closing quotation mark and makes your sentence into a question. In both cases, the position of the parenthetical citation is after the quotation but before the final sentence punctuation.

```
After documenting how plays receive critical and popular
attention, Knowles asks, "What are the alternatives to
canon-formation in Canadian drama?" (106). Doesn't the
reader become uneasy about any hope for a new method of
valuing plays when Knowles adds that the theatre
"functions as an institution in Canada" (92)?
```

Quotation Marks or Italics (Underlining)

The rules are simple:

- no indicators for unpublished work,

- quotations marks for material published inside something else, and

- italics (or the use of underlining to indicate italics) for separately published material.

So: Use no marks around the title of your essay. Use quotation marks around titles of short stories and titles of chapters in books, essays, songs, and poems that might not be published by themselves. Italicize (or underline) titles of books, periodicals, journals, collections of essays, plays, CDs, and long poems such as *The Rime of the Ancient Mariner.*

15

Writing a Research Paper

<table>
<tr><td>

Learning Objectives

When you've read this chapter you should be able to

➤ carry out a research project, using both primary and secondary materials;

➤ develop a good working thesis;

➤ locate materials in traditional print media and in online (or CD-ROM) databases;

➤ take notes for use in your essay;

➤ organize your notes into a standard essay, making it your own;

➤ incorporate quotation, paraphrase, and summary into your own development; and

➤ document your sources in correct MLA style.

</td></tr>
</table>

In the next chapter, we'll work through a case study of a research project. In this chapter, we discuss basic research methodology and documentation. You should read these chapters together, as they together describe current approaches to research and the product of that research.

WHAT RESEARCH IS, AND WHAT RESEARCH IS NOT

Hoping to scoop the market, an enterprising man thought he'd hit on a new way to sell honey. He included in each jar a dead bee as proof that the product was genuine. Some writers—even some professionals—seem to think that a hiveful of dead quotations or footnotes is proof of research. But research requires much more than the citation of authorities. What it requires, briefly, is informed, *thoughtful* analysis.

Because a research paper requires its writer to collect and interpret evidence—usually including the opinions of earlier investigators—people sometimes think that a research paper, unlike a critical essay, is not the expression of personal opinion. Such a view is unjust both to criticism and to research. A critical essay is not a mere expression of personal opinions; it offers evidence that supports the opinions and thus persuades the reader of their objective rightness. A research paper is in the final analysis largely personal because the author continuously uses his or her own judgment to

287

evaluate the evidence, deciding what is relevant and convincing. A research paper is not the mere presentation of what a dozen scholars have already said about a topic; it is a thoughtful evaluation of the available evidence, and a weaving together of this evidence according to a plan; so it is, finally, an expression of what the author thinks the evidence adds up to.

PRIMARY AND SECONDARY MATERIALS

The materials of literary research may be conveniently divided into two sorts: primary and secondary. PRIMARY materials or sources are the real subject of study; the SECONDARY materials are critical and historical accounts already written about these primary materials. For example, if you are concerned with Joy Kogawa's representation of the incarceration of Japanese-Canadians during World War II, you might want to read her novel, *Obasan,* and her other writing—these are primary sources. You might also consider other primary material such as newspaper articles of the period, records of the parliamentary debate, RCMP reports, and so on. But to understand a certain aspect of her work, you will also want to look at later biographical and critical studies about Kogawa and her novel, and at other studies of the historical events themselves—these are secondary sources.

FROM TOPIC TO THESIS

Almost every literary work lends itself to research. A study of the ghost of Caesar in Shakespeare's *Julius Caesar* (does it have a real, objective existence, or is it merely a figment of Brutus' imagination?) could lead to a study of Shakespeare's other ghosts (for instance, those in *Hamlet* and *Macbeth*), and a study of Elizabethan attitudes toward ghosts. Or, a reader of John Gray's *Billy Bishop Goes to War* might want to study the early critical reception of the play. Did the reviewers like it? More precisely, did the reviewers in academic journals evaluate it differently from those in popular magazines and newspapers? Or, what has Gray himself said about the play in the decades that have passed since he wrote it?

A Working Thesis

In the earliest stage of your research, then, you don't know what you will find, so you cannot yet formulate a thesis (or, at best, you can formulate only a tentative thesis). But you know that there is a topic, that it interests you, and that you are ready to begin the necessary legwork. It is crucial that you develop the skill of creating a WORKING THESIS, sometimes called a PRELIMINARY THESIS. With such a focus, you can narrow your search without prejudging the outcome—you will still create a final thesis when the material is gathered—but you will not wander for days in the library reading hundreds of related but unnecessary sources. This working thesis should be in thesis form (see Chapter 2), but the working thesis must be open-ended enough that the final thesis can go in one of many possible directions; otherwise, you will seek only material that fits your preconceptions. It is a tricky balance to learn, but it will greatly improve your research skills—and save you time.

LOCATING MATERIAL: FIRST STEPS

Here is a brief introduction to research in traditional sources. In the next chapter, we further discuss electronic sources, although you will likely also use electronic searches from the start. **Remember***:* Online search engines do not include older material, so you should also consult print versions when your research calls for investigation of earlier scholarship.

First, prepare a working bibliography, that is, a list of books and articles you must consult. The library catalogue is an excellent place to begin. Next, you'll need to move to various indices. Probably the best place to locate articles and books on literature is to consult the *MLA International Bibliography of Books and Articles in the Modern Languages and Literatures* (1922–). The index is also available on CD-ROM, and, in fact, the disc is preferable, since it is updated quarterly. Many colleges and universities now offer the *MLA International Bibliography* as part of their online resources, and this version is even more up-to-date. (Another excellent starting point, discussed later, is the group of electronic indices provided by *InfoTrac* or *EBSCOHost.*)

MLA International Bibliography lists scholarly studies—books as well as articles in academic journals—published in a given year. Because of the great number of items listed, the print version of the bibliography runs to more than one volume, but material on writing in English (including, for instance, Japanese authors who write in English) is in one volume. To see what has been published on Jack Hodgins in a given year, for example, you turn to the section on Canadian literature (as opposed to American, English, Irish, and so forth), and then to the subsection labelled 1900–99, to see if anything that sounds relevant is listed.

Because your time is severely limited, you probably cannot read everything published on your topic. At least for the moment, therefore, you will use only the last five or ten years of this bibliography. Presumably, any important earlier material will have been incorporated into some of the recent studies listed, and if, when you come to read these recent studies, you find references to an article that sounds essential written in, say, 1975, then read that article, too.

Although these indices include works on Canadian literature, you will want to also consult *The Canadian Periodical Index* (*CPI;* 1920–), an annual publication that lists articles in both scholarly journals and magazines. (The electronic version is an engine called *CPI.Q*). *Canadian Literature Index: A Guide to Periodicals and Newspapers* (1985–88) and the later *Canadian Literary Periodicals Index* (1992, 1997–) are also good general sources. (Some students use *Reader's Guide*, but it is generally inferior to these others.)

If you want to research a related but non-literary topic—such as the controversy over removal of Margaret Laurence's novel *The Diviners* from high school curricula—there may be no books, and there may be no information in the scholarly journals indexed in *MLA International Bibliography*. However, there will be information in *CBCA* (*Canadian Business and Current Affairs;* 1982–), which indexes literary and non-literary sources, and is available online and on CD-ROM.

This major source indexes more than 200,000 articles a year in Canadian scholarly journals, magazines, and newspapers in the fields of Literature, Business, Politics, History, and News Events. The electronic version includes over 20,000 full-text articles each year. This database subsumes the print counterparts, *Canadian Business Index, Canadian News Index, Canadian Magazine Index, Bibliography of Works on Canadian Foreign Relations*, and *Canadian Index*, but the print versions are also available. *Canadian Newsdisc* (1992), available online and on CD-ROM, is another important source. It contains full-text articles from 37 selected newspapers and television transcripts.

On many campuses, indices from *InfoTrac* (1985–) and *EBSCOHost* have become the preferred database vendors. *InfoTrac* includes the *Canadian Periodical Index*. A new version, *InfoTrac Total Access*, provides integrated searches among many products. *EBSCOHost* offers a number of databases, including *Canadian MAS*. These search engines change rapidly, so new sources may be available since this chapter was revised: This is another reason to also consult the traditional print and CD-ROM versions and to ask questions of reference librarians, who are up-to-date.

Other Bibliographical Aids

There are hundreds of guides to publications and to reference works. Some are more general; some are specific to literary topics. Here are a few examples of major print guides to literary analysis:

- *Contemporary Literary Criticism*
- *Profiles in Canadian Literature*
- *Book Review Index* (1965–); *Canadian Book Review Annual* (1975–)
- *A Bibliography of Canadian Folklore in English*
- *Canada on Stage: Canadian Theatre Review Yearbook*
- *Who's Who in Canadian Film and Television*
- *Canadian Writers and their Works: Poetry Series; Fiction Series*
- *Annual Bibliography of Commonwealth Literature* (1964–)
- *The Annotated Bibliography of Canada's Major Authors*
- *Poetry Index Annual* (1982–)
- *Modern English Canadian Prose*
- *Who's Who in Canadian Literature*

TAKING NOTES

Let's assume now that you have checked some bibliographies and that you have a fair number of references to read in order to gain a substantial knowledge of the evidence and the common interpretations of the evidence. Most researchers find it convenient, when examining bibliographies and the library catalogue, to write down each reference on an INDEX CARD—one title per card. On the card, put the author's full name (last name first), the exact title of the book or of the article, and the name of the journal (with dates and pages). Put it in proper MLA style now; you won't have to reconfigure it later. It's also a good idea to put the library catalogue number on the card to save time if you need to get the item for a second look.

Next, start reading or scanning the materials whose titles you have collected. Some of these items will prove irrelevant; others will prove valuable in themselves and also in the leads they give you to further references, which you should record on cards large enough to give you ample room (4" x 6," (100 x 152 mm) or half a piece of scrap paper). Be selective in taking notes.

The Photocopier and the Word Processor

The photocopier enables you to take home lots of material from the library (including material that does not circulate). Because it is easy to highlight or underline, however, you may be tempted to mark almost everything. That is, you may not *think* about the material, as you would if you were taking notes by hand, where you would have a powerful incentive to consider whether the material really is noteworthy. So, it is often more efficient

- to read the material in the library,
- to carefully select what pertains exactly to your working thesis, and
- to take note of it.

A word processor is useful not only in the writing process, but also in the early stages of research, when you are getting ideas and are taking notes. You can create files for each item (like electronic "cards"), make connections, organize (even using an outline view), and easily change your plan. It's a good idea to keep all these working files: Don't delete anything until the essay is complete and returned from your instructor. Keep earlier drafts of the essay in case of a later mishap: Computers and printers often fail.

Caution: Do not feel that you must use all of your notes. Your reader does not want to read a series of notes that are linked by thin connectives. This is a danger in using this method, especially if the notes are already neatly typed into files; don't set yourself up to produce a poor essay.

A Guide to Note Taking

- For everything you consult, *always specify the source*, so you later know exactly where you found that key point. The author's last name or the name and the first significant word of the title are usually enough.

- *Write summaries* (abridgements), *not paraphrases* (restatements).

- *Quote sparingly.* Remember: this is *your* paper. Quote particularly effective, important, or memorable passages that will provide authority to your final essay. Avoid long quotations: You are aiming to write your own essay, not to reproduce someone else's writing.

- *Quote accurately.* After copying a quotation, check your transcription against the original, correct any misquotation, and then put a check-mark after your quotation to indicate that it is accurate. (Recheck quotations when you type them into your essay: It is inaccurate and rude to put errors into another person's correct prose.) Verify the page number also, and then put a check on your note card, after the page number. If a quotation runs from the bottom of, say, page 306 to the top of 307, on your card put a distinguishing mark (for instance two parallel vertical lines after the last word of the first page), so that if you later use only part of the quotation, you will know the page on which it appeared.

- *Use ellipses* (as discussed in Chapter 14) to indicate the omission of any words within a sentence.

- *Use square brackets to indicate additions* (as discussed in Chapter 14).

- *Never change a word when you copy,* under the impression that you are thereby putting it into your own words. Notes of this sort may find their way into your paper; your reader will sense a style other than yours, and suspicions of plagiarism may follow. (For a detailed discussion of plagiarism, read further in the chapter.) Copy exactly and, later, decide whether to quote, paraphrase, or summarize.

- *In a corner of each note card write a brief key*—for example, "Blackfoot myths"—so you can later locate information at a glance.

- *Comment on your notes.* Consider it your obligation to *think* about the material, evaluating it and using it as a stimulus to further thought. For example, you might jot down, "Jones seriously misreads this passage," or "Leads on from Smith's comments—connect these ideas." It's a good idea to surround all your comments with double parentheses (( )) or a different colour pen.

DRAFTING THE PAPER

The difficult job of writing up your findings remains, but if you have taken good notes and have put useful headings on each card, you are well on your way.

- Read through the cards and sort them into packets of related material. Discard all notes, however interesting, that you now see are irrelevant to your paper. (Do not destroy them yet!) Go through the cards again and again, sorting and resorting, putting together what belongs together.

- Probably you will find that you have to do a little additional research—somehow you aren't quite clear about this or that—but after you have done this additional research, you should be able to arrange the packets into a reasonable and consistent sequence. You now have a kind of first draft or, at least, a tentative organization for your paper.

- Beware of the compulsion to include every note card in your essay; beware of telling the reader, "*A* says [. . .].; *B* says [. . .].; *C* says [. . .]."

- You must have a point, a thesis.

- Make sure your organization is clear to the reader. The final version of the paper should be a finished piece of work, without the inconsistencies, detours, and occasional dead ends of an early draft. Your readers should feel that they are moving toward a conclusion (by means of your thoughtful evaluation of the evidence) rather than merely reading an anthology of commentary on the topic. And so, if you are working through a number of critical opinions, we should get some such structure as:

```
There are three common views on [ . . . ].  The first
two are represented by A and B; the third, and by far
the most reasonable, is C's view that [ . . . ].  A
argues [ . . . ], but [ . . . ]. The second view,
held by B, is based on [ . . . ] and this
seems [ . . . ]. Although the third view, by C,
is not conclusive, it [ . . . ]. Moreover, C's
point can be strengthened when we consider a piece
of evidence that he does not make use of, the fact
that [ . . . ].
```

- Preface most quotations with a lead-in, such as "X concisely states the common view"; "Although Z asserts that [. . .]," or "A counters by suggesting [. . .]." Let the reader know where you are going, or, to put it a little differently, let the reader know how the quotation fits into your argument.

Remember that you should work from primary sources. It should be your paper. By using secondary sources you enrich your analysis, but keep a proper proportion between primary sources (the majority) and secondary sources (used selectively). Some people suggest marking up your penultimate draft with three colours of underlining (or highlighting on the word processor screen): say, red for primary material, blue for secondary material, and green for your own comments. If you see a lot more blue than red and green, you need to rethink the emphasis, the proportions. You should see a significant amount of green; otherwise, it isn't your own thinking.

Quotations and summaries should be accompanied by judicious analyses of your own so that by the end of the paper your reader has gained an idea of what previous writers have said, but also is persuaded that under your guidance she has seen the evidence, heard the arguments justly summarized, and reached a sound conclusion.

DOCUMENTATION

What to Document: Avoiding Plagiarism

Honesty requires that you acknowledge your indebtedness for material, not only when you quote directly from a work, but also when you appropriate an idea that is not common knowledge. Not to acknowledge such borrowing is plagiarism. If in doubt whether to give credit, give credit.

You ought, however, to develop a sense of what is considered common knowledge or *a priori* information. Definitions in a dictionary can be considered common knowledge, so there is no need to say, "According to *The Gage Canadian Dictionary*, a novel is [. . .]." (This is weak: It's unnecessary, and it's uninteresting.) Similarly, the date of first publication of, say, Frances Brooke's *The History of Emily Montague* can be considered common knowledge. Few can give it when asked—it's 1769—but it can be found in innumerable sources, and no one need get the credit for providing you with the date. The idea that Hamlet delays is also a matter of common knowledge. But if you are impressed by someone's argument that Claudius has been much maligned, you should give credit to that person.

Suppose you happen to come across Frederick R. Karl's statement in the revised edition of *A Reader's Guide to the Contemporary English Novel* (1972) that George Orwell was "better as a man than as a novelist." This is an interesting and an effectively worded idea—and it is certainly a loaded personal opinion. You cannot use these words without giving credit to Karl (or letting him take the blame). And you cannot retain the idea but alter the words, for example, to "Orwell was a better human being than he was a writer of fiction," presenting the idea as your own, for here you are simply lifting Karl's idea—and putting it less effectively. If you want to use Karl's point, give him credit and—since you can hardly summarize so brief a statement—use his exact words and put them within quotation marks.

What about a longer passage that strikes you favourably? Let's assume that in reading Diana Brydon's article, "The White Inuit Speaks," (*The Postcolonial Reader*, ed. Ashcroft, Griffiths and Tiffin 1995:136–42) you find the following passage interesting:

The current flood of books by white Canadian writers embracing Native spirituality clearly serves a white need to feel at home in this country and to assuage the guilt felt over a material appropriation by making it a cultural one as well. In the absence of comparable political reparation for past appropriations such symbolic acts seem questionable or at least inadequate. (141)

In your essay, you certainly cannot say, with the implication that these ideas and words are your own:

> The current appearance of books on Native
> spirituality by white Canadians may be explained by
> the fact that white Canadians need to feel at home in
> this country and feel guilty. Unless there are
> compensations for historical appropriation these
> questionable acts are only symbolic.

This example is simply lifting Brydon's ideas and making changes in the wording; it is simply a theft of Brydon's property. (The writer has stolen Brydon's car and given it a new paint job.) But even a larger change in wording is unacceptable unless Brydon is given credit for her work. The next example is still plagiarized:

> Guilt over past appropriation and a desire to feel at
> home may lead some white Canadians to embrace Native
> spirituality so that a shared culture may offset the
> historical theft of the land. Unless such acts are
> accompanied by compensation, however, they seem
> meaningless.

In this version, the writer still presents Brydon's idea as if it were the writer's own. What to do? Easy: **give credit** in any one of a number of ways. For example:

* By direct quotation, or direct quotation mixed with paraphrase:

> As Diana Brydon suggests, "the current flood of
> books by white Canadian writers embracing Native
> spirituality [. . .] serves a white need to feel
> at home [. . .] and to assuage the guilt" white
> people feel for taking the land "by making
> [the appropriation] a cultural one as well."
> Such "symbolic acts seem questionable or [. . .]
> inadequate" to Brydon (140).

* * *

> The reason there is an upsurge in writing about
> Native spirituality by white Canadians is the effort
> by these writers to "feel at home in this country and
> to assuage the guilt" they feel over "a material
> appropriation by making it a cultural one as well"
> (Brydon 140). Brydon argues that such "symbolic acts
> seem questionable or at least inadequate" unless
> white people also make "comparable political
> reparation" (140).

- Or by summary:

> Diana Brydon feels that symbolic acts that attempt a
> cultural appropriation of Native spirituality by
> white Canadians, and that have recently produced a
> large number of books on the subject, are question-
> able unless white Canadians match them with political
> recompense (140).

Notice that you must decide where to put the citation. Put it as close to the quoted material as possible, but after *all* material that comes from that source. The citation marks the division between borrowed material and your own voice, and you must place it carefully to indicate ownership (including your ownership of your own ideas).

How to Document

Documentation tells your reader exactly what your sources are. Until 1984, the standard form was the footnote. You will still see footnotes in some sources, but today parenthetical citations within the text are becoming the norm and it is these we will discuss at length. We will then briefly discuss current uses of notes.

Internal Parenthetical Citations
This is the style you should learn. Briefly, the idea is that the reader of your paper encounters an author's name and a parenthetical citation of pages. By checking the author's name in a Works Cited list, the reader can find the source.

Suppose you are writing about Thomas King's "Borders" (Appendix B). Let's assume that you have already mentioned the author and the title of the story—that is, you have let the reader know the subject of the essay—and now you introduce a quotation from the story in a sentence such as this. (Notice the parenthetical citation of page numbers immediately after the quotation.)

> The young narrator finds it fun to be trapped between
> borders. Even though "the car was not very
> comfortable," he enjoys "all that food" (365).

Turning to Works Cited, the reader, knowing the quoted words are by King, looks for King and finds the following:

```
King, Thomas. "Borders." Rpt. in Sylvan Barnet, Reid
     Gilbert, and William E. Cain, A Short Guide to
     Writing about Literature. 2nd Canadian ed. Don Mills,
     ON: Pearson, 2004. 359-367.
```

Thus the essayist is informing the reader that the quoted words ("the car was not very comfortable" and "all that food") are to be found on page 365 of this handbook.

If you have not mentioned King's name in some sort of lead-in, you will have to give his name within the parentheses so that the reader will know the author of the quoted words:

```
We know the young boy has learned a lesson when he says
that pride in his heritage "is a good thing to have, you
know" (King 364).
```

For EMBEDDED QUOTATIONS (those which run right into your sentence), citations are given immediately after the closing quotation mark, without any punctuation between author and page number—(King 364)—and then the necessary punctuation (usually a comma or a period) follows—(King 364).

You should follow standard rules of punctuation even when you are quoting. Hence,

```
     We appreciate the paradox of the woman's position
     because almost at the start of the story, in the
     third paragraph, we learn she decided "to persuade
     this man at the end of her voice" (13) to marry her;
     if she had not "used her voice like a hand" (13), she
     would have escaped his control, but met her own death
     by hanging.
```

Here, there is no punctuation after the first quotation (because none is needed in the sentence), and a comma comes after the second citation, because a comma is needed at this point in the sentence.

If punctuation is needed in a case where there is no citation, put commas and periods *inside* the quotation marks ("like a hand,"), put semi-colons and colons *outside* the quotation marks ("like a hand";), and put question marks and exclamation marks either *inside or outside*, depending on whether the mark is essential to your sentence or part of the quotation from the author:

```
     Atwood shows the woman's dilemma when she asks,
     "Who else is there to marry?" (13).
     With Atwood, we can ask, "Who else is there to
     marry" (13)?
```

For SET-DOWN QUOTATIONS (or LONG QUOTATIONS—those which are set off from your text by being indented ten spaces), put the parenthetical citation at the end of the quotation, one space *after* the period or other mark that ends the quotation. *No punctuation* follows the parenthesis in this case. Here is an example:

> In discussing "The Idea of a National Theatre," Denis
> Salter provides a concise history of the development of
> theatre in this country but consistently shows the
> assumptions built into that development. Salter sums up
> his position immediately in his opening:
>> A national theatre, like a national
>> literature, can never be ideologically
>> neutral. It emerges from a specific set of
>> moral, aesthetic, and political values, some
>> explicit, but most implicit, effective
>> precisely because they are so hard to discern.
>> All these values have been instrumental in the
>> formation of styles of performance, audience
>> expectations, the repertoire, and general
>> beliefs about the function of theatre in an
>> emergent culture. (71)
> It is these "beliefs" that Salter systematically
> explores, showing the early theatre of Canada to be "an
> effective instrument of trans-historical cultural
> imperialism" (89). Whether or not one agrees with his
> interpretation of each of his historical examples, it
> becomes clear that the overall thrust of the movement to
> form a national theatre was, as Salter argues, based in
> Eurocentric ideals.
>
>
>   Work Cited
> Salter, Denis.   "The Idea of a National Theatre."
>   Canadian Canons: Essays in Literary Value.
>   Ed. Robert Lecker.   Toronto: U of Toronto
>   P, 1991. 71-90.

This example points out a number of details you should note. Again, notice the difference in punctuation in embedded and set-down quotations. The indented quotation ends with a period, then there are two spaces, and then the citation in parentheses with no further punctuation. The last quotation is embedded, so the punctuation follows the citation. The repeated word "beliefs" is again shown to be Salter's word by quotation marks, but a second citation would be superfluous: The reader remembers having just read it.

Four additional points:

- The abbreviations *p.*, *pg.*, and *pp.* are not used in citing pages.

- If a story is very short—perhaps only a page or two—your instructor may tell you there is no need to keep citing the page reference for each quotation. Simply mention in a footnote that the story appears on, say, pages 13–14. Check with your instructor.

- If you are referring to a poem, your instructor may tell you to use parenthetical citations of line numbers rather than page numbers. MLA allows for this choice, or you may provide both, or use a footnote. Check with your instructor.

- If you are referring to a play with numbered lines, your instructor may prefer that you give act, scene, and line, rather than page numbers in the citation. Use Arabic (not Roman) numerals, separating each number by a period (3.2.118). Again, you can provide only line references, or lines and pages, or use a footnote combination. Check with your instructor.

Here are a few examples, all referring to an article by Robert Kroetsch, "The Fear of Women in Prairie Fiction: An Erotics of Space." The essay appeared in

```
Kroetsch, Robert. The Lovely Treachery of Words: Essays
     Selected and New. Toronto: Oxford UP, 1989. 73-83.
```

but all this information is given only in Works Cited, not within the text of your essay.

- You give the author's name in your text:

```
In his discussion of prairie fiction, Robert Kroetsch
asks how we can "establish any sort of close
relationship in a landscape--in a physical situation
--whose primary characteristic is distance?" (73).
```

Or:

```
Robert Kroetsch, in his discussion of prairie
fiction, asks how it is possible to establish a
close relationship in a landscape characterized by
distance (73).
```

- You do not give the name of the author in a lead-in:

```
Prairie fiction poses the question of how to
establish a close relationship in a space marked
by distance (Kroetsch 73).
```

- You use more than one work by an author. Here, you will have to identify which work you are using. You can provide the title in a lead-in:

```
In "The Fear of Women in Prairie Fiction: An Erotics
of Space," Kroetsch questions how we can "establish
any sort of close relationship in a landscape
```

```
[ . . . ] whose primary characteristic is
distance?" (73).
```

Or:

- You can provide the information in the parenthetic citation, giving a shortened version of the title—usually the first word, omitting *A, An,* or *The:*

```
According to Kroetsch, it is difficult to "establish
any sort of close relationship in a landscape [ . . . ]
whose primary characteristic is distance" ("Fear" 73).
```

Very occasionally, certain titles may require still another word or two for clarity. The rule is to move through the citation to the right, one word or aspect at a time, until you clarify to what you are referring. You would have to give a long reference, say, to either of two books if their titles were *Sharon Thesen's Poetry: Precision and Vision* and *Sharon Thesen's Poetry: Precision at the Point of Despair,* but this is an extreme example. (In very particular bibliographic essays you might need to go as far right as publication or edition information.)

Footnotes and Endnotes

There are still some uses for NOTES. If you are using only one source, your instructor may advise you to give the source in a footnote. (Check with your instructors to find out their preferred forms of documentation. It's the question to ask in the first class.)

If you use a footnote, elevate a small Arabic numeral above the final word of the sentence, like this.[1] If you are using a word processor, it will be able to format the note for you. Then give the citation after another raised numeral at the foot of the page (hence, footnote) or at the end of the document (endnote). The footnote begins by being indented five spaces, but second and subsequent lines are given flush left.

If you are using only one primary source and you do use a footnote, indicate in the note that all references will be to this source (as, "Subsequent references will be to this edition and appear in parenthesis in the text").

You may want to use a CONTENT NOTE, which is a note that gives extra useful information that would upset the coherence of your essay if you were to include it in the text. If you do, use a raised numeral in your essay and then prepare a separate page after the text and before the Works Cited page, called Notes. Put the material after a corresponding raised numeral on this page. A Content Note to an essay on King's "Borders" might say, for example:

```
¹The trickster figure is an important part of
Native mythology.  Called Coyote by many First Nations
People, the figure is also known as Raven and Nanabush.
He is an androgynous creature, given to playing tricks
on both men and women.  For a discussion of his
importance in Native literature, see Godard 184.
```

Any reference (like the Godard citation) *within* the note carries forward to the Works Cited list. In this list, then, you would find the title ("The Politics of Representation: Some Native Canadian Women Writers") and full publication information of Barbara Godard's essay in *Canadian Literature* 124–25 (1990): 183–221. Everything in the text—any Appendices and any Content Notes—refers forward to the citations in the Works List. This very important reference page is the last item in any essay.

The List of Works Cited

The key to your sources is the list that appears at the end of the essay. It can be called the *List of Works Cited, Works Cited*, or, if you have only one source, *Work Cited*. Here are the details:

- The list appears on a new page and continues the page numbering of your essay.

- The list is arranged alphabetically by author (last name first).

- If a work is anonymous, alphabetize it under the first word of the title unless the first word is *A, An,* or *The*, in which case alphabetize it under the second word.

- Each item begins flush left, but if an entry is longer than one line, subsequent lines in the entry are indented five spaces.

Sometimes, a Works Consulted list is added so that readers may easily look further into the primary and secondary material if they wish. A Works Consulted list muddies the water of what you actually used and what you "forgot" that you used—frankly, it encourages plagiarism. Avoid it.

For models of very many citations, consult Joseph Gibaldi, *MLA Handbook for Writers of Research Papers*, New York: Modern Language Association, latest edition. Updates are also available on the website, at www.mla.org. Here, however, we give examples of the most common kinds of citations you will use in literary essays.

MODELS FOR CITATION

Book Citations

1. A Book by One Author

```
Graveline, Frye Jean. Circle Works: Transforming
    Eurocentric Consciousness. Halifax: Fernwood, 1998.
```

Notice that the author's last name is given first, but otherwise the name is given as on the title page. Do not substitute initials for names written out on the title page or change the order. The name of a trade publisher is shortened (except in rare cases where two words are needed for clarity). For example: Little, Brown and Company is cited as *Little*. W. W. Norton and

Company becomes *Norton*. When the publisher is a University Press, abbreviate both *University* (U) and *Press* (P) and use the normal style of the university's name: *U of Victoria P*; *Guelph UP*. (Note that italics are used in these examples for emphasis only. In MLA documentation, only titles of separately published items—like books or plays or films, for example—are italicized.)

Take the title from the title page, not from the cover or the spine, but disregard unusual typography—for instance, the use of only capital letters or the use of *&* for *and*. Underline the title and subtitle with one continuous underline (or use italics), but do not underline the period. The place of publication is indicated by the name of the city. If the city is not well known or if two cities have the same name (for instance, Cambridge, Massachusetts, and Cambridge, England), add another locator: the name of the province in Canada, the state in the United States, or the country for the rest of the world. If the title page lists several cities, give only the first, or the one dictated by common sense. (This book lists a number of cities, but it is a Canadian edition, so *Don Mills, ON* seems most reasonable—it is also the first name in the list).

2. A Book by More than One Author

```
Eaton, Diane, and Garfield Neuman. Canada: A Nation
    Unfolding. Toronto: McGraw, 1994.
```

Notice that the book is listed under the last name of the first author (*Eaton*) and that the second author's name is then given in the normal order (*Garfield* before *Neuman*). Each name is separated by a comma. *If the book has more than three authors,* give the name of the first author only (last name first) and follow it with "et al." (Latin for "and others": *Peters, Helen, et al.*)

3. Two or More Works by the Same Author

Notice that the works are given in alphabetical order (*Fables* precedes *Myth*) and that the author's name is not repeated but is represented by three hyphens followed by a period and two spaces. If the author is the translator or editor of a volume, the three hyphens are followed not by a period but by a comma, then a space, then the appropriate abbreviation (trans. or ed.), then (two spaces after the period) the title:

```
Frye, Northrop. Fables of Identity: Studies in Poetic
    Mythology. New York: Harcourt, 1963.

---. The Myth of Deliverance: Reflections on
    Shakespeare's Problem Comedies. Intro. A. C.
    Hamilton. Toronto: U of Toronto P, 1993.
```

4. A Book in Several Volumes

You will want to cite the entire collection of volumes if you have used more than one. In this case, notice that the total number of volumes is given after the title. Within your essay you will parenthetically indicate a reference to the volume from which the quoted material comes; for instance, page 30 of volume 2 reads: (Klassen 2:30).

> Klassen, Ingrid, ed. <u>D'Sonoqua: An Anthology of Women</u>
> <u>Poets of British Columbia</u>. 2 vols. Vancouver:
> Intermedia, 1979.

If you have used only one volume of a multivolume work, the citation looks like this:

> Jerry Wasserman, ed. <u>Modern Canadian Plays</u>. 3rd ed.
> Vol. 1. Vancouver: Talonbooks, 1993-4. 2 vols.

(You may add the total number of volumes at the end, as here; it is not required but does give an idea of the scope of the work. Notice that this collection is also in a 3rd edition and that information comes before the volume number.)

In your parenthetical citation within the essay—(Wasserman 234)—you will therefore cite only the page reference, since the reader (on consulting the Works Cited) will understand that the reference is in volume 1.

If, instead of using the volumes as a whole, you used only an independent work within one volume—say a poem in volume 4—give the title, the volume in which it appears, and the pages it fills. Then, in the parenthetical citation you will not need to note the volume number. A citation for lines from Cohen's poem would appear as (Cohen 239) or (Cohen 240) or (Cohen 239–40) depending on which lines you chose and how many:

> Cohen, Leonard. "You Have the Lovers." <u>The Evolution of</u>
> <u>Canadian Literature in English: 1945-1970</u>. Ed. Paul
> Denham. Vol. 4. Toronto: Holt, 1973. 239-40. 4 vols.

5. A Book with a Separate Title in a Set of Volumes

> Wagner, Anton, ed. <u>The Developing Mosaic</u>. Vol. 3 of
> <u>Canada's Lost Plays</u>. Toronto: Canadian Theatre
> Review, 1980.

6. A Revised (or Later) Edition of a Book

> Geddes, Gary. <u>13 Canadian Poets X3</u>. 4th ed. Toronto:
> Oxford UP, 2001.

> Chaucer, Geoffrey. <u>The Works of Geoffrey Chaucer</u>.
> Ed. F. N. Robinson. 2nd ed. Boston: Houghton, 1957.

7. An Encyclopedia or Other Reference Book
A signed article in a familiar reference book:

> Blodgett, E. D. "Munroe, Alice." <u>The Canadian</u>
> <u>Encyclopedia</u>. Year 2000 ed. 1999.

An unsigned article:

> "Birney, Alfred Earle." <u>Encyclopedia of British</u>
> <u>Columbia</u>. Ed. Daniel Francis. Madeira Park, BC:
> Harbour, 2000.

This second entry is in a less familiar reference. In this case, give further publication information to help your reader locate the source, especially if there is only one edition.

A reference book:

> "Gzowski, Peter John." <u>Canadian Who's Who</u>. Vol. 36.
> 2001.

8. A Reprint, Such as a Paperback Version of an Older Hardcover Book

> Grove, Frederick P. <u>Over Prairie Trails</u>. 1922. New
> Canadian Library 1. Toronto: McClelland, 1957.

Notice that the entry cites the original date (1922) but indicates that the writer is using the McClelland and Stewart reprint of 1957. This example also shows the form for a book in a series; this is number 1 of the series.

9. An Edited Book Other than an Anthology

> Denham, Robert D., ed. <u>The Correspondence of Northrop</u>
> <u>Frye and Helen Kemp</u>, 1932-1939. Toronto: U of
> Toronto P, 1996.

> Keats, John. <u>The Letters of John Keats</u>. Ed. Hyder Edward
> Rollins. 2 vols. Cambridge, MA: Harvard UP, 1958.

10. A Work in a Volume of Works by One Author

> Trudeau, Pierre E. "The Just Society." In <u>Conversation</u>
> <u>with Canadians</u>. Toronto: U of Toronto P, 1972. 11-42.

11. An Anthology
You can list an anthology itself under the editor's name or under the title, depending on whether you mostly quote from works in the anthology or from the work of the editor (like the Introduction.) Remember to indicate the

meaning of the word you give in the parenthesis in your text: (*New*) to show it is the title (not W. H. New, a well-known Canadian critic) or (Thesen) to indicate the author. Thus:

```
The New Long Poem Anthology. Ed. Sharon Thesen. Toronto:
    Coach House, 1991.
```

```
Sharon Thesen, ed. The New Long Poem Anthology. Toronto:
    Coach House, 1991.
```

12. A Work in an Anthology (a collection of works by several authors)

Most often you are quoting from a work in the anthology. In that case, begin with the author and the title of the work you are citing, not with the name of the anthologist or the title of the anthology. The entry ends with the pages occupied by the selection you are citing:

```
Watson, Sheila. "Brother Oedipus." The Penguin Book of
    Modern Canadian Short Stories. Ed. Wayne Grady.
    Markham, ON: Penguin, 1982. 35-42.
```

```
Erin Mouré. "Blindness." A New Anthology of Canadian
    Literature in English. Ed. Donna Bennett and Russell
    Brown. Toronto: Oxford UP, 2002. 1115-16.
```

Normally, you will give the title of the work you are citing (probably an essay, short story, or poem) in quotation marks. If you are referring to a book-length work (for instance, a novel or a full-length play), underline (or indicate italics). Because it is inside an anthology, both its title and the anthology title will be underlined (italics): for example, *Jacob's Wake. Plays by Michael Cook*.

If the work is translated, after the period that follows the title, write "Trans." and give the name of the translator, followed by a period and then the name of the anthology and the rest of its citation.

Remember: the page span specified in the entry is the *entire selection*, not simply the pages you may happen to refer to within your paper.

13. Two or More Works in an Anthology: Cross-References

If you are referring to several works reprinted within one volume, instead of listing each item fully, simply link the author's name and the title of the work to the name of the anthologist(s) or editor(s) of the collection and then give the page span. This saves time. Of course, this cross-reference form requires that the anthology *itself* be cited elsewhere in the list under the name of the editor(s). Here are two selections and their anthology, in alphabetical order:

```
Ashcroft, Bill, Gareth Griffiths, and Helen Tiffin, eds.
    The Post-colonial Studies Reader. London and New
    York: Routledge, 1995.
```

Brydon, Diana. "The White Inuit Speaks: Contamination as
    Literary Strategy." Ashcroft, Griffiths and Tiffin
    136-42.

Hutcheon, Linda. "Circling the Downspout of Empire."
    Ashcroft, Griffiths and Tiffin 130-35.

14. A Translated Book

Marchessault, Jovette. Like a Child of the Earth. Trans.
    Yvonne M. Klein. Vancouver: Talonbooks, 1988.

If you are discussing the translation itself, as opposed to the book, list the
work under the translator's name:

Klein, Yvonne M., trans. Like a Child of the Earth. By
    Jovette Marchessault. Vancouver: Talonbooks, 1988.

15. An Introduction, Foreword, or Afterword, or Other Editorial Apparatus

Ashcroft, Bill, Gareth Griffiths, and Helen Tiffin.
    Preface. The Post-colonial Studies Reader. Ed
    Ashcroft, Griffiths, and Tiffin. London and New York:
    Routledge, 1995. xv-xvi.

Peraldi, François. Afterword. The Passions of Mister
    Desire (Selected Poems). By André Roy. Trans. Daniel
    Sloate. Montréal: Guernica, 1986. 75-81.

Usually a book with an Introduction or some such comparable material
is listed under the name of the author of the book rather than the name of the
author of the editorial material (see citation #6, to Chaucer). But if you are
referring to the editor's apparatus rather than to the work itself, use the form
just given. Quite often, if it is an Introduction or Preface, such apparatus is paginated with small Roman numerals (such as i–xiv).

The second example is an opportunity to show a number of contribu-
tors. Notice that this entry has an author (Roy), a translator (Sloate), and an
author of an Afterword (Peraldi). You must be careful to give credit to everyone who worked on the intellectual content of a book.

16. Reprint of a Scholarly Article

Give details of the original publication, as in the following example:

West, Paul. "Earle Birney and the Compound Ghost."
    Canadian Literature 13 (1962): 5-14. Rpt. in A Choice
    of Critics: Selections from Canadian Literature. Ed.
    George Woodcock. Toronto: Oxford UP, 1966. 131-41

17. Government Documents

There are a number of citations to different kinds of government (and corporate) documents. They aren't often used in literary essays, but sometimes provide background information (see Chapter 16). Unless a particular publisher is given (which might be a ministry or agency of government), use the generic publisher for the government. In Canada, the federal government publishes in Ottawa through *Information Canada*; provincial governments publish from their capitals through *Queen's Printer for [Name of Province]*. (In the US, *GPO*; in Britain, *HMSO*.) Here is a basic model:

```
Canada. Statistics Canada. Report on Japanese-Canadian
    Deportation. Ottawa: Information Canada, 1998.
```

Periodical Citations

18. An Article in a Scholarly Journal

Most journals are paginated consecutively; that is, the pagination of the second issue picks up where the first issue left off. Some journals begin each issue with a new page #1. The forms of the citations in Works Cited differ slightly.

A journal that uses continuous pagination:

```
Filewod, Alan. "Modernism and Genocide: Citing
    Minstrelsy in Postcolonial Agitprop." Modern Drama 44
    (2001): 91-102.
```

This article appeared in volume 44, which was published in 2001. Although journal volumes consist of 2-4 issues, you do *not* specify the issue number when the journal is paginated continuously.

For a journal that paginates each issue separately, add the issue number after the volume number. Otherwise, the citation is exactly the same: 44.1 (2001): 91-102.

A few journals, like *Canadian Literature*, use only issue numbers and are not arranged in volumes. Use the issue number as if it were a volume number.

```
Doyle, James. "Sui Sin Far and Onoto Watanna: Two Early
    Chinese-Canadian Authors." Canadian Literature 140
    (1994): 50-58.
```

19. An Article in a Magazine

A weekly magazine:

```
MacQueen, Ken. "The Lost Children." Macleans 21 Jan.
    2002: 22-24.
```

A monthly magazine:

```
Van Herk, Aritha. "Boxing the Critics: Sucker Punches,
    Shooting Niagara and Other Boy's Games of Criticism."
    Canadian Forum Dec. 1994: 32-35.
```

Notice that the volume number and the issue number are omitted for magazines.

20. An Article in a Newspaper

```
Fulford, Robert. "Portrait of an Author as a Fraud
    (Frederick Philip Grove)." Globe and Mail [Toronto]
    5 Apr. 1995, Natl. ed.: C1+.
```

When the city name is not included in the paper's name, it should be given after the title, in brackets: *[Toronto]*. Because papers appear in various editions, an edition name may be necessary: *(Natl.)*. Because newspapers usually consist of several sections, a section number may precede the page number: *C*. Because stories often continue from page to page, indicate the starting page and then, if it moves on, use a + sign.

21. A Book Review
Most often, reviews do not have a title:

```
Bennett, Susan. Rev. of Performing Women: Female
    Characters, Male Playwrights, and the Modern Stage,
    by Gay Gibson Cima. Essays in Theatre/Études
    Théâtrales 13 (1994): 73-75.
```

Notice the word *by* does not begin with a capital letter (as it does in other kinds of citations).

    If the review is unsigned, list it under the first word of the title, or the second word if the first word is *A, An,* or *The*. If an unsigned review has no title, begin the entry with "Rev. of" and alphabetize it under the title of the work being reviewed.

    If the review does have a title, give the title after the period following the reviewer's name: Bennett, Susan. "Title." Rev. of Performing Women [. . .].

Non-Print Citations

22. An Interview
A published interview:

```
Cone, Tom. Interview. The Work: Conversations with
    English-Canadian Playwrights. By Robert Wallace and
    Cynthia Zimmerman. Toronto: Coach House, 1982. 31-43.
```

A personal interview:

```
Jantzen, Dorothy. Personal interview. 3 Nov. 2000.
```

23. A Lecture

A titled speech at a conference or meeting:

> Acton, Tim. "ReFiguring Identities: Daphne Marlatt's <u>Ana
> Historic</u> and Sky Lee's <u>Disappearing Moon Cafe</u>." Cost
> of Marginality Sess. Race, Gender and the
> Construction of Canada Conf. U. of British Columbia,
> Vancouver. 21 Oct. 1995.

An untitled lecture in one of your classes. (Most of what your instructor tells you in a class is general knowledge within the discipline. Sometimes, however, your instructor makes a point that is her or his own view or interpretation; if you use it in an essay, you must give the professor credit):

> Saddlemyer, Ann. Lecture. English 431, sec. 2.
> University of Toronto. Toronto. 15 Oct. 1994.

24. A Television or Radio Program

> "Al Purdy." Narr. Adrienne Clarkson. Dir. John Gareau.
> <u>Adrienne Clarkson Presents</u>. Exec. prod. Adrienne
> Clarkson. CBC, Toronto. 7 Feb. 1991.

25. A Film or Videotape

> <u>The Hanging Garden</u>. Dir. Thom Fitzgerald. Perf. Chris
> Leavins, Terry Fox, Seanna McKenna, Troy Veinette,
> Kerry Fox. Cineplex Odeon Films Canada, 1997.

26. A CD or Sound Recording

> Ralph Markham, and Kenneth Broadway. Concerto in C Major
> for Two Pianos and Orchestra. By Vaughan Williams.
> <u>Sir Yehudi Menuhin: Vaughan Williams</u>. Royal
> Philharmonic Orch. Cond. Yehudi Menuhin. Virgin
> Classics, 1988.

27. A Performance

> <u>Age of Iron</u>. By Marie Humber Clements. Dir. Dennis
> Maracle. Firehall Theatre, Vancouver. 9 Oct. 1993.

Electronic Citations

The Modern Language Association provides guidelines for citing electronic sources. See the Frequently Asked Questions link at <www.mla.org>.

The basic rule is to provide as much publication information as possible in the traditional manner and to include the date the source was accessed and its location.

You sometimes locate periodical references directly on the Web via a URL, and usually through a leased database search engine at your college or university library. (Direct access through the Web often produces questionable or non-scholarly sources; be wary of simply searching the Web.) Note which form of entry you used. You give a URL if you used one; you give keywords or a search path if that is how you found the material.

Page Numbers

Noting page numbers is a problem with many electronic sources. If you use a Full-Text article and it provides page numbers, use them. *Tip:* If possible, download a full-text article in a graphic or PDF file format; you will then have an image of the original document with page numbers you can cite: (Gilbert 57). If you can't locate page numbers, then it becomes more difficult to cite the source. If possible, use paragraph counts: (Gilbert par. 5). If you can find neither, then you have to leave the page reference off. In a direct quotation this may be satisfactory, since the quotation marks indicate the span of quoted material. In a summary or paraphrase, however, it becomes difficult to "frame" the borrowing. In this case, you may have to repeat the author's name in the citation, even if it is already mentioned in a lead-in, in order to indicate where the source ends and your voice begins again; or you may set up the quotation with a detailed lead-in that indicates what exactly is being used. It is essential that the span of borrowed material be clearly marked, whatever kind of source you use.

Here are models of references you may use:

28. An Online Scholarly Project or Database

> The Canadian Literature Archive. Ed. David Aaronson and
>   Dennis Cooley. 4 Oct. 1994. U of Manitoba. 15 Sept.
>   2002 <http://www.umanitoba.ca/canlit>.

Note: There may not be an editor for such a project. In this case, Drs. Aaronson and Cooley created the *Canadian Literature Archive*, but these projects often continue with assistants or general departmental support.

29. A Work Within a Scholarly Project

> Kalsey, Surjeet. "Disowning Oneself." The Canadian
>   Literature Archive. Ed. David Aaronson and Dennis
>   Cooley. 4 Oct. 1994. U of Manitoba. 15 Sept. 2002
>   <http://www.umanitoba.ca/canlit>.

30. An Online Book Published Independently

Grove, Miss. <u>Little Grace, or, Scenes in Nova-Scotia</u>.
    Halifax: Mackenzie, 1846. 16 Mar. 2002
    <http://www.canadiana.org/cgi-bin/ECO/mtq?doc=68172>.

31. An Online Book within a Scholarly Project

Richardson, John. <u>Tecumseh, A Poem in Four Cantos</u>. 1842.
    <u>Canada Poetry Press Editions of Early Canadian Long</u>
    <u>Poems</u>. Ed. Douglas Daymond and Leslie Monkman. U of
    Western Ontario. 10 Feb. 2002
    <http://www.arts.uwo.ca/canpoetry/longpoems/Tecumseh/
    index-htm>.

32. An Online Government Document

British Columbia. Ministry of Management Services.
    <u>British Columbia Quarterly Population Estimates</u>:
    <u>1951-2002</u>. 4 Apr. 2002. 17 Sept. 2002
    <http://www.bcstats.gov.bc.ca/data/pop/pop/BCQrtPophtm>

33. An Article in a Scholarly Journal

Some journals available online are print journals which also publish an electronic version; some are e-journals which only appear online. Because you can't check other issues of online periodicals, you must assume they use non-continuous pagination and list the issue number as well as the volume number (34.2) if one is given. (*Canadian Literature* uses only issue numbers.)

Article available in an online database:

Williams, David. "Cyber Writing and the Borders of
    Identity: 'What's in a Name' in Kroetsch's <u>The</u>
    <u>Puppeteer</u> and Mistry's <u>Such a Long Journey</u>." Canadian
    Literature 149 (1996): 55-71. <u>CPI.Q</u>. Simon Fraser U
    Lib., Burnaby, BC. 18 Feb. 2002. Keywords: Mistry and
    Journey.

Hornby, Richard. "The Other Stratford." <u>Hudson Review</u>
    49.3 (1996): 468-74. <u>Academic Search Elite</u>.
    EBSCOHost. Capilano Coll. Lib. North Vancouver, BC.
    5 Jan. 2002. Keywords: Shakespeare and Canada.

Article in an e-journal:

> Kelly, Philippa. "Surpassing Stars: Shakespeare's
>   Mirrors." Early Modern Literary Studies 8.1 (2002):
>   32 pars. <http://www.shu.ac.uk/emls/08-1/
>   kellglas.htm>.

34. An Article in a Newswire or Newspaper
Unsigned:

> "Blanchett to Grace Atwood Adaptation." Globe and Mail
>   18 July 2001, metro ed.: R4. CBCA. U of British
>   Columbia Lib. Vancouver. 8 Sept. 2002. Keywords:
>   Atwood and "Alias Grace"

Signed:

> Perrin, Susan. "Facts, Fiction and Fables for Fall."
>   Globe and Mail 14 Sept. 2002. 12 Oct. 2002
>   <http://www.globeandmail.com>.

> McKay, John. "Michael Ondaatje Novel Named the Winner of
>   CBC's Battle of the Books." Canadian Press Newswire
>   23 Apr. 2002. CBCA. U of Alberta Lib., Edmonton. 18
>   Aug. 2002. Keywords: Ondaatje and Win*.

Note: The asterisk (*) is a truncation symbol or "wild-card": It causes the search engine to look for "win," "winner," "winners," winning," etc. (See Chapter 16 for more information on using search engines.)

35. Article in a Magazine

> Jones, Gordon. "The Hirsch Conundrum: Are All the Best
>   Young Directors Working in Newfoundland?" Performing
>   Arts & Entertainment in Canada 4 June 2002. 11 Sept.
>   2002 <http://www. Magomania.com/search/
>   show_article.epl?id=936>.

36. A Review

> Wigston, Nancy. "Inside From the Outside." Rev. of "One
>   Good Story, That One," by Thomas King. Toronto Star 8
>   Jan. 1994, final ed.: J15. Canadian Newsdisc.
>   Capilano Coll. Lib., North Vancouver, BC. 18 May
>   2002. Keywords: Story and King.

37. An Abstract

Grace, Sherrill. "Representation of the Inuit: From
    Other to Self." Theatre Research in Canada 21.1
    (2000): 38-48. Abstract. 2 Aug. 2002
    <http://www.lib.unb.ca/Texts/bin/
    getBack.cgi?directory=Backissues/abstracts/
    &Filename=vol21.htm>.

38. A Personal or Professional Site

Persky, Stan. Homepage. 19 Aug. 2002.
    <http://stanpersky.de/>.

39. Electronic Mail

Gilbert, Reid. "Re: Publication of Siting the Other."
    E-mail to Marc Maufort. 12 Apr. 2002.

Modenesi, George. E-mail to the author. 6 Sept. 2002.

40. An Online Posting

Listservs (Electronic Mailing Lists):

Knowles, Ric. "Canadian Shakespeare Archives." Online
    Posting. 16 Sept. 2001. Candrama. 17 July 2002
    <http://listserv.unb.ca/archives/candrama.html>.

MLA suggests you cite an archival version of online postings so it is easier for
your readers to find the reference.

Usenet (A Worldwide Bulletin Board):

Power, James D. "Reading Home from France." Online
    posting. 3 Mar. 2000. 1 Apr. 2001
    <news:alt.edu.literature.culture>.

41. Synchronous Communication

Young, Felicity. Engl. 304. Online discussion of The
    Orchard Drive, by Chris Grignard. 15 July. 2002.
    LinguaMOO. 16 July 2002
    <telnet://lingua.utdallas.edu:8888>.

SAMPLE ESSAY WITH DOCUMENTATION

Some research papers are largely concerned with the relation of a work to its original context. Several examples have been mentioned already, such as Elizabethan views of Julius Caesar or Joy Kogawa's representation of Japanese-Canadians during World War II.

But of course there are other kinds of research papers. One kind is chiefly concerned with studying a critical problem, for instance with deciding among a variety of interpretations of a literary work. A paper of this sort necessarily involves a certain amount of summarizing, but it is much more than a summary of those interpretations, since it evaluates them and finally offers its own conclusions.

Two things motivated Maya Birkel, the author of the following paper, to choose her topic. The first was a classroom discussion of whether Thompson captured authentic types of female self-identity in her characters. The second was a published essay that suggested that women's roles and identities are not fixed, but are fluid and changing. Ms. Birkel wanted to explore how the play shows types of women, some with static self-images, some with provisional ones, some growing to self-awareness.

Birkel took notes on index cards, both from the play and from secondary sources, and she arranged and rearranged her notes as her topic and her thesis became clearer to her. Here we print the final version of her essay, prefaced with the rough outline that she prepared before she wrote her first draft.

```
Lion similar to Tornado--both show women's identities
Chung: "T [...] challenges [...] unitary self [...]."
Characters seem to be put down, in bad relationships,
     but more is happening
Women trying to understand their world and their place
     --Sullivan and Hatch xv


T not a feminist writer
She rejects what men determine for women
BUT also rejects what other women construct for anyone--
     de Jongh here


Mandy in T makes a fiction of her life to please Bill
     goes against her own morals
     Mandy and Rose--children


Lion: Various women
```

```
***ISOBEL's PICTURES--run thru whole essay!  Women
see/make pictures.
Sue
Rhonda
Christine
Scarlett
Joanne
Isobel--moves away from everyone's image of women and
     her.
```
Moves to new picture of herself made just by herself.

Here is the final version of the essay. Notice the difference in style between spaced dots in the dialogue of the play—pauses put there by the playwright to help the actor speak the line—and [ellipsis dots in brackets] put into quotations by the essayist to indicate that she has used only part of a quotation.

```
Maya Birkel
English 210-01
Professor R. Gilbert
6 April 1996
         Judith Thompson's Pictures of Women
    In two of Judith Thompson's plays, Lion in the
Streets and Tornado, a recurring theme emerges,
offering a declaration of the female identity and
role.  Kathy Chung clarifies that "Thompson's theatre
challenges the notion of a unitary fixed self, show-
ing individual identities under attack, changing
conditions, and being constructed" (par.5).  The
truth of this statement becomes clear throughout
these plays.  Although the women in Thompson's Lion
in the Streets and Tornado first appear to be
characters entangled in demeaning, conflicting
relationships, it becomes apparent that much more is
transpiring under the surface of their turbulent
lives.  Revealed through each of the character's
upheavals, changes, and obstacles, they are, subse-
quently, left unsure in their knowledge of what
constitutes a woman and are forced to reassess and
reconstruct their definition--or "picture"--of their
feminine role and purpose in society.
    The development and portrayal of the women is
where the similarities in the two plays arise.  "To
be a woman in the twentieth century is to be a crea-
ture caught in a time of change, and change is an
```

opportunity for women to define themselves" (Sullivan and Hatch xv). Likewise, Thompson's females are caught in this changing world and are desperately trying to understand it. The obstacles, realizations, and conclusions they face seem to point to their common ground as women in a changing environment. In each case Thompson's women have been confronted--in a variety of ways--with the reality that their self-image, their "picture" is somehow false. Ultimately they are left to question what being a woman means and who defines their role. It is this question which the play attempts to answer.

Thompson is not a feminist playwright, however. She not only condemns and rejects "the male conception of what constitutes the female role and duty," but she also disregards the conformities that other females construct for the fellow members of their sex (de Jongh 87). Thompson's characters are exposed to the audience as "desperate human creatures," but this is not their spiritual end point: "it is rather the point where they begin a long, pre-ethical phase in the vale of soul making" (Toles 120). In the end, the realization in both of these plays--hopefully reached also by the audience--is that the only way to really live is to paint one's own "picture."

Women today have very different senses of their roles. In Tornado we are confronted by characters who each hold a very distinct "picture" of what it is to be a woman.

Mandy, for example, is a character with a very clear image of her female role: to be happily married. Everything is done to please her husband. She apparently even changed careers from being a real estate agent to a social worker because it better fit her image. Mandy lies about not wanting children in order to draw a portrait that conforms to her assumption of her husband's wishes: "it's the way I was brought up; if a man doesn't mention something . . . I . . . I wanted to please you, Bill, I didn't want to pressure you" (86). Consequently, she is living in a fiction that has been fabricated by someone else's ideals. Ironically, however, her husband wants more from this "picture" of a wife and marriage

than he admits; he does want children. As a result,
Bill has an affair with another woman who can fulfil
this need, a shared need that Mandy needlessly denies
herself.

When Mandy discovers her error, her original
"picture" is shattered. In order to salvage the only
part of her self-image that she values--her role as
wife--she is forced to restage the theatre of her
life. Sadly, Mandy discovers that she is biologi-
cally unable to bear a child, to move from the
"picture" of motherhood to its reality. In trying to
keep her husband she goes against all. Because all
her notions of womanhood are based on someone else's
ideals, she inevitably fails, though she goes against
all the morals, values, and laws that she was brought
up to respect in a desperate attempt to maintain the
lie.

The conflict of the play arises in these contrasting ideas of what a woman's role is. What Mandy
learns from the end, however, is that it is essential
to construct her own definition; her symbolic death
and rebirth at the end of the play signifies her
final realization.

Another subplot occurs between Mandy and Rose.
Rose is an example of a woman whose "picture" is, in
fact, her own. She is a character who, after
surviving the harshness of childhood sexual abuse,
has discovered her purpose as a person. Her
experience has taught her to be a good mother to her
children: "this is one thing I can do . . . I can
love them and I know how from my mom" (88). Seeing
Rose as an inferior being, Mandy tries to convince
her to have a tubal ligation. To Rose, however, an
operation would be a denial of her life's meaning,
believing that it is her purpose to help "all of the
unborn babies hangin' out there in limbo, they need
my hands to hold them" (89). Friction mounts with
this clash in ideals. Mandy's attempt to save her
own "picture" destroys Rose's.

The women in <u>Lion in the Streets</u> go through the
same confusion and disillusionment as those in
<u>Tornado</u>. In <u>Lion</u> there is an added character--
Isobel--who is a personification of this confused,

lost state in which the women find themselves after
the destruction of their "pictures" and the conse-
quent disruption of their lives. Isobel, who
actually calls her life a "pickshur" (15), is lost in
a world where she no longer belongs. As she and the
audience view each scenario they together come upon a
very important realization and conclusion about life.

Sue's picture of what a woman should be is quite
simple: she is a mother to her children. Yet the
disruption occurs when she discovers that her
husband's idea of what a woman should be is quite
different from her own. He does not want a "cartoon
mom" (22) any longer, but a woman who is sexually
desirable. Consequently he is having an affair with
his ideal woman and Lily--young, attractive,
worldly--is playing out the part. Acted out on the
telephone, their sexual life is pure fantasy, pure
theatre. Sue desperately attempts to regain her
husband's love by showing him that she could just as
easily conform to a picture such as his. Sadly, her
attempts are not welcomed as she loses all dignity as
she strips for him at a dinner party (24). She
grasps at the hope that her husband will come
crawling back to her, sick, and needing to be
mothered--returning her to a role she understands.

The day-care worker Rhonda's "picture" of her
female role and purpose consists of being a mother
and a day caregiver. She treats the children in her
day care the best that she knows how. However, her
image of a good caregiver does not coincide with that
of the "yuppie" mother, Laura (31). Another conflict
arises. Laura, again seeing her image as superior,
attempts to change Rhonda, yet Rhonda refuses to give
in to someone else's ideals. Taking control of her
life, she refuses to conform (31). Incidentally, in
doing this Rhonda instantly becomes Isobel's hero.

"The labelling of women in unhealthy relationships
as masochistic--that is, seeking and enjoying suffer-
ing--has long been standard practice [...] in our
culture" (Forward 523). The character Sherry demonstrates how false this statement is. She does not
submit because she enjoys the treatment, but rather
because she needs the potential "picture" that it
pretends to offer; she believes she will eventually

play the role of wife if she takes her boyfriend's
abuse. To avoid conflict she does and says what he
wants, conforming to his picture of woman as
temptress and unfaithful "slut." She keeps peace so
they both can live within their "pictures."

Christine at first appears to be a stable woman
with a good self-image: mother, provider, career
woman. She sees these roles as purposeful. However,
everything changes when she meets Scarlett, a character with "advanced cerebral palsy" (45). Scarlett
makes Christine realize that there is something missing from her complacent "picture." Unable to take
care of herself, and without physical freedom,
Scarlett is still able to have something that
Christine doesn't: "The way you, you talked to me
like that. Like, like, like you belong. In the
world. As if you belong. Where did you get that
feeling? I want it. I need it" (49). So Christine
tries to physically take it from her; her greed
"makes her a slave of the lion" (50) and she murders.
Christine realizes that even this "ugly geck" (45)
has something she doesn't. Her "picture" is void of
genuine purpose, meaning, and belonging.

Joanne has cancer and is faced with the fact that
one day soon she will not be in the picture any more:
"life going on without me" (34). So she wants literally to place herself in another play and in another
picture. She wants to drown as she has seen Ophelia
do in a pre-Raphaelite painting; "I want to die like
that . . . I wouldn't mind if you took maybe some
pictures of me like that" (35). It is a romantic
concept of death, and an image painted by someone
else of someone else. Her friend Rhonda tells her
how unrealistic she is: "you can't become a picture,
do you know what I mean?" (36). The irony is that
she can be a part of a picture, just not the one she
wants.

Isobel, the reoccurring and unifying character in
Lion, also had an ideal self-identity once. She was
an innocent child and her sense of self was equally
innocent: "this pickshur is niiice, nice! I looove
this pickshur, this pickshur is mine! Is my house,
is my street, my park, is my people!" (15). Yet this
picture was taken away from her when she was

assaulted and murdered and was replaced by one that
she does not understand. Lost, rejected, and uncertain of what to do, she decides to try and find a way
home. At the conclusion, she realizes the impossibil-
ity of her quest; "I AM DEADLY DEAD! Down! It was
night, was a lion, roar!! with red eyes; he come
closer, come closer, ROAR tear my throat out ROAR tear
my eyes out . . . ROAR I am kill!" (36). At first,
she attempts to find her lion and kill him in order to
protect other people. However, whenever she speaks of
killing, her body seems to take on lion-like qualities
itself. She realizes, at the end, that in killing the
lion, she herself would become one. In destroying his
life, she would deny him the right to change or create
his picture; she would take his life away as he took
hers. In not killing him she takes hold of her life
and remakes her picture: "I came back. I take my
life. I want you all to take your life. I want you
all to have your life" (63).

It is with these words that <u>Lion in the Streets</u>
ends. However, they could, just as easily, be the
concluding lines of Tornado. In these two plays we
see the problems and conflicts that arise when people
let their lives be constructed out of someone else's
ideals. In both plays Thompson urges her viewers not
to conform to any stereotypes, but to define their
own lives and to be responsible for their own happiness. For Thompson "the theatre has always been and
will continue to be the stage upon which women will
create new women" (Sullivan and Hatch xv). Judith
Thompson shows her "pickshurs" to be false and
destructive, and calls upon women to reimagine their
lives.

List of Works Cited

Chung, Kathy. Rev. of <u>Lion in the Streets</u>, by Judith
     Thompson. <u>Canadian Literature</u> 141 (1994): 12 pars.
     <u>CBCA</u>. Capilano Coll. Lib., North Vancouver, BC. 2
     Apr. 1996. Keywords: Judith Thompson and review and
     Canad*.

de Jongh, Nicholas. <u>Not in Front of the Audience</u>:
     <u>Homosexuality on Stage</u>. London and New York:
     Routledge, 1992.

Forward, Susan. "Men Who Hate Women and Why." <u>Fights,</u>
     <u>Feuds, and Heartfelt Hatreds: An Anthology of</u>
     <u>Antipathy</u>. Ed. Philip Kerr. New York: Viking, 1992.
     521-8.

Sullivan, Victoria, and James Hatch. Introduction.
     <u>Plays By and About Women</u>. New York: Random, 1973.

Toles, George. "'Cause you're the only one I want': The
     Anatomy of Love in the Plays of Judith Thompson."
     <u>Canadian Literature</u> 118 (1988): 116-28.

Thompson, Judith. <u>Lion in the Streets</u>. Toronto: Coach
     House, 1992.

---. <u>Tornado</u>. Toronto: Coach House, 1989.

✓ A Checklist: Reading the Draft of Your Research Paper

Begin by looking at the "big picture"—the essay as a whole. Do not begin by trying to find grammar errors or other small details. Ask yourself, or have a peer editor read your paper and ask you:

- ✓ Is the title informative, focused, and likely to attract attention?
- ✓ Does the paper develop your point, or does it just accumulate other people's ideas?
- ✓ Does the paper advance in orderly stages from the thesis? Can your imagined reader easily follow your thinking?
- ✓ Are generalizations supported by evidence?
- ✓ Are quotations introduced adequately?
- ✓ Are all of the long quotations necessary, or can some of them be effectively summarized?
- ✓ Are quotations discussed adequately rather than simply copied down?
- ✓ Are all sources given?
- ✓ Is the documentation in the correct form?
- ✓ Finally, are the grammar, syntax and spelling correct?

Read the paper aloud to hear how it sounds to another "ear." This technique can help you to find errors and pick up awkward or unclear diction.

16

New Approaches to the Research Paper: Literature, History, and the World Wide Web

Learning Objectives

When you've read this chapter, you should be able to

➤ see the links among literary analysis and other disciplines, particularly social and cultural history;

➤ conduct a preliminary search for information suitable to a short paper;

➤ conduct a thorough search for sources to use in expanding your argument to produce a longer paper;

➤ use library catalogues, print indices, abstracts, and library data bases; and

➤ use the Internet critically, evaluating sites carefully.

The previous chapter describes the traditional model and methods for writing a literary research paper. But literary research has recently become more wide-ranging and complicated, and a book like this one must devote a second chapter to it, in order to take into account important changes in the field of literary study and developments in technology. Students are now often asked to work with historical as well as literary materials, and to demonstrate skills in interdisciplinary learning. The New Historicism, as this methodology is called, blends various disciplines with historical documents and can richly illuminate literary texts. Like other fields, literary study is supplementing printed texts with electronic search tools, databases, and resources; literary analysis and research increasingly take place on the World Wide Web as well as in the library, and, in some cases, through e-mail and e-mail lists devoted to specific subject areas. Historical research can be very rewarding; it opens up new lines of inquiry as it teaches us about the contexts for literary works and enables us to respond to them in more complex ways. But we need the right strategies to perform this research effectively. Students in literature must now possess the insight and understanding to explore, and to make good choices when consulting, ever-multiplying amounts of information.

CASE STUDY ON LITERATURE AND HISTORY: THE INTERNMENT OF JAPANESE-CANADIANS

The best way to illustrate the new approach to literature and history, and to outline the process for identifying new kinds of resources, is through a case study. For this purpose, we have chosen the literature and history of the internment of Japanese-Canadians during World War II. This is a subject for research that a student might select, or be assigned, in a variety of courses. It would be a good topic to explore in an introductory literature course in which (for example) a group of contemporary poems on the subject, or Joy Kogawa's novel, *Obasan*, are studied. It might suit a course in Canadian or Asian-Canadian literature; a course in multicultural literature or in Canadian literature since World War II; or a senior seminar in twentieth-century literature and history. It would be a good topic in courses in ethnic and minority literatures, or in poetry and politics.

Many books, articles, and conferences have been devoted to the Japanese-Canadian internment—we can hardly do it justice here. This discussion will show the nature of the inquiry into the subject that you can undertake, beginning with literary texts and moving outward from them into history, and into print and electronic sources.

A reality for any student doing research on a Canadian topic is the fact that, often, fewer sources are available than for topics on American (or European) subjects. In this case study, students will quickly discover (especially on the web) that Japanese-Americans suffered a similar internment on the West Coast of the United States and that a large body of scholarship exists for the events in the U.S. In fact, it turns out that the University of Washington is a very large repository of archival information on the internment (including Canadian documents). However, research will disclose that a very significant body of documents and studies also exists on the Canadian experience. In fact, the amount of Canadian material on this subject is vast.

Be warned: It is dangerous (and politically naïve) to assume that everything in the American documents can be applied to the Canadian history. It is only rarely true that a subject is genuinely "borderless" in event, response, or consequence. Sometimes, however, similar episodes can be profitably compared in the two North American nations. In this case, some of the general historical background and some of the specific racial attitudes and their consequences can be extrapolated from the U.S. documents to the experiences of Japanese-Canadians—but not all. It is very important that Canadian students develop the critical skill to take background information from readily available American sources but evaluate such information against Canadian history, cultural attitudes, and law. (Consider, for example, the different responses of citizens in the two nations to the bombing of Pearl Harbor, which precipitated the evacuation, or to the different rights available to these nations' citizens in 1941.) It might generate an interesting essay to compare American and Canadian responses to the "hyphenated" Japanese citizens, but it would be a poor decision simply to call up easily found American

Web sites and other sources and to apply them uncritically to the history of Japanese-Canadians or the literature written by Japanese-Canadians. In fact, one of the most interesting revelations this research provides is the fact that, in many ways, the Canadian treatment of citizens of Japanese origin was harsher, and the subsequent treatment of these citizens after the war more reprehensible, than that experienced by Japanese-Americans.

LITERARY TEXTS

Reprinted below are three poems, as well as excerpts from a long poem and a novel. The first is Terry Watada's "VII. 1941 Minto," from *A Thousand Homes* (Stratford, ON: Mercury, 1995). The next two poems are haiku by anonymous members of the Slocan Haiku Club and are reprinted in Keibo Oiwa's edition, *Stone Voices* (Montreal: Véhicule, 1991). The third is an excerpt from Roy Kiyooka's poetic sequence *Wheels*, reprinted in Roy K. Miki, ed., *Pacific Windows: Collected Poems of Roy K. Kiyooka* (Vancouver: Talonbooks, 1997). The final text is a section from Joy Kogawa's famous novel, *Obasan* (Toronto: Penguin, 1983).

Terry Watada was born in 1951. He earned an MA in English, and then began work on a series of musical recordings, including *Hockey Night in Chinatown*, by Number One Son, a collective of Asian Canadian songwriters and performers. He writes a monthly column in *Nikkei Voice*, a national Japanese-Canadian newspaper. He is the author of four plays, a history of Jodo Shinshu Buddhism in Canada, poems, and stories. His collection of related stories, *Daruma Days*, traces the lives of *nisei* (second generation people of Japanese descent) in their relationships with *issei* (first generation immigrants). The stories explore the tensions felt by the *nisei*, who are trapped between cultures and values, and are grounded in their experiences in the camps. The City of Toronto awarded Watada the William P. Hubbard Award, in recognition of his work in race relations.

The poets of the Slocan Haiku Club were all internees who met to compose highly formal poems on given subjects, which were then judged by a master, who was also a prisoner. Writing the poems was an important means for many to retain contact with their ancient literary traditions, as well as a recreational activity that enlivened the boring life of the Slocan camp. In *Within the Barbed Wire Fence: A Japanese Man's Account of His Internment in Canada* (Toronto: U of Toronto P, 1980), Takeo Ujo Nakano reports that the club survived the closing of the camp and the removal of the internees to a smaller camp, and continued to the end of the war. Some two hundred pages of these short poems, those Nakano calls "the best haiku" (71), were collected in an anthology called *Tessaku no Seki* (*Loneliness within the Barbed Wire Fence*). The number of poems alone indicates the importance of this writing to those in the camp.

Roy Kiyooka was born in Moose Jaw, Saskatchewan, in 1926 and grew up in Calgary. Even though his family lived outside the "Protected Zone," they were considered to be enemy aliens, were fingerprinted, and were deprived of their civil rights. Roy Miki considers that Kiyooka was "profoundly disturbed by this radical estrangement from place" (304). Kiyooka had a varied career as painter, photographer, musician, filmmaker, and poet. He moved to Vancouver, where he taught at the University of British Columbia until he retired. He was nominated for the Governor General's Literary Award for his book *Pear Tree Pomes* and named an Officer of the Order of Canada in 1978. He died in 1994.

Joy Kogawa was born in Vancouver in 1935, the daughter of *issei*. She was raised in Vancouver, but she and her family were incarcerated and then relocated to the internment camp at Slocan and later to Coaldale, Alberta. She is very well known for her novel *Obasan*, which tells the story of a young woman, Naomi, caught in the racism of the war and sent to the camps. Kogawa is a Member of the Order of Canada. She taught school in Coaldale, Alberta, for one year and then studied music at the University of Toronto, moving on to study at the Anglican Women's Training College and the University of Saskatchewan. Kogawa was involved in the movement for redress from the Canadian government for its treatment of Japanese-Canadian citizens during World War II, a long emotional and political struggle she recounts in her novel *Itsuka* (1992). She is the author of several collections of poetry, essays, and children's literature including an account of life in the camps written for a juvenile audience, called *Naomi's Road* (1986). In the novel *The Rain Ascends* (1995), Kogawa considers another emotional issue of power and subjugation: the sexual abuse of children by a clergyman.

These authors were, directly or indirectly, victims of a series of Orders-in-Council, beginning with PC 9591 on December 7, 1942, which required Japanese nationals to register with the Registrar of Enemy Aliens by February 7, 1943. This historical fact renders Roy Kiyooka's boyhood memory of being fingerprinted by the RCMP intensely chilling: neither his nor the other texts under study are purely fictional. Even this preliminary research gives new colour to your reading of the literary texts.

Increasingly stringent orders culminated in PC 1486 (on February 27, 1943) which amended the *Defence of Canada Regulations* of 1941, giving the government the power to "authorize the detention" of "all persons" resident within a newly proclaimed "protected area" and to "require any or all persons to leave such protected area." Appendix VII, signed by Louis St. Laurent as Minister of Justice on March 7, 1942, imposed a curfew on "every person of the Japanese race," and ordered all Japanese-Canadians to leave the protected area, effectively "implementing the evacuation," as its subtitle states. Appendix VIII gave the British Columbia Security Commission the "duty" to "plan, supervise, and direct the evacuation [. . .] of all persons of the Japanese race." These orders, in the aftermath of the Japanese attack on Pearl Harbor in December 1941, began the detentions (initially in Hastings Park in Vancouver) and subsequent relocation of Japanese-Canadians to concentration camps in the British Columbia interior.

VII.1942. MINTO

Terry Watada

The land cut

the spirit like barbed wire.

It was my prison.

No bars

      just the haunted green and rock.

My son was alone.

> *My husband lies broken in pieces*
>
>   *in a Kamloops hospital*
>
> *and I lie in pain*
>
>   *in Vancouver.*
>
> *Even the sisters of mercy,*
>
> *who care for me, hate me.*

Lost, torn from those I love.

Let us dance in the moonlight

of wondrous imagination:

> *To my lonely wife—*
>
> *Do you see the autumn moon?*
>
> *I am sick like you*
>
> *and taken away from you,*
>
> *but I see the same clear sky.*

The glow of a night field

reflected in the eyes of an abandoned boy.   (58)

THEMES: EARLY SPRING; SPRING THAW

Anonymous: Slocan Haiku Club

Early spring

In time with the sunshine

Children are dancing

*

Thinking far

While gazing on

Early spring snow   (152)

from Wheels

Roy Kiyooka

i remember "JAPS SURRENDER!"

i remember all the flagrant incarceration/s

i remember playing dead Indian

i remember the RCMP finger-printing me:

I was 15 and lofting hay that cold winter day

what did i know about treason?

i learned to speak a good textbook English

i seldom spoke anything else.

i never saw the 'yellow peril' in myself

(Mackenzie King did)   (170)

from Obasan

Joy Kogawa

"You have to remember," Aunt Emily said. "You are your history. If you
cut any of it off you're an amputee. Don't deny the past. Remember

> everything. If you're bitter, be bitter. Cry it out! Scream! Denial is
> gangrene. Look at you, Naomi, shuffling back and forth between Cecil
> and Granton, unable either to go or to stay in the world with even a
> semblance of grace or ease."
>
> All right, Aunt Emily, all right! [. . .]
>
> If I search the caverns of my mind, I come to a collage of
> images [. . .]　(54).

Your goal is eventually to move to historical research, but first you must know the texts well. Consider the relationship of the structure—the length of the lines, the organization of the stanzas, the diction and imagery—to the dramatic situation and themes. Look carefully at the images, which are extremely important in haiku and poems growing from this tradition. Consider how the prose text differs from and is similar to the poetic texts. For help, reread the discussions of speaker, figurative language, and other key terms presented in Chapter 12 of this book, and refer to the checklist at the end of Chapter 12.

These texts suggest two related themes: the cultural and psychological prompting to endure hardship, to endure that which cannot be changed, and—conversely—the often painful need to remember and react (to Japanese heritage, homes in Canada, community, the joy of childhood, the atrocities of the evacuation, racist hatred). As well, each text speaks of community, both the racial community from which these people come and their new communities as Canadian citizens and as internees. We will hold these two potential theses in our minds as we begin our research.

Watada presents images of a spirit "cut" by the cold land that imprisons like "barbed wire," images of loneliness, racism, and loss of family. He also shows his protagonist urging her fellows to "dance" in "wondrous imagination," to hear her husband's poetic assurance that, although apart, the family sees "the same clear sky."

The excerpt from Kiyooka's work is from a longer sequence in which he is touring with his father and taking photographs. Suddenly, the lens turns back in time and he remembers the trauma of being fingerprinted, which reveals his boyhood self-identity as Canadian but immediately interrogates notions of community. The adult can no longer identify himself as confidently, or pretend that nothing happened during the war.

The haiku poems present a contrast between these two promptings. In one, traditional images of "spring" and "sunshine" present the stoic fact that children in the camps did dance, that life did go on. In the other poem, the local image of "early spring snow" draws the imagination to think "far"— back to happier days, perhaps, or away to a distant homeland, or back to life on the B.C. coast, or toward an uncertain future, or to family members.

You can begin to link the poems: Watada's protagonist is also "thinking far" to her "broken" husband in a Kamloops hospital and her own imminent death in a Vancouver hospital. She is also aware that her "son [is] alone." He is not dancing in the spring sunshine of the haiku. Is her call, "Let us dance," directed at the boy as well as herself, then? Must he simply endure? (In the next poem, he attends her cremation and responds with "curses" hidden "under the sheets" and a "quiet sobbing.") Her conflicted emotion is beautifully imagined in the final lines: the "glow" is "reflected in the eyes of an abandoned boy." Kiyooka's boy is not orphaned, but the fingerprinting already marks him out for the same tension between memory and action.

Kogawa relates this conflict directly. Aunt Emily, here and in *Itsuka*, insists upon recollection and open emotions, calling for a less traditional response to anger and injustice. No "quiet sobbing" for her. The contemporary Japanese-Canadian protagonist finally responds by allowing the "collage of images" to flood out. It is significant that she remembers her pain in images of her old home in Vancouver, taken away from the family and the community the government broke up. You should also notice that she speaks in images, recalling the literary tradition of the haiku and other Asian poetry, poetry that links geographical to psychological landscape. Noticing this stylistic device takes you back, of course, to first images of the first poem, the land cutting the spirit.

These are powerful texts even for a reader who knows only a little about the historical facts. But the poems become still more effective for a reader who knows in depth and detail about this episode in Canadian history, and who can bring this knowledge to a reading of the texts and present it in an analytical research paper.

THE SEARCH BEGINS

One form of *historical* research is to follow a traditional route for *literary* research. The literary resources and methods described in the previous chapter can lead to secondary sources on the authors and their writings, and to information about their careers, the work they have done, and its major themes.

Bibliographical Listing

By checking in the *MLA Bibliography* (see the previous chapter), you can locate bibliographical items such as the following, given simply as examples. (Note: These examples are in Works Cited format, as they would appear at the end of your essay.)

On Kogawa (from more than 68 entries):

Potter, Robin. "Moral—in Whose Sense?: Joy Kogawa's *Obasan* and Julia Kristeva's *Powers of Horror.*" *Studies in Canadian Literature* 15 (1990): 117–39.

Willis, Gary. "Speaking the Silence: Joy Kogawa's *Obasan.*" *Studies in Canadian Literature* 12 (1987): 239–49.

Jones, Manina. "The Avenues of Speech and Silence: Telling Difference in Joy Kogawa's *Obasan*." *Theory between the Disciplines*. Ed. Kreiswirth-Martin. Ann Arbor: U of Michigan P, 1990. 213–29.

On Kiyooka:

Ondaatje, Michael, et al. "Roy Kiyooka (1926–1994)." *Brick* 48 (1994): 13–34.

Other major indices are also helpful, and these are now available online. For example, EBSCOHost services such as *Academic Search Elite* or *Canadian MAS Full Text Elite* provide useful entries. *Canadian Business and Current Affairs Index*, which includes a broad category of sources including newspaper articles, lists 475 sources under the general subject heading, "Japanese-Canadians." A refinement of that subject to "Japanese-Canadians and internment" reduces the list to more directly useful sources. You need to learn some techniques to search and to refine your search: "play around" on the search engine at first and learn your way through the methodology. As well, remember that other disciplines will assist your search. For example, the *Social Sciences Index* provides general information on, say, racism in Canada. These indices can give you both specific sources (as above), or general information. Here are some examples:

Omatsu, Maryka. "Bittersweet Passage: Fifty Years after the Internment [. . .] an Insider Bares the Soul of the Japanese-Canadian Experience." *Canadian Forum* Sept. 1992: 15–16.

Ayukawa, Midge. "From Japs to Japanese-Canadians to Canadians." *Journal of the West* 38 (1999): 41–48.

Ramcharan, Subhas. "Racism, Nonwhites in Canada." *Canadian Review of Sociology and Anthropology*. 22 (1985): 589–91.

Through electronic access and interlibrary loan, you can get hold of almost any source, even if a library on campus does not carry it. But sometimes interlibrary loan can take a few days, a week, or more. Remember the importance of starting early on research projects. Request copies of everything while there is still time to examine it before your deadline.

Full-text Listings

A major benefit of these electronic database indices is that many entries are available in full text, meaning that you can download the entire article. This is true of articles from various categories of sources, but is particularly useful when your source is an article from a juried scholarly journal. In such a case, you get immediate access to the best scholarly material. This is a great boon to any researcher, but especially so if your library owns only a limited collection of periodicals.

There are often three levels of citation: the bibliographic listing, an expanded citation with abstract, and full text. Some entries boast all three. If the article you want is available in full text, you can get it instantly, without having to search through the library stacks or travel to another institution.

The biggest drawback of this feature, however, arises when you come to document the source. Full-text downloads rarely have page numbers and it becomes difficult to pinpoint the source, especially for paraphrases and summaries. The best solution is to use the paragraph number references discussed in the last chapter, and we urge you to count paragraphs and use this documentation style. If the article is available in print form in your library, choose that medium since the printed version does show page numbers. See the previous chapter for documentation models.

HISTORICAL SOURCES

The sources in the indices, while promising, may take for granted more than you know at this stage; the discussion and analysis presented in them assumes that readers *already* have the background that you are seeking to acquire. How can you begin to acquire a base of historical knowledge? *Start small.* Don't overwhelm yourself with more information than you can handle. Keep in mind as well that your aim is not to become a historian but, instead, to enrich your literary explorations with knowledge drawn from another field and set of sources.

Basic Reference Books (Short Paper)

It is best to begin with basic reference books, and you can get to them by consulting the following:

Balay, Robert. *Guide to Reference Books*. 11th ed. Chicago: American Library Association, 1996.

Blazek, Ron, and Elizabeth Aversa. *The Humanities: A Selective Guide to Information Sources*. 5th ed. Englewood, CO.: Libraries Unlimited, 2000.

This is an annotated guide to research sources in literature, art, and other fields in the humanities.

Or consult *ARBA Guide to Subject Encyclopedias and Dictionaries*, 2nd ed., 1997 and *First Stop: The Master Index to Subject Encyclopedias*, 1989.

Or, in the online library catalogue, check under the subject heading "history—dictionaries." (You can do the same thing for literature, for titles of reference works in that field.)

You can also refer to Jules R. Benjamin, *A Student's Guide to History*, 6th ed. (1994), and James R. Bracken, *Reference Works in British and American Literature*, 2 vols. (1990). See also M. J. Marcuse, *Reference Guide for English Studies* (1990), and James L. Harner, *Literary Research Guide*, 3rd. ed. (1998).

Browse in the reference section or, better still, talk to a reference librarian—he or she can be a valuable resource and often can direct you quickly to helpful books.

Such a search will point you to, among other sources, *The Oxford Companion to the Second World War* (Gen. Ed. I. C. B. Dear. Consultant Ed.,

M. R. D. Foot. Oxford and New York: Oxford UP, 1995). This guide is recent, prepared by eminent scholars, and published by a reputable press. It is a trustworthy source, and its entry on "Japanese-Canadians" (p. 634) is signed by the well-known historian, J. L. Granatstein. It is cross-referenced to a general entry on "Internment," and also leads to a longer article on the plight of Japanese-Americans that provides further relevant information. As well, the entry identifies two books for further reading:

Adachi, K. *The Enemy That Never Was: A History of the Japanese-Canadians*.
    Toronto: McClelland, 1976.

Roy, P. *Mutual Hostages: Canadians and Japanese during the Second World War*.
    Toronto: U of T Press, 1990.

Here is the entry from the *Oxford Companion* in full:

Japanese Canadians

The first Japanese came to Canada in 1877 and, although neither the Japanese nor the Canadian government encouraged the flow, by 1941 there were 23,000 people of Japanese origin in Canada, almost all living in British Columbia. Hard-working and slow to integrate, they stirred fears of the 'Yellow Peril' which increased exponentially as Japan turned expansionist in the 1930s. A Special Committee on Orientals, appointed in 1940, ordered registration of Japanese-Canadians and barred them from military service. There were, however, no plans for their evacuation from the coast or internment in event of war with Japan, though Canadian and American officials discussed the need for coordinated action at the Permanent Joint Board on Defense. After Pearl Harbor and the fall of Hong Kong, British Columbian fears increased, political and military leaders called for action, and on 14 January, 1942, Ottawa decided to move Japanese male nationals of military age inland. As Allied defeats continued, the pressure mounted; on 24 February, following the signing of an executive order by Roosevelt, which empowered the military to remove Japanese-Americans from the US West Coast, the government ordered evacuation of all Japanese-Canadians, men and women, citizens and aliens. Over the next months, their property confiscated, Japanese-Canadians were moved to inland communities, often very rough. Men worked on road gangs, though before long labour shortages led Ottawa to encourage them to move eastwards to Central Canadian manufacturing plants. Evacuation registrees along with Japanese patriots [sic] were interned. On 4 August 1944, Ottawa decided to repatriate 'disloyal' Japanese-Canadians to Japan and later to include those voluntarily seeking to return; after protests, 3,964 went. The remainder established new lives east of the Rockies. See also INTERNMENT.

Having researched a number of sources, at this point you should remind yourself of the boundaries of the assignment.

- What is the *length* of the essay? What is its *due date?*

- *How many* sources did the instructor state that you should use? Did he or she refer to specific kinds of sources that the paper should include—scholarly books and/or articles, other primary sources (literary texts, letters, autobiographies, journals), photographs, and so on?

- What should be the *proportions* of the essay? How much of it should consist of literary analysis, and how much of historical research and context?

For a short paper of three pages that treats one or both of the poems and provides some historical context, the above entry from *The Oxford Companion to the Second World War* may be all that you need. It reports what happened, where it happened, and why; emphasizes the outrage done to civil liberties; and highlights two cultural realities that bear on our texts: "[. . .] slow to integrate, they stirred fears of the 'Yellow Peril' [. . .]"(634). You can relate Granatstein's historical observation to the tradition of an inward-looking community that Kogawa and the haiku poets evoke. And you can easily see the racism that causes even the hospital workers to discriminate against Watada's narrator. Here, you have a historical detail that you can develop in your examination of the texts and, if the assignment is a longer one calling for more extensive research, that you can make the organizing principle for gathering and then sifting through sources.

It is important, then, to gain basic knowledge of the subject, so that you have a clear, accurate answer to your core question—in this case, "What was the internment?" But, at the same time, seek to locate in the overview of the subject an idea or issue that is connected to the themes of the specific literary works. *Connect* the literature and the history.

Getting Deeper (Medium or Long Paper)

The entry in the *Oxford Companion* is limited. It is brief and provides no bibliography beyond the two books for further reading. For a medium-length paper, you will need to search elsewhere for more information, and for additional bibliography.

In response to the question, "Where can I find out about the internment of Japanese-Canadians during World War II?" a reference librarian might recommend the *Canadian Encyclopedia*, which includes an entry on this subject titled "Japanese Canadians." (This encyclopedia is also available in a CD-ROM version, as we'll discuss later.) Subject-specific or -limited encyclopedias usually provide more information than general encyclopedias, so the librarian might also suggest the *Encyclopedia of British Columbia*, which contains an entry for "Japanese, Relocation of."

The Canadian Encyclopedia. Editor-in-chief James H. Marsh. Year 2000 ed. Toronto: McClelland, 1999.

Encyclopedia of British Columbia. Ed. David Francis. Madeira Park, BC: Harbour, 2000.

As well, the librarian might point to the electronic library subject catalogue. Searching by logical keywords, such as "Japanese-Canadian" and "Japanese-Canadian and internment" produces a lengthy list of sources. You need to use associative (Boolean) logic to search in library catalogues and you need to try various avenues; we discuss refined searches in more detail later in this chapter. A general search (often by "keyword") can give you a sense of the scope of your subject and quickly direct you to subheadings. One electronic search produced 27 useful subheadings; if you choose only "Japanese-Canadians evacuation and relocation 1942–1945," you will find eight useful sources.

It is tempting to go immediately to a catalogue search, but some preliminary research is usually a better starting point. If you go directly to the subject catalogue, you might not find an important book (if, say, your library does not own it), or you might not realize its importance. When a scholar like Granatstein recommends a study like Adachi's, you know it has value. It is a good idea, then, to start with reference books and then move to the catalogue.

When you do find a source in a catalogue, you will see on the entry a group of related subject categories. You can then use these further categories for your more complete subject search. The librarian can also assist you in identifying the phrases for the subject you are researching; the Library of Congress Subject Headings (LCSH) is another resource.

Now you can start to compile a bibliography of your own. But—here is a key point—note the dates of publication. You should be seeking sources as recent as possible to make certain that your knowledge is up-to-date. (We'll qualify this general advice later.) With a little research, you'll discover, for example, that the spring 2001 issue of the journal *West Coast Line* contains a literary-historical essay by Kirsten Emiko McAllister entitled "Held Captive: the Postcard and the Internment Camp." (The searches for this chapter were undertaken in the spring of 2002, so this article was completely up-to-the-minute research at the time of writing.)

McAllister's article provides a Works Cited list that includes sixteen sources, ten of which are more recent than Adachi's book. As well, this source lists Adachi's book as a 1991 publication, which tells us that there is a later edition than the 1976 edition cited in the *Oxford Companion*. You want to find the later edition, and when you do, you'll see in the Introduction, by Timothy Findley, the confirmation that "this book is more disturbing—and therefore more enlightening—than it was when it was first published in 1976" (x).

Adachi gives nine background chapters on the period 1867–1941, four chapters on the internment and its aftermath, two chapters of analysis, an Afterword by Roger Daniels (called "The Struggle for Redress"), photographs, notes, an appendix of historical documents, and an extensive bibliography. This is a first-rate book for your purposes; it is recently updated, and written by an accomplished scholar who is in full command of primary and secondary sources and whose bibliography will direct you authoritatively to other materials.

Your search will also disclose that Terry Watada has edited a collection called *Collected Voices: An Anthology of Asian North American Periodical Writing* (Toronto: HpF, 1997). In this collection, you will find an article by

Ayukawa Michiko Midge, "History of Nikku Pioneer Women," from the August 1990 *Nikkei Voice*, a Japanese-Canadian newspaper. In this essay, Michiko Midge tells us that by accepting "life's vicissitudes with *shikataganai* ('it can't be helped') [it] may appear as if they [the female evacuees] were just giving up. But it is a philosophy which, in that instance, helped them to carry on and make the best of a difficult situation. The women were stoic [. . .]" (n.pag).

Reading this opinion, you will recall our texts. Now you can appreciate the two-directional thrust of the haiku and Aunt Emily's call to rail against such stoic restraint. All through *Obasan*, Naomi struggles with this sense of private silence and her aunt's call—which we read in our excerpt—to break the code. In an epigram to her novel, Kogawa writes "There is a silence that cannot speak. There is a silence that will not speak. [. . .] I hate the staring into the night. [. . .] The sky swallowing the echoes." Read alongside Michiko Midge's comment, Kogawa's opening comment illuminates our understanding of the husband in Watada's poem who is "sick like you / and taken away from you,/ but I see the same clear sky." Your research is giving you context and authority with which to interpret the literary texts.

In Kirsten Emiko McAllister's article, we learn that postcards showing the camps were produced, and these are now emerging from archives and the personal family records of the descendants. McAllister describes one postcard that "captivates me": "it is as if one emerges from the edge of a forest, parting the softly-focused cedar fronds to reveal a nostalgic scene of *mura*—Japanese village. [. . .] the camps were set within a landscape that calls up the imagery of *furusato* ['old village']. Under the wash of its nostalgia, the boredom and uncertainty of confinement come to be recalled as the simplicity of life, and the rows of leaking cramped shacks as rustic" (28–29).

Now you can really begin to see the analytical value of historical sources. Details like these give a personal resonance to the conflicted landscape of Watada's poem, a prison that is also somehow a beautiful natural setting, almost Romantic: "just the haunted green and rock." The nostalgia of McAllister's postcard documents echoes the haiku: "Thinking far/ While gazing on/ Early spring snow." The fact that life in the camps was boring helps to explain the development of the haiku clubs, but also the wistful tone of the poems.

Our historical research teaches us about the *contexts* for these texts and alerts us to the power and precision of details that the writers include. Sometimes, too, it helps us to sense the pressure of feelings and thoughts that a writer or speaker is excluding, is holding back, or is reacting against. The more we learn about the camps, the more we can perceive what Aunt Emily is angry about, and what the mother in "VII. 1942 Minto" might be struggling to keep from speaking about.

Review

- Consult a range of reference books as you are getting launched on a literary-historical paper—it will take less time than you think, and it will be time invested wisely.

- Pay attention to when the books were published and how up-to-date they are in their suggestions for additional reading.

- Even as you acquire familiarity with the subject in general, take special note of where the historical record *makes connections* to the literature that you are studying. The real reward comes when you can perceive the relationship between history and the structure and the themes of the literary works.

Questions for Consideration.

In *The Enemy that Never Was* (1991), Ken Adachi states:

> Unlike the arid desert exile of the Japanese-American evacuees, encircled by barbed wire and military police in watch towers, the detention camps in the interior of British Columbia were another setting altogether. The were set against a splendid physical background, green pines and cottonwoods thrusting skyward, enfolding mountains looming through mists [. . .] ideal for a summer holiday [. . .]. But while a summer holiday, even a protracted one, was one thing, actually living there was another. All the interior camps were psychologically deceptive places in which to live. The magnificence of the outdoor setting and the echoes of a romantic past were but candy wrapping, hiding a grim reality. (251)

Write one or two paragraphs in which you connect Adachi's description to details in our literary texts. In your commentary, show how the historical context enhances the reader's response to and understanding of the texts.

Other Reference Sources

There are other routes to follow, especially for historical materials.

Humanities Abstracts, an index of articles in the humanities, with their contents summarized, is a good resource.

The ABSTRACT, or summary of the author's main points, is a valuable feature of this reference work. Abstracts appear in many indices (including online checklists such as *Academic Search Elite*) and vary in length and thoroughness.

Here is a sample abstract:

> Kirsten Emiko McAllister. "Narrating Japanese-Canadians In and Out of the Canadian Nation: A Critique of Realist Forms of Representation." *Canadian Journal of Communications* 24 (1999): 79–103.
>
> > During World War II the Canadian government implemented a systematic plan to rid British Columbia of over 22,000 Japanese-Canadians. Forty years later, Japanese-Canadians mobilized in a movement to demand redress. To make their case, they use realism with its objective research methods to prove that the government's actions violated their rights. But while realism helped them win their case, this paper claims that there were ramifications. While realism

made it possible to narrate Japanese-Canadians into the history of the Canadian nation as fully assimilated citizens, this implicitly accepted the nation's hostile construction of racial others. Through an analysis of the Japanese-Canadian film *Minoru: Memory of Exile*, this paper shows how difficult it is to shed realism once it is institutionalized, underlining the importance of developing a critical awareness of how it operates.

When you read an abstract, keep in mind that you are seeking sources that bear on the issues in the literary works that you have chosen to examine. The abstract may tell you about a source that, while interesting, is not pertinent to your research needs for this particular paper. For many topics, there is a great deal of material that you could draw upon if your time were limitless, but because you must use your limited time well, you should be focused and selective. Fasten on the best sources for the nature of the research task at hand. Look for keywords in titles of books and articles listed in bibliographies that offer clues about the author's point of view, approach, and treatment of the subject.

Individual journals usually have *index issues*. The journal *BC Studies*, for example, offers a Cumulative Index to numbers 1 to 120 that lists 19 articles on our subject. If you select a hopeful title, such as Werner Cohn's essay, "Persecution of Japanese-Canadians and the Political Left in British Columbia: December 1941–March 1942." *BC Studies* 68 (1985–86): 3–22, and locate the issue, you discover a full citation that gives you an idea of the length of the article and the quality of the journal, and then an abstract that helps you decide if the body of the text will contain information you need. Each of these steps—title, full entry, abstract—is designed to save you time by giving you enough information to keep going, or to stop.

Information databases, both in print form and online, are further sources. The National Library of Canada, for example, provides extensive "Canadian Information by Subject," which includes various sub-subjects of use to our search.

Some of these databases are commercial, such as *H-Canada: Canadian History and Studies*, and many of them are now available online. We'll discuss electronic sources in the next section.

Too Much Information?

At this point, you may be wondering, "How do I know when to stop?" A good question, but not one with a simple answer. We have known students who have become gripped by a subject and have read everything they can about it. But however excited about a subject you become, in the midst of a busy semester you will need to make choices and budget your time. Look back at the section on research where we urged you to create a "working thesis," which helps you to limit your search and your reading (page 288).

Stop when you have acquired the historical knowledge that strengthens your analysis of the literary texts—the knowledge that deepens your understanding of the issues that the authors have treated, and the knowledge that is sufficient for you to meet the terms (that is, the boundaries) of the assignment.

Question for Consideration

As you perform your research, you will often be confronted with lists of sources. It is important to become aware of how to evaluate these sources to determine which of the items on a list might be most relevant. Review the following items: the type of each source and its area of emphasis, the publication date (including the original date of any republished source), the status of the publisher, and the nature of the connection to the themes in the texts you plan to examine. Often, in Canadian research, you must also ask yourself whether you can read well enough in French or another language other than English to use a source written in that language. Not all of the following texts will prove to be useful to our particular project, though some will. Consider which you might plan to use:

Berger, Thomas R. *Fragile Freedoms: Human Rights and Dissent in Canada*. Toronto: Irwin, 1982.

Boyko, John. *Last Steps to Freedom: The Evolution of Canadian Racism*. 1995. Winnipeg: Schillingford, 1998.

Broadfoot, Barry. *Years of Sorrow, Years of Shame: The Story of the Japanese-Canadians in World War II*. Toronto: Doubleday, 1977.

Driedger, Leo. *Multi-Ethnic Canada: Identities & Inequalities*. Toronto: Oxford UP, 1996.

Enomoto, Randy, ed. *Homecoming '92—Where the Heart Is*. Winnipeg: National Assoc. of Japanese-Canadians, 1993.

Ito, Roy. *We Went to War: The Story of the Japanese-Canadians Who Served During the First and Second World Wars*. Etobicoke, ON: S-20 and Nisei Veterans Association., 1984.

Kobayashi, Addie. *Exiles in Our Own Country: Japanese-Canadians in Niagara*. Richmond Hill, ON: Nikkei Network, 1998.

Le Projet centenaire canadien-japonais. *Un rêve de richesse: Les Japonais au Canada 1877–1977*. Vancouver and Toronto: Le Projet centenaire canadien-japonais, 1978.

Okazaki, Robert K. *The Nisei Mass Evacuation Group and the P.O.W. Camp 101 Angler, Ontario: The Japanese-Canadian Community's Struggle for Justice and Human Rights During World War II*. Scarborough, ON: Markham, 1996.

ELECTRONIC SOURCES

CD-ROMs

Encyclopedias can give you the basics about a subject, but like all resources, they have limitations. An encyclopedia may not cover the subject that you are researching and will not cover it in adequate depth. Knowledge expands rapidly, and because it does, even a good encyclopedia lags somewhat behind current scholarship. A number of encyclopedias are now in CD-ROM form for use on a personal computer, and the CD makes searches for information easier. It may also mean that your version is more current as CD-ROMS are often cheaper to buy than print volumes. Many such encyclopedias can also be connected to the World Wide Web, where updated information and links to reference and research resources are listed. It is helpful to have the updated information and links, but only when they are reliable. More on this point in a moment.

Perhaps the most popular electronic encyclopedias are the *Grolier Multimedia Encyclopedia* and *Encarta*. The best general encyclopedia online is probably *Encyclopedia Britannica*. It is now available on library shelves, on CD-ROM, and free-of-charge online at <www.britannica.com>. Like *Grolier*, *Britannica* does not supply an entry on "internment"; you must first search the database, browsing through related items. In fact, the search is difficult because the database contains such a vast array of entries on minor topics—although a subject search engine is now provided. Of particular annoyance to many researchers is the fact that online advertisements keep taking over the screen!

Most online reference tools are American: you'd be better advised to consult the *McClelland and Stewart Canadian Encyclopedia: World Edition* (current edition 1999, 2 CDs). This electronic source has a 1700-word entry on our subject written by Ann Sunahara. The entry also gives five sources, some of which we've already found. Here is an excerpt:

Discrimination

From the beginning all Japanese Canadians, both Issei immigrants and their Canadian-born children, called Nisei (Nee-say), faced massive discrimination. Until the late 1940s, BC politicians pandered to white supremacists and passed a series of laws intended to force Japanese Canadians to leave Canada. All Japanese Canadians were denied the right to vote, including Canadian-born Nisei and Issei veterans of WWI who had served in the Canadian Army. Laws excluded Japanese Canadians from most professions, the civil service and teaching. Labour and minimum-wage laws ensured that employers would hire Asian Canadians only for the most menial jobs and at lower rates of pay than whites.

In the 1920s, the federal government tried to exclude Japanese Canadians from their traditional livelihood of fishing by limiting the number of their fishing licences. During the Great Depression of the 1930s, the BC government denied them logging licenses and paid Japanese Canadians only a fraction of the social assistance paid to whites. Before 1945, the Nisei could not enlist in the Canadian armed forces, since enlistment would give the vote to both the soldier and his wife [. . .].

Postwar Community

In the 1950s, through hard work and educational achievement, Japanese Canadians rebuilt their lives but, scattered across Canada, could not rebuild their community. The postwar economic boom and the rejection

> by Canadian society of racism as a political tactic opened new opportunities for Japanese Canadians. They moved rapidly into the urban and suburban middle class [. . .].
>
> By 1986, polls showed that 63% of Canadians supported redress and 45% favoured individual compensation.

The information about community, assimilation, and racism is directly useful to an essay about our literary texts.

One value of CD-ROM sources is that they provide quick cross-references to related subjects, dictionary definitions, or historical documents that might expand the information, or help you to understand a point. For example, the Sunahara article in the McClelland and Stewart CD-ROM is the same text as in the print version we discussed earlier, but phrases like, "War Measures Act" are "hot" and take you to additional entries that give more information. Online encyclopedias often provide active links to other Web sites. A problem, of course, is that these links are not always current. Finding an expired site, or receiving the message "Document contains no data" is a frustrating reality in web-based research.

There are two things to do when a link does not work:

1. Type in the link, but end with .edu or .com. or .org. The internal architecture of the site may have changed, but the information you are seeking might still be there, accessible through a different link.
2. Go to a search engine, such as Google (www.google.ca) or Infoseek (www.infoseek.com); type in the exact name of the site and see what you get. Sometimes the link that you tried at first will have expired, but you will manage, via a search engine, to reach the site under its name.

The Internet/World Wide Web

Because of the ease of using the Internet, with its access to electronic mail, newsgroups, mailing lists, and, especially, sites and links on the World Wide Web, many students now make it their first—and, unfortunately, too often their *only*—stop for research.

All of us, however, must be *critical* users of the materials we find on the Web. The Web is up-to-date *and* out-of-date, helpful *and* disappointing. It can be a researcher's dream come true and also a source of errors and a time-waster.

Let's work a bit on the literature and history of the internment by means of the Web and see what we discover. Start a search using a popular "search engine," such as Google, with the search phrase: *Japanese and internment*. Google is a better engine than, say, Yahoo!, which executes a much more limited search. Search engines make use of logical (Boolean) operators, such as *and, or, not,* and *near. And* searches the field for any uses of both keywords you have specified. *Or* searches for either of the keywords. *Not* enables you to restrict the search (eg. *minority not European*). *Near* looks for the keywords within a certain range (eg. 10 words) of one another. These operators can help you to tailor a search, and most search engines accept them and offer other refinements. Placing a phrase in quotations, for instance, means that the search will produce items using only that specific phrase (eg. "internment of Japanese-Canadians").

Search engines also use "wild cards," and these help you to extend the engine's very literal ability to associate words. The symbol you use as the "wild card" varies, and the search engine site will tell you what to type— $ or *, perhaps. For example, typing *Canada* will only find entries with the country's name and will usually miss *Canadian*, *Canadien*, *Canadienne*, and so on. If you type *Canad$* or *Canad**, you will uncover many more relevant sites. Use some common sense, however: typing only *Can$* will produce hundreds of useless sources containing words like *cannot* or *cannon*.

A good way to begin on the Web is to search for general information on your authors. We found biographical and bibliographical listings for each of the writers. It is very important to evaluate sites of this kind. We'll discuss critical assessment of sites later, but be careful that you haven't reached a "fan" site or an uploaded student project when you search for famous people. Look for reliable sponsors. For example, the University of Calgary English department maintains a site called "Canadian Poets" (<www.ucalgary.ca/UofC/faculties/HUM/ENCL/canada/poets>), where we found information about Roy Kiyooka, and we found information about Joy Kogawa on a site put up by the University of Northern British Columbia (<http://quarles.unbc.edu/kbeeler_html/research/kog4-html>). Because these sites are maintained by reputable academic agencies, they will contain accurate information on the authors. (Still, check the date of the last revision and update.)

The history and background research involves a much wider search. When we searched Google on May 1, 2002, using "Japanese-Canadians," we found 4,400 sites! (Yahoo! produced 3,120, by the way.) Obviously, you need to refine such a search. "Japanese-Canadians and internment" reduced the number to 1,410, which is still an impossible number of sites to evaluate. Adding "and racism" reduced the list to 398. You get the idea; as in the methodology for library search engines, it is necessary to try various sets of key-words and to refine your search.

What we did notice, however, is that two or three of the same sites appeared in each search; this probably means they are worth considering. We discovered, for example, that the National Association for Japanese-Canadians maintains a site, but examination of this URL proved disappointing. The association is undertaking many interesting activities, but we didn't gain much direct information for our project. As always, it is necessary to look critically at sites, including those that are frequently linked.

We learned that the University of Washington provides a site called "Japanese-Canadian Internment: Information at the University of Washington Libraries and Beyond," which proved to be useful to our project. (It was here that we discovered that the largest archive of information on the British Columbia issue is housed in a university in a neighbouring American state.) We also discovered the Canadian Race Relations Foundation site, which proved to be excellent. We discovered another very valuable source: Sophia University Institute of American and Canadian Studies in Tokyo produces the *Journal of American and Canadian Studies*. Issue 17 contains an outstanding article by

Masumi Izumi, of the Graduate School of American Studies, entitled "Lessons from History: Japanese-Canadians and Civil Liberties in Canada."

Because we already knew of its existence, we also checked the Canadian Archival Info Network site, which links a large number of Canadian museum and archive sites. This is the sort of lead a reference librarian can give you. Here is a description of each of the highly useful sources we found:

Japanese-Canadian Internment: Information at the University of Washington Libraries and Beyond

This extensive site provides an introduction by Linda Di Biase, including a reproduction of *Notice to all Japanese Persons and Persons of Japanese Racial Origin*, a photograph for which the site credits the Vancouver Public Library. (This tells us that information can also be obtained directly from that library.) The site has links: "General Materials"; "Roots of Racism"; "Internment and Redress"; and "Related Sites."

Clicking the "Related Sites" button gives us eleven links, some of which may be useful to our project. One, for example, takes us to the article by Werner Cohn in *BC Studies* that we had found earlier.

The "General Materials" button takes us to a useful bibliography with short abstracts. It includes some items we hadn't found previously. (However, on the day we visited the site, it hadn't been updated since August 1998.)

The "Roots of Racism" section provides an extensive list of sources with abstracts. It also reproduces a petition from 1897 and other material from Special Collections at the university; without the Web, we wouldn't be able to see these documents unless we visited Washington State.

The Canadian Race Relations Foundation Site

This site provides "fact sheets." One of these—"From Racism to Redress: The Japanese-Canadian Experience"—is a well-written, five-page overview with a timeline and a number of useful quotations from other sources and from historical documents. We learned, for example, that the estimated property loss to Japanese-Canadians was $50,000,000 in 1950 dollars and that the net loss was some $443 million. We learned that families were interned together in the U.S.A., while "in Canada, initially, families were separated." (You will remember the aching separation of mother, father, and child in Watada's poem: again, your research provides factual underpinnings for the poetic expression.) We learned that the U.S. government moved quickly in 1944–45 "to allow the return" of evacuees, but in Canada, internees "were forced to decide on deportation to Japan or relocation east of the Rockies."

These facts will need to be confirmed from another source because this site is unsigned, but you can expect them to be sound because of the authenticity of the sponsoring agency of this site. (In fact, Adachi and others do confirm these disturbing facts.)

This introduction lists ten sources, most of which we've already located by other means. Under another button, however, the site provides a further, more extensive bibliography with 40 entries, each with an abstract. This list is a very valuable find, particularly as some of the entries provide excerpts that allow you to get quickly to at least partial information. The site also provides a listing of videos and links to other Web sites.

"Lessons from History: Japanese-Canadians and Civil Liberties in Canada"

Izumi's article begins with an abstract in Japanese that makes it valuable for researchers in that country. But the long English essay that follows is one of the most thorough sources we found. Izumi lays out background history that we now know but didn't at the outset of our project—*when* you discover each source partly determines its value to your research.

After this overview, however, the essay discusses two events which Izumi feels are consequences of the internment: the adoption of the Canadian *Charter of Rights and Freedoms* in 1982 and the replacement of the *War Measures Act* with the *Emergencies Act* in 1988. Izumi claims that the participation of the Japanese in the Redress Movement "deserves to be recorded, because their experience provides a bitter, but precious lesson for Canadians, presenting an example of how tragedy can happen when racism is legitimized by political institutions."

Although the bulk of the article deals with events after the internment, it provides much history from the period we are researching, including interviews with survivors. The accounts of witnesses like Ms. Hide (Hyodo) Shimizu, who was the only Japanese-Canadian public school teacher before the Second World War, is moving: It gives us, again, personal history from which to read the fictional histories of Kogawa's Naomi or the real event which Kiyooka poeticizes. Izumi reports that "Some Nisei were qualified to teach," but could not get jobs in B.C. because "of the racial discrimination." We have more evidence for the hatred that "Even the sisters of mercy" felt for the Japanese, and the anger that Aunt Emily feels.

Ms. Shimizu reports that "I am a Christian woman, so I have forgiven, but it is very difficult to forget." One thesis we are considering involves the acts of remembering and forgetting, the tension between trauma and the sense of self. Kiyooka remembers the humiliation of being fingerprinted; it intersects with his memories of his father even though he is in another country and it is 1969, years after the incident. Roy K. Miki says of Kiyooka that the "internalized conflicts of the war years would never stray from the immediate reach of memory, though the artist RK remained wary of using its personal and historical specificities as subject-matter of his visual art [. . .]" (305). Kogawa remembers her family house in Vancouver, a memory she has repressed. In Izumi's article, Roger Obata recalls his own mother's horror at losing her house on four hour's notice and the looting of her personal belongings.

Obata provides a powerful detail that informs our other thesis about community and loyalties: He was in uniform as a Canadian soldier while his mother's home was being confiscated. This article, like all our findings, provides direct context for the literary texts.

The chief value to us, however, is not the essay itself, but the very extensive notes. Izumi offers 87 notes that hugely expand and qualify our bibliography. For example, we learn of a study written in 1948 by Forest E. La Violette, *The*

Canadian Japanese and World War II: A Sociological and Psychological Account (Toronto: U of Toronto P), which Izumi tells us "lacks a critical viewpoint on the evacuation policy itself," but does provide an opinion much more contemporaneous to the events. (Earlier, we urged you to use current research, and it is always a guiding principle. But there are particular applications in which research close in time to a historical event can give specific insight.) Izumi's notes warn us that Adachi's book—which has been our base source—"contains some errors in the description of the pre-W.W.II history" because Adachi could not read the Japanese language. This is an important caution for us! Izumi considers Adachi's section on the evacuation, however, to be "extremely valuable." This is the sort of up-to-date information and critical response that we need to evaluate our sources, to tell us what to use—and what to avoid—in a source. These notes qualify information we've learned elsewhere, provide myriad references we might explore (if we had time), and give us yet more sources.

This article is very useful, indeed. We might have found it anyway through a periodical index, but we did find it—almost by accident—on the Web. This demonstrates the often-surprising value of the Web, but reminds us that it is no substitute for a methodical library search.

Canadian Archival Info Network Site
On this government site, we found 23 records, including the University of Washington site once again. (Its presence on this authoritative site confirms that it will be a reliable source.) We pursued the following path and achieved the results indicated in the last line:

Virtual Exhibits

    British Columbia—27 sources

        British Columbia Government Provincial Archives Visual Records

        Online—110,000 images(!)

            Search Engine "J"

            Japanese Canadians—32 items

Of these 32 items, three were of direct use to our project, and, of these, two provided thumbnail contact sheets showing photographs we could use:

        C = 09837 Former Japanese Internment Camp, Lillooet

        I = 60959 Japanese-Canadian Internment Camp, showing school

These images can be downloaded for research purposes without charge.

Using the Web can lead to visual and archival resources such as this photograph, which might enhance your essay (perhaps placed in an appendix or used to illustrate a particular point in your text). Recall McAllister's comment on the imagery of *furusato* ["old village"]; you can relate her comment and

Japanese-Canadian internment camp, showing school and housing, at Lemon Creek, south of Slocan City. Courtesty of BC Archives.

this drab photograph to the literary texts. Remember the section from Adachi's history in which he compares "summer holiday" settings to the "grim reality" of the camps (251). Once again, your research offers historical balance to the psychological conflicts suffered by the protagonists in our literary texts. You are gathering enough interrelated evidence to make strong points.

In these instances, the Web turns out to be an excellent resource. Wherever you might be, you can undertake research in the University of Washington's holdings, or enter the British Columbia Archives. You can read primary and secondary materials, view photographs and artwork, and download them for papers and presentations. Many universities and government agencies have well-designed sites like these.

Some Reminders

- Each search engine has its own forms and criteria, and each has its own categories and indexes. Consult the Help pages for each search engine so that you will perform your search as effectively as possible. A handy guide is Randolph Hock, *The Extreme Searcher's Guide to Web Search Engines*, 2nd. ed, 2001.

- Web sites are a supplement to print sources, not a substitute for them, and the search tools and bibliographic pathways to print sources are now easier to negotiate than are those for the Web. Keeping this point in mind, we recommend to students that for each Web site they consult, they should consult three print sources.

✓ A Checklist for Evaluating Sources on the World Wide Web

The case study we have presented in this chapter proves the value of integrating literary analysis and historical research. It also shows that for sources on the World Wide Web, as with print sources, you must do the following:

✓ Evaluate what you have located and gauge how much or how little it will contribute to your literary analysis and argument.

✓ Consider the agency that sponsors the site, the qualifications of the author, and the breadth and currency of the information.

✓ Be wary of sites that are overly graphic or interactive: we are looking for scholarly work, not technological wizardry. Take note of whether the URL includes *.edu*; such sites are likely to be more scholarly than others. Sites with a tilde (~) are untrustworthy since the tilde is a way for someone to add on to an existing site.

✓ Be wary of sites that seem useful because they contain a university name: Very often the essays on such sites are written by students who have completed a project such as yours for a class assignment. They may be excellent essays (as yours will be), but they may also be barely adequate essays or even contain errors.

Focus the topic of your research as precisely as you can before you embark on a Web search. Lots of surfing and browsing can sometimes turn up good material, but using the Web without a focus can prove distracting and unproductive. It takes you away from library research (where the results might be better) and from the actual planning and writing of the paper.

When considering a Web site, ask the following questions:

✓ Does this site or page look as if it can help me in my assignment?
✓ Whose site or page is this? Is the author an expert or another student?
✓ What is the intended audience?
✓ What is the point of view? Are there signs of a specific slant or bias?
✓ What are the levels of detail and quality of the material presented?
✓ Is the material well-constructed and well-organized?
✓ Is the text well-written?
✓ Can this Web information be corroborated or supported by print sources?
✓ When was the site or page made available? Has it been recently revised or updated? *Note:* Your browser will enable you to get this information; look for Page Info.
✓ Can the person, institution, company, or agency responsible for this site or page receive e-mail comments, questions, and criticisms?

DOCUMENTING ELECTRONIC SOURCES IN MLA STYLE

Many Web sites and pages are not prepared according to the style and form in which you want to cite them. Sometimes the name of the author is unknown, and other information may be hard to come by as well. Pagination is particularly difficult to ascertain. And it is worth repeating that while you may cite the source, including the URL accurately, you cannot be certain that the site will exist at this URL (or at all) when your readers attempt to access it for themselves. Using scholarly databases, of course, makes it less likely that your sources will disappear: This is yet another reason to shy away from general Web sites and to use sites maintained by reliable agencies. But these difficulties aside, perhaps the main point to remember is that a source on the Web is as much a source as a book or article that you can track down and read in the library. If you have made use of it, you must acknowledge that you have done so and include the bibliographic information, as fully as you can, in your Works Cited for the paper.

In Chapter 15, we provided guidance for making citations and gave models. The examples of electronic citations are useful and you should reread that section now. We will conclude this chapter by noting additional print and electronic resources that can aid you in a literary and historical project like the one we have undertaken on the Japanese-Canadian internment.

SOME ELECTRONIC SEARCH ENGINES AND DIRECTORIES

All-In-One Search Page

<www.albany.net/allinone>

Gathers together search forms for all search engines.

The Argus Clearinghouse

<www.clearinghouse.net>

A directory of subject guides to resources; especially useful for scholars.

Britannica Internet Guide

<www.ebig.com>

A directory of sites reviewed by the *Encyclopedia Britannica.*

Canadian Information by Subject

<www.n/c-bnc.ca/caninfo/ecaninfo.htm>

Developed by the National Library of Canada.

Galaxy

<www.einet.net>

A directory for resources in many subjects and fields, including "Humanities—Literature."

Google

<www.google.ca>

Perhaps the best general search engine available outside a reference library.

Libweb: Library World Wide Web Servers

<sunsite.Berkeley.EDU/Libweb>

Lists more than 2,000 home pages of libraries in over 70 countries.

Yahoo!

<www.yahoo.com and www.yahoo.ca>

A guide by subject to the Web, with links to other sites and an array of search engines.

PRINT DIRECTORIES

The following books include listings of Web sites on a wide range of topics; as the titles suggest, a number also supply tips and suggestions for effective research. Such books can be great time savers in identifying for you the names and URLs of sites you can consult for your research. Rather than the hundreds, even thousands, of sites that a search engine might turn up, these books will be much more focused and selective in their listings. Their limitation is that however carefully they have been compiled, they always fall behind the ever-changing nature of the Web.

Calishain, Tara. *Official Netscape Guide to Internet Research*. Research Triangle Park, N.C.: Ventana, 1997.

Clark, Michael. *Cultural Treasures of the Internet*. 2nd ed. Upper Saddle River, N.J.: Prentice Hall, 1997.

Carroll, Jim, and Rick Broadhead. *Canadian Internet Directory and Research Guide*. Don Mills, ON: Stoddart, 2002.

Hahn, Harley. *Harley Hahn's Internet and Web Yellow Pages: 1998*. 5th ed. Berkeley, CA.: Osborne McGraw, 1997.

Krol, Ed, and Bruce C. Klopfenstein. *The Whole Internet User's Guide and Catalog*. Belmont, CA: Wadsworth, 1996.

Levine, John R., Carol Baroudi, and Margaret Levine Young. *The Internet for Dummies*. 4th ed. San Mateo, CA: IDG Books, 1997.

Morris, Evan. *The Book Lover's Guide to the Internet*. Rev. ed. New York: Fawcett, 1998.

Rositano, Dean J., Robert A. Rositano, and Jay Lee. *Que's Mega Web Directory*. Cupertino, CA: Que, 1996.

Stout, Rick. *The World Wide Web Complete Reference.* Berkeley, CA: Osborne McGraw, 1996.

Print Articles on Literature, History, and the World Wide Web

The magazines *Wired* and *Choice* provide expert overviews of Web (and CD-ROM) resources for research, in particular for literature and history. *Choice* 34 (1997) is a special, "Web Issue" supplement. Other journals also provide Internet information. These sources describe the kinds of material now available and supply bibliographies.

For example:

New Technologies and the Practice of History. A special issue of *Perspectives: American Historical Association Newsletter* 36.2 (1998).

O'Malley, Michael, and Roy Rosenzweig. "Brave New World or Blind Alley? American History on the World Wide Web." *The Journal of American History* 84. 1 (1997): 132–55.

As well, you could consult:

Browner, Stephanie, et al., eds. *Literature and the Internet: A Guide for Students, Teachers, and Scholars.* New York: Garland, 2000.

Trinkle, Dennis A., and Scott A. Merriman. *The History Highway 2000: A Guide to Internet Resources.* 2nd ed. Armonk, NY: Sharpe, 2000.

EVALUATING WORLD WIDE WEB RESOURCES

The following sites, prepared by research librarians, provide excellent advice for evaluating Web sites and the materials they contain:

Bibliography on Evaluating Web Information

<www.lib.vt.edu/research/evaluate/evalbiblio.html>

A bibliography of 17 articles on evaluating sources—available on line.

Evaluating Internet Resources

<www.albany.edu/library/internet/evaluate.html>

Thinking Critically about Discipline-Based World Wide Web Resources

<www.library.ucla.edu/libraries/college/instruct/discp.htm>

Thinking Critically about World Wide Web Resources

<www.library.ucla.edu/libraries/college/instruct/critical.htm>

Recommended Web sites for Scholarly Citation and the Internet/World Wide Web

Addison-Wesley Web site

<www.awl.com>

For Humanities matters, this site links to:

Longman Web site

<www.longman.awl.com/englishpages/ >

Includes a range of resources in five areas: Online Citation Guide; Composition; Literature; Basic Skills; Technical Writing.

MLA on the Web

Includes a link to a site of guidelines for MLA (Modern Language Association) documentation style (e.g., Citing Sources from the World Wide Web).

17

Essay Examinations

Learning Objectives

When you've read this chapter, you should be able to

➢ prepare for the most common types of essay exam questions; and

➢ approach an essay examination without fear.

WHAT EXAMINATIONS ARE

An examination not only measures learning and thinking, but also stimulates them. Even so humble an examination as a short-answer quiz—chiefly a device to coerce others in your class to do the assigned reading you've already completed—is meant as a sort of push. Of course, internal motivation is far superior to external, but even a quiz can have a beneficial effect. Students know this; indeed, they often seek courses with quizzes to force themselves to complete the reading. (Teachers often teach a new course for the same reason: to become knowledgeable about, say, Chinese-Canadian literature—perhaps the work of Fred Wah or jam. ismail—knowing that despite lofty intentions we may not seriously confront the subject unless we are under the pressure of facing a class.)

In short, examinations force us to acquire learning and then to convert learning into thinking. Sometimes, when you are preparing for the final examination, the fog lifts—a pattern emerges. The experience of reviewing and then of writing an examination, though fretful, can be highly exciting as connections are made and ideas take on life. Further, we are often more likely to make imaginative leaps when trying to answer questions that other people pose to us, rather than questions we pose to ourselves. And although questions posed by others cause anxiety, once they have been confronted we often make yet another discovery—a self-discovery, a sudden and satisfying awareness of powers we didn't know we had.

WRITING ESSAY ANSWERS

Let's assume that you have read the assigned material, marked the margins of your books, made summaries of the longer readings and of the classroom comments, reviewed all this material, and had a decent night's sleep. Now you are facing the examination sheet.

Here are seven obvious but important practical suggestions:

- Take a moment to jot down, as a sort of outline or source of further inspiration, a few ideas that strike you after you have thought a little about the question.

- Answer the question: If you are asked to compare two characters, compare them; don't just write two character sketches. Take seriously such words as *compare, summarize,* and especially *evaluate.* A direction such as *discuss* doesn't actually guide you and probably shouldn't be used by examiners. But since it often is, remember that this instruction asks you to *find a thesis of your own* and to use the examination material to illustrate or argue it.

- Try turning the question into an affirmation, for example, by turning "In what ways does the poetry of Michael Ondaatje resemble his fiction?" into "Michael Ondaatje's poetry resembles his fiction in that [. . .]."

- Don't waste time summarizing at length what you have read unless asked to do so—but, of course, you may have to give a brief summary in order to support a point. The instructor wants to see that you can *use* your reading, not merely that you have *done* the reading.

- Budget your time. Do not spend more than the allotted time on a question.

- Be concrete. Illustrate your arguments with facts—the names of authors, titles, dates, characters, details of plot, and quotations if possible.

- Leave space for last-minute additions. If you are writing in a booklet, write only on the right-hand pages so that on rereading you can add material at the appropriate place on the left-hand pages. Don't be afraid to add (or delete) using the editing marks discussed in Chapter 14.

HINTS ON COMMON TYPES OF ESSAY QUESTIONS

Beyond these general suggestions, we can best talk about essay examinations by looking at the five commonest sorts of questions.

A Passage To Explicate

See Chapter 3. As a short rule, look carefully at the tone (speaker's attitude toward self, subject, and audience) and at the implications of the words (their connotations and associations), and see whether a pattern of imagery or other pattern is evident. Remember that an explication is not a paraphrase (a putting into other words) but an attempt to show the relations of the parts by calling attention to implications. Try to avoid simply moving in order through the piece of writing; organize your explication around the thesis you devise.

A Historical Question

Example: "Trace the influence of the English Romantic poets on the Confederation poets."

Offer a nice combination of argument and evidence; that is, support your thesis by concrete details (names, dates, and even brief quotations). A discussion of the Confederation poets' debt to British Lake District Romanticism cannot be convincing if it does not specify certain works and certain characteristics. If you are asked to relate a writer or a body of work to an earlier writer or period, list the chief characteristics of the earlier writer or period, and then show *specifically* how the material you are discussing is related to these characteristics. If you quote some relevant lines from the works, your reader will feel that you know not only titles and stock phrases but also the works themselves.

A Quotation to Discuss or Evaluate

Read the quotation very carefully, and in your answer take account of *all* the quotation. If, for example, the quoted critic has said, "W. O. Mitchell in his fiction always [. . .] but in his talks and lectures rarely [. . .]," you will have to write about fiction and nonfiction, it will not be enough to talk only about Mitchell's novels or only about his speeches. Watch especially for words such as *always, for the most part, never;* that is, the writer of the quotation may use some important qualification. This is not being picky; true thinking involves making subtle distinctions, yielding assent only so far and no further. And (again) be sure to give concrete details, supporting your argument with evidence.

A Comparison (or Contrast)

Example: "Compare the role of the mother in Michel Tremblay's fiction and plays."

See pages 40–43. A comparison of Tremblay plays and novels might treat two examples of each, devoting the first half to one genre and the second to the other. There is always the danger that the essay may break into two parts. You can guard against this weakness by announcing at the outset that you will treat one genre first, then the other; by reminding your reader during your treatment of the play that certain points will be picked up when you get to the novel; and by briefly reminding your reader during the treatment of the novel of certain points already made in the treatment of the play

A stronger essay might first treat one issue or image in a play (say, in *Les Belles Soeurs*) and then turn to the same issue or image in a novel (say, in *The Fat Woman Next Door Is Pregnant*). This alternating plan is usually stronger, with clearer focus.

A FINAL WORD

Above all, do not panic. Do your reading; prepare for the exam; take in an outline or notes if you are allowed them, and then—strange as it may sound—try to enjoy yourself. Writing is difficult, but it can be among the most rewarding things you will ever do.

Appendix A

ARABY

James Joyce

North Richmond Street, being blind,[1] was a quiet street except at the hour when the Christian Brothers' School set the boys free. An uninhabited house of two stories stood at the blind end, detached from its neighbors in a square ground. The other houses of the street, conscious of decent lives within them, gazed at one another with brown imperturbable faces.

The former tenant of our house, a priest, had died in the back drawing-room. Air, musty from having long been enclosed, hung in all the rooms, and the waste room behind the kitchen was littered with old useless papers. Among these I found a few papercovered books, the pages of which were curled and damp: The *Abbot,* by Walter Scott, *The Devout Communicant* and *The Memoirs of Vidocq.*[2]

I liked the last best because its leaves were yellow. The wild garden behind the house contained a central apple-tree and a few straggling bushes under one of which I found the late tenant's rusty bicycle-pump. He had been a very charitable priest; in his will he had left all his money to institutions and the furniture of his house to his sister.

When the short days of winter came dusk fell before we had well eaten our dinners. When we met in the street the houses had grown sombre. The space of sky above us was the colour of everchanging violet and towards it the

[1] **blind** a dead-end street

[2] The *Abbot* was one of Scott's popular historical romances. *The Devout Communicant* was a Catholic religious manual; *The Memoirs of Vidocq* were the memoirs of the chief of the French detective force.

lamps of the street lifted their feeble lanterns. The cold air stung us and we played till our bodies glowed. Our shouts echoed in the silent street. The career of our play brought us through the dark muddy lanes behind the houses where we ran the gauntlet of the rough tribes from the cottages, to the back doors of the dark dripping gardens where odours arose from the ashpits, to the dark odorous stables where a coachman smoothed and combed the horse or shook music from the buckled harness. When we returned to the street light from the kitchen windows had filled the areas. If my uncle was seen turning the corner we hid in the shadow until we had seen him safely housed. Or if Mangan's sister came out on the doorstep to call her brother in to his tea we watched her from our shadow peer up and down the street. We waited to see whether she would remain or go in and, if she remained, we left our shadow and walked up to Mangan's steps resignedly. She was waiting for us, her figure defined by the light from the half-opened door. Her brother always teased her before he obeyed and I stood by the railings looking at her. Her dress swung as she moved her body and the soft rope of her hair tossed from side to side.

Every morning I lay on the floor in the front parlour watching her door. The blind was pulled down to within an inch of the sash so that I could not be seen. When she came out on the doorstep my heart leaped. I ran to the hall, seized my books and followed her. I kept her brown figure always in my eye and, when we came near the point at which our ways diverged, I quickened my pace and passed her. This happened morning after morning. I had never spoken to her, except for a few casual words, and yet her name was like a summons to all my foolish blood.

Her image accompanied me even in places the most hostile to romance. On Saturday evenings when my aunt went marketing I had to go to carry some of the parcels. We walked through the flaring streets, jostled by drunken men and bargaining women, amid the curses of labourers, the shrill litanies of shopboys who stood on guard by the barrels of pigs' cheeks, the nasal chanting of street-singers, who sang a come-all-you about O'Donovan Rossa,[3] or a ballad about the troubles in our native land. These noises converged in a single sensation of life for me: I imagined that I bore my chalice safely through a throng of foes. Her name sprang to my lips at moments in strange prayers and praises which I myself did not understand. My eyes were often full of tears (I could not tell why) and at times a flood from my heart seemed to pour itself out into my bosom. I thought little of the future. I did not know whether I would ever speak to her or not or, if I spoke to her, how I could tell her of my confused adoration. But my body was like a harp and her words and gestures were like fingers running upon the wires.

One evening I went into the back drawing-room in which the priest had died. It was a dark rainy evening and there was no sound in the house. Through one of the broken panes I heard the rain impinge upon the earth, the

[3]Jeremiah O'Donovan (1831–1915), a popular Irish leader who was jailed by the British for advocating violent rebellion. A "come-all-you" was a topical song that began "Come all you gallant Irishmen."

fine incessant needles of water playing in the sodden beds. Some distant lamp or lighted window gleamed below me. I was thankful that I could see so little. All my senses seemed to desire to veil themselves and, feeling that I was about to slip from them, I pressed the palms of my hands together until they trembled, murmuring: *O love! O love!* many times.

At last she spoke to me. When she addressed the first words to me I was so confused that I did not know what to answer. She asked me was I going to Araby.

I forget whether I answered yes or no. It would be a splendid bazaar, she said; she would love to go.

—And why can't you? I asked.

While she spoke she turned a silver bracelet round and round her wrist. She could not go, she said, because there would be a retreat that week in her convent. Her brother and two other boys were fighting for their caps and I was alone at the railings. She held one of the spikes, bowing her head towards me. The light from the lamp opposite our door caught the white curve of her neck, lit up her hair that rested there and, falling, lit up the hand upon the railing. It fell over one side of her dress and caught the white border of a petticoat, just visible as she stood at ease.

—It's well for you, she said.

—If I go, I said, I will bring you something.

What innumerable follies laid waste my waking and sleeping thoughts after that evening! I wished to annihilate the tedious intervening days. I chafed against the work of school. At night in my bedroom and by day in the classroom her image came between me and the page I strove to read. The syllables of the word *Araby* were called to me through the silence in which my soul luxuriated and cast an Eastern enchantment over me. I asked for leave to go to the bazaar on Saturday night. My aunt was surprised and hoped it was not some Freemason[4] affair. I answered few questions in class, I watched my master's face pass from amiability to sternness; he hoped I was not beginning to idle. I could not call my wandering thoughts together. I had hardly any patience with the serious work of life which, now that it stood between me and my desire, seemed to me child's play, ugly monotonous child's play.

On Saturday morning I reminded my uncle that I wished to go to the bazaar in the evening. He was fussing at the hallstand, looking for the hatbrush, and answered me curtly:

—Yes, boy, I know.

As he was in the hall I could not go into the front parlour and lie at the window. I left the house in bad humour and walked slowly towards the school. The air was pitilessly raw and already my heart misgave me.

When I came home to dinner my uncle had not yet been home. Still it was early. I sat staring at the clock for some time and, when its ticking began to irritate me, I left the room. I mounted the staircase and gained the upper part of the house. The high cold empty gloomy rooms liberated me and I went from

---

[4]Irish Catholics viewed the Masons as their Protestant enemies.

room to room singing. From the front window I saw my companions playing below in the street. Their cries reached me weakened and indistinct and, leaning my forehead against the cool glass, I looked over at the dark house where she lived. I may have stood there for an hour, seeing nothing but the brown-clad figure cast by my imagination, touched discreetly by the lamplight at the curved neck, at the hand upon the railings and at the border below the dress.

When I came downstairs again I found Mrs Mercer sitting at the fire. She was an old garrulous woman, a pawnbroker's widow, who collected used stamps for some pious purpose. I had to endure the gossip of the tea-table. The meal was prolonged beyond an hour and still my uncle did not come. Mrs Mercer stood up to go: she was sorry she couldn't wait any longer, but it was after eight o'clock and she did not like to be out late, as the night air was bad for her. When she had gone I began to walk up and down the room, clenching my fists. My aunt said:

—I'm afraid you may put off your bazaar for this night of Our Lord.

At nine o'clock I heard my uncle's latchkey in the halldoor. I heard him talking to himself and heard the hallstand rocking when it had received the weight of his overcoat. I could interpret these signs. When he was midway through his dinner I asked him to give me the money to go to the bazaar. He had forgotten.

—The people are in bed and after their first sleep now, he said.

I did not smile. My aunt said to him energetically:

—Can't you give him the money and let him go? You've kept him late enough as it is.

My uncle said he was very sorry he had forgotten. He said he believed in the old saying: *All work and no play makes Jack a dull boy.* He asked me where I was going and, when I had told him a second time he asked me did I know *The Arab's Farewell to His Steed.*[5]

When I left the kitchen he was about to recite the opening lines of the piece to my aunt.

I held a florin tightly in my hand as I strode down Buckingham Street towards the station. The sight of the streets thronged with buyers and glaring with gas recalled to me the purpose of my journey. I took my seat in a third-class carriage of a deserted train. After an intolerable delay the train moved out of the station slowly. It crept onward among ruinous houses and over the twinkling river. At Westland Row Station a crowd of people pressed to the carriage doors; but the porters moved them back, saying that it was a special train for the bazaar. I remained alone in the bare carriage. In a few minutes the train drew up beside an improvised wooden platform. I passed out on to the road and saw by the lighted dial of a clock that it was ten minutes to ten. In front of me was a large building which displayed the magical name.

I could not find any sixpenny entrance and, fearing that the bazaar would be closed, I passed in quickly through a turnstile, handing a shilling to a weary-

[5] "The Arab to His Favorite Steed" was a popular sentimental poem by Caroline Norton (1808–77).

looking man. I found myself in a big hall girdled at half its height by a gallery. Nearly all the stalls were closed and the greater part of the hall was in darkness. I recognised a silence like that which pervades a church after a service. I walked into the center of the bazaar timidly. A few people were gathered about the stalls which were still open. Before a curtain, over which the words *Café Chantant* were written in coloured lamps, two men were counting money on a salver. I listened to the fall of the coins.

Remembering with difficulty why I had come I went over to one of the stalls and examined porcelain vases and flowered teasets. At the door of the stall a young lady was talking and laughing with two young gentlemen. I remarked their English accents and listened vaguely to their conversation.

—O, I never said such a thing!

—O, but you did!

—O, but I didn't!

—Didn't she say that?

—Yes! I heard her.

—O, there's a . . . fib!

Observing me the young lady came over and asked me did I wish to buy anything. The tone of her voice was not encouraging; she seemed to have spoken to me out of a sense of duty. I looked humbly at the great jars that stood like eastern guards at either side of the dark entrance to the stall and murmured:

—No, thank you.

The young lady changed the position of one of the vases and went back to the two young men. They began to talk of the same subject. Once or twice the young lady glanced at me over her shoulder.

I lingered before her stall, though I knew my stay was useless, to make my interest in her wares seem the more real. Then I turned away slowly and walked down the middle of the bazaar. I allowed the two pennies to fall against the sixpence in my pocket. I heard a voice call from one end of the gallery that the light was out. The upper part of the hall was now completely dark.

Gazing up into the darkness I saw myself as a creature driven and derided by vanity; and my eyes burned with anguish and anger.

Appendix B

BORDERS

Thomas King

When I was twelve, maybe thirteen, my mother announced that we were going to go to Salt Lake City to visit my sister who had left the reserve, moved across the line, and found a job. Laetitia had not left home with my mother's blessing, but over time my mother had come to be proud of the fact that Laetitia had done all of this on her own.

"She did real good," my mother would say.

Then there were the fine points to Laetitia's going. She had not, as my mother like to tell Mrs. Manyfingers, gone floating after some man like a balloon on a string. She hadn't snuck out of the house, either, and gone to Vancouver or Edmonton or Toronto to chase rainbows down alleys. And she hadn't been pregnant.

"She did real good."

I was seven or eight when Laetitia left home. She was seventeen. Our father was from Rocky Boy on the American side.

"Dad's American," Laetitia told my mother, "so I can go and come as I please."

"Send us a postcard."

Laetitia packed her things, and we headed for the border. Just outside of Milk River, Laetitia told us to watch for the water tower.

"Over the next rise. It's the first thing you see."

"We got a water tower on the reserve," my mother said. "There's a big one in Lethbridge, too."

"You'll be able to see the tops of the flagpoles, too. That's where the border is."

359

When we got to Coutts, my mother stopped at the convenience store and bought her and Laetitia a cup of coffee. I got an Orange Crush.

"This is real lousy coffee."

"You're just angry because I want to see the world."

"It's the water. From here on down, they got lousy water."

"I can catch the bus from Sweetgrass. You don't have to lift a finger."

"You're going to have to buy your water in bottles if you want good coffee."

There was an old wooden building about a block away, with a tall sign in the yard that said "Museum." Most of the roof had been blown away. Mom told me to go and see when the place was open. There were boards over the windows and doors. You could tell that the place was closed, and I told Mom so, but she said to go and check anyway. Mom and Laetitia stayed by the car. Neither one of them moved. I sat down on the steps of the museum and watched them, and I don't know that they ever said anything to each other. Finally, Laetitia got her bag out of the trunk and gave Mom a hug.

I wandered back to the car. The wind had come up, and it blew Laetitia's hair across her face. Mom reached out and pulled the strands out of Laetitia's eyes, and Laetitia let her.

"You can still see the mountain from here," my mother told Laetitia in Blackfoot.

"Lots of mountains in Salt Lake," Laetitia told her in English.

"The place is closed," I said. "Just like I told you."

Laetitia tucked her hair into her jacket and dragged her bag down the road to the brick building with the American flag flapping on a pole. When she got to where the guards were waiting, she turned, put the bag down, and waved to us. We waved back. Then my mother turned the car around, and we came home.

We got postcards from Laetitia regular, and, if she wasn't spreading jelly on the truth, she was happy. She found a good job and rented an apartment with a pool.

"And she can't even swim," my mother told Mrs. Manyfingers.

Most of the postcards said we should come down and see the city, but whenever I mentioned this, my mother would stiffen up.

So I was surprised when she bought two new tires for the car and put on her blue dress with the green and yellow flowers. I had to dress up, too, for my mother did not want us crossing the border looking like Americans. We made sandwiches and put them in a big box with pop and potato chips and some apples and bananas and a big jar of water.

"But we can stop at one of those restaurants, too, right?"

"We maybe should take some blankets in case you get sleepy."

"But we can stop at one of those restaurants, too, right?"

The border was actually two towns, though neither one was big enough to amount to anything. Coutts was on the Canadian side and consisted of the convenience store and gas station, the museum that was closed and boarded up, and a motel. Sweetgrass was on the American side, but all you could see was an overpass that arched across the highway and disappeared into the prairies. Just hearing the names of these towns, you would expect that Sweetgrass, which is a nice name and sounds like it is related to other places such as Medicine Hat and Moose Jaw and Kicking Horse Pass, would be on the Canadian side, and that Coutts, which sounds abrupt and rude, would be on the American side. But this was not the case.

Between the two borders was a duty-free shop where you could buy cigarettes and liquor and flags. Stuff like that.

We left the reserve in the morning and drove until we got to Coutts.

"Last time we stopped here," my mother said, "you had an Orange Crush. You remember that?"

"Sure," I said. "That was when Laetitia took off."

"You want another Orange Crush?"

"That means we're not going to stop at a restaurant, right?"

My mother got a coffee at the convenience store, and we stood around and watched the prairies move in the sunlight. Then we climbed back in the car. My mother straightened the dress across her thighs, leaned against the wheel, and drove all the way to the border in first gear, slowly, as if she were trying to see through a bad storm or riding high on black ice.

The border guard was a old guy. As he walked to the car, he swayed from side to side, his feet set wide apart, the holster on his hip pitching up and down. He leaned into the window, looked into the back seat, and looked at my mother and me.

"Morning, ma'am."

"Good morning."

"Where are you heading?"

"Salt Lake City."

"Purpose of your visit?"

"Visit my daughter."

"Citizenship?"

"Blackfoot," my mother told him.

"Ma'am?"

"Blackfoot," my mother repeated.

"Canadian?"

"Blackfoot."

It would have been easier if my mother had just said "Canadian" and been done with it, but I could see she wasn't going to do that. The guard wasn't angry or anything. He smiled and looked towards the building. Then he turned back and nodded.

"Morning, ma'am."

"Good morning."

"Any firearms or tobacco?"

"No."

"Citizenship?

"Blackfoot."

He told us to sit in the car and wait, and we did. In about five minutes, another guard came out with the first man. They were talking as they came, both men swaying back and forth like two cowboys headed for a bar or a gunfight.

"Morning, ma'am."

"Good morning."

"Cecil tells me you and the boy are Blackfoot."

"That's right."

"Now, I know that we got Blackfeet on the American side and the Canadians got Blackfeet on their side. Just so we can keep our records straight, what side do you come from?"

I knew exactly what my mother was going to say, and I could have told them if they had asked me.

"Canadian side or American side?" asked the guard.

"Blackfoot side," she said.

It didn't take them long to lose their sense of humour, I can tell you that. The one guard stopped smiling altogether and told us to park our car at the side of the building and come in.

We sat on a wood bench for about an hour before anyone came over to talk to us. This time it was a woman. She had a gun, too.

"Hi," she said. "I'm Inspector Pratt. I understand there is a little misunderstanding."

"I'm going to visit my daughter in Salt Lake City," my mother told her. "We don't have any guns or beer."

"It's a legal technicality, that's all."

"My daughter's Blackfoot, too."

The woman opened a briefcase and took out a couple of forms and began to write on one of them. "Everyone who crosses our border has to declare their citizenship. Even Americans. It helps us to keep track of the visitors we get from the various countries."

She went on like that for maybe fifteen minutes, and a lot of the stuff she told us was interesting.

"I can understand how you feel about having to tell us your citizenship, and here's what I'll do. You tell me, and I won't put it down on the form. No-one will know but you and me."

Her gun was silver. There were several chips in the wood handle and the name "Stella" was scratched into the metal butt.

We were in the border office for about four hours, and we talked to almost everyone there. One of the men bought me a Coke. My mother brought a couple of sandwiches in from the car. I offered part of mine to Stella, but she said she wasn't hungry.

I told Stella that we were Blackfoot and Canadian, but she said that didn't count because I was a minor. In the end, she told us that if my mother didn't declare her citizenship, we would have to go back to where we came from. My mother stood up and thanked Stella for her time. Then we got back in the car and drove to the Canadian border, which was only about a hundred yards away.

I was disappointed. I hadn't seen Laetitia for a long time, and I had never been to Salt Lake City. When she was still at home, Laetitia would go on and on about Salt Lake City. She had never been there, but her boyfriend Lester Tallbull had spent a year in Salt Lake at a technical school.

"It's a great place," Lester would say. "Nothing but blondes in the whole state."

Whenever he said that, Laetitia would slug him on his shoulder hard enough to make him flinch. He had some brochures on Salt Lake and some maps, and every so often the two of them would spread them out on the table.

"That's the temple. It's right downtown. You got to have a pass to get in."

"Charlotte says anyone can go in and look around."

"When was Charlotte in Salt Lake? Just when the hell was Charlotte in Salt Lake?"

"Last year."

"This is Liberty Park. It's got a zoo. There's good skiing in the mountains."

"Got all the skiing we can use," my mother would say. "People come from all over the world to ski at Banff. Cardston's got a temple, if you like those kinds of things."

"Oh, this one is real big," Lester would say. "They got armed guards and everything.

"Not what Charlotte says."

"What does she know?"

Lester and Laetitia broke up, but I guess the idea of Salt Lake stuck in her mind.

The Canadian border guard was a young woman, and she seemed happy to see us. "Hi," she said. "You folks sure have a great day for a trip. Where are you coming from?"

"Standoff."

"Is that in Montana?"

"No."

"Where are you going?"

"Standoff."

The woman's name was Carol and I don't guess she was any older than Laetitia. "Wow, you both Canadians?"

"Blackfoot."

"Really? I have a friend I went to school with who is Blackfoot. Do you know Mike Harley?"

"No."

"He went to school in Lethbridge, but he's really from Browning."

It was a nice conversation and there were no cars behind us, so there was no rush.

"You're not bringing any liquor back, are you?"

"No."

"Any cigarettes or plants or stuff like that?"

"No."

"Citizenship?"

"Blackfoot"

"I know," said the woman, "and I'd be proud of being Blackfoot if I were Blackfoot. But you have to be American or Canadian."

When Laetitia and Lester broke up, Lester took his brochures and maps with him, so Laetitia wrote to someone in Salt Lake City, and, about a month later, she got a big envelope of stuff. We sat at the table and opened up all the brochures, and Laetitia read each one out loud.

"Salt Lake City is the gateway to some of the world's most magnificent skiing.

"Salt Lake City is the home of one of the newest professional basketball franchises, the Utah Jazz.

"The Great Salt Lake is one of the natural wonders of the world."

It was kind of exciting seeing all those colour brochures on the table and listening to Laetitia read all about how Salt Lake City was one of the best places in the entire world.

"That Salt Lake City place sounds too good to be true," my mother told her.

"It has everything."

"We got everything right here."

"It's boring here."

"People in Salt Lake City are probably sending away for brochures of Calgary and Lethbridge and Pincher Creek right now."

In the end, my mother would say that maybe Laetitia should go to Salt Lake City, and Laetitia would say that maybe she would.

We parked the car to the side of the building and Carol led us into a small room on the second floor. I found a comfortable spot on the couch and flipped through some back issues of *Saturday Night* and *Alberta Report*.

When I woke up, my mother was just coming out of another office. She didn't say a word to me. I followed her down the stairs and out to the car. I thought we were going home, but she turned the car around and drove back towards the American border, which made me think we were going to visit Laetitia in Salt Lake City after all. Instead she pulled into the parking lot of the duty-free store and stopped.

"We going to see Laetitia?"

"No."

"We going home?"

Pride is a good thing to have, you know. Laetitia had a lot of pride, and so did my mother. I figured that someday, I'd have it, too.

"So where are we going?"

Most of that day, we wandered around the duty-free store, which wasn't very large. The manager had a name tag with a tiny American flag on one side and a tiny Canadian flag on the other. His name was Mel. Towards evening, he began suggesting that we should be on our way. I told him we had nowhere to go, that neither the Americans nor the Canadians would let us in. He laughed at that and told us that we should buy something or leave.

The car was not very comfortable, but we did have all that food and it was April, so even if it did snow as it sometimes does on the prairies, we wouldn't freeze. The next morning my mother drove to the American border.

It was a different guard this time, but the questions were the same. We didn't spend as much time in the office as we had the day before. By noon, we were back at the Canadian border. By two we were back in the duty-free shop parking lot.

The second night in the car was not as much fun as the first, but my mother seemed in good spirits, and, all in all, it was as much an adventure as an inconvenience. There wasn't much food left and that was a problem, but we had lots of water as there was a faucet at the side of the duty-free shop.

One Sunday, Laetitia and I were watching television. Mom was over at Mrs. Manyfinger's. Right in the middle of the programme, Laetitia turned off the set and said she was going to Salt Lake City, that life around here was too boring. I had wanted to see the rest of the programme and really didn't care if Laetitia went to Salt Lake City or not. When Mom got home, I told her what Laetitia had said.

What surprised me was how angry Laetitia got when she found out that I had told Mom.

"You got a big mouth."

"That what you said."

"What I said is none of your business."

"I didn't say anything."

"Well. I'm going for sure, now."

That weekend, Laetitia packed her bags, and we drove her to the border.

Mel turned out to be friendly. When he closed up for the night and found us still parked in the lot, he came over and asked us if our car was broken down or something. My mother thanked him for his concern and told him that we were fine, that things would get straightened out in the morning.

"You're kidding," said Mel. "You'd think they could handle the simple things."

"We got some apples and a banana," I said, "but we're all out of ham sandwiches."

"You know, you read about these things, but you just don't believe it."

"Hamburgers would be even better because they got more stuff for energy."

My mother slept in the back seat. I slept in the front because I was smaller and could lie under the steering wheel. Late that night, I heard my mother open the car door. I found her sitting on her blanket leaning against the bumper of the car.

"You see all those stars," she said. "When I was a little girl, my grandmother used to take me and my sisters out on the prairies and tell us stories about all the stars."

"Do you think Mel is going to bring us any hamburgers?"

"Every one of those stars has a story. You see that bunch of stars over there that look like a fish?"

"He didn't say no."

"Coyote went fishing, one day. That's how it all started." We sat out under the stars that night, and my mother told me all sorts of stories. She was serious about it, too. She'd tell them slow, repeating parts as she went, as if she expected me to remember each one.

Early the next morning, the television vans began to arrive, and guys in suits and women in dresses came trotting over to us, dragging microphones and cameras and lights behind them. One of the vans had a table set up with orange juice and sandwiches and fruit. It was for the crew, but when I told them we hadn't eaten for a while, a really skinny blonde woman told us we could eat as much as we wanted.

They mostly talked to my mother. Every so often one of the reporters would come over and ask me questions about how it felt to be an Indian without a country. I told them we had a nice house on the reserve and that my cousins had a couple of horses we rode when we went fishing. Some of the television people went over to the American border, and then they went to the Canadian border.

Around noon, a good-looking guy in a dark blue suit and an orange tie with little ducks on it drove up in a fancy car. He talked to my mother for a while, and, after they were done talking, my mother called me over, and we got into our car. Just as my mother started the engine, Mel came over and gave us a bag of peanut brittle and told us that justice was a damn hard thing to get, but that we shouldn't give up.

I would have preferred lemon drops, but it was nice of Mel anyway.

"Where are we going now?"

"Going to visit Laetitia."

The guard who came out to our car was all smiles. The television lights were so bright they hurt my eyes, and, if you tried to look through the windshield in certain directions, you couldn't see a thing.

"Morning, ma'am."

"Good morning."

"Where you heading?"

"Salt Lake City."

"Purpose of your visit?"

"Visit my daughter."

"Any tobacco, liquor, or firearms?"

"Don't smoke."

"Any plants or fruit?"

"Not any more."

"Citizenship?"

"Blackfoot."

The guard rocked back on his heels and jammed his thumbs into his gun belt. "Thank you," he said, his fingers pattering the butt of the revolver. "Have a pleasant trip."

My mother rolled that car forward, and the television people had to scramble out of the way. They ran alongside the car as we pulled away from the border, and when they couldn't run any farther, they stood in the middle of the highway and waved and waved and waved.

We got to Salt Lake City the next day. Laetitia was happy to see us, and, that first night, she took us out to a restaurant that made really good soups. The list of pies took up a whole page. I had cherry. Mom had chocolate. Laetitia said that she saw us on television the night before and, during the meal, she had us tell her the story over and over again.

Laetitia took us everywhere. We went to a fancy ski resort. We went to the temple. We got to go shopping in a couple of large malls, but they weren't as large as the one in Edmonton, and Mom said so.

After a week or so, I got bored and wasn't at all sad when my mother said we should be heading back home. Laetitia wanted us to stay longer, but Mom said no, that she had things to do back home and that next time, Laetitia should come up and visit. Laetitia said she was thinking about moving back, and Mom told her to do as she pleased, and Laetitia said that she would.

On the way home, we stopped at the duty-free shop, and my mother gave Mel a green hat that said "Salt Lake" across the front. Mel was a funny guy. He took the hat and blew his nose and told my mother that she was an inspiration to us all. He gave us some more peanut brittle and came out into the parking lot and waved at us all the way to the Canadian border.

It was almost evening when we left Coutts. I watched the border through the rear window until all you could see were the tops of the flagpoles and the blue water tower, and then they rolled over a hill and disappeared.

Appendix C

Glossary of Literary Terms

The terms briefly defined here are for the most part more fully defined earlier in the text. Hence many of the entries below are followed by page references to the earlier discussions.

ABSURD, THEATRE OF THE plays, especially written in the 1950s and 1960s, that call attention to the incoherence of character and of action, the inability of people to communicate, and the apparent purposelessness of existence

ACCENT stress given to a syllable

ACT a major division of a play

ACTION (1) the happenings in a narrative or drama, usually physical events but also mental changes (for example, a move from innocence to experience); (2) less commonly, the theme or underlying idea of a work (9)

ALLEGORY a work in which concrete elements (for instance, a pilgrim, a road, a splendid city) stand for abstractions (humanity, life, salvation), usually in an unambiguous, one-to-one relationship. The literal items (the pilgrim, and so on) thus convey a meaning, which is usually moral, religious, or political. A caution: Not all of the details in an allegorical work are meant to be interpreted.

ALLITERATION repetition of consonant sounds, especially at the beginnings of words (*free, form, ph*antom) (224)

ALLUSION an indirect reference to a work of art, religion, literature, or culture outside the text; hence, a reference to the Bible or a well-known painting

ANALYSIS an examination, which usually proceeds by separating the object of study into parts (12, 40)

ANAPEST a metrical foot consisting of two unaccented syllables followed by an accented one Example, showing three anapests: "As I came / to the edge / of the wood"

ANECDOTE a short narrative, usually reporting an amusing event in the life of an important person

ANTAGONIST a character or force that opposes (literally, "wrestles") the protagonist (the main character)

APOSTROPHE address to an absent figure or to a thing as if it were present and could listen ("O rose, thou art sick!"); an honorific address ("Oh, sire.") (214–15)

APPROXIMATE RHYME only the final consonant sounds are the same, as in *crown/alone*

ARCHETYPE a theme, image, motive, or pattern that occurs so often in literary works it seems to be universal. Examples: a dark forest (for mental confusion), the sun (for illumination). There is also a critical approach called ARCHETYPAL (OR MYTH) CRITICISM; see Chap. 8 (110–11)

ASIDE in the theatre, words spoken by a character in the presence of other characters, but directed to the spectators, that is, understood by the audience to be inaudible to the other characters

ASSONANCE repetition of similar vowel sounds in stressed syllables Example: *light/bride*

ATMOSPHERE the emotional tone (for instance, joy or horror) in a work, most often established by the setting

BLANK VERSE unrhymed iambic pentameter, that is, unrhymed lines of ten syllables, with every second syllable stressed (234–35)

CAESURA a strong pause within a line of verse

CANON a term originally used to refer to those books accepted as Holy Scripture by the Christian church. The term has come to be applied to literary works thought to have a special merit by a given culture, for instance the body of literature traditionally taught in colleges and universities. Such works are sometimes called "classics," and their authors are "major authors." Until recently, the canon consisted chiefly of works by dead white males—partly, of course, because middle-class and upper-class white males were in fact the people who did most of the writing in the Western hemisphere, but also because white males were the people who chiefly established the canon. Not surprisingly the canon-makers valued (or valorized or "privileged") writings that revealed, asserted, or reinforced the canon-makers' own values. From about the 1960s, feminists and others argued that these works had been regarded as central not because they were inherently better than other works but because they reflected the interests of the dominant culture, and that other work, such as slave narratives and the diaries of women, had been "marginalized." In fact, the literary canon has never been static (in contrast to the Biblical canon, which has not changed for more than a thousand years), but it is true that certain authors have been permanent fixtures. This is partly because they do indeed support the values of those who control the high cultural purse strings, and partly because these books are rich enough to invite constant reinterpretation from age to age.

CATASTROPHE the concluding action, especially in a tragedy

CATHARSIS Aristotle's term for the purgation or purification of the pity and terror supposedly experienced while witnessing a tragedy

CHARACTER (1) a person in a literary work (Romeo); (2) the personality of such a figure (sentimental lover, or whatever). Characters (in the first sense) are sometimes classified in E. M. Forster's terms, as either **FLAT** (one-dimensional) or **ROUND** (fully realized, capable of surprising the reader or viewer) (6, 141–46)

CHARACTERIZATION the presentation of a character, whether by direct description, by showing the character in action, or by the presentation of other characters who help to define each other (194–96)

CLICHÉ an expression that through overuse has ceased to be effective. Examples: acid test, sigh of relief

CLIMAX the culmination of a conflict; a turning point, often the point of greatest tension in a plot (44)

CLOSE READING rigorous reading with attention to detail; close reading is the first step to any analysis of a text

CLOSURE the sense of ending in a work. Early literature always provided a neat closure to resolve any tensions and finish the plot (see *comedy*); contemporary art often refuses closure, urging the reader or viewer to take responsibility for the significance of the work

COMEDY a literary work, especially a play, characterized by humour and by a happy ending or an ending which resolves conflict (often in a return to the status quo) (38)

COMPARISON AND CONTRAST to compare is strictly to note similarities; to contrast is to note differences. But *compare* is now often used for both activities (41)

COMPLICATION an entanglement in a narrative or dramatic work that causes a conflict

CONFLICT a struggle between a character and some obstacle (for example, another character or fate) or between internal forces, such as divided loyalties (139)

CONNOTATION the associations (suggestions, overtones) of a word or expression. Thus both "seventy" and "three score and ten" mean "one more than sixty-nine," but because "three score and ten" is a biblical expression, it has an association of holiness; see *denotation* (214, 269)

CONSISTENCY BUILDING the process engaged in during the act of reading, of re-evaluating the details that one has just read in order to make them consistent with the new information that the text is providing (6)

CONSONANCE repetition of consonant sounds, especially in stressed syllables. Also called half-rhyme or slant rhyme. Example: *arouse/doze*

CONVENTION a pattern (for instance, the 14-line poem, or sonnet) or motif (for instance, the bumbling police officer in detective fiction) or other device occurring so often that it is taken for granted. Thus it is a convention that actors in a performance of *Julius Caesar* are understood to be speaking Latin, though they are, in fact, speaking English. Similarly, the **SOLILOQUY** (a character alone on the stage speaks his or her thoughts aloud) is a convention, for in real life sane people do not talk aloud to themselves

COUPLET a pair of lines of verse, usually rhyming

CRISIS a high point in the conflict that leads to the turning point

CRITICAL THINKING a careful way of thinking and writing that follows the rules of formal logic, testing premises and conclusions and avoiding fallacies

CRITICISM the analysis or evaluation of a literary work

CULTURAL MATERIALISM; CULTURAL CRITICISM criticism that sets literature in a social context, often of economics or politics or gender. Borrowing some of the methods of anthropology, cultural criticism usually extends the canon to include popular material, for instance comic books and soap operas

DACTYL a metrical foot consisting of a stressed syllable followed by two unstressed syllables. Example: *underwear*

DECONSTRUCTION a critical approach assuming that language is unstable and ambiguous and is therefore inherently contradictory. Deconstruction attempts to remove the privilege which speech has enjoyed over writing and to show that all language systems are attempts to find a stable "centre" where none really exists. Deconstruction locates the "free play of signification" between binary meanings, allowing both meanings to coexist. See Chap. 8. (107)

DEIXIS a "pointing out" or "pointing to" in literature and, especially, in drama. Verbal deixis includes pronouns like "here" and "now"; physical deixis employs *index*

DENOTATION the dictionary meaning of a word. Thus *soap opera* and *daytime serial* have the same denotation, but the connotations (associations, emotional overtones) of *soap opera* are less favorable. (214, 269)

DÉNOUEMENT the resolution or the outcome (literally, the "unknotting") of a plot (139)

DIALOGUE exchange of words between characters; speech

DICTION the choice of vocabulary and of sentence structure. There is a difference in diction between "One never knows" and "You never can tell." (50)

DOCUMENT, TO; DOCUMENTATION the careful citation (reference to) the author and source of any borrowed material used by a writer. Without correct documentation, an essay is plagiarized

DOCUMENTARY a style of film or play (or even poem) which *aims* to create a true "document" of a subject—for example, the Inuit People in the famous film *Nanook of the North* (1922)—although it may use fictional elements. Of course, the documentary employs its own literary conventions and sometimes creates biased or false images which are made to appear true because of they are presented as "document." *Nanook of the North* is now considered to give a false view of Inuit people. The early work of the National Film Board was largely documentary.

DRAMA (1) a play; (2) conflict or tension, as in "The story lacks drama" (17)

DRAMATIC IRONY see **IRONY**

DRAMATIC MONOLOGUE a poem spoken entirely by one character but addressed to one or more other characters whose presence is strongly felt (205)

EFFACED NARRATOR a narrator who reports but who does not editorialize or enter into the minds of any of the characters in the story

ELEGY a lyric poem, usually a meditation on a death

END RHYME identical sounds at the ends of lines of poetry

END-STOPPED LINE a line of poetry that ends with a pause (usually marked by a comma, semicolon, or period) because the grammatical structure and the sense reach (at least to some degree) completion. It is contrasted with a *run-on line*

ENJAMBMENT a line of poetry in which the grammatical and logical sense run on, without pause, into the next line or lines (229)

EPIC a long narrative, especially in verse, that usually records heroic material in an elevated style

EPIGRAM a brief, witty poem or saying

EPIGRAPH a quotation at the beginning of a work, right after the title, often giving a clue to the theme

EPIPHANY a "showing forth," as when an action reveals a character with particular clarity, or a protagonist suddenly understands his plight or its consequence

EPISODE an incident or scene that has unity in itself but is also a part of a larger action

ESSAY a work, usually in prose and usually fairly short, that purports to be true and that treats its subject tentatively

EXPLICATION a line-by-line unfolding of the meaning of a text (31)

EXPOSITION a setting-forth of information. In fiction and drama, introductory material introducing characters and the situation; in an essay, the presentation of information, as opposed to the telling of a story or the setting forth of an argument (130)

EYE RHYME words that look as though they rhyme, but do not rhyme when pronounced. Example: *come/home*

FABLE a short story (usually involving speaking animals) with an easily grasped moral

FARCE comedy based not on clever language or on subtleties of characters but on broadly humorous situations. In classic farce, sudden changes of location or cast, and sudden revelations shift the action and create the comedy

FEMINIST CRITICISM an approach especially concerned with analyzing the depiction of women in literature, the reappraisal of work by female authors, and the manner in which women read. There are many schools of feminist criticism and a long history. See Chap. 8

FICTION an imaginative work, usually a prose narrative (novel, short story), that reports incidents that did not actually occur. The term may include all works that invent a world, such as a lyric poem or a play

FIGURATIVE LANGUAGE words intended to be understood in a way that is other than literal. Thus *lemon* used literally refers to a citrus fruit, but *lemon* used figuratively refers to a defective machine, especially a defective automobile. Other examples: "I'm on cloud nine," "A sea of troubles." Literally, such expressions are nonsense, but writers use them to express meanings inexpressible in literal speech. Among the commonest kinds of figures of speech are **APOSTROPHE**, **METAPHOR**, and **SIMILE**. (131)

FILM; FILMIC an imaginative work recorded by camera on a strip of celluloid that is played by means of projected light. Video shares some similarities with the form, as does **DRAMA**, but there are important characteristics of film particular to the genre

FLASHBACK an interruption in a narrative that presents an earlier episode

FLAT CHARACTER a one-dimensional character (for instance, the figure who is only and always the jealous husband or the flirtatious wife) as opposed to a round or many-sided character

FOIL a character who makes a contrast with another, especially a minor character who helps to set off a major character

FOOT a metrical unit, consisting of two or three syllables, with a specified arrangement of the stressed syllable or syllables. Thus the iambic foot consists of an unstressed syllable followed by a stressed syllable. For a list of the kinds of feet, see Chap. 12

FORESHADOWING suggestions of what is to come (44)

FORMALIST CRITICISM an approach that assumes that the work of art is a carefully constructed artefact with a meaning that can be perceived, and agreed on, by all competent readers. Literary criticism, in this view, is an objective description and analysis of the work. See Chap. 8

FOURTH WALL a term used of the "well-made" play where a fourth wall seems to have been removed to allow the audience to view into a naturalistic set

FREE VERSE poetry in lines of irregular length, usually unrhymed

GAP a term from **READER-RESPONSE CRITICISM,** referring to a reader's perception that something is unstated in the text, requiring the reader to fill in the material. Filling in the gaps is a matter of **CONSISTENCY-BUILDING**. Different readers may fill the gaps differently, and readers may even differ as to whether a gap exists at a particular point in the text. (6)

GAZE a term from film and drama criticism sometimes used in other literary analysis. The gaze refers to the "eye" of the viewer or reader that looks with a particular point of view upon a subject in the work. **FEMINIST CRITICISM** often speaks of the "male gaze."

GENRE kind or type, roughly analogous to the biological term *species*. The four chief literary genres are nonfiction, fiction, poetry, and drama, but these can be subdivided into further genres. Thus fiction obviously can be divided into the short story and the novel, and drama obviously can be divided into tragedy and comedy. But these can be still further divided—for instance, tragedy into heroic tragedy and bourgeois tragedy, comedy into romantic comedy and satirical comedy. Today, genre borders are disappearing. In Canada, the New Rhetoric School sees genre as an agent of larger discourses; see Chap. 1

GESTURE physical movement, especially in a play (190)

HALF-RHYME repetition in accented syllables of the final consonant sound but without identity in the preceding vowel sound; words of similar but not identical sound. Also called NEAR RHYME, SLANT RHYME, APPROXIMATE RHYME, and OFF-RHYME. See **CONSONANCE**. Examples: *light/bet; affirm/perform*

HERO, HEROINE the main character (not necessarily heroic or even admirable) in a work; cf. **PROTAGONIST**

HEROIC COUPLET an end-stopped pair of rhyming lines of iambic pentameter

HISTORICAL CRITICISM the attempt to illuminate a literary work by placing it in its historical context. See Chap. 8

HUBRIS, HYBRIS a Greek word, usually translated as "overweening pride," "arrogance," "excessive ambition," and often said to be characteristic of tragic figures (185)

HYPERBOLE figurative language using OVERSTATEMENT, as in "He died a thousand deaths" (223)

IAMB, IAMBIC a poetic foot consisting of an unaccented syllable followed by an accented one. Example: *alone*

ICON one of Peirce's sign-functions. An icon stands in for something it directly resembles. In current use, the word means a **SIGN** that stands for something so fully that it has almost replaced the thing itself. Hence, Marilyn Monroe or Madonna become iconic signs for certain constructions of the category "woman"; Brad Pitt or Elvis for certain notions of "man."

IMAGE, IMAGERY imagery is established by language that appeals to the senses, especially sight ("deep blue sea") but also other senses ("tinkling bells," "perfumes of Arabia") (5, 216)

IMAGE PATTERN a series of repeated or related images which tie together to provide structure within a work

INDETERMINACY a passage that careful readers agree is open to more than one interpretation. According to some poststructural critics, because language is unstable and because contexts can never be objectively viewed, all texts are indeterminate (6)

INDEX one of Peirce's sign-functions. An index "points to" characterization by reference to a physical sign (costume, gait, posture, etc.)

INNOCENT EYE a naive narrator in whose narration the reader sees more than the narrator sees

INTERNAL RHYME rhyme within a line

INTERPRETATION the assignment of meaning to a text (77-82)

INTERTEXTUALITY all works show the influence of other works. No matter how original an author thinks she is, she inevitably brings to her own story a know-ledge of other stories, for example, a conception of what a short story is, and, speaking more generally, an idea of what a story (long or short, written or oral) is. In opposition to formalist critics, some contemporary critics emphasize the work's *intertextuality*, that is, its connections with a vast context of writings and all aspects of culture, and in part depending also on what the reader brings to the work. In this view, then, no text is self-sufficient, and no writer fully controls the meaning of the text. Because we are talking about connections of which the writer is unaware, and because *meaning* is in part the creation of the reader, the author is by no means an authority.

IRONY a contrast of some sort. For instance, in **VERBAL IRONY** or **SOCRATIC IRONY**, the contrast is between what is said and what is meant ("You're a great guy," meant bitterly). In **DRAMATIC IRONY** or **SOPHOCLEAN IRONY**, the contrast is between what is intended and what is accomplished (Macbeth usurps the throne, thinking he will then be happy, but the action leads him to misery), or between what the audience knows (a murderer waits in the bedroom) and what a character says (the victim enters the bedroom, innocently saying, "I think I'll have a long sleep") (18)

LESBIAN AND GAY CRITICISM (QUEER THEORY; QUEER CRITICISM) considers texts with homosexual characters or action, or which may be read from a gay or lesbian subject position. As male and female writers and critics read texts differently, the term QUEER CRITICISM is used by some critics to capture a homosexual and resistant subject position without investing it with gender. Lesbian criticism is often connected in important ways with FEMINIST CRITICISM. Queer theory considers the notion of human sexuality itself and asks questions concerning its cultural construction. See Chap. 8

LITOTES a form of understatement in which an affirmation is made by means of negation: "He was not underweight," meaning "He was grossly overweight."

LYRIC POEM a short poem, often songlike, with the emphasis not on narrative but on the speaker's emotion or reverie (96)

MAGIC REALISM a highly stylized form of narrative (often seen in Latin American writing and now popular in many countries including Canada) in which apparently "real" action and characters are juxtaposed with fantastic or mythical or imaginative characters without any seeming incongruity. The blend stretches the definitions of the "real."

MARXIST CRITICISM the study of literature in the light of Karl Marx's view that economic forces, controlled by the dominant class, shape the literature (as well as the law, philosophy, religion, etc.) of a society. See Chap. 8

MASK a term used to designate the speaker of a poem, equivalent to PERSONA or VOICE (205)

MEANING critics seek to interpret "meaning," variously defined as what the writer intended the work to say about the world and human experience, or as what the work says to the reader irrespective of the writer's intention. Both versions imply that a literary work is a nut to be cracked, with a kernel that is to be extracted. Because few critics today hold that meaning is clear and unchanging, the tendency now is to say that a critic offers "an interpretation" or "a reading" rather than a "statement of the meaning of a work." Many critics today would say that an alleged interpretation is really a creation of meaning. (4)

METADRAMA a play that refers to itself or breaks the dramatic illusion to comment on itself or the audience; a technique of exposing the theatricality of the work

METAFICTION a novel or story that refers to itself or exposes the techniques of language and structure by which it is composed

METANARRATIVE the overarching story in which a person or society operates. Some believe huge stories (of history, religion, culture, gender, etc.) to be literally true, others see them as literary/social constructs that form a narrative in which we live

METAPHOR a kind of figurative language equating one thing with another: "This novel is garbage" (a book is equated with discarded and probably inedible food), "a piercing cry" (a cry is equated with a spear or other sharp instrument)

METONYMY a kind of figurative language in which a word or phrase stands not for itself but for something closely related to it: *sabre-rattling* means "militaristic talk or action." The term is being used differently today in a more complex manner related to METAPHOR to imply comparisons in which the referent is not assumed to be fixed (213)

METRE a pattern of stressed and unstressed syllables. A line of poetry can be named for the number of stresses it contains; hence, a line with five feet is termed pentametre, a line with three feet is called trimetre, one with four feet, tetrametre and so on; see Chap. 11

MONOLOGUE a relatively long, uninterrupted speech by a character

MONTAGE in film, quick cutting (245); in fiction, quick shifts

MOOD the atmosphere, usually created by descriptions of the settings and characters

MOTIF a recurrent theme within a work, or a theme common to many works

MOTIVATION grounds for a character's action (195)

MYTH (1) a traditional story reflecting primitive beliefs, especially explaining the mysteries of the natural world (why it rains, or the origin of mountains); (2) a body of belief, not necessarily false, especially as set forth by a writer. Thus one may speak of Yeats or Robertson Davies as myth-makers, referring to the visions of reality that they set forth in their works

NARRATOR; NARRATIVE a narrator is one who tells a story (not the author, but the invented speaker of the story); a narrative is a story (an anecdote, a novel). On kinds of narrators, see **POINT OF VIEW**

NATURALISM an attempt to delve into the inner workings of "real" things, including the human body; a technique of showing apparently "real" elements in a literary work, of making things look like they do in everyday life and taking interest in their workings. Compare **REALISM**

NEW CRITICISM see **FORMALIST CRITICISM**

NEW HISTORICISM a school of criticism holding that the past cannot be known objectively. According to this view, because historians project their own "narrative"—their own invention or "construction"—on the happenings of the past, historical writings are not objective but are, at bottom, political statements. See Chap. 8

NOVEL a long work of prose fiction, especially one that is relatively realistic

NOVELLA a work of prose fiction longer than a short story but shorter than a novel, about 40 to 80 pages

OBJECTIVE POINT OF VIEW a narrator reports but does not editorialize or enter into the minds of any of the characters in the story

OCTAVE, OCTET an eight-line stanza, or the first eight lines of a sonnet, especially of an Italian sonnet

OCTOSYLLABIC COUPLET a pair of rhyming lines, each line with four iambic feet

OMNISCIENT NARRATOR a speaker who knows the thoughts of all of the characters in the narrative

ONOMATOPOEIA words (or the use of words) that sound like what they mean. Examples: *buzz, whirr* (232)

OPEN FORM poetry whose form seems spontaneous rather than highly patterned

OXYMORON a compact paradox, as in "mute cry," "a pleasing pain."

PARABLE a short narrative that is at least in part allegorical and that illustrates a moral or spiritual lesson (39)

PARADOX an apparent contradiction, as in Jesus' words: "Whosoever will save his life shall lose it; but whosoever will lose his life for my sake, the same shall save it" (224)

PARAPHRASE a restatement that sets forth an idea in diction other than that of the original (31, 53)

PARODY a humorous imitation of a literary work, especially of its style (9, 56–57)

PASTICHE a mix of elements; in postmodernism, **PASTICHE** refers to a set of borrowings that no longer carry the intent or belief system of the originals, an empty borrowing, sometimes playful

PERFORMATIVE; PERFORMATIVITY an action or speech-act by which we cause something to come into being. Hence, a doctor's statement, "I'm sorry, you have cancer" not only reports a fact, but reconstructs the auditor into the role of "patient," or "victim," with serious consequences. Feminist, gay and lesbian critics argue that gender itself is a performative, established by repeated actions and attitudes, rather than arising in any essential quality of the biological beings, male or female

PERIPETEIA a reversal in the action (185)

PERFECT (OR EXACT) RHYME differing consonant sounds are followed by identical stressed vowel sounds, and any further following sounds are also identical (*row-toe; meet-fleet; buffer-rougher*)

PERSONA literally, a mask; the "I" or speaker of a work, sometimes identified with the author but usually better regarded as the voice or mouthpiece created by the author (131)

PERSONIFICATION a kind of figurative language in which an inanimate object, animal, or other nonhuman is given human traits. Examples: "the creeping tide" (the tide is imagined as having feet), "the cruel sea" (the sea is imagined as having moral qualities) (214)

PETRARCHAN (OR **ITALIAN**) **SONNET** a poem of 14 lines, consisting of an octave often rhyming *abbaabba*) and a sestet (usually *cdecde* or *cdccdc*)

PLOT the episodes in a narrative or dramatic work—that is, what happens. (But even a lyric poem can be said to have a plot; for instance, the speaker's mood changes from anger to resignation.) Sometimes *plot* is defined as the author's particular arrangement (**SEQUENCE**) of these episodes (also called *sjuzet*), and *story* (or *fabula*) is the episodes in their chronological order

POEM; POETRY an imaginative work in metre or in free verse, usually employing figurative language

POINT OF VIEW the perspective from which a story is told—for example, by a major character or a minor character or a fly on the wall; see also **NARRATIVE, NARRATOR, OMNISCIENT NARRATOR** (5, 155–63)

POST-COLONIAL CRITICISM a critical approach which examines aesthetic values in terms of the historical processes of imperialism and colonialism. Post-colonial critics first studied the effects of imperialism on modern nations; post-colonialism now offers useful ways of reading the relationship of power to race, gender and other social issues. In Canada, the approach is often employed to study the idea of national identity. See Chap. 8

POSTMODERNISM the term first came into prominence in the 1960s, to distinguish the contemporary experimental writing of such authors as Samuel Beckett and Jorge Luis Borges from such early twentieth-century classics of modernism as James Joyce's *Ulysses* (1922) and T. S. Eliot's *The Waste Land* (1922). Although the classic modernists had been thought to be revolutionary in their day, after World War II they seemed to be conservative, and their works seemed remote from today's society. Postmodernist literature, though widely varied and not always clearly distinct from modernist literature is given to parody and pastiche—and more closely related to the art forms of popular culture than is modernist literature.

PROSODY the principles of versification (227)

PROTAGONIST the chief actor in any literary work. The term is usually preferable to *hero* and *heroine* because it can include characters—for example, villainous or weak ones—who are not aptly called heroes or heroines

PROVERB a pithy short saying which stays in memory by capturing a commonplace (67, 69–70)

PSYCHOLOGICAL CRITICISM a form of analysis especially concerned both with the ways in which authors unconsciously leave traces of their inner lives in their works and with the ways in which readers respond, consciously and unconsciously, to works. See Chap. 8

PYRRHIC FOOT in poetry, a foot consisting of two unstressed syllables

QUATRAIN a stanza of four lines

READER-RESPONSE CRITICISM criticism emphasizing the idea that various readers respond in various ways and therefore that readers as well as authors "create" meaning. See Chap. 8

REALISM presentation of plausible characters (usually middle class) in plausible (usually everyday) circumstances, as opposed, for example, to heroic characters engaged in improbable adventures

RECOGNITION a discovery, especially in tragedy—for example, when the hero understands the reasons for his or her fall—or a sudden realization by the reader or viewer of a meaning in the work or a dimension of character. Also called ANAGNORISIS and DISCOVERY

RESOLUTION the dénouement or untying of the complication of the plot

REVERSAL a change in fortune, often an ironic twist (185)

RHYME similarity or identity of accented sounds in corresponding positions, as, for example, at the ends of lines: *love/dove; tender/slender* (18, 231–32)

RHYTHM in poetry, a pattern of stressed and unstressed sounds; in prose, some sort of recurrence (for example, of a motif) at approximately identical intervals (229-231)

ROMANCE narrative fiction, usually characterized by improbable adventures and love

ROUND CHARACTER a many-sided character, one who does not always act predictably, as opposed to a "flat" or one-dimensional, unchanging character

RUN-ON LINE a line of verse whose syntax and meaning require the reader to go on, without a pause, to the next line; an ENJAMBED line

SATIRE literature that entertainingly attacks folly or vice; amusingly abusive writing which seeks to amend what it sees as wrong (56–57)

SCANSION description of rhythm in poetry; metrical analysis

SCENE (1) a unit of a play, in which the setting is unchanged and the time continuous; (2) the setting (locale, and time of the action); (3) in fiction, a dramatic passage, as opposed to a passage of description or of summary

SELECTIVE OMNISCIENCE a point of view in which the author enters the mind of one character and for the most part sees the other characters only from the outside (156)

SEMIOTICS the study of SIGNS. Semiotic criticism looks for language and physical signs in literature and drama, exploring how sounds, words, and physical objects are part of a system of signification that allows us to communicate and perceive our world. Signs are signifiers, pointing to a thing signified.

SENTIMENTALITY excessive emotion, especially excessive pity, treated as appropriate rather than as disproportionate (99–116)

SEQUENCE (1) a series, either of events in the action or points in an essay; (2) a group of related scenes in a film

SESTET a six-line stanza, or the last six lines of an Italian sonnet

SETTING the time and place of a story, play, poem, or film (37)

SHAKESPEAREAN (or **ENGLISH**) **SONNET** a poem of 14 lines (three quatrains and a couplet), often rhyming *ababcdcdefefgg*

SHORT STORY a fictional narrative, usually in prose, rarely longer than 30 pages and often much briefer

SIGN see **SEMIOTICS**

SIGNIFYING PRACTICE a system of discourses creating verbal, visual and written TEXTS from all aspects of human existence which help to frame (or control) human consciousness; signifying practices are often part of cultural METANARRATIVES (75)

SIMILE a kind of figurative language explicitly making a comparison—for example, by using *as, like,* or a verb such as *seems* (211)

SOCIAL CONSTRUCTION the notion that aspects of human life and personality and gender are constructed by forces of culture and society, rather than essential. See **METANARRATIVE**

SOLILOQUY a speech in a play, in which a character alone on the stage speaks his or her thoughts aloud

SONNET a lyric poem of 14 lines; see **SHAKESPEARIAN SONNET**, **PETRARCHAN SONNET**

SPEAKER see **PERSONA** (205)

SPECTATORIAL EXPERIENCE, or **SPECTATORSHIP** the relationship between viewer and object being viewed, especially in theatre and film. Psychological criticism and performance theories are very concerned with this relationship

SPONDEE a metrical foot consisting of two stressed syllables

STAGE DIRECTION a playwright's indication to the actors or readers—for example, offering information about how an actor is to speak a line

STANZA a group of lines forming a unit that is repeated in a poem

STEREOTYPE a simplified conception, especially an oversimplification—for example, a stock character such as the heartless landlord or the kindly old teacher. Such a character usually has only one personality trait, and this is boldly exaggerated; the stereotype is usually pejorative. Contrast *type*, a character who also embodies a single trait, but whose characterization is neutral

STREAM OF CONSCIOUSNESS the presentation of a character's unrestricted flow of thought, often with free associations, and often without punctuation

STRESS relative emphasis on one syllable as compared with another (71)

STRONG ENDING a line ending with a stress

STRONG RHYME rhyme of one-syllable words (*lies/cries*) or, if more than one syllable, words ending with accented syllables (*behold/foretold*)

STRUCTURALISM a critical theory holding that a literary work consists of conventional elements that, taken together by a reader familiar with the conventions, give the work its meaning. Structuralists normally have no interest in the origins of a work (i.e., in the historical background, or in the author's biography), and no interest in the degree to which a work of art seems to correspond to reality. The interest normally is in the work as a self-sufficient construction

STRUCTURE the organization of a work, the relationship between the chief parts, the large-scale pattern

STYLE the manner of expression, evident not only in the choice of certain words (for instance, colloquial language) but in the choice of certain kinds of sentence structure, characters, settings, and themes

SUBPLOT a sequence of events often paralleling or in some way resembling the main story (17)

SUMMARY a synopsis or condensation (52)

SYMBOL a person, object, action, or situation that, charged with meaning, indirectly suggests another thing (for example, a dark forest may suggest confusion, or perhaps evil). Usually a symbol is less specific and more ambiguous than an allegory. A symbol usually differs from a metaphor in that a symbol is expanded or repeated and works by accumulating associations. It also refers to the third of Peirce's three sign-functions. In Peirce's theory there is no direct or physical relationship between a symbol and that which it represents. (See **ICON** and **INDEX**.)

SYNECDOCHE a kind of figurative language in which the whole stands for a part ("the law," for a police officer), or a part ("all hands on deck," for all persons) stands for the whole (213)

TALE a short narrative, usually less realistic and more romantic than a short story; a yarn

TEXT any writing, but particularly a writing which is given meaning by its reader; in contemporary criticism **TEXT** is more often used than a term like **LITERATURE** (75)

THEME   what the work is about; an underlying idea of a work; a conception of human experience suggested by the concrete details (5, 163–64, 189–90, 241, 245–46)

THESIS   the point or argument that a writer announces and develops. A thesis differs from a **TOPIC** by making an assertion. "The fall of Oedipus" is a topic, but "Oedipus falls because he is impetuous" is a thesis. (20–22, 288–89)

THESIS SENTENCE   a sentence summarizing, as specifically as possible, the writer's chief point (argument and perhaps purpose); see also **TOPIC** (20–21)

THIRD-PERSON NARRATOR   the teller of a story who does not participate in the happenings

TONE   the prevailing attitude (for instance, ironic, genial, objective) as perceived by the reader. Notice that a reader may feel that the tone of the persona of the work is genial while the tone of the author of the same work is ironic.

TOPIC   a subject, such as "Hamlet's relation to Horatio." A topic becomes a **THESIS** when a **PREDICATE** is added to this **SUBJECT**, thus: the topic "Hamlet's relation to Horatio" becomes "Hamlet's relation to Horatio helps to define Hamlet." (25)

TRAGEDY   a serious play showing the protagonist moving from good fortune to bad and ending in death or a deathlike state (38, 184–87)

TRAGIC FLAW   a supposed weakness (for example, arrogance) in the tragic protagonist. If the tragedy results from an intellectual error rather than from a moral weakness, it is better to speak of "a tragic error" (186)

TRAGICOMEDY   a mixture of tragedy and comedy, usually a play with serious happen-ings that expose the characters to the threat of death but that ends happily

TRANSITION   a connection between one passage and the next

TRIPLET   a group of three lines of verse, usually rhyming

TROCHEE   a metrical foot consisting of a stressed syllable followed by an un-stressed syllable. Example: *garden*

TROPE   a figure of speech or other figurative element

UNDERSTATEMENT   a figure of speech in which the speaker says less than what he or she means; an ironic minimizing, as in "Well, you've done fairly well for yourself" said to the winner of the 6/49 jackpot. Also called *meiosis*. Contrast **HYPBERBOLE** (223)

UNITY   harmony and coherence of parts, absence of irrelevance

UNRELIABLE NARRATOR   a narrator whose report a reader cannot accept at face value, perhaps because the narrator is naive or is too deeply implicated in the action to report it objectively

VERSE   (1) a line of poetry; (2) a stanza of a poem

VERS LIBRE   free verse, unrhymed poetry

VOICE   see **PERSONA**, **STYLE**, and **TONE** (45, 131, 205)

WEAK ENDING   a line ending with an extra unstressed syllable

WEAK RHYME   a rhyme of two or more syllables, with the stress falling on a syllable other than the last. Examples: *fatter/batter; tenderly/slenderly*

WHITE SPACE   in poetry, a space on the page with no text. This space is "read" as part of the poem, causing a pause, or emphasis, or a linkage

WORKING THESIS   an open-ended sentence (but still a true thesis sentence) which limits research while leaving the investigation open. Sometimes it is a good idea to write out the opposing directions the research may take you: for example, "(Although/Because) Canada was at war with Japan in World War II, the incarceration of Japanese-Canadians (was an immoral act/was a justified military action)."

Credits

Index of Authors, Titles, and First Lines of Poems

Subject Index

working bibliography,
289–90
See also Web search
strategies
research paper
analysis and
interpretation,
287–88
documentation, 294–96
drafting, 292–94
revision, 321
sample essay, 315–21
resolution, 139
response, literary, 55–56
restrictive information, 261
review, 57–62
courtesy, 62
notes, 58
sample, 59–61
sincerity, 45
writing suggestions,
57–58, 62
See also evaluation
revision
of draft, 24
of paragraphs, 278–79
of research paper, 321
rhyme, 231–32
rhythm, 229–30
rising action, 139, 191
romantic comedy, 187
rose, as symbol, 216–17
run-on line, 229

satiric comedy, 187
scansion, 228
search engines, 289,
340–41, 347–48
search engines. *See also*
Web search strategies
secondary materials, 288
selective omniscient,
155–57
self, ideal (*moi*), 114–15
semi-colon, 262, 263
semiotic criticism, 196
sentences
economy in, 271–72
mood, 259
parallels, 272–73
subject, 255
subordination, 273–74
types of, 258

voice, 259
sentimentality, 99–102
separation, of words, 281
sestet, 233
set-down quotations, 298
setting, 149, 175–76
stage, 198–200
Shakespearean sonnet,
233–34
sign, 107, 141
significance, vs. meaning, 5
signifier. *See* sign
similie, 211
soliloquy, 201
Sophoclean irony, 185
sound patterning
blank verse, 234
free verse, 234–35
rhyme, 231–32
stanzaic patterns,
233–34
sound of sense
(wordplay), 271
speaker
and author, 205
identifying, 206–8
tone, 207, 240
writing about, 207–8
spectatorial economy, 111
spectatorial experience,
190–91
speculative essay. *See*
expressive essay
spelling, spell checkers, 26,
27
spondee (spondaic), 228
square bracket, 282
stage directions, 196–97
stanzaic patterns, 233–34
story, vs. theme, 164
stream of consciousness,
15
strong ending, in poetry,
229
strong rhyme, 232
structure
comparison, 41–42
in literature, 38
logical structure, 222–24
narrative structure,
221–22
poem, 33–34, 217–24,
227–35

repetitive structure, 221
style, of essayist
analysis, 135–36, 176
sample essay on, 136–38
sample work, 132–35
subject catalogue,
electronic library, 334
subjective case, 260
subjective view, 109
subjunctive mood, 259
subordinate clauses. *See*
dependent clauses
subordination, 273–74
summary, 52–53
symbolic characters, 195
symbolism
in fiction, 150–51
imagery and, 216–17
sample essay, 151–55
writing about, 176,
247–51
symmetry, 39
synechdoche, 213
syntax, 254–55

taste, personal, 94
technical language, 50
tense, 257
present tense, use of, 30
shift in, 265
tercet. *See* triplet
tetrametre, 228
texts, 75–76
theatre, 177
review, 57–62
theme
of drama, 189–90
of fiction, 163–64
of films, 245–45
of poems, 241
sample essays, 166–67,
169–73
vs. thesis, 164
thesis
consistent argument, 49
formation of, 20–22, 43
vs. theme, 164
thesis sentence, 20
working thesis, 288
Thinking Critically about
Discipline-Based
World Wide Web